Human Rights in American Foreign Policy

PENNSYLVANIA STUDIES IN HUMAN RIGHTS

Bert B. Lockwood, Jr., Series Editor

A complete list of books in the series is available from the publisher.

Human Rights
in American Foreign Policy

From the 1960s to the Soviet Collapse

Joe Renouard

PENN

UNIVERSITY OF PENNSYLVANIA PRESS

PHILADELPHIA

Published by
University of Pennsylvania Press
Philadelphia, Pennsylvania 19104-4112
www.upenn.edu/pennpress

Printed in the United States of America
on acid-free paper
10 9 8 7 6 5 4 3 2 1

Library of Congress Cataloging-in-Publication Data

Renouard, Joe, author.
    Human rights in American foreign policy : from the 1960s to the Soviet collapse / Joe Renouard.
        pages cm. — (Pennsylvania studies in human rights)
    ISBN 978-0-8122-4773-2 (alk. paper)
    1. United States—Foreign relations—1945–1989. 2. United States—Foreign relations—1989–1993. 3. Diplomacy—Moral and ethical aspects—20th century. 4. Human rights—Government policy—United States—20th century. 5. Cold War. I. Title. II. Series: Pennsylvania studies in human rights.
JZ1480.R465 2016
327.1′1—dc23
                                                    2015022968

For my family

What has for centuries raised man above the beast is not the cudgel but an inward music: the irresistible power of unarmed truth.
—Boris Pasternak

Contents

Introduction: A Riot in Washington

November 15, 1977, began like most any other fall day in Washington. The morning temperature hovered in the upper forties, and the forecast called for an afternoon high of around sixty. It had been unusually cool in the District of late, and residents welcomed the return of warmer weather. On Capitol Hill, the 95th Congress was working through its customary autumn slate of committee hearings and legislative proposals, with staffers poring over reams of bills on foreign affairs, the economy, and the more mundane matters of congressional governance. At the White House, President Jimmy Carter's morning was taken up with the usual round of cabinet meetings and advisers' briefings, as well as an interview with *New York Times* foreign affairs columnist C. L. Sulzberger.

The central item on Carter's agenda that day was an official visit by the head of state of Iran, Shah Reza Pahlavi. The United States had maintained a special relationship with the Shah for a quarter of a century, and the new American president was eagerly anticipating his first meeting with this longtime ally. In accordance with the Shah's importance to the United States, the White House planned to pull out all the stops with a state dinner, policy meetings, and multiple photo ops with the Shah and his elegant wife, Empress Farah. The United States had many reasons to value the Shah's friendship. Not only did he provide a steady source of oil, but he had solidified relations with Israel and the large Arab states of Egypt and Saudi Arabia, and he stood as a reliable bulwark against Soviet ambitions along the two nations' fifteen-hundred-mile border. In return for the Shah's secular anticommunism, oil, and Western orientation, the United States had provided him with modern weapons, diplomatic support, and favorable trade deals.

There was just one problem: the Western-leaning, Western-educated Shah was no Western liberal. He had ascended the throne in 1941, and he had seen his power greatly augmented in 1953 following a U.S.-backed coup. In the ensuing years he had ruled more like an eighteenth-century absolutist than a twentieth-century democrat. Iran's political institutions were ill-equipped to accommodate dissent or a political transition, and its security agency, SAVAK, was widely accused of imprisoning, torturing, and even killing dissidents. The Shah deemed these authoritarian measures necessary for a feudal society making the transition to modernity, but in the 1970s more and more Western critics were speaking out against such methods. True, the Shah was hardly the worst human rights abuser in the world. His ambitious modernization program had benefited many Iranians, and he had recently implemented a set of limited legal and social reforms.[1] But his one-party government was neither liberal nor democratic.

The Shah's human rights record had been of little interest to American policymakers, but Jimmy Carter was a new kind of executive. He had campaigned on a promise to bring moral values to governance, and since his inauguration he had pursued an ambitious human rights policy. This activism put him into a difficult position. If he publicly confronted the Shah, he would damage the vital U.S.-Iran relationship. But if he ignored the Shah's transgressions, he would risk losing credibility for *all* of his policies, including human rights. With U.S.-Iran ties and his own policies in flux, Carter hoped to steer a middle course by publicly supporting the Shah, continuing the special relationship, and addressing Iranian human rights in private.

In keeping with the tradition of state visits to the White House, the schedule called for a welcoming reception on the South Lawn. Such ceremonies were common, but this time thousands of pro- and anti-Shah demonstrators were expected, and the presence of two opposing groups created the potential for violence. By ten o'clock that morning, around eight thousand had arrived. The anti-Shah crowd was an unusual mix of students, Marxists, Muslims, and liberals who were united only in their loathing of the Shah. Well-known figures from the 1960s antiwar movement proclaimed Iran to be America's worst police-state ally, while an Iranian student group declared that "the U.S. government, multinational corporate interests, and the Shah" were "engaged in an orchestrated effort to mask the reality of oppression in Iran." The pro-Shah group, meanwhile, was composed of expatriate Iranian students, professionals, and diplomats. Rumors abounded as to who was funding the demonstrations, with each side predictably accusing the other of dubious backing and malevolent motives.[2]

Tensions were high on the Ellipse just south of the White House, where upward of three thousand people were split into pro- and anti-Shah camps with a line of mounted police between them. Many in the anti-Shah group wore masks to avoid (so they said) being photographed and identified by the Shah's secret police. As each side eyed the other nervously and exchanged insults, the match that lit the dynamite was the arrival of the Shah. When he was ushered out to the South Lawn and his twenty-one-gun salute rang out over the Ellipse, all hell broke loose. The anti-Shah demonstrators attacked the Shah's supporters with rocks, bottles, fists, and wooden planks that were piled up for construction of the upcoming Christmas "Pageant of Peace." The younger members of the pro-Shah contingent fought back. Outnumbered and in danger, the police fired tear gas to disperse the crowd.

A few hundred yards away on the South Lawn, the ceremony's well-dressed attendees quickly realized that something was amiss. Carter later recalled hearing in the distance "the faint but unmistakable sounds of a mob" before the gathering was enshrouded in tear gas.[3] While his esteemed visitor daubed at his eyes with a handkerchief, Carter spoke of America's historical ties to Iran, after which the Shah reciprocated by rather ominously stating, "We shall stay, hopefully, always together because basically we believe in the same principles."[4] The entourage then retired to the White House. Back on the Ellipse, the police succeeded in separating the two groups and shepherding them out of the area. All told, there were 124 injuries. The police took extra precautions throughout the remainder of the Shah's visit, including placing riot police inside the White House fences and sharpshooters on the roof.

Unfortunately for Carter and the Shah, the world news media paid little attention to their words on the South Lawn, instead focusing on the riot—the bloodiest in Washington since the Vietnam War—and its effect on the august ceremony. Newspapers around the world published front-page photos of the dignitaries wiping away tears as Carter spoke at the podium. The footage shocked Iranians, who had never seen their leader in such apparent peril. Many took the riot as evidence that American support for the Shah was on the wane; why else, they asked, would the Americans have allowed these protests to take place? "We learned last night," said one Iranian in Washington, "that news of our protest efforts had reached home, and the people were rejoicing. When they saw the Shah wipe his eyes from the tear gas, they thought we had gassed [him]!"[5]

At that evening's state dinner, Carter tried to make light of the demonstrations. "One thing that I can say about the Shah," he quipped, "he certainly knows how to draw a crowd."[6] But critics saw very little to laugh about. How could Carter reconcile his desire for close relations with his supposed interest in human rights? Was it not appropriate, they asked, to press the Shah strongly on liberal reforms in Iran? Despite these criticisms, Carter was hardly outspoken in public or in private. Behind closed doors, he asked the Shah if he could ease his domestic security policies, and the latter replied with an unequivocal no. He had to enforce Iran's laws, he told the president, in order to prevent the spread of communist influence. Most opponents of his regime, he claimed, were "Marxists, anarchists wearing masks."[7] Although Carter would have liked to see more substantive reforms, his administration prioritized a strong, stable Iran, and the Shah seemed the best bet to ensure just that. Because Carter had no viable alternative to the Shah's rule, human rights would remain, for the time being, a distant priority.[8] He offered his visitor a warm toast at the state dinner, praising the Shah's "enlightened leadership" and extolling Iran as a "stabilizing influence" in the Middle East. "We look upon Iran's strength as an extension of our own strength," Carter declared, "and Iran looks upon our strength as an extension of theirs."[9]

The violence surrounding the Shah's Washington visit brought home to President Carter and his allies the problems they faced in trying to make human rights an integral part of American diplomacy. The demonstrations also symbolized the troubles that the Shah, and America, would soon face in Iran. Although the Washington protests were about much more than Iran's lack of democracy and civil liberties, they signaled the level of Iranian dissatisfaction with the Shah, and they showed Jimmy Carter that a "moral" foreign policy was easier to proclaim than it was to implement. Neither leader could have known just how little time the Shah had left. Demonstrators soon took to the streets of Teheran calling for everything from a parliamentary democracy to an Islamic theocracy. After a year of unrest, the Shah fled his country in January 1979 and Iran became an Islamic republic, ending 2,500 years of the Persian monarchy. On November 4, 1979—almost exactly two years after the Washington protests—Iranian students stormed the U.S. embassy in Teheran and set off the 444-day hostage crisis. Carter later wrote of the 1977 Washington riot, "That day . . . was an augury" that soon "there would be real grief in our country because of Iran."[10]

Carter's ambiguous position on human rights in Iran exemplified American ambiguity toward human rights practices worldwide after 1945.

Time and again, Americans were faced with a quandary: Should they stand up for liberal, democratic principles and human rights everywhere? Or should they follow a more pragmatic course in pursuit of a narrow set of national interests? Did superpower status oblige the United States to promote human rights around the world? Should America simply lead by example rather than "meddling" in other nations' affairs? Did moral concerns even belong in foreign policy? How Americans answered these questions is the subject of this book.

Human Rights from Tet to Tiananmen Square

This study explains the emergence and institutionalization of human rights in American foreign policy between 1967 and 1991. The modern international movement rose from the ashes of the Second World War, but for two decades the U.S. government was only a minor participant. It was in the quarter century between the late 1960s and the Cold War's end that presidents, legislators, foreign service officers, and bureaucrats embarked upon a sustained, though hardly consistent, campaign to address abuses in the Soviet Union, Iran, Chile, South Korea, and dozens of other countries. The most important distinction between these activities and Washington's traditional diplomatic representations was that human rights diplomacy was carried out on behalf of foreign nationals, not American citizens. Defending American lives and property was a customary role for U.S. officials; addressing the well-being of other nations' citizens was not. In this new era, Congress held hearings on international human rights, cut aid to abusive regimes, passed "sense of the Congress" resolutions, assailed presidential indifference, and required the executive to produce detailed human rights reports. Presidents and diplomats used a combination of private diplomacy (usually with "friendly," pro-American clients), sanctions, and public criticism (usually with communist or nonaligned nations) to move governments toward more humane practices. Nongovernmental organizations (NGOs) expanded in number and influence, raising awareness among politicos and the public alike. These efforts had a notable impact on American diplomacy in the latter years of the Cold War and beyond.

This book addresses several problems in modern American diplomacy and politics. It sheds light on the domestic sources of foreign policy and the conflict between the executive and legislative branches. It explains why human rights policies emerged as such attractive political solutions and considers why these policies were so difficult to implement. It explains why some causes were more prominent in Washington than others. It explores the role of non-state actors in the policymaking process and in the publicizing of human rights abuses. Most important of all, this book challenges readers to ponder America's role in the modern world. The story told here exemplifies the classic struggle between the realist tradition in foreign affairs, which emphasizes the pursuit of power, stability, and the national interest, and the idealist tradition, which promotes multilateralism, humanitarianism, and international law. President Richard Nixon crystallized the former sentiment with the mantra, "We deal with governments as they are, not as we would like them to be."[11] President Jimmy Carter articulated the latter tradition when he stated, "Human rights is the soul of our foreign policy because human rights is the very soul of our sense of nationhood."[12]

Although the narrative herein begins before the Tet Offensive of 1968 and extends a few years beyond the Tiananmen Square massacre of 1989, Tet and Tiananmen are conveniently alliterative signposts for the sweeping changes of the Vietnam War era and the Cold War's end. Within this time frame, American interest in global human rights was especially evident in three major turning points—the late 1960s, 1973, and the late 1980s. In the early Cold War era, support for authoritarian anticommunist regimes occasioned little comment. Even as late as 1965, few Americans questioned the assumptions behind President Lyndon Johnson's decision to send troops into South Vietnam and, for a brief time, the Dominican Republic. But as the war in Vietnam became increasingly costly in blood and treasure, domestic support diminished and policymakers were confronted with uncomfortable questions about the war's wholesale violence and its effect on civilians. The bombing campaigns and atrocities like the My Lai massacre spurred a public conversation on the justice of the fight, and the image of the United States as a beacon of freedom was challenged, and occasionally supplanted, by the image of America as an agent of suffering. As more and more observers suggested that the United States was fighting an unjust, unwinnable war, a parallel concern emerged that Washington was exacerbating repression through its support of illiberal, undemocratic regimes worldwide. When congressional liberals began to defect from the Cold War consensus by demanding a drawdown of the Vietnam commitment, they also shed light on America's many other troublesome relationships. They focused first on the autocratic regimes in Greece and Brazil.

Other "friendly" states (Iran, South Korea, and Indonesia, among others) also attracted activists' attention in the late sixties and early seventies, as did humanitarian crises in Biafra and Bangladesh. Likewise, legislators challenged the budding U.S.-Soviet détente by publicizing the Soviet Union's mistreatment of dissidents and Jews. As a result, the Soviet Jewry movement emerged as the most significant, broad-based human rights movement of the 1970s.

Beginning in 1973, policymakers' and activists' attention shifted to South America. General Augusto Pinochet's military coup d'état against President Salvador Allende of Chile was a watershed moment, in part because of the Pinochet regime's brutality and in part because of the widespread (though flawed) perception that the United States had orchestrated Allende's overthrow. Alongside the Soviet Jewry issue, the Pinochet coup and its aftermath arguably did more than any other overseas event to propel the human rights push in Washington. This same year, Congressman Donald Fraser (D-MN) held the first generalized human rights hearings in congressional history, and a group of legislators sponsored the first of dozens of bills that would eventually curtail aid to anticommunist dictatorships. For the remainder of the decade—especially during the presidency of Jimmy Carter—activists and policymakers would spotlight abuses in South America's Southern Cone (Chile, Argentina, Uruguay, Paraguay) and Eastern Europe, with a few other regions occasionally coming into focus.

The second half of the 1980s saw the most wide-ranging efforts of all. The first administration of President Ronald Reagan (1981–1985) generally tolerated allied governments' excesses in the name of Cold War pragmatism, but Reagan's second term signaled a substantial departure. In conjunction with the global democracy trend and the waning East/West ideological conflict, the executive and legislative branches and both political parties backed human rights and democratization efforts across a wider swath of the globe than at any time before or since. In this relatively short period, policymakers and activists took up causes in East Asia, the Soviet Union, Eastern Europe, South and Central America, and South Africa. Political divisions remained, but it is hard to deny that American policymakers did a great deal in the late eighties to promote liberal reforms and democratic transitions. The dissolution of the Soviet Union and the end of the Cold War then constituted a final breaking point. After 1991, absent a competing superpower or even an alternative ideological vision, the political salience of human rights waned noticeably in Washington, while the violations of nonstate actors increased in prominence.

Into the Human Rights Era: The 1970s as a Turning Point

The story of the international human rights movement is long, complex, and largely beyond the purview of this book.[13] Much more germane to this study is the question of why and how human rights concerns became a part of American foreign policy. Within the post-1945 time frame, there is general scholarly agreement that the 1970s was a defining decade, from the standpoints of both American politics and international activism. Simply put, before this time international human rights mattered very little in most world capitals, but perceptions and policies changed so much in the seventies that scholars now refer to this as the decade of the human rights "breakthrough," and even "revolution."[14] In a provocative turn of phrase, Samuel Moyn has suggested that the global human rights movement was "the last utopia"—a largely post-1970 phenomenon that was viable as a program and lexicon only in the context of the failure of earlier social orders and utopian ideologies.[15]

Several factors combined to create a more congenial environment for human rights concerns in the late 1960s and 1970s. This period's aberrant rise in civil conflicts, military coups, and outright atrocities drew international attention, and may have convinced some Americans that the United States should play a stronger role in protecting civilians. Civil wars and genocides plagued Bangladesh, Burundi, and Cambodia, while undeclared civil struggles ("dirty wars") afflicted Argentina, Chile, and Uruguay.[16] There were military dictatorships in Brazil, Greece, and Indonesia, and violent racial and political conflicts in South Africa, Uganda, and Rhodesia. Civil wars increased in intensity, with the late sixties and early seventies seeing a nearly threefold increase in worldwide battle-related deaths over the previous decade. (The numbers remained high until 1991, after which they dropped precipitously.)[17] A tidal swell of NGO activity and news coverage helped bring these issues to the attention of Western governments and publics.

Concurrent with the rise in civil violence was the retreat of liberal democracy. Between 1950 and 1975, the proportion of nations with functioning parliamentary systems declined. At the dawn of the seventies, communist governments in Eastern Europe and Asia seemed as resolute as ever, while right-wing autocracies were ubiquitous in much of the rest of the world. Across the global South, notes Roland Burke, there was a marked expansion of authoritarianism, including twenty-six coups in Africa in the

1960s, mostly in the decade's final few years. As Kathryn Sikkink has pointed out, in Latin America alone upward of a dozen nations underwent a wave of repression from the 1960s to the 1980s that was unprecedented in the twentieth century. "In virtually all cases," she writes, "the repression was carried out under military regimes that had come to power through the wave of coups that swept the region in the 1960s and 1970s. . . . We have to go back to the colonial and independence periods to find comparable violence."[18]

The Cold War thaw and President Richard Nixon's détente policy also helped fuel human rights interest in Washington. Nixon and his closest foreign policy adviser, Henry Kissinger, pursued détente with the Soviet Union as a means of preventing nuclear war, limiting the arms race, and containing Soviet ambitions. The Soviets, meanwhile, sought recognition, Western technology, arms control agreements, and respect for existing borders. A mutually beneficial relationship developed. Soviet Ambassador Anatoly Dobrynin later recalled that Soviet-American relations "reached a level of amity in 1973 never before achieved in the postwar era."[19] Neither set of leaders cared to make human rights a part of this process, but the close relationship facilitated American influence in the internal affairs of the Eastern Bloc. The most prominent legislative attempt to wield this influence was the Jackson-Vanik amendment to the 1974 Trade Act, which tied U.S.-Soviet trade to Soviet Jews' right to emigrate. The Cold War thaw also increased the potential for action against nominal American allies. In earlier years, dictators' probusiness and anticommunist credentials were enough to earn a passing grade from American policymakers, a sentiment summarized in a senior official's alleged comment about a morally dubious ally: "He may be a son of a bitch, but he's OUR son of a bitch." The quote's origins are apocryphal, but no matter; it captures an element of truth in America's ties to unsavory autocrats like Nicaragua's Anastasio Somoza, the Dominican Republic's Rafael Trujillo, and Yugoslavia's Josip Broz Tito.[20] But in the 1970s Americans grew much less tolerant of undemocratic practices in noncommunist states. Détente shaped American diplomacy and the human rights movement until the very end of the 1970s, only to reappear in a different form in the late 1980s under Ronald Reagan and Mikhail Gorbachev.

Among the most important domestic factors was the conflict between the executive and legislative branches. As the bipartisan foreign policy consensus began to unravel in the wake of the Vietnam stalemate, Congress fought to reclaim a central role, and both parties found a convenient weapon in human rights causes. When Democrats controlled Congress and Republicans held the White House, liberals took the lead by attacking American support for right-wing dictators. Conservatives in both parties then adopted this rhetoric and embraced causes of their own. They, too, were sharply critical of presidential foreign policy, and they routinely publicized Soviet abuses in order to attack Nixon's détente policy and Reagan's rapprochement with Gorbachev. Conservatives also lambasted Jimmy Carter's human rights policy as an "abandonment" of anticommunist allies.

Another major spur to human rights policies was a phenomenon that contemporaries dubbed the "ethnic revival." As a result of long-term social transformations, Americans of a variety of lineages experienced a profound reawakening of ethno-religious pride and identification, and many entered the public arena to assert their identities and lobby on behalf of their overseas kin. This lobbying occasionally took the form of human rights advocacy in communist countries (Poland, the Soviet Union, Cuba) as well as a few noncommunist polities (South Africa, Northern Ireland, Turkey/Cyprus). Because traditional party lines had fractured and the "ethnics" constituted large voting blocs in key districts, both parties paid a great deal of attention to ethnic lobbies and voters.

Changing perceptions of the U.S. foreign aid program were yet another influence. One of the most effective methods by which the United States could penalize abusive regimes was cutting military and economic aid. Aid cuts grew not only from the increasing attention paid to rights violations, but also from growing dissatisfaction with weapons proliferation and the entire U.S. foreign aid program. Congress first approved Marshall Plan aid to Europe in 1948, and in the ensuing years the United States allocated billions in economic and security assistance to dozens of nations. But in the 1960s, legislators engaged in heated debates over the purpose of foreign aid, and they began to tighten the rules governing aid allocation and arms exports. By the time congressional liberals drafted the first human rights laws in the 1970s, aid cuts were deemed acceptable. Unsurprisingly, these cuts were heavily politicized. Liberals were more likely to oppose military aid to authoritarian governments, while conservatives sought cuts in economic aid to poor countries.

Of course, the increasing acceptance of human rights norms did not grow out of the political realm alone; it also grew from newer, contested perceptions of individualism, rights, permissiveness, and racial and sexual matters. The growing interest in human rights abroad paralleled the increasing acceptance of the "mosaic" character of the American nation, as well as the cautious acceptance of ethnic and racial factors in the making of foreign policy. Human rights became a part of the foreign policy process at the same time that the American political system was becoming more pluralistic. By the 1970s, Americans had tackled many of their most troublesome domestic civil rights issues, and they were now willing to cast their reform energies overseas. The Cold War thaw allowed them to do just that. As the scholar-politician Michael Ignatieff has argued, "The international human rights revolution abroad would have been inconceivable without the rights revolution at home."[21] Although domestic racial conflicts persisted, mainstream opinion increasingly rejected racism. It is no coincidence, then, that the two most broad-based human rights efforts of the era—the Soviet Jewry movement and the movement against apartheid in South Africa—were challenges to racially exclusionary policies. Irrespective of the complexities of these cases, Americans generally interpreted them as matters of racial injustice. The changing norms of the post–World War II era were also closely tied to the information revolution, which improved the investigatory process and facilitated the distribution of information to policymakers, the media, and the public. Television humanized faraway suffering, while computers, fax machines, and satellite technology expanded and quickened information gathering, data analysis, and communication.

American human rights policymaking also developed alongside, and often in conjunction with, the era's other social movements. The 1970s saw the continuation of a robust activist culture amid a variety of new rights claims, from women's liberation to Chicano Power. Even European American "ethnics" began to claim the language of "rights" and "identity" as a means of distinguishing themselves from white, Protestant Americans. Kenneth Cmiel referred to these movements when he wrote that the 1970s was not "a moment of flagging liberal energy," but rather "a moment of more basic political restructuring."[22] This restructuring created new possibilities for rights claims in a variety of realms. Yet although some antiwar and civil rights activists did parlay their experiences into other causes, the movements of the sixties hold little explanatory power for the emergence of human rights diplomacy. There are, in fact, few clear connections between the earlier activism and later human rights efforts.[23]

All of these influences—détente, the Vietnam War, domestic social movements, the ethnic revival—took place against the backdrop of American social and political life in the 1970s. Many remember this decade rather wistfully as the era of leisure suits, disco, and tragicomic popular culture antiheroes like Evel Knievel. (One study of the period was ironically titled *It Seemed Like Nothing Happened.*)[24] The political and diplomatic memories, though, are less sanguine. The Cambodia Incursion, the Fall of Saigon, Watergate, gas lines, the Iran hostage crisis, and stagflation collectively symbolized economic weakness, military impotence, and cultural failure. These disappointments did not create the human rights movement, but they did fuel debates over America's role in the world. Some "neo-isolationists," who took these failures as signs that American power was limited, embraced human rights as a cheaper, less invasive form of global involvement. Others continued to see the United States as a superpower with a national mission to spread liberal, democratic values. These observers lamented the "moral weaknesses" that underpinned the political and military losses, and they saw human rights as a way of renewing America's commitment to its founding principles. Thus political figures who advocated moral concerns were tapping into both the public's resentment of Washington and the concomitant popular demand for positive ideas.

And indeed, while the human rights policies of 1967–1991 developed from unique contemporary circumstances, they also fell within a much longer tradition of American moralism. This moral strain, which had been a part of American life since the colonial era, began to merge with the nation's diplomacy early in the twentieth century. After 1945, efforts on behalf of anticommunism, national self-determination, democracy promotion, and international economic development were routinely justified in moral terms, even when many such goals clearly reflected superpower self-interest. In light of this heritage, American interest in persecuted foreign nationals from 1967 onward is easier to understand.

Major Claims

My position in this book is academic rather than activist. I do not presume that moral principles belong, ipso facto, at the center of diplomacy. I acknowledge that humanitarian concerns have arrived relatively recently in the history of international affairs, and I recognize that in centuries past, diplomacy was carried out in pursuit of royal, imperial, tribal, or national interests with little or no regard for such concerns. I also acknowledge that although international covenants define basic rights standards that all governments should respect, they prescribe few effective enforcement mechanisms. After 1945, states *chose* to be concerned with other nations' internal practices; they were rarely *obliged* to do so.

Thus I am implicitly challenging scholars who assert that American human rights policymaking has been defined by inaction, hypocrisy, and double standards. Julie Mertus argues that the divide between Washington's high-minded rhetoric and its relative inactivity amounts to a political "bait and switch" in conjunction with a high degree of inconsistency and insincerity.[25] Clair Apodaca sees "paradox" and an "erratic evolution" in American policies. She asserts that American political leaders have "routinely dismissed, deferred, or rejected human rights issues," while the public has been willing to ignore faraway violations for "the delusion of security."[26] David Forsythe, too, has found an "ambivalent and inconsistent" record in America's dealings with authoritarian states.[27] Others have highlighted America's record of nonaccession to multilateral covenants, or have criticized U.S. support to a succession of autocrats, from Ferdinand Marcos and Nicolae Ceaușescu to Suharto and Mobutu Sese Seko.[28]

These authors argue, to varying degrees, that the United States did not go far enough in its efforts to protect human rights worldwide. This is a defensible position for an activist, but it is rather presumptuous for a scholar of diplomacy. When asserting that human rights should play a more prominent role in American foreign relations, these authors are often correct on the facts. Clearly the United States has had relationships with many undemocratic governments. But writers who assail American "hypocrisy" do so at the risk of ignoring context and experience. The history of international affairs is one of alliances, allegiances, partnerships, and friendships that are constantly in flux; friends quickly become enemies, and vice versa. This has been true for centuries: consider Lord Palmerston's assertion that Britain had no permanent allies, only permanent interests, and Thomas Jefferson's admonition against entangling alliances for the United States.

One is bound to see "hypocrisy" or "double standards" in American human rights policies if one believes that consistency is a realistic goal. In fact, consistency is an impossible standard. It is proper, of course, to probe the extent of U.S. support to authoritarian regimes and to assess whether such support facilitates abuse. But we should acknowledge the broad array of American national interests, as well as each nation's unique customs, traditions, and economic and security needs. Moreover, considering the relative paucity of democracies for much of the past century, a zealous determination to deal only with nations that shared America's political traditions and social values would have isolated the United States from most of the world. Critics of American inaction also tend to downplay the social complexities that engender authoritarian forms of government. Although many regimes have blatantly violated their citizens' rights, it has also often been the case that these governments were responding to serious threats from dangerous neighbors, homegrown terrorists, or armed insurgencies.

I offer four major claims. First, although the Cold War was only one chapter in the long human rights narrative (and can, in fact, be considered marginal to this evolution), it was central to the story of human rights in American foreign policy. American human rights politics were deeply embedded in Cold War ideological divisions and domestic political conflicts. These divides were reflected in the selectivity of policies and rhetoric, especially conservatives' tendency to condemn left-wing governments in Eastern Europe and liberals' tendency to target right-wing governments in Latin America. Beyond those two regions, authoritarian governments were either dealt with lightly (South Korea, for example) or not at all (China, Saudi Arabia, Cambodia). American participation in the antiapartheid movement in the 1980s was a rare exception to these regional preferences. Although some activists claim that the mainstream of the international movement was unconcerned with political ideologies, in reality activism and policymaking were imbued with ideological biases and preferences.[29] Cuba, South Africa, Pinochet-era Chile, and postrevolutionary Nicaragua were especially notable battlegrounds. Policymakers and activists on the right tended to overstate or misrepresent Cuban and Nicaraguan abuses while downplaying those in Chile and South Africa, and those on the left tended to do the opposite. Despite this selectivity, all sides claimed to be furthering not just American interests, but also *human* interests.

The Cold War thus stimulated *and* inhibited the global movement.[30] Americans consistently denounced communist governments' abuses after 1945, but many also tolerated allies' abuses in the name of the global ideological struggle. (Such "allies" could even include communist regimes, such as those in Yugoslavia and Romania, that demonstrated their independence from Moscow.) After the sixties, when American activists and legislators questioned Washington's support to undemocratic regimes, these governments increasingly defended their (often blatantly repressive) policies as "anticommunist" or "antiterrorist." Meanwhile, Eastern Bloc activists also shamed their governments for not living up to constitutional guarantees. Some of these activists sought reformed socialism, while others wanted to emulate Western democracies.

Second, this story is defined by a high degree of politicization, and even opportunism. Every part of the policymaking process was politicized, from congressional hearings and foreign aid debates to democracy promotion initiatives and visits of foreign dissidents. Irrespective of politicians' true feelings (and many were surely motivated, at least in part, by genuine humanitarian concern), "human rights" was a useful oppositional strategy. Virtually every presidential candidate criticized his opponents' human rights positions. Congressional advocates' political motives included their desire to attack executive policies, please local constituencies, or enhance their own publicity. In turn, presidential administrations fought pitched battles with Congress and activists over American priorities and their own interpretations of a "moral" foreign policy. As the movement grew, policy-makers faced difficult choices concerning what they might gain or lose by their own participation. A few, like Congressman Donald Fraser, partici-pated wholeheartedly and pushed the movement forward, though they did not necessarily gain politically. Others, like Senator Henry Jackson (D-WA) and Senator Edward Kennedy (D-MA), participated selectively and often enhanced their influence in the process. Those who tried to ignore the movement—Henry Kissinger, for example—had to defend their reliance upon older standards of diplomacy while also paying lip service to new norms. One thing remains clear: few policymakers had an electoral man-date to take up human rights, though some did claim one. Fraser, Jackson, Kennedy, and President Carter *chose* to champion international human rights, much as they might have chosen to champion education or inter-state highways.

Third, in light of the mixed motives behind American policies and rhet-oric, as well as these policies' varied outcomes, human rights activity in Washington cannot be explained by any single analytical model—not *real-ism*, *idealism*, *paternalism*, *paradox*, *bait and switch*, or otherwise. There were simply too many unique cases worldwide and too many interests driv-ing American involvement. Some human rights actions were aimed at alle-viating suffering, while others were outward projections of U.S. power, interests, or domestic anxieties. Some policies saved the American taxpayer money, while others hindered trade and hurt American business. Some policies challenged communist adversaries, while others pressured allied governments. Some human rights problems were deemed appropriate for American intervention, while many of the most egregious cases were ignored.

Yet although no single model or label can encompass the totality of American human rights policymaking, we can parse out a few general patterns. American policies and proclamations were largely in the national interest—more precisely, in the interest of some Americans—not simply in the interest of altruism or humanitarianism. The United States protested the actions of governments with which policymakers disagreed, and, with a few notable exceptions, policymakers avoided criticizing those governments they considered "friendly." If legislators or presidential administrations wanted to weaken a government, they used human rights and democracy policies; if they wanted to strengthen a government, they did not. This was especially true with respect to the Soviet Union. When the United States pressed the Kremlin to free political prisoners and liberalize emigration, it was a direct challenge to Soviet laws. Thus Moscow's leaders were generally correct in their belief that American activism was aimed, at least in part, at challenging the Soviet state. As for Washington's dealings with nominal allies, policymakers' chiding was generally intended to strengthen these governments, unless the leaders in question had lost popular support, in which case some in Washington would support a regime change. Policymakers then often blurred the line between encouraging reforms and interfering in events. When the United States supported democratic transitions in Haiti, the Philippines, and Chile in the 1980s, it was effectively choosing sides by working against the incumbents and quickly backing their successors.

When we consider American foreign relations in toto, international human rights concerns were secondary to more traditional interests like security, trade, international stability, strong bilateral relationships, regional hegemony, and anticommunism. Put another way, although Washington's human rights efforts were noteworthy, they were not quite revolutionary. American national security always trumped human rights, and policymakers were reluctant to hinder commerce. Important trading partners were rarely sanctioned for long. Likewise, those nations that fell outside of America's primary economic sphere were seldom a part of human rights debates in Washington. There were some exceptions to these rules: human rights sanctions against Chile and Argentina hurt some American businesses, and antiapartheid policies in the 1980s conflicted with other economic and security interests in the Southern Africa region. But these were aberrations, and the sanctions in question only transpired after months or years of difficult political wrangling.

Another natural consequence of these priorities was that policymakers opted for bilateral policies over multilateral ones. Many Americans had long harbored deep suspicions of multilateral agreements and organizations like the League of Nations (pre-1939) and the United Nations (post-1945). Consequently, although the United States established groundbreaking bilateral human rights policies in the 1970s, Americans were far less willing to embrace multilateral policies. The U.N. human rights treaties languished in the Senate for years, while many U.N. bureaus became sounding boards for nonaligned and communist governments' criticisms of the Western democracies. As the United Nations lost credibility in the human rights field, national legislatures like the U.S. Congress took on a more significant role. Global human rights concerns were addressed more effectively through the traditional mechanisms of bilateral relations than through multilateral forums.

My final major claim is that inconsistency was central to human rights policymaking and enforcement. The U.S. government's inability to create a strong, consistent set of policies that applied equally to all nations was a natural outcome of the fractiousness of politics and the sheer variety of interests competing for attention in Washington. This inability further stemmed from a series of problems that beset the human rights movement from the very start. The entire post-1945 regime of universal rights and international law was defined by a conflict—some considered it a *contradiction*—between the rights of states and the rights of individuals. Because national sovereignty is one of the oldest and most fundamental principles of international law, the new emphasis on individual integrity clearly implied a radical reinterpretation of sovereignty. Furthermore, while the Universal Declaration of Human Rights proclaimed the inviolability of the individual, the U.N. Charter's second article reinforced the primacy of national sovereignty and sovereign equality. Authoritarian regimes thus relied on the maxim that a nation's "internal affairs" were its own business, while activists touted the individual as the basic building block of international relations.

Another source of seemingly "inconsistent" behavior grew out of disagreement over the precise definition of a human right. Beyond the most basic matters of individual inviolability—freedom from torture, freedom from extrajudicial execution, and the like—there was no consensus. Activists also found that several cultural, ideological, and religious traditions challenged Western definitions. The impoverished citizens of developing nations were arguably more interested in economic growth than in freedom of expression or religious pluralism. And while the Western democracies exalted individual liberty and corporal integrity, Marxists assailed this as "bourgeois ideology" and instead touted social equality, also known as "economic, social, and cultural rights." Likewise, cultural relativists and pluralists argued that every culture had a unique conception of rights and obligations, while the postcolonial perspective asserted that human rights were a "neo-imperialistic" imposition upon non-Western societies. In the words of the scholars Adamantia Pollis and Peter Schwab, the liberal human rights doctrine was "a Western construct with limited applicability" to the belief systems, values, and needs of much of the world's people.[31] Islam offered yet another challenge to the notion of universality through its strict moral code and the tenets of Sharia law. These divides—East/West, collective/individual, capitalist/Marxist, religious/secular—were never simple binaries.[32] Many in the West, for example, defended the legitimacy of economic and social rights. Nevertheless, these conflicts consistently hampered activists' efforts.

For Washington policymakers, these disputes were overshadowed by the far more important debate over the national interest. While activists argued that human rights promotion was in America's interest, conservative cold warriors and advocates of traditional diplomacy asserted that the United States should support any stable, anticommunist government. In their eyes, cutting military aid and arms sales destabilized allies, hurt American businesses, and decreased Washington's leverage but did not prevent regimes from obtaining aid and weapons elsewhere. Was it not preferable, conservatives asked, to maintain cordial relations with undemocratic governments and, if necessary, use private diplomacy to persuade them to reform gradually? The diplomatic corps, too, found much to dislike about human rights rules. Foreign service officers (FSOs) were trained to cooperate with foreign governments, but new laws and practices forced them to broach uncomfortable subjects with their hosts.

In response to these criticisms of morality in foreign policy, activists offered an alternative vision of the national interest—one that included the well-being of other states' citizens. Some argued that liberal democracies made better, more stable allies. Others claimed that ties to oppressive governments hurt America's reputation and even spurred foreign policy setbacks, as when revolutionaries overthrew U.S.-backed regimes in Iran and Nicaragua. Most activists, though, justified their vision by pointing to humanism and the American liberal tradition. The United States, they argued, should pursue human rights because this was the right thing to do and because these were consistent with the nation's founding principles. Realists countercharged that none of these justifications gave much guidance on when and where to apply such ideals, and even activists had to admit that there was a profound difference between desiring a freer, more democratic world, and taking up a national mission to spread liberty and democracy. Some activists argued that America was duty-bound to act because it was a powerful nation that could use its vast economic resources, diplomatic leverage, and even the threat of military force to change other governments' behavior. But as activists and policymakers would discover time and again between 1967 and 1991, there were limits to American power, and policymakers were rarely able to convince other governments— or other U.S. government agencies, for that matter—to do exactly what they wanted.

One final observation: human rights NGOs were only of marginal importance to Washington policymaking in comparison with their importance to the global movement. This is not to say that human rights NGOs were ineffective; it is, rather, to say that other non-state actors played a more substantial role in America. The number and variety of NGOs concerned with international human rights were remarkable. Hundreds of ethnic associations, churches, synagogues, private foundations, and labor unions occasionally worked on behalf of human rights causes, from the Polish-American Congress and the National Conference on Soviet Jewry to the National Council of Churches and the AFL-CIO. As for the major human rights organizations—Amnesty International, Human Rights Watch, and Freedom House, among others—they did help deter abuses by conducting research, providing information to policymakers, and shaming governments into freeing prisoners and commuting sentences. But dealing with Washington was only one aspect of their methodology, and their efforts paled in significance to those of other non-state actors.

This book explores those human rights causes that had the most resonance in Washington, as well as those that illustrated broader trends in the policymaking and activist communities. For reasons of space, I have omitted detailed discussions of cases for which American efforts engendered few substantive policies. I have also left out details about multilateral human rights bodies like the U.N. Human Rights Commission and the Conference on Security and Cooperation in Europe (Helsinki) follow-up meetings. Not only have other scholars already explored these subjects in great depth, but bilateral relationships have been much more integral to the story of American human rights policymaking.

Chapter 1

The Crisis of Confidence

This chapter explores the domestic and international milieus in which human rights violations became a concern of the American people and their government. Early in the Cold War, policymakers' fear of communism overshadowed their global humanitarian concerns, but by the late sixties many more Americans were questioning their nation's ties to undemocratic, anticommunist regimes. This chapter takes a close look at Greece and Brazil, which fell under dictatorial rule in the sixties and became two of the earliest human rights causes in Washington. It also places Richard Nixon and Henry Kissinger's realist foreign policy alongside activists' and legislators' increasing attention to human rights violations. The Nixon administration's critics raised questions about the lack of democracy and individual liberty in Eastern Europe, South America, and elsewhere, but Nixon and Kissinger remained steadfast in their defense of realpolitik. China also stands out in this story for the almost complete absence of Western attention to its violations during the Sino-American rapprochement of the early 1970s.

Prologue: Human Rights After 1945

The broad-based international human rights movement that began to coalesce in the middle of the twentieth century drew on diverse origins. Paul Gordon Lauren has aptly described this movement as the convergence point of multiple premodern and modern "visions."[1] With a nod to some notable antecedents, its roots lay in the ideals of the eighteenth-century Enlightenment and the French and American revolutions. In the ensuing two centuries, growing wealth and interdependence in the Western world spurred the aspirations of the middle class, workers, women, and ethnic and religious minorities. In the twentieth century, the horrors of two world wars fueled calls for more substantial civilian protections in international law, while advances in communication and transportation increased interconnectedness and the proliferation of liberal ideas.

The carnage of the Second World War—especially the wholesale slaughter of civilian populations—threw into sharp relief the need to address the failures of the Versailles peace and to establish and enforce international rights standards. Accordingly, between 1945 and 1950 the world community created a set of regional frameworks and multilateral covenants.[2] This period saw a significant change in attitudes toward basic rights and the proper composition of international law, as evidenced by such milestones as the U.N. Charter (1945), the Nuremberg case law (1945–1949), the Universal Declaration of Human Rights (1948), the Genocide Convention (1948), and the European Convention on Human Rights (1950). The Universal Declaration became the blueprint for national and regional policies, and it remains the most commonly cited document in the human rights pantheon. In effect, a new global vision posited that citizens and states could rightly concern themselves with the well-being of other states' citizens. The international community was giving unprecedented attention to what Susan Sontag called "the pain of others."[3]

American policymakers' active involvement in these efforts reflected a major shift in domestic attitudes toward internationalism. The failings of prewar unilateralism (or "isolationism") made the World War II generation far more willing to accept the burdens of Great Power status. Americans were thus at the forefront of the creation and maintenance of the United Nations, the Security Council, the International Monetary Fund, and the World Bank. The Cold War then convinced most of the remaining conservatives and unilateralists that faraway events could have dire consequences for American security, and this new, activist attitude became manifest in the Marshall Plan, the North Atlantic Treaty Organization (NATO), and President Harry S. Truman's containment doctrine.

Yet despite America's democratic traditions and its leading role in postwar standard-setting, American humanitarian activism waned after 1950. A combination of Cold War concerns, political realism, lingering isolationism, and domestic racial conflicts kept human rights at the margins of American diplomacy. A general consensus emerged that Washington would back undemocratic but anticommunist leaders in the developing world while also working to undermine or depose left-leaning regimes. Political disagreements remained, but they concerned means, not ends. A 1950 memo from diplomat George Kennan to Secretary of State Dean Acheson regarding Latin America demonstrates policymakers' tendency to deemphasize democracy and individual rights in favor of the struggle against communism. "We cannot be too dogmatic," argued Kennan, "about the methods by which local communists can be dealt with" in Latin America. "Where the concepts and traditions of popular government are too weak" to fend off aggression, "then we must concede that harsh governmental methods of repression may be the only answer; that these measures may have to proceed from regimes whose origins and methods would not stand the test of American concepts of democratic procedure; and that such regimes and such methods may be preferable alternatives, and indeed the only alternative, to further communist successes."[4]

True to Kennan's directive, American leaders of the fifties and sixties typically chose pragmatism and realism over vague standards of universal rights and a costly push for liberal democracy. As the presidential adviser William P. Bundy has written, the moral problem of backing dictators "hardly troubled an America engrossed in what she saw as a major job of preserving the national independence of new nations and protecting them from . . . totalitarian methods of government."[5] Many saw multilateral human rights instruments as threats to U.S. sovereignty, or worried that embracing such instruments would lead other nations to criticize racial segregation in America. Still others simply asserted that moral concerns did not belong in diplomacy, or pointed out that even the best of intentions could generate unforeseen consequences. "How often," wrote the realist scholar and political adviser Hans J. Morgenthau in 1960, "have statesmen been motivated by the desire to improve the world, and ended by making it worse? And how often have they sought one goal, and ended by achieving something they neither expected nor desired?"[6]

The Cold War thus had a dual effect on international human rights promotion. On the one hand, "rights" assumed a new respectability as Washington and Moscow promoted competing visions of state obligations. On the other hand, national security ideologies were defined in part by repressive domestic policies.[7] Cold War anticommunism differed from human rights activism, though at times the two overlapped. Anticommunism stimulated the work of ethnic activists who sought to curb authoritarianism in their ancestral homelands, but these desires went unrequited in the fifties and six-ties because East/West relations were so poor. America's support of auto-cratic, anticommunist regimes also hindered global liberal and democratic developments. This is not to say that Americans were uninterested in civil and political liberties; it is simply to say that their interest was not global in scope. The unique civil rights struggle of African Americans was only inciden-tally "transnational" for much of the fifties and sixties, though civil rights–era violence did serve as fodder for communist propaganda outlets—unwanted attention that may have speeded the passage of federal civil rights legislation.[8]

As America's postwar human rights momentum was nipped in the bud, such concerns were largely ignored in the making of foreign policy. True, Americans remained genuinely concerned about communist governments' transgressions, and criticism of totalitarianism was, in a broad sense, a com-mentary on individual liberty. American political rhetoric and public opin-ion posited a "free world" struggle to contain communism, and in the 1960s Congress did hold a few hearings on religious intolerance in the East-ern Bloc. But Americans aimed their reformist energies at solving the nation's considerable racial problems, not international human rights vio-lations. According to the policymaking logic of the day, human rights were the business of bodies like the U.N. Commission on Human Rights (UNHRC), not Congress or the president. As the activist Aryeh Neier has argued, multilateral human rights instruments "barely registered on the consciousness of even those most preoccupied with struggles over rights in the U.S."[9]

The few global human rights issues that confronted the Lyndon Johnson administration (1963–1969) were generally relegated to the U.N. mission. Johnson allowed his representatives to issue mild criticisms of some com-munist governments, but he did little else, even on behalf of popular causes. Soviet anti-Semitism, for example, spurred the formation of NGOs, rallies in several American cities, and regular pickets at the Soviet embassy, but Washington's official sympathy was not matched by political will or diplo-matic initiatives.[10] Such issues were still embedded in a Cold War ideologi-cal framework: just as Soviet propagandists attacked American racism, Americans attacked Soviet anti-Semitism. The Johnson administration encouraged direct appeals from private organizations, but in the absence of a closer East/West working relationship Americans could do little to help Soviet citizens. Besides, few in the mid-1960s believed that letters to the Kremlin would change Soviet internal policies. After the 1967 Arab-Israeli

War, activists' attention shifted from anti-Semitism to Soviet-Jewish emigration, and this interest would prove to have effects far beyond anyone's expectations. (Richard Nixon would continue President Johnson's hands-off approach, but he would find it much harder to sustain his priorities in the face of the Soviet Jewry movement.)

The Johnson administration also avoided a leading role in South Africa and Rhodesia. The global interest in these two states demonstrated that national self-determination and racial equality were two of the most prominent rights claims of the fifties and sixties.[11] Many nations, NGOs, and multilateral forums attempted to undermine the South African system of apartheid—white-minority political rule and de jure white social and economic domination—through resolutions, economic sanctions, and boycotts. President Kennedy halted U.S. arms sales to South Africa in 1962, and the following year the U.N. Security Council passed a voluntary arms embargo. The Johnson administration continued Kennedy's policy, but was unwilling to go beyond concurrence with the international status quo. Near the end of his presidency, Johnson even sought better relations with Pretoria in response to the rise of a radical bloc in the United Nations.[12]

Nor did the United States take the lead when the white-dominated government of Southern Rhodesia declared unilateral independence from the United Kingdom in 1965 as a means of forestalling a transition to independence and all-but-inevitable black rule. The United States endorsed a British-authored sanctions resolution, and Johnson issued an executive order prohibiting Rhodesian chrome imports and American oil and arms exports. He cited the principles of majority rule and national self-determination, though it seems that his chief concerns were domestic African American and liberal opinion, Anglo-American relations, and relations with other African states. Johnson's U.N. ambassador, Arthur Goldberg, suggested that the United States was obliged to support U.N. sanctions, because to do otherwise would inhibit Johnson's domestic racial policies and hurt American businesses in Africa. But with Johnson's attention on Vietnam and Europe, his administration followed the British lead and used American influence only behind the scenes. "There are times when the best policy is to sit things out on the sidelines," advised one insider. "Any efforts on our part to straighten things out . . . will be at best useless, at worst counter-productive. So let's be nice, generous, friendly—and aloof." Secretary of State Dean Rusk similarly advised Johnson that Rhodesia was "first a U.K. problem, then a U.N. problem, and only then is it a U.S. problem."[13]

Some Americans opposed the chrome embargo. Not only did it force American manufacturers to buy from the Soviet Union, but Rhodesia and South Africa were anticommunist and arguably better potential allies than the other African states. (Johnson even had to politely refuse Rhodesian volunteers for service in Vietnam.) "I know the Negro has been putting pressure on to break relations with Rhodesia," one Texan wrote to Johnson in 1967, "but why should we quit buying from a democratic country and buy from our known enemy?" Senator Sam Ervin (D-NC) argued that the U.N. Charter did not authorize "interference" in a member state's affairs. "Rhodesia is just as much a part of the British Empire as the state of Texas is a part of the United States," he asserted.[14] Few of these critics spoke of the troubling moral issue of white-minority rule, though in light of the many violations taking place in Africa, they were perhaps justified in asking why the United States was sanctioning Rhodesia and embargoing arms to South Africa while otherwise ignoring most of the continent. The Kennedy and Johnson administrations clearly feared losing the friendship of new African states, while Johnson especially worried that a weak policy would alienate African Americans.

It was not until the end of the sixties that American policymakers began to seriously consider the role international human rights should play in American foreign policy. It is perhaps fitting that 1967–1968 proved to be a turning point in the human rights story, for this stands as the modern watershed *sine pari* of social upheaval, antiwar protests, political assassinations, radical youth movements, and "long, hot summers" of racial antagonism. Tensions extended far beyond American shores, with violent demonstrations and government crackdowns taking place in locales as disparate as Paris, Berlin, Prague, Chicago, and Mexico City. It was also a turning point for American race relations and the civil rights movement. The assassination of Martin Luther King, Jr., in April 1968 precipitated the last of the 1960s riots and ushered in a new set of domestic civil rights goals and conflicts.

In the realm of foreign relations, 1967–1968 witnessed the collapse of the Vietnam consensus and the weakening of the containment paradigm. Every presidential candidate—as well as President Johnson, who withdrew from the race—agreed that America had to rethink its global approach. As the neoconservative writer Irving Kristol noted in May 1968, "Everyone is to some extent aware that American foreign policy, after this [Vietnam] trauma, will never again be the same."[15] The Cold War became an altogether different struggle, one in which policymakers sought creative ways of decreasing overseas commitments. Other contemporary events also had broad ramifications. The April 1967 military coup in Greece brought a shocking end to democracy in a NATO member nation, while the Soviet arms buildup and the August 1968 Warsaw Pact invasion of Czechoslovakia convinced American leaders to strengthen transatlantic ties. Not coincidentally, 1967–1968 arguably witnessed the initial stirrings of détente, first between East and West Germany and later between the United States and the Soviet Union.[16] Inspired in part by these developments, some legislators and activists began to challenge the security-centered goals of the containment doctrine.

Vietnam and the End of Consensus

The new diplomatic possibilities of the late sixties emerged from the failure of older ideas. The containment principle, which originated as President Truman's short-term solution to the problem of communist insurgency in Greece and Turkey in 1947, was the blueprint for American security policy for twenty years. It was not until the Vietnam War became a stalemate that critics began to mount a serious challenge to the containment paradigm. Congressional liberals were ahead of the curve with their moral criticism of Johnson's Vietnam policy and their fear that the war would undermine the Democrats' domestic agenda. Early in 1966, before it had become fashionable to criticize the war effort, Senator Eugene McCarthy (D-MN) expressed uncertainty and some bewilderment about the bombing of North Vietnam, noting the "serious problem" that Americans were "called upon to make a kind of moral commitment to an objective or to a set of purposes which we do not clearly understand."[17] Within two years, McCarthy's sentiments had entered the mainstream. The White House and the Pentagon had long claimed that victory was imminent, but the January–February 1968 Tet Offensive showed that the Vietnamese communists were still able to mount deadly attacks. From that point forward, a majority of Americans consistently told pollsters that the war was a mistake.[18] The straightforward assumptions undergirding containment had been replaced by nagging questions, and even disillusionment; the optimism that had accompanied Johnson's electoral victory in 1964 and his Great Society program in 1965 now seemed a distant memory. When Johnson announced in March 1968 that he would not run for reelection, his attempt to deliver a message of national unity was overshadowed by his ominous tone. "There is division in the American house now," he said. "There is divisiveness among us all tonight."[19]

The war's chief influence on the human rights story was its effect on the American self-image. For a people accustomed to believing in their nation's basic decency, the war presented a difficult moral quandary. The bombing campaigns, attrition tactics, and search-and-destroy missions not only revived age-old questions about the rights of civilians during wartime, but also convinced many Americans that their nation had become an agent of suffering. Defense Secretary Robert McNamara reflected these misgivings when he wrote to President Johnson in May 1967, "The picture of the world's greatest superpower killing or seriously injuring 1,000 non-combatants a week, while trying to pound a tiny backward nation into submission on an issue whose merits are hotly disputed, is not a pretty one. It could conceivably produce a costly distortion in the American national consciousness and in the world image of the United States."[20] President Nixon would later fuel these controversies by expanding the war into Cambodia and Laos and periodically stepping up bombing of North Vietnam. Macabre stories trickling back from combat veterans also spurred questions about the rights of Vietnamese prisoners and American troops alike. For many Americans, the callousness of the war was summed up in what one officer allegedly told a reporter following an artillery barrage on the village of Bến Tre during the Tet Offensive: "It became necessary to destroy the town to save it."[21] The source of the quote went unverified, and in fact may not have existed, but the statement became part of the war's mythology nonetheless. Beyond the stories and rumors were the television and print images of the fighting. It is difficult to prove the impact that news coverage had on public opinion about the war, but there is little doubt that war footage and the Pulitzer Prize–winning images of Eddie Adams and Nick Ut humanized the violence and spawned greater public scrutiny of military decisions in a way that print journalists could not.[22]

Martin Luther King, Jr.'s, April 1967 antiwar sermon was a fascinating moment in this national transition. Not only was this a turning point in King's civil rights crusade, symbolizing as it did his movement away from mainstream activism, but his phrasing also anticipated human rights activists' critique of American foreign policy in the years to come. He offered a moral criticism that emphasized the war's unjustness and ultimately asked Americans to ponder their nation's capacity to cause, or prevent, suffering in the world. He lamented the violence, the civilian victims, and especially the paradox that America's rhetoric of high moral purpose could not mask its support of a corrupt, unpopular government. Despite American promises of peace, democracy, and land reform, he asserted, the Vietnamese people "languish under our bombs." Children were "running in packs on the streets like animals . . . degraded by our soldiers as they beg for food," while others were "selling their sisters to our soldiers, soliciting for their mothers." What did Vietnam's poor think of us, asked King, "as we test our latest weapons on them, just as the Germans tested out new medicine and new tortures in the concentration camps of Europe?" America, he proclaimed, desperately needed a "radical revolution of values. . . . When machines and computers, profit motives and property rights are considered more important than people, the giant triplets of racism, materialism, and militarism are incapable of being conquered."[23]

The controversial My Lai massacre arguably influenced Americans' perceptions of their cause in Vietnam more than any single event. My Lai was a South Vietnamese village where American soldiers killed as many as five hundred civilians during a raid in March 1968. The killing was kept secret for many months, but the story eventually made its way to the Pentagon's top brass. The Army charged several soldiers with misconduct in September 1969, and two months later investigative journalist Seymour Hersh broke the story to the public. In the longest trial in Army court martial history, upward of two dozen officers and enlisted men were charged with premeditated murder and related crimes, though only Lieutenant William Calley was convicted. He was sentenced to life in prison in March 1971 but served only eighteen weeks at Leavenworth followed by three and a half years of house arrest.

The story may not have had such resonance if it had not been for the public release of official photos that clearly showed that most of the victims were unarmed women and children. Once the photos were published, National Security Adviser Henry Kissinger and Defense Secretary Melvin Laird privately bemoaned the impossibility of "sweep[ing] the whole thing under the rug."[24] The administration feared that the story could lead to reprisals on American POWs, hinder the ongoing peace talks, and provide "grist for the mills of antiwar activists." In terms of their ability to bring the violence of the war home to Americans, the pictures were among the most powerful and disturbing in the history of war photography. After seeing them in *Time*, presidential adviser Daniel Patrick Moynihan suggested that the images had irrevocably changed the war effort. "I fear the answer of too many Americans will simply be that this is a hideous, corrupt society," he counseled Nixon. "It is America that is being judged."[25]

As the news media publicized the trials and courts martial between 1969 and 1971, My Lai provoked a great deal of soul-searching and painful questions. Were the soldiers acting on orders against a legitimate threat? Or had the war driven ordinary American boys to become hardened killers capable of slaughtering women and children without remorse? The public reaction was divided and highly politicized. One side saw in the massacre an illustration of America's dark side writ globally. They were troubled that American soldiers had killed so many innocents, and angry that only one person was convicted of war crimes. "We sense, all of us," wrote a columnist, "that our best instincts are deserting us, and we are oppressed by a dim feeling that beneath our words and phrases, almost beneath our consciousness, we are quietly choking on the blood of innocents."[26] A former Marine wrote to his senator, "I am today ashamed to be an American. . . . I feel unclean." The journalist Peter Steinfels asserted that My Lai was "a cancer in the conscience of America. . . . Is this nation taking a mass 'Manson murder' to its heart as an act of patriotic duty, of soldierly duty? Are our consciences that stunted, our sensitivities so shriveled?"[27]

On the other side, many refused to believe that a "massacre" had taken place, or simply chalked My Lai up to the ugly realities of war. Some believed that the defendants were being railroaded and that the good name of the United States and its military were being besmirched by the news media and foreign enemies. *National Review* assailed the "collective madness" of media outlets whose "irrational and irresponsible comment" threatened the Vietnam mission more than all the antiwar protestors combined.[28] Others denied that America's cause in Vietnam was unjust or that American society was "sick." "I feel [Lt. Calley] is being railroaded," wrote an Army veteran to his senator. "You congressmen sent us over there, now damn it back us up. War is war. This is a cold cruel fact."[29]

The Nixon administration knew that many Americans sought to punish the perpetrators, but it was also clear that domestic public opinion favored Calley. When Nixon commuted Calley's sentence, one of the prosecuting attorneys complained directly to the president and expressed shock that so many Americans did not seem to grasp the trial's legal and moral underpinnings—that it was "unlawful for an American soldier to summarily execute unarmed and unresisting men, women, children, and babies."[30] Nixon did not defend Calley, but in his memoir he attacked his own opponents for politicizing the affair and for ignoring North Vietnamese war crimes. "Calley's crime was inexcusable," wrote Nixon, but "the whole tragic episode was used by the media and the antiwar forces to chip away at our efforts to build public support for our Vietnam objectives."[31] In fairness to Nixon, although his commutation may have seemed insensitive relative to the magnitude of the massacre, he was asking a valid question about the biases behind his opponents' outrage. But then, it was also true that the soldiers at My Lai had killed hundreds of innocents, and Americans could not punish other nations' war criminals as easily as they could punish Lieutenant Calley.

In addition to the My Lai investigations, several forums publicized allegations of human rights violations and atrocities in Southeast Asia. In 1971, a group called Vietnam Veterans Against the War held a public "Winter Soldier Investigation," which featured three days of antiwar testimony from Vietnam veterans of all services. The recurring themes in these testimonies were American brutality, arbitrary violence, and violations of the rights of the Vietnamese. Former Marine William Crandall's opening statement set the tone of the event: "We went to preserve the peace and our testimony will show that we have set all of Indochina aflame. We went to defend the Vietnamese people and our testimony will show that we are committing genocide against them. We went to fight for freedom and our testimony will show that we have turned Vietnam into a series of concentration camps."[32] Critics charged that the allegations were sensationalized or that these veterans were anti-American; others rationalized the violence as an unfortunate reality of war. Whatever the truth, the testimonies were further ammunition for those questioning the morality of U.S. foreign policy. In the eyes of some observers, the war had placed the United States into the ranks of the world's human rights abusers. When a congressional committee asked the former presidential adviser James C. Thomson, Jr., in 1972 whether a U.S. withdrawal might precipitate a bloodbath in Vietnam, he replied, "It strikes me that the bloodbath danger has to be put in the context of the daily bloodbath we have inflicted on three countries."[33]

For more and more Americans, this moral criticism of the war—its violence, its uncertain purpose, and its ability to turn young men into killers—evolved seamlessly into indignation that the United States was supporting autocratic regimes worldwide. Daniel Patrick Moynihan aptly noted in 1970 that the younger generation, in particular, was "marked by the belief that its government is capable of performing abhorrent deeds."[34] Prominent congressional activists of the 1970s and 1980s like Donald Fraser and Tom Harkin saw Vietnam as the prime motivator for public and congressional examinations of America's human rights record. In Harkin's case, this inspiration came in 1970, when as a congressional aide he saw firsthand the infamous "tiger cages" and political prisoners in South Vietnam's Con Son prison.[35]

Yet although it is tempting to draw a neat causative line from America's Vietnam experience to the human rights activism of the seventies, we should be careful not to overstate the case. The war's opponents rarely framed their charges in the language of "human rights," and a substantial proportion of Americans continued to support the war effort all the way to the 1973 peace accords. Moreover, as American troop numbers dropped after 1968, so did public attention. In reality, a relatively small number of activists and congressional liberals channeled their outrage about carpet bombing and tiger cages into a broader criticism of American ties to autocracies worldwide.[36] Nevertheless, given the scope of America's long experience in Southeast Asia—a quarter century of involvement, a decade of combat, seven million tons of bombs dropped, nearly three million Americans serving in country, and more than two hundred thousand of them killed or wounded—the war undoubtedly played at least some part in spurring the human rights movement in Washington. The Vietnam tragedy had a considerable impact on American political and cultural life, and it continued to influence foreign policy well into the 1990s.

In the larger human rights story, the war's effect on Americans' self-image was only the tip of a very large iceberg. Multiple political, military, and economic failures in the late 1960s and 1970s ushered in a decade-long drop in public trust that was often described as a "crisis of confidence." This crisis did not "cause" human rights activism in any clear sense, but it did confirm for many Americans what the Vietnam debacle had already suggested: that their nation was no longer exceptional. All signs seemed to point to a decline in American power. As the Bretton Woods system collapsed and the American economy entered a period of uneven growth and high inflation, the U.S. standard of living dropped from first to tenth in the world. American industry faced major challenges from Japan and West Germany—a decline in industrial prowess that paralleled the disturbing decay of America's cities. The long gas lines and exorbitant heating bills spawned by the energy crises brought home Americans' reliance on imported oil, while the humiliating hostage crisis at the end of the seventies revealed the nation's impotence when confronting hostility overseas. For the Anglophone Western world, the crisis of confidence may have been more perception than reality.[37] But these economic and political shocks did deepen Americans' feelings of powerlessness in international affairs while also contributing to political apathy, mistrust of government, and alienation from the democratic process. As John Lewis Gaddis has noted of this era's anxious insularity, "Americans seemed mired in endless arguments with themselves."[38]

This air of gloom had a foreign policy corollary that went beyond Vietnam and the Johnson and Nixon administrations' "credibility gap." Just as Americans were increasingly unsure of their nation's greatness, they were also less willing to believe in its "goodness"—that is, that the United States was a nation that did good things. Every era has its problems and its social critics, but it does appear that Americans grew more pessimistic at the turn of the seventies. The Harris Alienation Index rose from 29 percent in 1966 to 59 percent in 1974, and remained relatively consistent for the next two decades.[39] A group of university students told Henry Kissinger in 1971 that their peers felt "alienation" and "really wanted nothing to do with the system." There was "a general withdrawal from governmental processes," they said; young people were "no longer willing to believe."[40] Gonzo journalist Hunter S. Thompson more colorfully illuminated the public's contempt for the political culture when he wrote of President Johnson, "When the history books are written he will emerge in his proper role as the man who caused an entire generation of Americans to lose all respect for the presidency, the White House, the Army, and in fact the whole structure of government. . . . And then, to wrap it all up another cheapjack hustler moved into the White House."[41] The Watergate crisis of 1973–1974 further fueled citizens' mistrust of their leaders. In a 1974 poll, 71 percent of respondents believed "things are going badly in the country" and 88 percent mistrusted "the people in power."[42] Yet despite this extensive list of problems, liberal democratic principles remained important to American national identity. Although fewer Americans believed that their nation could easily solve international problems, many hoped that traditional principles could triumph where flawed individuals had failed.

Crises of Democracy: Greece and Brazil

At the turn of the seventies, several international crises helped bring human rights and humanitarian issues to the attention of the American public.

As a result of decolonization, nationalism, ideological struggles, and other factors, the world witnessed an increase in civil conflicts, military coups, famines, and human rights abuses in dozens of countries. These conflicts had a considerable impact on the nascent global human rights movement, and they spurred American political interest in overseas suffering. As activists and the news media publicized abuses, Americans began to ask tough questions about their country's role. Advocates drew attention not only to the Eastern Bloc, but also to noncommunist states like Iran, South Korea, South Africa, and Paraguay.

Two cases were particularly significant to our story. Washington's dealings with the dictatorships in Greece and Brazil demonstrate how America's Cold War strategy evolved at the end of the sixties into a more nuanced approach to allied nations. Both were authoritarian regimes accused of torture, yet both were also considered important strategic partners. Greece was a NATO ally and the historical "cradle of democracy," while Brazil was a growing economic player in a region beset by ideological divisions and left-wing insurgencies. American ties to these governments engendered tough questions from policymakers and the growing activist community about possible U.S. complicity in human rights abuses. Such questions had rarely been broached before, but the 1967–1973 period saw a significant drop in congressional and public compliance with executive foreign policy.

These two cases show the extent to which America and its politics changed in the sixties. At middecade, America's chief overseas interests were curbing leftist activity and promoting economic growth, but by decade's end there was mounting concern about allies' lack of civil liberties. With respect to Greece and Brazil, this concern took the form of pressure to end military rule, restore constitutional government, and respect individual rights. By 1970, a notable transatlantic movement against Greek and Brazilian torture was forming, and this activism in turn contributed to the development of a broad-based, global human rights movement in the seventies.[43] Meanwhile, congressional liberals used Greece and Brazil to make the case for a new foreign policy standard. But these two cases also show how difficult it was for activists to succeed amid America's multitude of interests and its division of powers. More Americans were talking about human rights at the turn of the seventies, but national security and geostrategy still took precedent.

The Greek crisis arose in April 1967, when a group of colonels seized power in Athens, dissolved the parliament, and formed a ruling junta under the guise of protecting the state against a left-wing insurgency. The coup was the culmination of decades of political instability, during which socialists, conservatives, monarchists, and other factions had jockeyed for power. Although such volatility was a hallmark of Greek political life, the 1967 coup was widely perceived as a shocking end to democracy in the region that had originated the concept. Over the course of seven years, the junta was accused of arbitrary arrests, detentions without trial, torture, and a multitude of other police-state tactics. The initial Western reaction to the coup was overwhelmingly negative. While European governments called for a return to democracy, escaped dissidents brought allegations of extrajudicial internment and torture. Amnesty International sent two prominent lawyers to investigate these allegations in 1968, and their report catalogued the regime's physical and psychological tactics against an estimated three thousand political prisoners. In November 1969, the European Commission asserted in a damning twelve-hundred-page report that the Greek authorities had done virtually nothing to stop the security apparatus from using torture. Similar journalistic and NGO investigations helped make Greece one of the era's major causes célèbres. "Hardly a day passes," stated the *New York Times* in May 1969, "without fresh evidence from objective sources of tortures inflicted on Greek political prisoners that recall the excesses of Nazis and communists."[44] But despite the negative publicity, the junta did not change its tactics. The colonels recoiled from this outside "interference," and they promised to do whatever it took to preserve "public order and security."[45]

America's role in this unfolding Greek tragedy was long a source of controversy. The United States first took a major interest in Greek affairs in 1947, when President Truman asked Congress to appropriate aid to prevent a communist takeover. The Marshall Plan channeled additional dollars, and in 1952 Greece joined NATO. Successive presidential administrations continued economic support and worked to integrate Greece into the Western alliance. These were key turning points in the shift from British to American hegemony in the Eastern Mediterranean, and the United States remained Greece's chief patron up to the time of the 1967 coup. But were U.S. policymakers or covert operatives to blame for the slide into authoritarian rule? Greek liberals, monarchists, and Marxists assigned a preponderance of blame to the United States from the very start. Among the best-known critics was the politician Andreas Papandreou, who assailed the United States for providing arms under the aegis of NATO necessity and "arming to the teeth the military mafia which usurped the government of our country." Speaking in Washington, he claimed that the level of arbitrary violence in Greece "surpasses the tortures which have been perpetrated at Dachau," and he openly blamed the U.S. government for the coup.[46]

Papandreou's version of events was accepted by much of the Greek public, but it greatly overstated American influence. Evidence of significant American involvement has never materialized.[47] Indeed, in the coup's wake U.S. Ambassador Philips Talbot privately decried "the rape of Greek democracy" and cabled Washington that Greeks would "long rue this day's events, whose long range effects are hard to foresee."[48] The initial State Department assessment of the new rulers succinctly encapsulated America's dilemma in the human rights era. "We must walk a narrow line," it read, "between resisting [the junta's] embrace and at the same time cooperating with it sufficiently to serve our national interests, which includes gradually moving the government towards constitutional government." The administration would have to protect America's global image, retain leverage with the new government, press for the release of political prisoners, and avoid close identification with the regime because, President Johnson's advisers concluded, "the memory of the 'rape of democracy' will undoubtedly . . . haunt the perpetrators."[49] Johnson temporarily suspended full diplomatic relations and halted the delivery of over $30 million worth of heavy weapons.

But geopolitical considerations soon won out. In the eyes of American strategists, Greece was much like South Korea—an allied state in a dangerous neighborhood with many vital interests at stake. Greece and Turkey constituted NATO's eastern flank, and Greece bordered communist Albania, Bulgaria, and Yugoslavia. At a time when other regional ports were turning away the U.S. Navy, Greece was providing key facilities. Meanwhile, the June 1967 Six-Day War between Israel and its Arab neighbors had demonstrated Greece's value as a bridge to the increasingly important Middle East.[50] The United States also sought to strengthen NATO in the wake of wavering commitments from France, Denmark, and Norway. American strategists feared that undue pressure would push the Greek junta to withdraw from the alliance, a move that would isolate Turkey and open it to Soviet pressure. The 1968 Warsaw Pact invasion of Czechoslovakia further cemented the value of NATO, and even led the United States to partially lift the Greece arms embargo. Owing to Greece's strategic position, the

Greek colonels realized that remaining friendly toward NATO was a key to retaining power.[51]

This, then, was the dilemma for American policymakers: how to maintain the Western alliance, and keep Greece in it, while demonstrating misgivings about military rule and police-state tactics. The heavy arms embargo was not bearing fruit, in part because France was supplying the junta with weapons and because, as James Miller has demonstrated, the junta was unwilling to imperil its rule to placate U.S. concerns.[52] President Johnson, whose hands were tied with Vietnam and a daunting set of domestic troubles, encouraged the junta to restore democracy, but he also accepted them as anti-Soviet allies and loyal NATO members. This essentially became America's long-term policy. Although few in Washington were happy with the colonels, the United States tilted in their favor and went on to offer them various forms of support over the next seven years despite their political and civil excesses.

The administration did worry about how Johnson's political base would respond to a restoration of relations, and they feared that congressional liberals would cut aid in an attempt to force the junta's collapse. Thus Johnson pointed out Greece's importance to Israel, as well as the junta's promise to reinstate democracy. "I believe we can make a convincing case that the foreign policy considerations should override our understandable distaste for doing business with a military regime in a country like Greece," advised National Security Adviser Walt Rostow.[53] At the end of 1967, the administration resumed normal diplomatic relations with the understanding that there would be progress on press freedom, resolution of political prisoner cases, a new constitution, and parliamentary elections. Given the unfavorable attitude among many in Congress and the press, the State Department expected the regime to implement more reforms.[54] But at the junta's one-year point (April 1968), U.S. embassy assessments were pessimistic. Bilateral relations were marred by doubts and disappointments, wrote the ambassador, and "we have not been totally convinced of the regime's intention to remain in power only temporarily." The embassy also believed some activist claims that the regime was abusing detainees. Nevertheless, Johnson's advisers concluded that he had few options. As Rostow put it, "The government will probably be in power for some time, so we will have to deal with it."[55] Consequently, late in 1968 the administration decided on a partial resumption of military shipments. "The time has come to separate our NATO relationship from our disapproval of domestic Greek politics," read the policy memo. "It doesn't make sense to let our security relationships with Greece . . . deteriorate further."[56]

From a public relations standpoint, the obvious problem was that American recognition of the junta looked like tacit support for authoritarian rule. The junta's activities had a limited impact on an American public consumed by everyday problems and the war in Vietnam, but Greece did get some attention from a nascent American activist movement. Limits to democracy and civil liberties received the first and most continuous criticism, but accusations of torture also occasionally came into view. As Barbara Keys has argued, American liberals put torture allegations at the center of their anti-junta activism and in the process transformed the broader debate about U.S. support to dictatorships.[57] Yet the torture accusations also brought to light a question that would consistently influence debates in the human rights era. Since news reports often contradicted one another and methods of verification were limited, which claims should be believed? In most such cases, the answer to this question spoke volumes about an individual's ideological stance. If policymakers wanted to maintain an alliance or friendship, they accepted at face value the offending government's denials and its promises of reform. But if policymakers sought to alter the relationship, they did not accept the denials. In fairness to the skeptics, there were plenty of politicized allegations of rights violations, and the realities of modern propaganda could turn even reasonable people into doubters. But given the large number of firsthand accounts in Greece, by the decade's end many in Washington were willing to accept that torture was happening and that the United States should address it.[58]

Liberals in Congress took the lead. Their pronouncements and hearings focused on Greece's lack of democracy, but also veered into broader human rights territory by bringing up torture and civil liberties. Citing America's "guilt by association," they called for aid cuts until constitutional government was restored. They also argued that although Americans had no right to tell Greeks how to run their affairs, the U.S. government had a right to withhold American tax dollars. Several even assailed the national security argument by charging that the Greek military was ineffective. "The military value of Greece to the Western Alliance is today negligible," argued a group of congressmen. "The army has turned into a military shambles, however efficient it may be as a political machine."[59] In March 1968, Senator Claiborne Pell (D-RI) urged the administration to hold off on aid allocations until there were specific signs that Greece was respecting freedom of dissent. Senator Eugene McCarthy similarly declared that the U.S. government was supporting "an overweighted military establishment . . . not content with fulfilling its purely military function so well defined by Aristotle nearly 2,400 years ago."[60] A personal visit to Athens convinced Congressman Donald Fraser that American interests were not being served and that Greece was "a full-blown police state."[61] He and other activists added an oblique Greece reference into the 1968 Democratic Party platform.

These questions about aid to a dictatorship soon made their way into the Senate Foreign Relations Committee (SFRC), whose deliberations showed that a significant proportion of legislators was now willing to tie U.S. aid to other nations' political liberties. Senator Pell proposed cutting all weapons and military assistance until Greek citizens had approved a new constitution, but others sought to preserve regional order and minimize overseas commitments. Senator Stuart Symington (D-MO) lamented the dictatorship's actions, but he maintained that military aid prevented a Vietnamesque boots-on-the-ground commitment. The Greek government "may not be just exactly what we want," he argued, "but it is better to have them running the government today than it would be to have chaos in Greece." Senators Bourke Hickenlooper (R-IA) and Karl Mundt (R-SD) questioned American efforts to change distant societies. "This is paternalism at its worst," argued Mundt, "and I think we ought to oppose it." Senator Joseph Clark (D-PA) used moral reasoning to support Pell: "The Greek government represents everything that American democracy is opposed to. It is fascist, it is totalitarian, and they will use these arms to put down their own people. . . . It is a tyranny of the worst sort." Senator Frank Church (D-ID) went even further by assailing the entire foreign aid philosophy as "a massive meddling program." The United States, he charged, was "trying to organize and run and mold and fashion and influence every government in the world . . . either by the aid we give or the aid we withhold."[62]

Several NGOs and journalists emerged in the late sixties to join the dissenting legislators. Organizations like the Washington Committee Friends of Greece and the Council for Democracy in Greece protested the restoration of relations. "Any attitude short of condemnation [by the United States] will be interpreted . . . as approval and in many quarters as active cooperation with the dictatorship," cautioned one such organization. Another warned that continued military aid would put the United States "in a posture of favoring a dictatorship over proven democratic allies and over the freedom of the Greek people."[63] When the Greeks announced a continuation of martial law and press censorship in March 1968, the *New York Times* accused the administration of "appeasing" the junta despite Greece's questionable value to NATO and of "[doing] everything it can to provide the Athens junta with the prestige and respectability it has hungered after."[64]

Despite these reservations, most legislators supported the status quo in the belief that cutting aid would reduce American leverage and catalyze Greece's tilt toward another benefactor. Besides, they reasoned, junta rule was better than disorder or civil war. Public and journalistic criticism demonstrated that the foreign policy consensus was weakening, but it still seemed a safer bet to maintain the relationship. Johnson's announcement that he would not run for reelection further weakened activists' cause during 1968. It remained to be seen if a new president would choose the path of stronger bilateral relations, a diminished U.S. commitment, or—as activists hoped—strong pressure to end torture and restore democracy.

Another of this period's earliest human rights causes was the international campaign against authoritarianism and torture in Brazil.[65] The Brazilian military deposed the left-leaning President João Goulart in 1964 in response to growing unrest and the perceived threat of a leftist takeover, and for the next twenty-one years a succession of military leaders ruled with varying degrees of coercion. Like Greece, the Brazil case shows the change in American attitudes from the Cold War assumptions of the mid-1960s to Washington's more complicated global assessment at the decade's end. American policymakers were generally supportive of the military regime early on, but by 1968–1969 the regime had fewer friends in Washington. Nevertheless, even as the containment consensus was evaporating, American policymakers were reluctant to alter the status quo and punish Brazil for perceived human rights violations.

The 1964 coup was engineered by Brazilians and generally welcomed in Washington. At a time when American policymakers feared another Fidel Castro in the hemisphere, President Goulart was considered too far left. In the words of a National Security Council (NSC) adviser, "We don't want to watch Brazil dribble down the drain while we stand around waiting for the election."[66] The Johnson administration used economic measures to weaken Goulart, and when Brazil's political and economic troubles culminated in a crisis, the administration offered arms and ships to the Brazilian military. Once Goulart was overthrown, Johnson recognized the new regime almost immediately and told the American people that the Brazilians had saved their republic from Marxist forces.[67] The United States saw Brazil's military government as a defender of U.S. interests—anticommunism, stability, and economic development—with progress toward democracy a distant concern.

This Cold War mind-set dominated thinking about such regimes in the mid-sixties. The U.S. embassy expressed satisfaction that the new government had rooted out "communists and other extremists" from government and labor unions and had maintained a semblance of political and economic stability. Even the relatively liberal Senator J. William Fulbright (D-AR) was willing to give the military government the benefit of the doubt. In a 1965 meeting with the Brazilian foreign minister, Fulbright agreed that some form of authoritarianism was "almost necessary" in the early stages of a poor nation's development as a form of "collective discipline" that permitted a country to "focus on its real problems."[68] Both the State Department and USAID preferred a return to constitutionalism in the hope that this would stabilize the economy, but they had little concern for the individual rights of Brazilian citizens. The regime became a solid American ally and supported the United States in many international endeavors, including voting with the United States in the United Nations, isolating Castro in Latin America, assisting in the 1965 Dominican crisis, and offering gifts of coffee and medicine to South Vietnam.[69]

Brazilian military rule occasioned little political comment in the United States until 1967–1968, when critics began to ask tough questions about America's authoritarian clients. Early in 1968, the State Department advised against a Washington visit from Brazilian President Artur da Costa e Silva, arguing that his regime demonstrated "authoritarian tendencies" and had not built a credible political base. In light of President Johnson's troubles with South Vietnam and Greece, advisers believed that a close association with the Brazilian regime would be a political liability.[70] The real turning point in American perceptions came late in 1968, when a wave of urban terrorism led the Brazilian government to implement Institutional Act 5 (IA-5), a strict measure that dissolved the National Congress and state legislative assemblies, bolstered censorship, and strengthened the state's ability to detain suspects. IA-5 ushered in the most repressive period of the twenty-one-year dictatorship, and was the impetus for a more substantial American conversation on repression in Brazil. As we have seen with respect to Greece, many legislators were no longer willing to tolerate long-standing Cold War excuses for allies' excesses. They expressed misgivings about everything from nation-building in South Vietnam to the Alliance for Progress in Latin America because these endeavors seemed to be doing very little for *any* American interest, whether military, economic, or humanitarian.

Much like the Greek case, the State Department had a hard time formulating an official American response to IA-5. Most foreign service officers (FSOs) viewed it with revulsion, but they had to conduct a delicate balancing act between expressing concern, maintaining the relationship, and respecting Brazilian sovereignty. There were several matters on the bilateral ledger, including USAID project loans, fighter aircraft sales, and a pending coffee agreement. The sums were considerable: Brazil received $2 billion in U.S. aid between 1964 and 1970, the third highest amount behind South Vietnam and India.[71] Exchanges between Washington and the U.S. embassy in Brasilia give us some insight into the dilemma. An embassy official reported to Secretary Rusk that although IA-5 was harsh and the generals were "nationalistic and narrow," these leaders were also fundamentally favorable to the United States. Rusk agreed that the administration would have to reassure Latin American democrats without pushing Brazil "into further irrational acts affecting our relations" and without "publicly shaking our finger." Rusk also saw these issues in civilizational terms—that is, that Brazilian customs could not be compared to those of the world's established democracies. "Brazil's needs and performance cannot be measured against North American or northwest European standards of constitutional democracy," he asserted, "nor even easily expressed in Anglo-Saxon terms."[72] Such sentiments betrayed a basic ignorance of Brazilian society, and even reflected common Western conceptions of the developing world. But from Washington's perspective, the bewildering, cyclical political extremes of South America—conflict and instability followed by authoritarianism and order—made it easy to dismiss the dictatorship as a necessary evil.

The junta's leaders were more than willing to exploit this perspective by insisting that Americans did not understand Brazil's problems. As a military official told the U.S. Army attaché, "Writers who refer to the democratic anxieties and aspirations of eighty million Brazilians are dreaming if they believe that most of our population even suspects what democracy in the U.S. sense is."[73] Such justifications fit a common pattern among authoritarian regimes. Aware that their practices would offend sensibilities in Washington, they pled that they had acted in the interest of stability and to quell leftist insurgents. They were not simply acting to retain power, they argued, but were protecting their people from terrorist violence and revolutionary agitation. Finally, if national security and anticommunism were not strong enough justifications for North American liberals, the junta asserted that they were offering Brazilian solutions to Brazilian problems—and emphasizing that Americans could not easily grasp their cultural traditions and methods.

The official U.S. reaction to IA-5 was cautious. The Johnson administration first decided to steer a middle course by making a public statement of concern and announcing that the program of aid to Brazil was "under review." The embassy maintained normal contacts and privately expressed regret at the curbing of civil liberties. But with Congress and the public now more closely scrutinizing allies' activities and Washington's commitments, President Johnson had to be more forthright. His administration thus signaled U.S. disapproval by withholding some weapons, $50 million in aid funds, and $125 million in loans. As in Greece, the possibility of more significant measures would have to wait until Johnson's exit from office, but the broader significance was that the events in Brazil fueled pessimism in Washington that Latin America was evolving politically. The U.S. embassy noted that the government had "moved to a virtual out-and-out military dictatorship" and that "labor, church, students, journalists, intellectuals, and most politicians are shaken and temporarily cowed." Given such poor prospects, embassy specialists argued, the United States would be best served by a passive approach. Genuine political development could be achieved only "as an extremely long-range result of other fundamental social and cultural improvements," wrote one embassy official. "We must recognize that our influence on internal political events is marginal at best."[74]

Nixon, Kissinger, and the Perils of Realpolitik

It would be impossible to understand the emergence of human rights in American foreign relations without understanding the policies of President Richard Nixon (1969–1974) and his closest adviser, Henry Kissinger. The two men are remembered for several international accomplishments, including détente with the Soviets, rapprochement with China, and extrication of the United States from Vietnam. Their human rights record, though, is not held in such high regard. Nixon famously eschewed moralism, choosing instead a more traditional realpolitik quest for peace, stability, and an international balance of power. Yet Nixon and Kissinger played a central, though unintended, role in the era's human rights politics. First, their pursuit of better relations with the Soviet Union facilitated American influence in the internal affairs of the Eastern Bloc. The Cold War thaw encouraged congressional and NGO interest in human rights causes, and it increased the potential for action against communist, anticommunist, and nonaligned states. Second, Nixon and Kissinger's obstinacy in the face of the growing movement only galvanized their political opponents to work harder. Kissinger, in particular, was a foil for both liberal human rights activists and conservative anticommunists. A third Nixon influence was his attempt to bring white, working-class "ethnics" into the Republican fold. Owing to the period's shifting voting patterns, these ethnics became a valuable commodity in presidential and congressional elections. Politicians were willing to give extraordinary attention to ethnics' interests, including human rights in their ancestral homelands.

Despite his administration's disdain for what he considered moralistic interference in presidential diplomacy, Nixon did show some signs of flexibility. He saw a place for humanitarianism in foreign affairs, but only if these issues did not conflict with his central foreign policy goals. He supported ratification of the Genocide Convention, backed relief efforts in war-torn Biafra and Burundi, and supported the idea of a U.N. human rights commissioner and a State Department humanitarian bureau. But a nominal response to natural and manmade disasters was not the same as having an active human rights policy. Nixon wanted to leave these matters to the United Nations, the State Department, and humanitarian agencies while the White House and NSC handled important bilateral issues among powerful nations.

Nixon's foreign policy was more pragmatic than ideological. He adhered to a traditional "balance of power" model and argued that the United States should work closely with the Soviet Union and regional powers like Japan, Britain, and China. He paid little attention to much of the rest of the world, except in response to crises. "There are certain countries that matter in the world and certain countries that don't matter in the world," he told his chief of staff in 1972. "After you've dealt in two summit meetings, one in Peking and the other in Moscow . . . it is really terribly difficult to deal with even a country as important as Mexico."[75] From President Johnson's failings, Nixon learned to divert the public's attention from the Vietnam War. True, he maintained the American commitment to South Vietnam, especially in 1969–1970, and he later approached the Soviets and the Chinese for help in ending the war. But he did not let Vietnam dominate his presidency as it had dominated that of his predecessor.

Nixon also rejected Wilsonian idealism. As he told a reporter shortly before the 1968 election, Americans needed to recognize that "the American-style democracy that we find works so well for us may not always work well for others." This criticism of liberal internationalism was inspired in large measure by the moralistic rhetoric that accompanied the defense of South Vietnam. To Nixon, the United States was in no position to interfere in other nations' domestic affairs. "That doesn't mean that I am opting for military dictatorships," he noted. "[But] for the United States to attempt to say that, well, this nation or that nation doesn't have the kind of a government that we think is what we would want for it, . . . that is more than we can take on our plate." America could perhaps use its influence on behalf of certain freedoms, "but I don't think we can impose it."[76] As president, he summarized these ideas in blunt terms to one of his ambassadors: "We hope that governments will evolve toward constitutional procedures but . . . we deal with governments as they are."[77] This is not to say that Nixon was without optimism. He was, after all, a middle-class Californian who retained at least some of the idealism typical of his generation of political leaders. Yet he maintained a healthy distance from the moral perspective in international affairs. Soviet foreign minister Andrei Gromyko later said of Nixon's diplomacy, "He always presented himself as a pragmatist . . . a man who preferred to keep discussions on a purely practical level."[78]

Nixon laid out his administration's international policies in a series of four massive foreign policy reports to Congress between 1970 and 1973. The first report's opening sentence captured its essence: "The postwar period in international relations has ended." The Vietnam War was winding down; European and Asian economies were challenging the United States; and Moscow and Beijing were engaged in a bitter struggle for leadership of the communist world. Although the United States needed to live up to its commitments, argued Nixon, America's friends would have to shoulder more of the burden. The United States "cannot and will not conceive all the plans, design all the programs, execute all the decisions and undertake all the defense of the free nations of the world."[79] Although some observers equated this "Nixon doctrine" with isolationist retrenchment, Nixon emphasized that America's military would remain formidable.

Human rights concerns were entirely absent from the foreign policy reports, with the exception of a brief mention of U.N. priorities in the fourth report (May 1973).

Henry Kissinger was at the center of the foreign policy nexus even longer than was Nixon. As national security adviser (1969–1975) and secretary of state (1973–1977), he acted as a constant antagonist to human rights advocates. An academic schooled in the diplomacy of Metternich and Talleyrand, Kissinger was a strong believer in traditional interstate relations and the balance of global power. And like Nixon, he preferred to deal with only the most powerful nations; the developing world mattered little to him, excepting those places where the United States and the Soviets battled by proxy. Kissinger tended to believe that the United States should maintain relations with key states, no matter how illiberal or undemocratic their governments were. In a 1966 essay that would become remarkably self-referential, he argued that a true statesman's view of human nature "is wary; he is conscious of many great hopes which have failed." To the statesman, "gradualism is the essence of stability" and "maintenance of the existing order is more important than any dispute within it."[80] Kissinger carried these attitudes into the Nixon administration. As he told a group of business leaders in 1971, the administration sought to "reduce dogmatic hostilities around the world. Our policies are not idealistic, moralistic. We do not plead altruism—a tendency far too common in the history of American foreign affairs."[81]

Kissinger's Machiavellian streak went hand in hand with his pessimistic view of human nature. Growing up Jewish in prewar Germany, he witnessed firsthand the weakness of the Weimar Republic and European democracies in the face of the Nazis' rise. This lesson in the fragility of democracy may explain, in part, his later willingness to deal with undemocratic governments like those in Beijing and Moscow. And on a personal level, he was more than a little arrogant. "I've always acted alone," he told a journalist in an unguarded moment. "Americans like the cowboy who leads the wagon train by riding ahead alone on his horse. . . . This amazing, romantic character suits me."[82] And although Kissinger was a tremendous asset to the Nixon administration, he was difficult to maintain, and his carefully cultivated public image of cool rationality masked his mercurial emotions.[83] A Nixon speechwriter suggested that "the care and feeding of Henry was one of the greatest burdens of [Nixon's] presidency, but he was worth it."[84] Nixon himself was blunter, once telling an aide, "There are times when Henry has to be kicked in the nuts. Because sometimes Henry starts to think that he's president. But at other times you have to pet Henry and treat him like a child."[85]

Kissinger's diplomatic style matched his pragmatism. Because he believed in maintaining personal relationships with important leaders, he was unlikely, to say the least, to assail someone for human rights violations. He argued that American attacks on the Soviets' record would make superpower conflicts only more likely and that similar criticism of anticommunist states would alienate allies. The real job of diplomacy, he asserted, was to hammer out bilateral agreements based on mutual interest, not to make grand pronouncements of principle that would have no long-term effect. Even when President Nixon supported humanitarian assistance in war-torn regions, Kissinger was largely indifferent. As we will see, scholars, journalists, and activists have not merely criticized Kissinger's indifference to humanitarianism; several have even accused him of complicity in human rights violations through his support of authoritarian regimes in Chile, Indonesia, and elsewhere.[86]

From our twenty-first-century perspective, Nixon and Kissinger come across as singularly unsympathetic, even antagonistic, toward human rights matters. But it is worth considering their position in a broader historical context. These men practiced a form of diplomacy that had served European and American statesmen for centuries. Only in rare cases had other states' internal practices concerned executive policymakers in Washington. We must also acknowledge that many domestic and foreign observers applauded Nixon's foreign policy and his rejection of the American imperium. His détente with Moscow was generally popular in 1972–1973, and he was commended for the opening to China and the accords that finalized America's Vietnam withdrawal. A relatively small number of Americans wanted Nixon to pursue a more moral course that included human rights judgments. It is perhaps most accurate, then, to say that Nixon and Kissinger were transitional figures whose training and worldview did not prepare them for the human rights activism of the 1970s. The movement was so new and unusual that they tended to believe it was politically driven and largely irrelevant to the real work of diplomacy.

The post-1968 Cold War thaw—of which the U.S.-Soviet détente was an integral part—was the international political foundation on which American human rights policies were built. Moderates in the American and Soviet camps had been trying to engineer a détente since the 1950s, but a viable working relationship had always eluded them. By the late sixties, divisions in both alliances made for a more congenial superpower climate. Sino-Soviet tensions peaked in 1969, when the two nations became engaged in a series of bloody border clashes. Meanwhile, Yugoslavia, Romania, Albania, and Czechoslovakia expressed varying degrees of independence from Moscow. Coincident with this lack of unity in the communist world, France pursued a more unilateral course and withdrew from the NATO integrated military command. And in a process known as *Ostpolitik*, West German Chancellor Willy Brandt cultivated relations with East Germany and the Soviet Union. Owing to these splits, East/West tensions reached a postwar nadir at the end of the sixties.

Richard Nixon entered the White House amid these shifting alliances. Despite, or perhaps because of, his anticommunist credentials, he was willing to negotiate with the communist states that were, as he put it, "too powerful to ignore."[87] In his 1969 inaugural address he signaled to the world, "After a period of confrontation, we are entering an era of negotiation. Let all nations know that during this administration our lines of communication will be open."[88] Because Moscow and Beijing needed Western technology, trade, and recognition, détente would be a logical means to several ends. It would strengthen NATO and prevent America's European allies from becoming too independent. An engagement with the Soviet Union and China would also allow Nixon to play the two countries against one another. He further hoped to increase his political capital through bold international maneuvers. If he could secure arms limitation agreements, an opening to China, and support in ending the Vietnam War, it would all but ensure his reelection. The more agreeable international environment would then allow Americans to cut defense spending and usher in what Nixon called "a generation of peace." Thus détente with the Soviet Union and rapprochement with China became Nixon's top priorities after his first two years in office. Through a combination of ideological flexibility and pragmatism amid changing circumstances, Nixon and his Soviet counterparts overcame the limitations faced by their predecessors and produced numerous results, from trade and arms control agreements to cultural exchanges and joint scientific ventures.

The administration's emphasis on interstate peace and order would often conflict with the goals of human rights activists. Indeed, although East/West propaganda continued in the détente era, the U.S. and Soviet governments reduced the ideological sniping that had defined the Cold War for over two decades. In the parlance of the day, détente implied noninterference in a nation's internal affairs. Or as Michael Ignatieff has asserted, it "traded rights for order."[89] Nixon and Kissinger came to accept the Soviet Union as a world power whose leaders were more interested in preserving international stability than in fomenting Marxist revolutions. The Soviets, too, argued that détente had nothing to do with individual rights or Westernization of the Soviet Union. A typical *Pravda* editorial of the period asserted that détente should be defined by a "comparison of ideas and facts . . . and must not be turned into a conscious incitement of mistrust and hostility, the falsification of reality or, least of all, subversive activity."[90]

Yet although Nixon, Kissinger, and the Soviets preferred not to make human rights issues a part of détente, they could not control all of the forces unleashed by the Cold War thaw. Détente opened the Eastern Bloc to scrutiny from NGOs, Congress, and ordinary American citizens, and in the long run activists in both East and West became significant actors in international relations. Many observers also held out hope that trade liberalization, educational exchanges, and scientific cooperation would improve the flow of ideas and perhaps decrease repression in the East. Such a decrease would ultimately require activism *within* Eastern Bloc nations, but détente's proponents argued that liberalization was more likely if East/West relations improved. State Department experts counseled that détente could even imperil the Soviet system in the long run. An adviser reminded Kissinger in 1970 that "any loosening of Moscow's control brings East European attempts to reassert independence. In this sense . . . détente is far more dangerous potentially for them than for us." The United States could influence Eastern Europe because these people wanted Western technology, capital, and goods—things that the Soviet Union could not provide. "Détente and greater freedom of action in Eastern Europe go hand in hand," the adviser concluded.[91] Despite this belief in potential benefits for Eastern Europeans, Nixon and Kissinger were unwilling to dwell on it publicly for fear of inflating expectations. They were somewhat more willing to tout these benefits as détente met more resistance after 1972, but they did not want their goals to be overshadowed by concern for human rights.[92] Nevertheless, while they did not seek to change these societies, détente did offer new opportunities for a wide array of actors to promote reforms in the Eastern Bloc.

Nixon's opening to China did not have the same effect on human rights promotion. Despite years of Beijing's abuses, Western activists and politicians paid far less attention to China than they did to the Soviet Union between 1949 and the 1989 Tiananmen Square massacre. On those occasions when Beijing relaxed its grip through mild liberalization programs, some citizens pressed for greater reform, and their assertiveness was invariably met by renewed repression.[93] Nixon was hardly alone in disregarding human rights in China; indeed, his White House predecessors and successors acted in much the same way. Because China had long been closed off from the West, Westerners did not have an accurate sense of just how oppressive Mao Zedong's regime was. When Westerners did hear about Chinese abuses, many dismissed them with the fallback logic that China was geographically distant and culturally enigmatic—that is, that "they do things differently there." Unlike the Soviet Union, China did not pose an existential nuclear threat to the United States. Also, more Americans traced their lineage to ethnic groups in the Soviet orbit and thus were more aware of Soviet violations than Chinese ones. Human rights concerns did not fundamentally alter the long-term trend of closer Sino-American relations, from rapprochement (1971–1972) to diplomatic recognition (1979) to conditional most-favored-nation (MFN) trade status (1980) to permanent MFN status and billions of dollars in annual trade.

The February 1972 Nixon/Mao summit took up trade, exchanges, and regional matters, and was completely unencumbered with talk of Beijing's internal policies.[94] This was consistent, of course, with Nixonian realpolitik. As early as 1969, Kissinger was telling the press, "We have always made it clear that we have no permanent enemies and that we will judge other countries, and specifically countries like communist China, on the basis of their actions and not on the basis of their domestic ideology."[95] In Nixon's eyes, rekindling relations with a large communist country was a delicate mission that could be derailed by a focus on humanitarian issues. He sought only a basic rapprochement that could foster opportunities in other areas.

Although most contemporary observers applauded the opening, the preponderance of evidence shows that Nixon and Kissinger were willing to give up far more than they received. The administration proposed diplomatic recognition of China and support for Beijing to assume the Security Council seat of America's old ally, Taiwan. They also volunteered a timeline for a unilateral U.S. withdrawal from Vietnam. "After a peace is made [in Vietnam]," said Kissinger in private, "we will be 10,000 miles away, and [Hanoi] will still be there."[96] Kissinger went on to provide the Chinese with a great deal of classified information over the next few years. The historian

Robert Dallek confirms that "Nixon was eager to flatter Mao," even to the point of telling the Chairman that his writings "moved a nation and have changed the world."[97] Meanwhile, Mao's government was more than willing to have its humanitarian record ignored. China had endured a long history of outside interference, and "human rights" seemed to many Chinese merely another form of foreign meddling. Mao's government had earlier pieced together the Five Principles of Peaceful Coexistence in its relations with India—equality, territorial respect, nonaggression, peaceful coexistence, and mutual noninterference in internal affairs—and by the time of Nixon's opening, these had become China's foreign policy guidelines. In the human rights era, and especially after 1989, Beijing would defend its domestic policies by elevating the "noninterference" principle to the top of the list.

Not everyone was smitten with the summit or the new Sino-American relationship. Some American conservatives were angry, as were some European and Asian allies. The British ambassador to the United States thought the Sino-American joint communiqué had about it a "distinct whiff of 'peace in our time.'"[98] After observing Nixon toast Chinese officials at a state dinner, conservative commentator William F. Buckley concluded that it "was as if Sir Hartley Shawcross had suddenly risen from the prosecutor's stand at Nuremberg and descended to embrace Goering and Goebbels."[99] But even these criticisms were more "anti-red" than pro–human rights, and most Americans were happy with the summits.

Why did Nixon and Kissinger offer Mao so much? Nixon was far more concerned with electoral politics at home than he was with gaining concessions. If he could forge a Sino-American working relationship, he would score political points for being a foreign policy visionary and gain crucial leverage against the Soviets—both developments that would boost his re-election chances. We must also consider Nixon and Kissinger's Western worldview. Both men had studied European history and Great Power diplomacy, but knew comparatively little about China. After the summit, Beijing invited congressional delegations to China, and in the next seven years before formal U.S. recognition, around one hundred American legislators visited. Before one such delegation departed, Nixon cautioned them to avoid linking trade with the political relationship, though he admitted that they were linked in an unspoken way because of America's economic power. "We don't have to like each other's systems to work with them," he concluded. "Frankly, they don't have anything to sell us."[100]

Given Nixon and Kissinger's willingness to concede so much to achieve a rapprochement, Mao's treatment of the Chinese people was nowhere near Nixon's agenda. The only humanitarian matter raised at the entire summit was the plight of four American pilots who had been imprisoned after their planes were shot down during the Korean and Vietnam Wars. Zhou Enlai was clearly interested in removing this obstacle; Beijing released one of the prisoners immediately and freed the others the following year.[101] Kissinger later had an exchange with Zhou regarding missing American soldiers and journalists in Southeast Asia, though even here he clarified that he was not making a formal representation, but rather "a personal request" for information. True to his style, Kissinger also showed his hand by noting that the issue was only for public consumption and would not interfere with the relationship. "The families ask us if we have asked you the question," he told Zhou. "If we could say at a press conference that we have asked you and you have assured us that there are no missing in action, that would be sufficient."[102] But although the release of the imprisoned pilots and the search for missing soldiers and journalists were humanitarian matters, they had nothing to do with the rights of the Chinese people. Indeed, negotiating for the release of one's own nationals was a routine aspect of bilateral diplomacy. Margaret MacMillan concludes that the 1972 U.S.-China breakthrough was good for both countries, but she adds that it is possible to ask whether Nixon and Kissinger were too eager for a rapprochement. They offered the lion's share of concessions, and they made some promises that they could not keep.[103] The budding relationship had virtually no impact on Chinese internal policies, nor would it in the years to come.

The Ongoing Crisis of Greek Democracy

President Nixon's preference for realpolitik formed the basis of his policy toward the Greek junta. He was willing to listen to different opinions during his first year in office, but it was not long before he decided to continue, and eventually augment, American support. Nixon publicly backed a return to democracy, but in keeping with his noninterference principle, and because he saw Greece as a bulwark against Soviet power and an important link to the Middle East, he worked to strengthen relations and keep it within NATO. In the words of a senior official, "We have a better chance to influence the [Greek] government to change if we continue to work with them than if we turn our back to them." Thus Nixon lifted the arms embargo and instructed Ambassador Henry Tasca to stay out of Greek internal affairs.[104] The Greek government reciprocated with a beneficial homeporting agreement for U.S. Navy vessels, but uncomfortable questions about America's ties to a dictatorship and the efficacy of "quiet diplomacy" became more common in Washington. Nixon's desire for democracy in Greece may have been genuine, but he did little to bring it about.

Some Americans and Greeks lobbied Nixon to cut ties at the outset of his presidency, and both pro- and anti-junta advocates used anticommunism to bolster their arguments. "You are respectfully asked whether you can tolerate any longer the violation of human rights of your Greek allies and friends," implored a former Greek politician and torture victim. "Increasing hatred boosts the communist cause and may turn Greece into another Vietnam." But others asked Nixon to restore ties and end the arms embargo. Congressman Edward Derwinski (R-IL), who was angry that "the American liberal establishment" had ostracized Greece, argued that "logic and American national interest" necessitated full U.S. support. Meanwhile, the junta's leaders pled for support with a combination of polite inquiries and thinly veiled threats. A bitter Greek general told his American counterpart that U.S. inaction imperiled his nation. "When you at last decide to give us the weapons," he said, "you will probably find no one here to use them."[105] But while it was true that Greeks faced some internal threats, the junta also overstated the problem in order to maintain power, and sometimes even to justify abuse of civilians. The communists in the Western world were "using the students as a spearhead," argued the deputy prime minister. These were "children [who] smoked marijuana and had little sense of reality." Urging resumption of full political and military ties, Prime Minister Georgios Papadopoulos argued that the regime had remained loyal to NATO and had prevented an economic collapse, a communist takeover, and a civil war. The junta was moving toward democracy, he asserted to Nixon, but it would have to do so at its own pace.[106]

Early on, the Nixon administration lobbied for a democratic restoration in the belief that this would enhance stability. In April 1969, Secretary of State William Rogers pressed the foreign minister on a political timetable and on the release of Greece's eighteen hundred political prisoners, arguing that the United States considered "evolution toward representative government and the application of civil liberties" as important steps. A harsh State

Department assessment found that America's reputation had "to some extent become identified with that of the junta." There had been no meaningful progress on democracy or on promised economic and social programs, yet the junta seemed to be relying on the U.S. need for Greek facilities. (Europeans, meanwhile, were criticizing the regime while profiting from arms sales.)[107] By the end of Nixon's first year, Ambassador Tasca was advising that there was no alternative to the dual policy of public support mixed with private encouragement for a return to democracy. Because the colonels were maintaining domestic stability and following a foreign policy generally consistent with America's, Tasca advised against a "self-defeating" policy of military aid cuts and "quixotic public criticism."[108]

Beyond the domestic political issues at stake, Nixon considered Greek democracy irrelevant to the bilateral relationship. At a time when the United States was the only NATO member granting military aid to Greece (several were selling weapons), he lifted the embargo on heavy weapons in September 1970 in response to a Greek timetable to restore democracy. "The [anti-junta activists'] idea is that the U.S. shouldn't give arms and then the Greeks would change," said Nixon privately. "They'd change alright, but the wrong way. . . . We need the Greeks. . . . We don't like the government, but we'd like its successor less."[109] This resumption of arms shipments forced the administration to defend the regime and to put a positive spin on Greek events, even to the point of stating in September 1970, with scant evidence, that torture had ceased and that political prisoner numbers were falling. Behind the scenes, the United States was dissatisfied with the Greeks' authoritarianism and their "public relations ineptness," but Greece's strategic importance and loyalty to the alliance remained the focal point of Nixon's policy.[110] It is clear, then, that security and continuity overrode any sharp public tones on democracy and human rights. Because Nixon and Kissinger had little interest beyond regional security and the possibility that bad press would hurt their overall foreign policy, from 1970 onward their Greece policy was entwined with détente. The "noninterference" position became a broad cover for Nixon's desire to free the United States from unwanted commitments, but for better or worse, the United States was now more closely identified with the junta. When Defense Secretary Laird visited Greece in October 1970, his meetings were interrupted by a nearby bomb, and the following month a bomb damaged the statue of Harry Truman in downtown Athens.

In light of Nixon's unwillingness to pressure the junta, legislators proposed several solutions. Congressional liberals challenged the administration's line that Greece was fulfilling its NATO obligations. Congressman Don Edwards (D-CA) asserted that Greece's NATO status was "an excuse for U.S. inaction" because of Greece's minimal military value, while Congressman Fraser argued that Nixon's approach contradicted American tradition and alienated America's friends.[111] In 1969–1970, Senator Pell's and Vance Hartke's (D-IN) proposals to deny new aid were nixed in close votes amid strong lobbying by the Departments of State and Defense. The proposals prompted Kissinger to clarify U.S. aims in private: "We do not give military aid to support governments, but because a country is important to the U.S."[112] Appropriations committees also scrutinized NATO ties and military aid. Congressman Wayne Hays's (D-OH) 1971 amendment to ban such aid to Greece was a significant milestone in congressional assertiveness, though it allowed the president to grant a waiver on national security grounds, which he did.

In addition to this legislative interest, public opinion ran a wide gamut between those who decried congressional liberals' "interference" in Greek affairs and those who criticized support to an authoritarian regime. One of Congressman Fraser's constituents told him to "quit whipping the government of a country that is trying to do a good job. . . . Let's give the few rightist countries of the world a chance to prove their mettle before we castigate them."[113] Another voter wrote to Senator Henry Jackson, "That the U.S. even recognizes such a repressive dictatorship as the Greek junta is unbelievably hypocritical for a country purporting to be the bastion of freedom in the world. . . . How can we fight totalitarianism of the left while condoning and even aiding totalitarianism of the right?"[114] Greek Americans were similarly divided. A Greek Orthodox archbishop wrote to Secretary Rogers that America's interests "should be with the people [of Greece], and not in the hands of the leaders who form an unacceptable, self-imposed, and self-perpetuating oligarchy."[115] But most favored the status quo. "Is it not a little ridiculous," wrote a Greek-American voter to Congressman Fraser, "to concern ourselves with the internal affairs of Greece at a time when all congressmen should be devoting all their time and energy to solving the many problems that plague our country?"[116] The Order of AHEPA at first lamented the dictatorship's emergence, but soon accepted the argument that communists had threatened Greece and that military aid should continue. "Greece today is our lone ally in that part of the world," asserted AHEPA's president, and "Greek internal politics are the business of the Greek people."[117]

Congress and the administration then locked horns over the 1971 decision to homeport part of the U.S. Navy's Sixth Fleet and ten thousand military and civilian personnel in Athens-Piraeus. Homeporting was intended to increase regional capabilities and improve morale by minimizing long family separations, but many interpreted the choice as support for the junta. Two critics, Congressmen Benjamin Rosenthal (D-NY) and Lee Hamilton (D-IN), were eventually proved correct in arguing that the homeporting decision would embolden the colonels. One year after the decision, the dictatorship was still in power, anti-Americanism in Greece was on the rise, and there was no democratic transition in sight. Unless the United States paid more attention to political considerations, argued Rosenthal, "We will not have much prestige left in Greece to use in the difficult times ahead."[118] State Department analysts privately admitted that the regime had stepped up its efforts to emphasize American dependence on Greece. "It is difficult to look to the future with optimism," they concluded.[119] Since the lack of democracy was now the major bilateral problem, Secretary of State Rogers and the U.S. embassy ramped up both private diplomacy and public statements. Rogers even took an indirect stab at the colonels by giving a prodemocracy speech to a group of American FSOs and their families in Greece on July 4, 1972. "Democracy is one of those clear and incisive Greek words that are part of the Western vocabulary," he stated. "It means simply: rule by the people and for the people."[120]

The final turning point in the Greek junta's story came in November 1973, when the hard-line clique of Colonel Dimitrios Ioannidis seized power. Ioannidis's accession spurred a revealing discussion between Kissinger and his aides, who realized that this backsliding would make the Nixon/Kissinger policy look like a failure. When Ambassador Tasca (correctly) predicted that the regime would not last long and recommended continuing a public prodemocracy stand, Kissinger asked why this was in America's interest. With so few democracies in the world, why was America being charged with holding Greece to democracy, but not Yugoslavia, Morocco, or Algeria? "Where else are we requiring governments to specify dates for elections?" he asked. "Why is it in the American interest to do in Greece what we apparently don't do anywhere else?" Kissinger then laid out perhaps the clearest statement of his foreign policy beliefs in light of the era's new human rights demands: "The Department of State doesn't have a Political Science Division. It conducts the foreign policy of the United States. It deals with any government—communist or non-communist—within the context of the foreign-policy objectives of the United States. That way you don't get caught with each individual government in giving approval and disapproval. Why is that wrong?" Ambassador Tasca argued that Greece was receiving so much attention because it had a unique position in Europe and because people believed that the United States could influence it. Kissinger accepted that Greece could be considered a special case, but he argued that the administration should stand by its principles and let the chips fall where they may. "We can survive congressional hearings if we know what's right," he concluded.[121]

The colonels' end came about over Cyprus. When the junta fomented an uprising against the centrist Cypriot president, Archbishop Makarios, Turkey invaded the island in 1974, which in turn created a whole new set of human rights problems. The invasion was the death knell for the Greek junta. After it collapsed in July 1974, democracy was restored, Greece withdrew from the NATO command structure for six years, and Greek anti-Americanism remained strong for a generation. In the final analysis of America's dealings with Greece during the Johnson and Nixon years, it is clear that realism consistently trumped liberal idealism. As *New York Times* correspondent C. L. Sulzberger, an early defender of the junta, wrote of Nixon's policy in 1973, "All the U.S.A. stands for has been hurt by this; but not our national interests."[122] The Greek story also demonstrates the U.S. government's limited ability to promote democracy, even among its allies. James Miller has correctly argued that Greece's failure to create a stable democracy between 1950 and 1974 was largely the work of Greek politicians, military leaders, and the monarchy. Yet the United States bears some responsibility. President Johnson, President Nixon, and much of Congress continued to support a dictatorship that was abusing its population. Nixon, in particular, was largely indifferent to these abuses, even when a firmer American position might have encouraged more substantial changes in Greek policies.[123]

Latin America's Cold War: The Brazilian Dictatorship

Latin America was not a high priority for Richard Nixon and Henry Kissinger. Not only was Nixon generally uninterested in the global South, but he also considered the Western Hemisphere to be beyond the realm of Soviet and Chinese interest. Mark Atwood Lawrence is correct in asserting that the two men sought "low-key preservation of the status quo"—a posture that often meant relying on dictators to maintain stability and fend off leftist threats. This policy succeeded insofar as Marxist influence did not expand into South America on their watch, but in the long run their support to oppressive regimes arguably sowed the seeds of multiple crises.[124] Nixon's approach to Brazil must be considered in the context of détente, traditional American paternalism, and South America's civil struggles. As we have seen, Latin American democracy took a hit in the sixties and seventies. And despite Nixon's relative inattention, there was no denying America's unique regional interests and its overwhelming economic and political influence. As Greg Grandin has shown, while Washington backed land reforms and social welfare programs in postwar Europe and Japan, policymakers considered such programs to be dangerous in Latin America. Instead, writes Grandin, the United States "inevitably sided with reactionary civilian and military forces as a bulwark against communism." True, the United States often had little or no involvement in the region's coups and atrocities, but it also rarely discouraged them.[125]

Although South America was a low Nixon priority, he recognized Brazil as an important regional ally with a growing economy. Early in his presidency, he sent his erstwhile opponent for the Republican presidential nomination, Governor Nelson Rockefeller of New York, on a regional tour to collect information and shore up relations with Latin American republics. While in Brazil, Rockefeller was willing to ask tough questions about political rights and censorship, and he toured the empty Brazilian Congress in order to demonstrate American concern over the suspension of political activity.[126] Rockefeller's report to the president was rather moderate in its recommendation to recast trade and lending to reflect broader national interests rather than narrow business interests. Yet the report's grim tone accurately reflected the range of problems in the region and the level of hemispheric skepticism about America's intentions. Rockefeller also provocatively suggested that these nations' internal security problems had spurred the authoritarian trend. "Governments everywhere are struggling to cope with often conflicting demands for social reform and economic growth," he wrote. "Subversive forces working throughout the hemisphere are quick to exploit and exacerbate each and every situation." He recommended continued military aid and increased arms sales to meet these security challenges.[127]

Some observers have assailed both the Rockefeller mission and the report. The journalist A. J. Langguth asked why Nixon had sent the scion of the Rockefeller steel empire to assess an impoverished region teeming with anti-imperialist and anti-*yanqui* sentiment. (Riots broke out when Rockefeller visited Colombia and Ecuador, causing Chile and Venezuela to cancel their invitations.) Considering the millions Rockefeller had invested in Latin America, wrote Langguth, it was not surprising that he praised the security forces.[128] Walter LaFeber similarly criticized Rockefeller's conclusion that South American militaries were "the essential force for constructive social change." The preponderance of military coups in the 1960s seemed to have rendered such a sentiment painfully outdated.[129]

These observers were correct in pointing out Rockefeller's liberal capitalist biases. His report emphasized economic and security policies that would strengthen the rule of law, protect property, and stimulate growth— controversial ideas in a region beset by endemic poverty and wealth disparities. But Rockefeller's critics understated the level of civil violence in the region. Significant rural, leftist, guerrilla insurgencies developed early in the sixties in Peru, Bolivia, Guatemala, Venezuela, and Colombia. The defeat of many of these groups (symbolized by the capture and execution of Ernesto "Che" Guevara in Bolivia in 1967) led rebels to transition to urban guerrilla activity. By decade's end, several such Cuba-supported groups operated in the Southern Cone, including the Tupamaros (Uruguay), MIR (Chile), FAR (Argentina), and ALN (Brazil). These organizations, which tended to draw young members from the educated urban classes, used bombings, kidnappings, assassinations, and sabotage to undermine what they perceived as bourgeois decadence and elite domination.[130] Later, they would focus their acts on repressive military governments.

True enough, these militant groups' violent acts did not excuse the excesses of which South America's military governments were guilty. On balance, the region's authoritarian governments and allied paramilitaries (aka "death squads") were responsible for more suffering than were terrorist groups. But one cannot comprehend the region's downward spiral toward authoritarianism without understanding the threat (or at least the perception of such) posed by these groups. Washington policymakers were not alone in fearing another Cuba-like revolution in Latin America; many Latin American citizens had similar fears. Nor can we understand how Americans perceived authoritarianism and human rights matters without understanding the high-profile nature of some insurgents' crimes. The left-wing FAR in Guatemala killed U.S. Ambassador John Gordon Mein and two U.S. military advisers in 1968. Two years later the group killed the West German ambassador and kidnapped and released the U.S. labor attaché. The Brazilian Marxist group MR-8 kidnapped and later released the U.S. ambassador, Charles Elbrick, in 1969. The following year, Brazilian rebel groups kidnapped Swiss, West German, and Japanese diplomats, and the Popular Revolutionary Vanguard shot the U.S. consul, Curtis C. Cutter, during a botched kidnapping attempt.

The kidnappers asserted that they were acting to undermine oppressive governments and to free imprisoned compatriots. The kidnappings usually involved a negotiation for the release of political prisoners. (In Cutter's case, the would-be captors had written a false confession in which Cutter "admitted" he was a CIA agent instructing Brazilians in methods of torture. The note also sentenced Cutter to death.)[131] Such acts did not endear insurgent groups to foreign publics. Among the most sensational cases was the Tupamaros' kidnapping and murder of the USAID police adviser Dan Mitrione in Uruguay in 1970. His death has been the source of much controversy because of his possible role in training military and police in torture methods.[132] But at the time of his death, Americans heard a simpler story of a public servant whose murder at the hands of Marxist terrorists left his nine children without a father. Simply put, the guerrillas were unlikely to win friends in Washington by killing U.S. citizens. These groups' other acts of violence against the state, civilians, and businesses got less attention from the American public than did diplomats' kidnappings, but they were great fodder for military juntas that wanted to justify their repression. Perceptions mattered. Human rights activists saw right-wing governments and militaries as the sources of many South American problems, while conservatives and practitioners of realpolitik pointed out that much of South America was embroiled in undeclared civil wars. How one perceived these civil struggles said much about one's perception of the human rights movement and of human rights as a goal of American foreign policy.

Nixon followed many of Rockefeller's recommendations on Brazil. He sought to bolster the relationship by restoring the suspended aid and accepting the generals' claim that there was no torture. In the meantime, Brazil's economic growth—upward of 9 percent in 1970 alone—strengthened the regime's domestic and international legitimacy and deflected some attention from its excesses. Observers began to refer to the Brazilian economic "miracle." Thomas E. Skidmore has correctly concluded that American policymakers made "at most a half-hearted attempt" to pressure the Brazilians in 1968–1969, during which the generals success-fully waited out the bad publicity.[133] The Nixon administration routinely argued that Brazilian political evolution would come about with further economic growth, and also claimed to be using private diplomacy to nudge the dictators toward reforms. But since America's traditional business and security interests were arguably being met, the administration was unwill-ing to go much further. Not only was there no consensus that Washington must promote political development, but Brazil was merely one among many authoritarian states in the world. Nixon could count on minimal domestic resistance considering the American public's limited awareness of Brazilian affairs.

A small number of academics, clergy, exiled Brazilians, and liberal Cath-olics responded by building a network to publicize the junta's violations. This movement became a groundbreaking part of the human rights push in Latin America and beyond.[134] Using information they received from their contacts in Brazil, these activists wrote articles and submitted testimony to congressional committees and the Inter-American Commission for Human Rights (IACHR). They also formed an NGO, the American Committee for Information on Brazil, as a means of collecting and verifying victims' testi-monies.[135] Established NGOs also became active. The International Com-mission of Jurists released a scathing criticism of the junta's tactics in 1970, and Amnesty International soon had nearly two hundred active prisoner cases in Brazil.[136] At a time when torture was not widely reported in the mainstream press, activists' legwork led to numerous reports on Brazilian torture in 1970–1971, including dozens of articles in the *New York Times* and *Washington Post*. Critics highlighted not only the self-evident immoral-ity of the junta's tactics, but also America's guilt by association. A *Washing-ton Post* editorial stated that the United States was "in danger of getting itself caught up on the side of the oppressors, forced to choose wrong."[137] Two syndicated columnists similarly lamented the "tragedy" that America's support of Brazil was "keep[ing] in unchecked power the most repressive regime in the Western Hemisphere."[138]

The burgeoning movement against torture might have had more reso-nance in Washington had it not been for the November 1970 election of the left-wing reformer Salvador Allende as president of Chile. Not only did this event throw a new wrinkle into Nixon's approach to South America, but as Tanya Harmer has argued, the 1970–1973 Allende presidency was a watershed in hemispheric affairs in that it augmented the "inter-American

Cold War" at a time when the Washington-Moscow relationship was at its most agreeable. Following Allende's accession, it soon became clear that there would be no North-South parallel to the East/West détente. Instead, Allende aligned with Cuba, while the United States aligned with Brazil and the Southern Cone regimes. As Harmer has suggested, these right-wing leaders were hardly pawns of the United States, but rather increasingly took "ownership" of the Cold War in their region.[139]

The Nixon administration offered mild, private encouragement for a parliamentary transition in Brazil, and they acknowledged that the torture allegations were at least partially true. But if there was any indignation about torture in the administration, it took a backseat to the desire for stability. "An aroused [Brazilian] public could well give rise to a deep division within the government on how to deal with the [torture] problem," suggested the State Department, "in the process possibly weakening the government's hold on the country."[140] Nixon summarized his approach in a December 1970 meeting with the U.S. ambassador to Brazil, William Rountree. In a world filled with undemocratic states, argued Nixon, the United States would have to be "realistic and deal with governments as they are." He wanted Rountree to ensure that the Brazilian government and military "do not get the impression that we are looking down our noses at them because of their form of government."[141] The administration would consult with Brazil on political developments, but Nixon drew a clear line at addressing the status of individual Brazilians. When the U.S. embassy received requests to inquire about imprisoned Brazilians, they turned these down as interventions in Brazil's internal affairs.[142] The Nixon administration considered economic development to be America's chief long-term interest in Latin America. Meanwhile, Brazil's economic growth and its diminishing reliance on U.S. aid meant a concurrent decrease in U.S. leverage.

While the administration strengthened relations with Brasilia, congressional liberals grew increasingly vocal. As chair of the Senate subcommittee on Latin America, Senator Frank Church built a reputation as one of the chief political gadflies of the era on the subject of military aid. In 1969, he suggested the unprecedented step of cutting such assistance to Brazil, arguing that military aid fueled anti-Americanism, alienated the American public, and "raise[d] the question of what the United States really stands for." Church also assailed the Alliance for Progress, to which the United States had contributed $8 billion while nine nations in the region had suffered military takeovers.[143] President Emílio Médici's enduring grip on power encouraged more legislators to shed the spotlight on Brazil in 1970, including Senator Edward Kennedy, who embarked on a public campaign against U.S. support to human rights abusers. "Reports of official terrorism and torture [in Brazil] are mixed with incidents of violence committed by opponents of the regime who are denied access to legitimate political channels," said Kennedy on the Senate floor. America's support for the regime, he argued, was laying bare the gap between America's ideals and Washington's policies. In so arguing, Kennedy was making a clear leap from America's Vietnam experience to its support of other anticommunist regimes. "We now face a deep crisis in the spirit of the American people because of our support of an unpopular government in an unjust cause in Vietnam," he asserted. "Our unquestioning endorsement of a government that accepts torture of political prisoners can only exacerbate this crisis."[144] In retrospect, Kennedy was on the cutting edge in his attempts to loosen America from its Cold War assumptions, though he oversimplified events in Brazil. In reality, many of the victims he championed were also willing to use violence against civilians.

The Brazilian junta lashed out at Senator Kennedy, "international agents of subversion," and the "morbid and sensationalist" foreign press. Regime representatives admitted that there had been instances of mistreatment, but they pledged that this was not official policy and that alleged "political prisoners" were actually incarcerated terrorists. Besides, they argued, other regimes did much worse. The general message was that outsiders did not understand the threats that Brazil faced. "Do people think this is a picnic?" said the finance minister to an American official. "These terrorists are a bunch of murderers. . . . We all live in fear."[145] The Brazilian regime also continued to make the case that things were different in Latin America. "I do not believe that the public is interested in any change in the present regime," a Médici deputy told a reporter. "The truth is that political liberty, in the sense of liberty to elect the government, is not one of the values sought by our people."[146] The regime was at least correct in arguing that many foreign critics were working from secondhand information, often had no specialized knowledge of Brazil, and downplayed the violence posed by insurgents. But the regime's other rejoinders were spurious. In stating that human rights violations were not unique to Brazil, they were essentially admitting guilt. And in focusing their propaganda on a chimerical "conspiracy" of foreign criticism, they were ignoring the substantial wellspring of legitimate domestic opposition. The combination of Kennedy's statements and the negative international press reports fueled the Brazilian opposition's call for investigations and reforms.

Concern then shifted to possible U.S. complicity in torture through USAID's Office of Public Safety (OPS), which had provided funds and training to police forces in several nations since 1957. Because the OPS had trained thousands of Brazilian police officers in law enforcement and interrogation techniques, activists shed light on the small U.S. Naval Mission that was housed in Brazil's Navy Ministry. Some prisoners claimed that Brazilian security officers had tortured them in this building, and a few added that they had heard American voices in the corridors. Others said that the Brazilian interrogators claimed to have been trained by the CIA. The State Department, meanwhile, vehemently denied that torture was on the agenda of the training programs.[147]

It was one thing for American activists to point out that their government was supporting a repressive regime; it was another thing entirely to claim that Americans were training foreign nationals how to torture, or even participating in torture themselves. At the very least, it was significant that so many now believed that their government was directing such morally questionable actions. However, CIA activities were closely guarded, and even congressional committees did not find evidence that implicated the agency or OPS. Langguth published some of the victims' claims in his 1978 book *Hidden Terrors*, though he did not uncover much hard evidence that Americans were directly involved in torture. It is now clear that torture was happening in Brazil and that the CIA and State Department were aware of it, but much of the rest is speculation or hearsay.[148] Recently declassified CIA interrogation manuals are intriguing, though confirmation of direct CIA abuse has been harder to come by.[149]

But this focus on American culpability deflects attention from the story's central truth: that Brazilians were abusing Brazilians. Even if some Americans were involved in police training, to claim that they were the architects of extensive detainee abuse is to betray a marked ignorance of Brazil's troubled, violent history. More important than the claim that Americans were torturing or training others to do so was the perception—both in the United States and in South America—that American support was empowering dictatorial regimes to abuse civilians. The OPS became infamous because of its training in South Vietnam, and activists and journalists naturally began to scrutinize OPS ties to a host of Latin American

nations. (A decade later, activists would raise similar questions about counterinsurgency training at the U.S.-funded School of the Americas.)

In 1971, Senator Church chaired SFRC hearings on U.S.-Brazil relations. Together with the debate over aid to Greece, these hearings were
among the earliest congressional efforts to investigate and limit U.S.
involvement in other governments' human rights violations. The hearings
would last only three days and would include only government witnesses,
but the modest agenda could not obscure the provocative precedent. As
soon as Senator Church announced his plans, representatives of the Brazilian government and American businesses unsuccessfully petitioned the
State Department to stop it. As it turned out, the hearings were somewhat
traditional in the sense that the committee did not seek to change Brazilian
society or protect the rights of Brazilian citizens. "How Brazilians organize
their own affairs and how they treat each other are not proper concerns of
the U.S. Senate," said Church, but the actions of U.S. agencies in Brazil
were "proper concerns of all Americans."[150]

The liberal Senator Claiborne Pell—another early advocate of limiting
aid to undemocratic governments—had a testy exchange on these points
with USAID's chief public safety adviser in Brazil, Theodore D. Brown.
"The thing that arouses me and arouses American public opinion a good
deal," said Pell, "is this use of physical torture. Why is it the Brazilians . . .
use torture as a police method when it will alienate their friends and allies
around the world?" Brown first replied that he was "not personally aware"
of torture, and then tacitly acknowledged the problem: "Why certain people do things, that is a difficult question for me to answer, sir. . . . Why do
some people beat their wives?" Senator Church then got into a row with
Ambassador Rountree over President Nixon's policy of dealing with all governments. "We not only deal with them," said Church, "we extend lavish
amounts of money. . . . Can we simply say it matters not what the state of
freedom is in any country?" Church went on to succinctly lay out the moral
dilemmas Americans faced in the human rights era. "When I go to American colleges and talk to young people," he told the ambassador, "they ask
why have we spent two billion dollars in Brazil when the government there
is dictatorial in character, run by military men, any number of Brazilians
are said to be mistreated in the jails, where there are recurrent reports of
human torture."[151]

The congressional hearings process had long served as an opportunity
for legislators to question the executive branch on policy matters, but the

Church hearings went much further in highlighting the level of skepticism about the moral value of foreign aid. Church and Pell not only doubted that the large aid allotment to Brazil did anything for the United States, but they were unimpressed with the administration's claims of private diplomacy, and argued instead for strong public condemnation. The hearings were also a different kind of conversation because the senators had been receiving information from nongovernmental sources. Because activists and NGOs had done so much research and writing on Brazil, the senators did not have to rely on the State Department.[152]

Congress did not cut direct aid in 1971, but these hearings set an important precedent for the threat of cutoffs based on human rights concerns. Congress soon terminated USAID funds for Brazilian police training, and the OPS pulled out of Brazil. (Congress would phase out the entire program in 1974.) These hearings also increased the congressional momentum against such regimes in Latin America. In 1971–1972, Senator John Tunney (D-CA), Congressman Donald Fraser, and Congressman Ronald Dellums (D-CA) proposed Brazilian aid cuts until the IACHR could prove that torture had been eradicated. These proposals received no more than about one-third support in each house, but they demonstrated a growing liberal challenge to Nixonian realpolitik.[153] Meanwhile, the State Department was hardly unified. Ambassador Rountree, who was clearly troubled by the overwhelming evidence of torture, supported diplomatic intercession. Unfortunately for him, when he commented to Washington on the "essentiality of making [U.S. disapproval] clear on appropriate occasion and in appropriate manner," his superior wrote in the memo's margin, "i.e. never, and by saying nothing."[154]

The mounting congressional opposition did not prevent the administration from rolling out the red carpet when President Médici visited Washington in December 1971. With both governments seeking to halt the leftward drift in the hemisphere, Secretary Rogers advised Nixon that the visit would provide an opportunity to influence Brazil's leadership, as "the Brazilians' objectives parallel our own." Rogers even put a positive spin on the junta's domestic achievements. Although many "thinking Brazilians" were "impatient with the slow pace of return to democratic procedures," the wider public was "enthusiastic about Brazil's progress." Terrorism had been reduced, Brazil's economy had grown, and the regime had permitted some direct congressional and municipal elections.[155] State Department FSOs in Brazil concurred. In the words of a U.S. embassy report, "large segments of Brazilian opinion [are] willing to accommodate themselves to authoritarian government, tainted with chronic, if occasional, abuses of individual rights, so long as it is accompanied by prosperity and a sense of accomplishment."[156]

At their first meeting, Médici implored Nixon not to neglect South America, where the danger from homegrown, Cuba-backed insurgencies was so dire that it "could blow up at any time." Nixon agreed that regional insurgencies were a problem, and he assured Médici that the United States would maintain a strong front against Cuba. But otherwise he was cautious, asking many questions but promising little. Twice he pointed out that Congress controlled foreign aid, and he frankly noted that many American legislators wanted to limit ties in the belief that Brazil was "not democratic enough." Médici denied that Brazil was a military dictatorship (he cited as proof the nation's relatively small army), and he emphasized that the position of Brazil and its neighbors was so tenuous that they needed U.S. military support.[157] Considering that Nixon twice brought up the lack of democracy, we might be tempted to believe that he had misgivings about supporting an undemocratic government. But it is more likely that he simply wanted to clarify that Congress had to be taken seriously and that he did not have a free hand to aid allies as he wished. He may also have been preoccupied by his more important upcoming meetings in Beijing and Moscow. Either way, with respect to Brazil he was essentially caught between three of his central policy positions. He sought to aid anticommunist allies and avoid involvement in their internal affairs, all while decreasing America's overseas commitments.

At their second meeting, it became clear that the price for Nixon's support was Brazil taking a leading role in policing the Americas. The two leaders found common cause in curbing the activities of Fidel Castro, the region's guerrillas, and Salvador Allende in Chile. Médici strongly agreed with Nixon's statement that the two countries must work to "prevent new Allendes and Castros," and he made it clear that Brazil intended to play a key role in preventing left-wing incursions. Nixon then made vague promises of U.S. back-channel funding if the Brazilians moved to undermine or overthrow Allende. Each side saw these meetings as a great success—the Brazilian foreign minister even told American officials that the visit "far exceeded our fondest expectations."[158] Nixon was pleased with the Brazilian leadership from the standpoint of hemispheric security, and he and Secretary Rogers were privately effusive in their praise of Médici. "He's quite a fellow, isn't he," said Nixon. "I wish he were running the whole continent." Rogers agreed: "God, I'm glad he's on our side." The Brazilians did go on to interfere in their neighbors' political affairs, and Médici became far more active than Nixon in fighting communism in South America.[159]

But not everyone was happy with the Médici visit or the state of U.S.-Brazil relations. The Committee Against Repression in Brazil erected a large sign outside the White House that read, "Stop U.S. Dollar Complicity with Brazilian Torturists." A Brazilian student briefly disrupted Médici's speech at the Organization of American States by yelling, "Long live free Brazil—stop the tortures!" The *New York Times* suggested that Nixon's public inclusion of Brazil among America's closest allies "will be taken in Latin America as bestowing Washington's blessings on the less attractive aspects of the junta's record."[160] Even some Brazilian military leaders had misgivings, including one general who lamented that the Americans wanted Brazil to "do the dirty work" in the region.[161]

Although the Nixon administration did not alter its position, the Brazilian case showed that a focused antitorture campaign could raise public awareness of suffering, essentially turning a Brazilian domestic issue into an international concern. Activists' testimony and images reached the news media and Congress, and this rise in awareness forced the executive branch to reexamine bilateral relations. Antitorture activism on behalf of Brazilian political prisoners contributed to a much broader international movement against torture, including Amnesty International's groundbreaking global campaign in 1973.[162] These activities would lay the foundations for a strong international reaction to one of the era's major turning points: the Chilean military's September 1973 overthrow of Salvador Allende. As for Brazil, incidences of torture and disappearances would decrease under the government of General Ernesto Geisel (1974–1979), in part because of international criticism and in part because most of the armed resistance had been subjugated. Many exiles would return following a 1979 amnesty, though the Brazilian military government would remain in power until 1985.

Chapter 2

The Congressional Challenge and
the Ethnic Revival

Washington politics in the 1970s were defined by an inordinate amount of conflict between the executive and legislative branches. As part of a broad-based effort to limit the power of the executive and claim a more prominent position in the foreign policymaking process, legislators played a key role in bringing human rights concerns to Washington. Indeed, Congress became the linchpin by transforming earlier questions about support to authoritarian regimes into firm statutory demands to alter these relationships. Through a variety of measures, the U.S. government became the first in the world to write human rights standards into its bilateral foreign policy laws. Between 1973 and 1979, legislators invoked the power of the purse and amended the Foreign Assistance Act to assess the human rights situation in every nation receiving aid, and they approved over two dozen bills that addressed foreign nations' human rights practices. Congress also passed country-specific legislation that influenced relations with upward of twenty nations between 1973 and 1984.[1]

These moves heartened activists, and at times may even have influenced human rights practices in target countries. But congressional activism was a double-edged sword. Not only did much of this activity antagonize foreign governments, but it also spawned awkward questions about policymakers' intentions and the limits to American power. Were these pursuits solely intended to improve human rights practices, or were they politically motivated? How could Congress measure success? What if new laws conflicted with American commercial or security interests? And where did legislators draw the line between suitable and unsuitable causes? This chapter explores these questions and explains the pivotal role Congress played in the human rights story. It also highlights those legislators who took the lead in bringing these concerns into the diplomatic realm. Activists and journalists played an important part in providing information and pressuring the powerful, but Congress had the power to pass laws and directly challenge the executive branch. The clearest cases of executive-legislative conflict over human rights in the Nixon-Ford years were the Pinochet dictatorship and the Soviet Jewry movement. This chapter also examines ethnic interest groups' involvement in the major causes of the seventies.

Congressional assertiveness grew from several sources. Congress had earlier granted President Johnson extraordinary power to wage war and expand social programs, but the combination of endemic domestic problems and the Vietnam stalemate led legislators to openly lambaste the "imperial presidency." President Nixon aggravated this animosity through his secretive, executive-centered diplomacy. A set of legislators then emerged with a program that one senator defined as "new internationalism"—a posture aimed at demilitarizing foreign policy and pursuing new international priorities.[2] In 1970, Congress repealed the Tonkin Gulf Resolution and restricted Nixon's use of the military in Southeast Asia—the first ever vote to limit troop deployments during wartime. Three years later, the War Powers Act required congressional approval for all American military activities. Congress also assumed some oversight of intelligence and pressured President Ford into banning involvement in political assassinations.[3] In perhaps the most famous (or infamous) assertion of legislative dominion, Congress refused emergency funds for the final defense of South Vietnam in 1975. These moves led William Bundy to write of these years, "Consensus on foreign policy has disappeared perhaps beyond recall."[4]

International human rights became a significant battleground in this executive-legislative conflict. The executive had never been required to consider human rights in bilateral relations, but in light of the Nixon administration's adherence to realpolitik, legislators took the lead in placing these issues onto the agenda. They used the hearings process to gather information and to build support for pending legislation; they mandated human rights requirements in trade and foreign aid; and they passed nonbinding "sense of the Congress" resolutions, which functioned as public position statements on everything from civil liberties in South Korea to religious persecution in the Soviet Union. Congress also required the State Department to create a new human rights bureau and compile "country reports" that would assess the domestic situation within every country receiving assistance.

Legislators were motivated by their constituents' concerns, by personal political ambitions, and, presumably, by a degree of genuine concern for suffering peoples. But while we cannot prove what was in their hearts, it is easier to demonstrate that their respective positions lined up with their ideological beliefs and their political interests. Liberal Democrats Donald Fraser, Edward Kennedy, and Frank Church took the first major steps by chairing hearings and sponsoring resolutions to limit military assistance to authoritarian regimes of the right.[5] Conservatives then latched onto the trend to attack détente, left-wing regimes, and economic aid to developing nations. Coalitions occasionally formed across party lines, but rarely across ideological lines. Conservative Democrats were more likely to align with conservative Republicans than liberals of their own party on anti-Soviet proposals. Likewise, some moderate and liberal Republicans were troubled by American support of dictatorships, and thus were often willing to join with liberal Democrats (though liberal Republicans were a rarity by the end of the 1970s). Members of Congress also prioritized specific regions. Conservatives generally fixated on the communist regimes of Eastern Europe, while liberals focused on the right-wing regimes of Latin America. Beyond Latin America and Europe, Congress largely ignored violations in the Middle East and East Asia, though they occasionally spotlighted American allies Iran, South Korea, the Philippines, and Indonesia. Africa was also generally ignored, with the exception of Uganda in 1978–1979 and South Africa during the 1980s antiapartheid movement.

The Foreign Aid Battleground

A major factor in the growing congressional interest in human rights was the long-standing debate over America's program of international economic and military assistance. Foreign aid—the voluntary transfer of public resources from one nation to another—was central to the human rights story because cutting aid was among the most effective methods by which members of Congress could create *and* enforce a human rights policy. If private diplomacy or public criticism failed to alter an abusive government's behavior, legislators could withhold funds in order to encourage reforms. The aid-cutting trend and the human rights movement developed for many of the same reasons. The Cold War thaw allowed policymakers to step outside of the assumptions that had long governed aid allocation. At the same time that policymakers were growing wary of overextending the nation's commitments, the economic troubles of the seventies seemed a poor context for the U.S. government to dispense dollars around the world. Foreign aid was always controversial, and policymakers debated it for two decades before they began debating human rights. Consequently, by the time Congress began passing human rights laws in the mid-seventies, legislators had already grown comfortable with the notion of aid cuts.

The unraveling of the foreign aid consensus predated, and in some ways contributed to, the dissolution of the containment doctrine. In most years up to the mid-1960s, foreign aid exceeded 1 percent of GNP; during the Marshall Plan it even exceeded 2 percent. But when the Vietnam War effort began to look prohibitively costly, more Americans questioned the principles undergirding aid programs. Senator Fulbright, who called foreign aid "one of the most vexing problems of American foreign policy," joined with congressional liberals to savage the manner in which the paternalistic aid commitment to South Vietnam had evolved into a military commitment.[6] In the sixties, liberals further argued that foreign assistance was too closely linked to American economic interests and anticommunism. Although aid to South Vietnam financed infrastructure and schools, it also funded the poorly conceived strategic hamlet program and the authoritarian police apparatus. Legislators asked why South Vietnamese leaders seemed unable to improve their popularity or increase their democratic attributes despite being granted such large sums. One early attempt to address these problems, Title IX of the Foreign Assistance Act (1966), proposed making "political development" (loosely defined as more democratic procedures and institutions) a part of USAID decisions. But the effort was not sustained, and USAID's mandate remained economic development, not the promotion of democracy.[7]

Human rights concerns had little influence on aid debates in the 1960s, but policymakers did question aid to regimes that exhibited poor political development or expressed anti-Americanism. Many liberals and moderates disagreed that a government's anticommunist credentials were a proper litmus test for receiving aid. These critics argued that aid should only go to the poorest countries or to democracies, a position they justified on both strategic and moral grounds. Meanwhile, conservatives' criticism of foreign aid was an integral part of their opposition to post-1945 liberalism. Republicans had been somewhat amenable to aid early in the Cold War, but in the sixties they lambasted the exorbitance of aid levels and marveled at how few strings were attached. The United States, they argued, was giving too much money to too many countries, an attitude exemplified in a 1966 Republican campaign slogan: "Why are we losing our money AND our friends?" These misgivings did not stem from recipient nations' human rights records, but rather nations' relative alignment with American interests and anticommunism.[8] Many American voters, too, supported cuts in the interest of anticommunism, isolationism, countering anti-Americanism, or trimming the budget. A constituent wrote to Senator Henry Jackson in 1970, "In every country that we have given aid to that says 'Go Home Yankee,' take them off the list of being permitted to receive foreign aid." Another wrote, "Let's build a healthy prosperous America if we have a lot of money to spend and the hell with the damned foreigners, let them fend for themselves. . . . Besides, the more we donate to them, the more they despise Americans."[9] That same year, one congressman succinctly described how this new isolationism had affected Congress: "The congressional climate in support of American economic overseas commitments has never been more inhospitable."[10] Due in part to these reservations, foreign aid declined throughout the seventies and eighties, dropping as low as 0.25 percent of GNP, and this downward trend continued into the twenty-first century.[11]

Richard Nixon's approach to the aid dilemma was consistent with his wider foreign policy goals. Publicly, he assured Americans that there were sound moral reasons for foreign aid, but his real interest was using aid to prevent developing nations from turning toward socialism or nonaligned anti-Americanism. He also sought to shift more of the aid burden to America's allies, multilateral institutions, the private sector, and the developing nations themselves. Reducing direct aid would be a way for the United States to loosen itself from troublesome entanglements and avoid being "blackmailed," he asserted, though he did not see democracy as a necessary yardstick for aid allocation. "If you go down that road," he said to Kissinger, "you will have to cut off aid to two-thirds of the ninety countries in the world that get it."[12] In 1971, the Senate rejected the foreign assistance bill for the first time ever. Emergency legislation allotted some funds, but for the next several years budgets were lower than usual. "Neo-isolationism" was clearly a factor in these trends. Whereas the prior generation of liberals had supported the use of dollars to build up the developing world, those in the 1970s were far more likely to focus on

America's domestic ills. The American public, too, was rejecting broad plans for global melioration. In a 1976 Gallup poll, 23 percent of respondents called themselves "predominantly" or "completely" isolationist, compared with just 8 percent in 1964. Only 7 percent of respondents identified themselves as "completely internationalist" in 1976, while 30 percent had done so in 1964.[13]

Nevertheless, cutting aid and arms exports was controversial on many levels. Military aid constituted the bulk of American foreign assistance, and foreign military sales were among the nation's largest exports. Such aid and sales strengthened alliances, allowed friendly regimes to defend themselves, prevented the United States from having to commit troops, and helped keep American defense contractors in the black. Not only were American leaders reluctant to abandon long-standing friendships, but after Vietnam they also sought to reduce direct military commitments. Indeed, military aid allocations were a relatively reliable measure of America's foreign policy priorities. As policymakers shifted their attention away from Asia and toward the Middle East at the dawn of the 1970s, aid to South Vietnam, South Korea, and Taiwan fell considerably, while Israel and Egypt leaped to the top of the list.[14]

Arms sales and security assistance decisions were long unencumbered by human rights considerations, but in the seventies policymakers began to ask why the United States was lavishing so many dollars and weapons upon blatantly abusive regimes. As we have seen, Senator Kennedy offered one of the earliest such laments in his 1970 criticism of the U.S. approach to Latin America, where military governments were ruling eleven republics with substantial U.S. support.[15] Kennedy's statement was noteworthy because he was challenging the Cold War security imperative of arming anticommunist regimes, and he was questioning the moral implications of exporting arms that might be used against civilians—a perspective that grew directly out of the debates over aid to Greece and Brazil. Kennedy's opponents countered that this aid protected American interests and that reducing it would call into question American power and reliability. The Nixon and Ford administrations generally supported military assistance, and they further argued that any state with a need would eventually find a supplier. "You cannot have military governments that you don't give arms to," said Kissinger privately. "They're going to get it sooner or later from somebody else."[16] This disagreement would soon be taken up in earnest by the entire Congress, and the new human rights legislation would prove to be a major sticking point between the executive and legislative branches.

Congressional Hearings, Human Rights Laws, and the Dissidents

The hearings process emerged as a key congressional method of challenging the executive. As Robert D. Johnson has pointed out, committee hearings were the only routine public forum in which one branch of government could directly challenge another branch to defend its policies.[17] In the first half of the 1970s, Congress used the process to uncover secret government activities and to assume greater control over defense, covert operations, and foreign policy. In 1971, Senator Sam Ervin investigated allegations that the U.S. Army had spied on civilians. The SFRC then investigated the activities of the State Department and American corporations in Chile. Most significant of all, the 1973–1974 Watergate hearings inhibited Nixon's presidential abilities and revealed a complex web of illegal and unethical activities. After Nixon's resignation, the Church Committee and the Pike Committee looked into unscrupulous CIA and FBI activities. All told, these hearings presented Americans with uncomfortable truths about their government, and they spurred legislative action to rein in the power of the executive and reorient foreign policy.

Human rights hearings grew out of this milieu. Earlier attention to Greek and Brazilian internal policies set an important precedent for the threat of aid cutoffs based on human rights concerns, but these inquiries were not connected to a broader movement, nor did they engender substantive legislation. It was not until 1973–1974 that Congress institutionalized human rights hearings as a means of challenging the executive, drafting human rights laws, and laying out an alternative to realpolitik. The SFRC's 1973 confirmation hearings on Henry Kissinger's nomination as secretary of state were unexpectedly germane to this burgeoning conversation. An array of groups opposed his nomination, including conservatives who blamed him for the shortcomings of détente and liberals who derided his secretiveness and his possible complicity in human rights violations. Summing up the view from the left, one university professor testified that "illicit wiretapping, deception of Congress and of the American people, secret and massive bombing, and deep involvement in the most brutal use of armed violence against human beings" were sufficient reasons to deny his confirmation. Some senators used the forum to highlight the administration's secrecy, while others questioned its amoral foreign policy. Senator Edmund Muskie (D-ME), a 1972 presidential candidate and Nixon critic, assailed the administration's "style of operation" in foreign affairs, for which the United States had "paid a serious and possibly dangerous price." Meanwhile, Kissinger defended his realism. "If we adopt as a national proposition the view that we must transform the domestic structure of all countries with which we deal," he asserted, "then we will find ourselves massively involved in every country in the world."[18] Despite the criticisms, the committee recommended his confirmation, and the full Senate confirmed him by a vote of seventy-eight to seven. The nay votes included such unlikely bedfellows as the liberal Democrat George McGovern (SD) and the conservative Republican Jesse Helms (NC).

While the SFRC was considering Kissinger's nomination, Congressman Donald Fraser became the first to conduct hearings for the express purpose of publicizing international human rights violations.[19] These investigations helped establish him as the preeminent congressional advocate of the seventies. Fraser seems to have been driven to activism more by contemporary events and his personal beliefs than by the interests of voters in his Minneapolis district. Although his constituents were generally moderate to liberal, few had a direct ethnic or religious connection to overseas victims. What is clear is that Fraser was greatly affected by the Vietnam War, the worldwide rise in military coups and civil wars, and America's ties to undemocratic regimes.

The Fraser-chaired Subcommittee on International Organizations and Movements—also known as the Fraser Committee—held fifteen landmark hearings on international human rights from August to December 1973. Over forty witnesses testified, including legislators, foreign service officers (FSOs), and activists. The subcommittee's final report, *Human Rights in the World Community: A Call for U.S. Leadership*, made a strong claim that "the human rights factor is not accorded the high priority it deserves in our country's foreign policy." The report's authors conceded that it should not be the only factor, but argued that it should hold a higher priority if Americans wanted to retain global leadership and encourage the spread of democracy. Many of their conclusions were thinly veiled criticisms of the Nixon-Kissinger foreign policy, as when they assailed "proponents of pure

power politics" for too readily accepting dictators who "unabashedly vio-
late almost every human rights guarantee pronounced by the world community." In several cases—torture in Brazil and Chile, racial discrimination
in Southern Africa, the massacres in Bangladesh and Burundi—the subcommittee found the U.S. response to be lacking. They proposed a combination of public statements, private diplomacy, evenhanded laws, and a
more active State Department.[20]

Not everyone on the committee agreed with the report. Republicans
H. R. Gross of Iowa and Edward Derwinski of Illinois distanced themselves
from it, and L. H. Fountain (D-NC) lambasted the report for "presum[ing]
to have the answer for the prevention of nearly every form of human rights
violation in the world today."[21] Fraser also received mixed messages from
his constituents. "I cannot tell you how glad and excited I was," wrote one
supporter, "to read that you had introduced resolutions . . . in the interests
of human decency and dignity for God and man. . . . Thank God for you."
But another accused him of hunting for publicity and wasting money in
the full knowledge that "no amount of hearings . . . is going to change the
Greeks, Burundians, or the Northern (or for that matter Southern) Irish."
Fraser also had critics on the political left. "This country must get its own
house in order before it goes out proselyting [sic]," wrote one voter.
"Nowhere have human rights been more abused than in Southeast Asia,
where this nation has rained terror out of the skies. . . . The right to be free
of U.S. bombs falling on one's person is a very important human right,
don't you agree Mr. Fraser?"[22] The sheer variety of such criticisms illustrates
how unusual Fraser's pursuit was in 1973, though these difficult questions
would also continue to perplex policymakers in the years ahead. Irrespective of these reservations, the Fraser Committee hearings influenced the
human rights tide in Congress, and many of the committee's recommendations later became law. Fraser went on to hold over 150 hearings on over
forty countries. Although congressional liberals spearheaded this budding
congressional revolt, conservative Republicans like Senator Helms and neoconservative Democrats like Senator Henry Jackson soon adopted similar
rhetoric to assail détente's compromises and its inattention to Soviet
persecution.

While this discontentment was brewing in Congress, Eastern Bloc dissidents like Andrei Sakharov and Aleksandr Solzhenitsyn were becoming
Western causes célèbres and impediments to détente. Solzhenitsyn was the
most prominent symbol of Soviet writers' diminished opportunities during

the Brezhnev era. He was persecuted throughout the 1960s and was expelled from the Union of Soviet Writers before winning the Nobel Prize in Literature in 1970. Soviet leaders considered him a menace because he criticized their policies on moral grounds, and he similarly troubled the Nixon administration because he asserted that détente equaled tacit Western acceptance of Soviet totalitarianism. In his provocative Nobel acceptance speech, he exhorted, "Newspaper headlines still display: 'No Right to Interfere in Our Internal Affairs,' whereas there are no internal affairs left on our crowded earth! And mankind's sole salvation lies in everyone making everything his business: In the people of the East being vitally concerned with what is thought in the West, the people of the West vitally concerned with what goes on in the East."[23]

After Solzhenitsyn was banished from the Soviet Union in 1974, he became a political and intellectual pawn in America, and with his arrival came increasing awareness of dissidents' plight. As the Czech writer Milan Kundera later sardonically said of Solzhenitsyn's influence, Western intellectuals finally "started to believe, after a fifty-year delay, that in communist Russia there were concentration camps."[24] Much of the dissidents' appeal lay in their malleability as symbols. Stefan-Ludwig Hoffmann notes that the dissident figure became an "object of projection" for the right, left, and center—"each claimed the dissident and thus the language of human rights for their own political objectives."[25] And indeed, Solzhenitsyn's dour image seemed to be everywhere in America, as legislators of all political stripes latched onto his coattails. President Nixon noted the writer's "great courage," but otherwise steered clear of him for fear of threatening détente. "I look back to the years of confrontation," Nixon told reporters, "and I find that men like [Solzhenitsyn], as a matter of fact, rather than being sent to Paris, would have been sent to Siberia or probably worse."[26] Senator Jackson savaged this logic by arguing that Nixon and Kissinger had "obscured the relationship between détente and human rights" by implying that American support for dissidents and *refuseniks* would somehow increase the chance of nuclear war.[27]

In 1975, Solzhenitsyn embarked on a U.S. tour that kicked off with a speaking engagement at the AFL-CIO convention in Washington. Organizers suggested a meeting with President Ford, but in order to avoid antagonizing the Soviets, Kissinger convinced the president not to meet with the writer. Ford suffered mightily as a result of the snub—so much, in fact, that the presidential mailroom did not receive a single letter or telegram supporting his decision.[28] Ronald Reagan, who had his eye on the 1976 presidential election, attacked the administration, and Senator Jackson capitalized on the snub by bringing Solzhenitsyn to speak to a large gathering in the Senate.[29] Behind the scenes, Ford called Solzhenitsyn "a goddamn horse's ass" and complained that the writer was gunning for publicity.[30]

But although Ford took a public beating, perhaps he had a point. Few questioned Solzhenitsyn's authority to speak about tyranny, for his life had been riddled with suffering. After surviving combat in the Second World War, he spent nearly a decade in Stalin's Gulag, almost died of cancer, and then faced years of harassment for his writing. But what were Americans to make of his exhortation that "mankind's sole salvation lies in everyone making everything his business?" What practical guidance did this open-ended demand give to policymakers dealing in the real world of interstate relations? It was not altogether clear then, or in the years to come, that such a claim could even apply to the diplomatic realm.

The Solzhenitsyn affair and the slew of congressional hearings showed that members of Congress could wage public human rights diplomacy. In the long run, though, concrete legislative measures would have a much greater impact on foreign policy. Simply put, in the 1970s Congress used its powers to make international human rights practices a concern of the U.S. government. At first, legislators were chiefly concerned with the Soviet Union and those nations that received American military aid—Greece, Brazil, Chile, South Korea, the Philippines, and a few others—and in time the list grew to include dozens of states. Aid cuts also reflected the popular demand for reductions in both foreign aid and the defense budget. Yet despite congressional success in pushing bilateral human rights requirements, Americans remained skeptical about multilateral arrangements and international organizations. This combination of bilateral activism and multilateral inaction created some confusion in the international community, and even led to accusations of hypocrisy.[31] Nevertheless, the wave of congressional legislation signaled a remarkable trend.

Just as 1973 was a turning point in the hearings process, so was it a moment of fundamental change in legislative activism. Against the backdrop of Watergate, the Pinochet coup, and the publication of Solzhenitsyn's *Gulag Archipelago*, Congress took its first major steps. Chile became a particular obsession of Democratic legislators. Congressmen Fraser, Benjamin

Rosenthal, and Robert Drinan (D-MA) joined with Senators Edward Kennedy and James Abourezk (D-SD) to sponsor several resolutions that suggested (but did not mandate) that the president deny economic or military aid to any government that "practices the internment or imprisonment of that country's citizens for political purposes."[32] As it became clear that the Nixon and Ford administrations were ignoring these resolutions, Congress took the unprecedented step of explicitly linking U.S. military assistance to foreign governments' human rights records. The Foreign Assistance Act of 1974 banned military aid to Chile and placed a ceiling on military aid to South Korea, unless the president could certify that Santiago and Seoul were making "substantial progress" in the observance of human rights standards.[33] The act also prohibited the United States from aiding or training foreign police forces, and it eliminated the controversial Office of Public Safety (OPS).

These trends were amplified by the Democrats' gain of forty-nine House and five Senate seats in the 1974 election. These victories grew primarily from anti-Republican sentiment in the wake of Watergate, but the election results strengthened the human rights cause nonetheless. "Watergate baby" Democrats like Senator Tom Harkin (IA), Congressman Christopher Dodd (CT), and Congressman Edward Koch (NY) would make it even harder for Ford and Kissinger to pursue their foreign policy goals. Yet although the election results forced Kissinger to take congressional activists more seriously, his candid comments showed that he truly did not understand their perspective. He interpreted the human rights resolutions as left-wing and neoconservative challenges to his steady and reasonable geopolitical aims. "These guys don't want to stand for human rights," he barked in a staff meeting, "they want grandstand plays. They want public humiliation of other countries." To Kissinger, the activists embraced a contrarian philosophy that would weaken the United States while doing little for human rights. "What do they want?" he asked. "They want us to cut off aid. . . . They want us to be anti-Philippine, anti-Korean, anti-Chilean. Pro what? Castro? I don't know what they want us to be pro."[34]

Kissinger was more agreeable in person. In his meetings with legislators, which he only agreed to out of necessity, he touted private diplomacy and defended the necessity of maintaining relations with unsavory governments "no matter how unpleasant it might seem." But his visitors expressed misgivings over military aid when the threat to America was unclear. Because Santiago was further away than Moscow, Fraser quipped, "I can't really associate [Chile] with a landing in any time in the future on the beaches of California." Kissinger agreed that few developing nations posed a direct security threat, but he argued that the "increasingly radicalized" world posed a long-term danger.[35] But his exhortations ultimately meant little to congressional activists, largely because the administration did not alter its policies. Yet although it is tempting to interpret Kissinger's sentiments as an undistilled rejection of human rights activism, it is more accurate to say that he was defining national security broadly and the American national interest narrowly, while his interlocutors were doing the opposite. Irrespective of legislators' cause, he wanted them to stay out of the foreign policy game.

South Korea's special relationship with the United States made it a particularly difficult human rights case. NGOs had documented evidence of political imprisonment and torture under the government of President Park Chung-hee, but the nation's precarious position between North Korea, China, and the Soviet Union had long prevented an outcry in Washington. Growing congressional activism and the unpopularity of foreign aid then convinced the Ford administration to encourage Korean reforms, but the administration's public line emphasized security. "Obviously we do not approve of Korea's policies on human rights," said a Ford spokesman, but the prevention of war was "the first and most important step toward the maintenance of human liberties."[36] When Ford made a quick stop in Seoul in November 1974, President Park emphasized the existential threat from the North and alluded to the need for tough domestic measures and continued American support. "Although some of our people complain," he said of his policies, "we need to develop prosperity and security to deal with the peculiar North Korean type of communism." Since Ford was not seeking a new diplomatic problem, he simply reaffirmed the American commitment and left it to the U.S. embassy to offer private encouragement for democratic reforms.[37]

The April 1975 Fall of Saigon and Phnom Penh altered Washington's outlook on the Asia-Pacific region and further fueled activists' frustrations. Fearing that the twin communist victories would have regional repercussions, Ford and Kissinger sought to strengthen ties with President Park, Ferdinand Marcos in the Philippines, and Suharto in Indonesia. Korea and the Philippines were the subject of a very telling Fraser Committee exchange in June 1975. Congressman Fraser asserted that American soldiers did not die to establish an authoritarian South Korea, and he questioned whether South Korea and the Philippines were really vital to U.S. security. Assistant Secretary of State Philip Habib was willing to criticize Seoul and Manila's repressive measures—a far cry from the denials the administration would have issued a few years earlier—but he clarified that the security relationship was unchanged in light of the North Korean threat, the loss of Vietnam and Cambodia, and the continuing need for bases in the Philippines.[38] Ever the realist, Kissinger even asked Thailand's foreign minister to pass a conciliatory message to the communist Khmer Rouge. Although the group had begun a genocidal campaign in Cambodia, Kissinger believed that they could be a counterweight to America's erstwhile enemy in Vietnam. "Tell the Cambodians that we will be friends with them," he said. "They are murderous thugs, but we won't let that stand in our way."[39]

The administration's relationship with the government of Indonesia would engender one of the most controversial decisions of the Ford presidency. Suharto was an anticommunist ally and a champion of stability, but he was also an autocrat whose jails held over thirty thousand political prisoners. Indonesia's actions in the neighboring territory of East Timor were another matter of concern. East Timor was a Portuguese colony until the 1974 Carnation Revolution brought democracy to Portugal and independence to its imperial possessions. Fearing a takeover by the Marxist group FRETILIN and its military wing, FALINTIL, Suharto considered preemptively invading and occupying the region. When he met with Ford and Kissinger in December 1975, they assured him that they would not hinder the effort. "We will understand and will not press you on the issue," said Ford. "We understand the problem and the intentions you have." Kissinger suggested that a quick resolution of the problem would be best for both countries, and he added that the administration would be able to handle the American reaction "if whatever happens happens after we return [to Washington]."[40] Indonesia then invaded and began a brutal, long-term occupation. The United States condemned the invasion in the U.N. Security Council and temporarily halted new military aid, while legislators debated whether Suharto was illegally using American military equipment in an offensive war. But the Ford administration did little else, preferring instead to interpret the occupation as an Indonesian domestic issue.

In Washington, the political prisoner problem was more prominent than was East Timor. With Congress willing to withhold aid if there was no progress on prisoners, Suharto assured the administration that he was working on releases, and Kissinger and Ford chose to believe him. So soon

after the fall of South Vietnam and Cambodia, they were far more interested in continuing American assistance and using private persuasion to
resolve the political prisoner problem. When Suharto visited Washington
in 1975, congressional pleas to address the issue went unheeded. As Habib
advised Kissinger, such representation would only "sour the atmosphere"
and would be "misunderstood by Suharto, whose government is at least
moving in the right direction on this issue."[41] As for East Timor, Washington's indifference had much to do with the continuing adherence to a Cold
War outlook in East Asia, but there was also a surprising lack of global
sympathy for the East Timorese due to the perception that this was an
anticolonial struggle. In Samuel Moyn's words, because the East Timorese
had framed their cause in a now-obsolete anticolonial nationalism, they
"therefore fell outside the pale of empathy."[42] Near the end of Ford's presidency, he increased military aid to Suharto, and Suharto's government
announced a three-year phased release of the prisoners.[43] Some legislators
and NGOs tried to shed light on America's relationship with the regime,
but Indonesia remained a marginal concern in Washington. Neither Congress nor the executive would seriously consider sanctions over East Timor
until the 1990s. Meanwhile, upward of a hundred thousand died in Indonesia's occupation between 1975 and 1999.

Although Congress did not sanction Indonesia, it did pass several new
human rights laws in 1976, including one that prohibited security assistance
to any government that engaged in "a consistent pattern of gross violations
of internationally recognized human rights." President Ford vetoed the bill,
but he signed a compromise that declared these human rights standards to
be "the policy of the United States." Although the law was intended to
limit presidential power, Congress created exceptions for "extraordinary
circumstances" and for cases in which providing aid was in America's
national interest. These proved to be major sticking points in the years to
come. As a result, only in rare instances was aid actually cut. Moreover,
most of the world's worst offenders were not receiving any American aid,
and thus were not affected by the law. The Ford administration's unwillingness to invoke the spirit of this era's resolutions led Congress to take more
control. It granted itself decision-making power on arms transfers and the
use of American military advisers, and it passed country-specific laws to
block arms sales and military aid. Ford vetoed the arms bill, arguing that
its "well-intended but misguided" provisions would not promote human
rights but would certainly weaken the president's leverage.[44] Nevertheless,

legislators further angered the administration by reducing military aid to Turkey, Uruguay, Angola, Chile, and South Korea. Congress was even more successful in limiting economic aid and loans to offending governments through such laws as the 1975 Harkin Amendment, which banned economic assistance to consistent violators unless the aid directly benefited the needy.

While Congress was redefining the nation's bilateral relationships, it was also writing new requirements for the State Department. The most significant was the mandate for an annual study of human rights practices in each nation that received U.S. aid—an effort that stemmed, in part, from the State Department's slow responses to congressional and NGO queries. These reports would set a global precedent: no other government in the world was required by law to document foreign nations' human rights practices. Congress also pressed the State Department to establish a new position to coordinate human rights and humanitarian activities. Within a few years, they created a new bureau and elevated the coordinator position to the level of assistant secretary.

The release of the first individual country reports in 1976–1977 elicited a mixed response. The governments in question bristled at the attention, while activists criticized the reports' inadequacy and bias. Amnesty International found them "disconcerting," "inadequate," and riddled with distortions.[45] A similar reaction greeted the first complete set of country reports in 1978. The State Department's first human rights coordinator, James M. Wilson, noted that the initial reaction in most of the affected countries was "mostly severe . . . all were clearly unhappy."[46] But in the long run the reports gained in quality and credibility, and their annual release became a major event in Washington. In response to conservatives' protests, Congress later expanded the mandate to include reports on communist governments.

These requirements dramatically expanded America's involvement in international human rights, but they also created a new set of challenges. For starters, there were definitional difficulties. With respect to the Harkin Amendment on economic aid, for example, policymakers debated how to define aid that would "directly affect needy people." Did this include, say, agricultural research programs to increase crop yields, or aid for vocational teacher training? Another obvious downside to the new laws was the inevitable backlash in foreign capitals. The new rules forced the diplomatic corps to do work that ran counter to their traditional mandate. As David Forsythe has noted, the creation of the human rights bureau was coolly received in the State Department because FSOs were trained to maintain friendly relations with their host governments.[47] Naturally, the State Department's regional bureaus typically underreported abuses or overemphasized "positive" signs of liberalization.

The new requirements also spurred discord within the State Department itself, especially between Kissinger and the new human rights bureaucrats. Considering that Kissinger's attitude fluctuated between wholly uninterested and completely hostile, the officers in James M. Wilson's human rights office were often unsure of their mandate.[48] It did not help their morale that Kissinger referred to them as "theologians" and "bleeding hearts" and frequently ignored their recommendations. In 1975, he told the Chilean foreign minister that the State Department was "made up of people who have a vocation for the ministry. Because there were not enough churches for them, they went into the Department of State."[49] The country reports mandate caused perhaps the most conflict. Unsurprisingly, Kissinger opposed the requirement in principle. There was an "original sin" in the world, he argued, and the United States should not be in the business of judging its allies. He also saw the mandate as a wedge issue: if the State Department caved to Congress, he insisted that it would imperil the entire Ford/Kissinger foreign policy.[50] A member of the human rights office countered that the administration should be more forthright for both practical and moral reasons. Human rights now mattered to Americans and to the global community; it was "no longer a bleeding heart issue presided over by fairies in Geneva." With liberal democracy imperiled worldwide, the United States had to fight against being identified as "the protector of repressive regimes."[51]

Although NGOs played an important role in the international movement at this time, they were always fighting for more access in Washington.[52] Most NGOs preferred to maintain at least some distance between themselves and the governments with which they interacted. The nominally "nonpartisan and nonpolitical" Amnesty International USA (AIUSA), for example, did not want to be too closely identified with U.S. foreign policy, though they did seek to influence it. NGOs' political activities were also limited by law. In order to sustain tax-exempt status, nonprofits could not campaign for individual candidates, influence legislation, or ask a legislator to cut aid to a government. Despite these statutory limits, NGOs did become more prevalent in Washington, and they made an important contribution by conducting research, distributing their findings, meeting with policy-makers and staffers, and asking policymakers to speak out for specific dissi-dents. In a short period in 1975, for example, Amnesty's Washington office provided information to a congressional delegation heading to the Soviet Union, pressed the State Department to accept more Chilean refugees, asked legislators to send telegrams to the Soviet ambassador on behalf of the dissident Sergei Kovalev, and testified before congressional committees after observing trials in South Korea and Chile.[53]

As NGOs grew in prominence and political influence, they also suffered from the stigma of political bias. One pair of scholars has argued that the most influential NGOs exhibited a "principled neutrality" by focusing on both right-wing and left-wing governments.[54] There was some truth to this claim in the long run, but many organizations and activists in the 1970s took a rather circuitous path to impartiality, if they did so at all.[55] A 1974 internal Amnesty International USA audit found that the organization had, indeed, focused on noncommunist and nonaligned states. AI was working on over 350 cases in Brazil, Chile, and Guatemala, but only 13 in Cuba. It was handling nearly 300 cases in South Vietnam, South Korea, and Taiwan, but only 14 in North Vietnam and North Korea, and none in China. These lopsided numbers surely had much to do with relative access to informa-tion and to governments, though activists' political leanings also played a part. Realizing that the organization had violated its policy of evenhanded-ness, its leaders reinforced the long-standing rule that each campaign would embrace three prisoners—one in a Western-aligned state, one in a commu-nist-aligned state, and one in a nonaligned state. The organization also made some efforts to recruit members from the political right, though the opposition of its executive director, David Hawk, spoke volumes about his perspective on such matters. "My suspicion is," he argued, "most right-wingers, particularly those most concerned with the political imbalance of our image don't give two shits about intellectual freedom or political and conscientious imprisonment."[56]

Augusto Pinochet's Chile

Congressional activism was spurred, in part, by global events. And of all the human rights causes of the 1970s and 1980s, few had as much resonance in Washington and in the global activist community as the Chilean dictatorship of General Augusto Pinochet. Indeed, Chile was one of the three major causes célèbres of the era alongside Soviet Jewry and South African apartheid. This attention stemmed from the Pinochet regime's undeniable abuses, but it also reflected ideological predilections. Just as American conservatives singled out the Soviet Union for special criticism, so African states targeted South Africa, Arab states targeted Israel, and the world's left-wing governments targeted Chile.

As we have seen, Salvador Allende's 1970 election as president of Chile was an important moment in U.S.-Latin America relations. The Nixon administration considered Allende a problem for several reasons. He was not a member of the Chilean Communist Party, but he agreed with some of the party's ideas and had ties to many of its members. And although he received only a plurality of votes (just over one-third), his coalition government embarked on an ambitious program of social welfare and economic reforms that he called "the Chilean path to socialism"—*La Vía Chilena*. Among the decisions that put his government at odds with industrial nations was the nationalization of copper mines owned by the U.S.-based Anaconda and Kennecott corporations. Nixon and Kissinger had never given much thought to South America, but they believed that Allende's victory could embolden the region's left-wing rebels and even make Chile a base for Cuban and Soviet operations.

Consequently, Nixon and his advisers generally agreed that Allende's ouster would be good for American national interests. Nixon and Kissinger's intelligence group worked with the Chilean military to hatch a coup plot, but the plan was abandoned when Chilean conspirators killed the army's commander in chief during a botched kidnapping. The administration then worked with other governments to undermine the Chilean economy and marginalize Allende with economic and political measures. The administration also assured the Chilean military that they would receive American support if Allende was toppled. As international investors withdrew their capital, Chile became economically isolated and was able to secure significant support only from Cuba.[57] Although the United States did not play a central role in the coup d'état of September 11, 1973, the White House certainly welcomed it. The coup and the regime it established were brutal. The new rulers dissolved the Chilean Congress, sent members of the Allende government into remote detention centers, and arrested, interrogated, and tortured thousands of suspected "enemies" in the

National Stadium. Around twelve hundred were killed before the year was out. Over the course of seventeen years, the Pinochet dictatorship would imprison and torture thousands and would kill perhaps five thousand. Around two hundred thousand Chileans would flee the country.[58]

The coup was a watershed moment in the human rights story in that it helped transform the varied causes of the early 1970s into an international movement. Many activists have reflected on the foundational significance of these events. "Human rights entered my vocabulary on September 11, 1973," recalled the head of the Washington Office on Latin America, "when it was suddenly denied to one-third of the Chilean population."[59] Given this prominence, it is worth exploring why, exactly, the Pinochet regime became the bête noire of the global activist community for the remainder of the 1970s and 1980s. The answer goes beyond any objective measure of human suffering. Without question, the Pinochet dictatorship was terribly abusive in the coup's immediate aftermath, but at least a dozen other countries—Uganda, North Korea, Burundi, and Cambodia, to name only the most notorious—were arguably far worse in the seventies. "If the 1970s were a highpoint of human rights campaigns," notes Jan Eckel, "they were just as conspicuous for the many non-campaigns in the face of egregious mass murders." Why, then, did activists pay so much attention to Chile? Eckel suggests that the answer has much to do with the Pinochet regime's intransigent, unapologetic posture in international forums and in public relations. Chile was also a relatively open society, which meant that the world was privy to more accurate information about Pinochet's abuses. Equally significant was Chile's long tradition of democracy and its image as a civilized, Western nation.[60] Eckel misses two other significant factors. The fact that right-wing military men had overthrown a left-wing government in a highly visible coup gave the Pinochet dictatorship a heavily ideological cast. Then there was the widespread perception that the United States had masterminded the coup. This combination of presumed U.S. support to rightists who violently overthrew a left-wing reformer made the Pinochet regime a target for communist and socialist governments, left-liberal activists, academics, journalists, and Latin American opposition figures.

Although the United States did not engineer the coup, many in Chile and elsewhere assumed that Washington's hands were dirty. Not only did America have a long history of hemispheric interventions, but contemporary congressional investigations had already exposed some of the CIA's activities in the region. More importantly, there was an obvious mutual antagonism between Washington and the Allende government. Then there were the many rumors that accompanied the coup—that American pilots were flying the planes that strafed the presidential palace, that the CIA chief was in Santiago the day of the coup, that CIA assassins killed Allende. But while several scholars have disproved the accusations, the rumors became their own truth.[61] Allende's fall spurred an outpouring of polemical literature that laid the blame for Chile's downward spiral at America's doorstep.[62] The CIA did use over $6 million to fund opposition parties and candidates between 1970 and 1973—a clear violation of sovereignty—but the coup was the work of Chileans. The Chilean people were deeply divided in the face of Allende's controversial economic program, and the nationalization program killed foreign investment. The legend of American involvement in the coup would continue for decades, including even statements of guilt from uninformed American officials.[63]

Irrespective of the Nixon administration's limited role in Allende's fall, there is no denying Nixon's post-coup support to Pinochet. Much of the global left therefore blamed Nixon and Kissinger, much as they had blamed Washington for the Greek coup six years earlier. Even many American citizens believed that their government had committed terrible crimes in Chile. As Congress began to hold public hearings on Chile, America's open political system bolstered the impression of U.S. complicity. The fact that so many Americans were willing to believe that their government had toppled and even killed Allende was a telling indication of the extent to which Americans had lost faith in their leaders. Some of this was partisan grandstanding of the "What did the president know, and when did he know it?" variety, but much of it also stemmed from genuine feelings of apprehension and guilt. One scholar has convincingly argued that there was a general "sense of culpability" in the United States and that the Chile situation was a watershed in Americans' changing views of their nation's foreign policy.[64]

By contrast, the Nixon administration saw the coup as a victory over leftism, radicalism, and Cuba's regional ambitions. Nixon sent private cables of support to Santiago only days after the coup and recognized the Pinochet government two weeks later. The administration granted a $24 million wheat credit—eight times the amount offered to Allende—and added USAID housing guarantees, Food for Peace funds, and Inter-American Development Bank loans. Economic aid rose from $3.3 million in 1973 to nearly $100 million by 1975.[65] The administration justified these actions in the name of American economic and strategic interests, while further emphasizing that they did not judge governments by their domestic policies. Nixon also privately justified his backing of the region's authoritarian regimes by noting the lack of democracy in Latin America. "All of Latin America's not any good at government," he told an adviser. "They either go to one extreme or the other . . . dictatorship on the right or one on the left."[66]

Nixon did not particularly like Pinochet's rough methods, but he considered the regime good for American interests. Three weeks after the coup, as information about human rights abuses flooded into Washington, Kissinger told his staff that the administration should not put itself in the position of defending the regime's actions, but should instead understand that "however unpleasant they act, the government is better for us than Allende was."[67] Ambassador David Popper echoed Kissinger's sentiments the following year, calling Pinochet's accession "a change for the better" for U.S. interests. "A hostile regime has been replaced by one which is avowedly friendly," he informed his superiors.[68] In response to criticism about supporting Pinochet, Kissinger privately barked that an anti-American government had been overthrown: "In Eisenhower's day it would have been celebrated!"[69]

The harsh congressional reaction to the coup and its aftermath suggested that Chile would be a touchstone issue in the human rights era, as well as a test of activists' and policymakers' differing ideological beliefs. Two weeks after the coup, Senator Edward Kennedy declared that Nixon's support to Pinochet was simply "the latest symbol of our willingness to embrace a dictatorial regime that came to power in a bloody coup." Kennedy and Fraser failed in their attempt to cut aid to Chile, but they did pass a bill asking the president to use his power and that of the IACHR to press for human rights improvements. Kennedy also convinced the administration to admit more Chilean political refugees.[70] The general tenor of the discussion had changed completely from the 1960s. Legislators were now skeptical of the administration's explanations, as evidenced by Congressman Benjamin Rosenthal's dressing down of an assistant secretary during a congressional hearing: "I fear you are going to go down the road in a few months toward normal relations with this government on the theory that the people decided. The people didn't decide."[71]

In other hearings held just after the coup, lawyers, professors, and NGOs testified that torture and political imprisonment were rampant, and that the U.S. embassy had not been a place of refuge for people in danger.

By the time the committees reconvened in June 1974, Congress was clearly emboldened by Nixon's Watergate-induced weakness. Deputy Assistant Secretary of State Harry Shlaudeman argued that human rights had to be weighed against the relationship as a whole. Military aid and arms sales should continue, he asserted, because these weapons contributed to regional stability "in a balanced and nonpartisan way." He admitted that Chile was undemocratic for the time being, but asserted that it was not a totalitarian state and that "there is no jackbootism." A dubious Congressman Fraser shot back that "totalitarian" was a highly appropriate moniker, as the generals had taken power in a coup, dissolved the parliament, and imprisoned people without charge.[72]

Evidence from Pinochet's records suggests that his regime believed such criticisms to be an ephemeral, communist-inspired attempt to interfere in Chilean affairs. In Pinochet's words, congressional criticism demonstrated both American "imperialism" and "the extremely active campaign that international Marxism has loosed" against Chile. Only at the end of 1974 did Pinochet and his advisers appear to grasp the varied sources of human rights concern.[73] In retrospect, it seems absurd that an undeniably repressive regime would use the "communist conspiracy" canard to fend off criticism, but Pinochet was right about at least one thing. Chile *was* being judged by a different standard, though the Nixon and Ford administrations did not join the global ostracizing of Santiago. When a large majority in the United Nations, including eight Western states, reprimanded Chile in October 1974, the United States abstained on the grounds that Pinochet's record was improving. Referring to the sponsor states' own authoritarian tendencies, an American representative further argued that the vote demonstrated the United Nations' double standards.[74] The administration was clearly intimating that left-wing governments were not standing up for human rights, but rather singling out a right-wing adversary.

Throughout 1974 and 1975, Congress and NGOs became increasingly distressed at the Nixon and Ford administrations' insistence upon maintaining ties with Pinochet. Revelations of Kissinger's private callousness fueled the criticism. The journalist Seymour Hersh leaked an earlier memorandum in which Kissinger had said of Allende, "I don't see why we need to stand by and watch a country go communist due to the irresponsibility of its own people."[75] The German-born Kissinger may have been reflecting on how his native land had fallen to the Nazis due to the German people's "irresponsibility"—that is, totalitarianism via the ballot box. But whatever his point, his unfortunate wording confirmed activists' suspicions about U.S. intervention into Chilean affairs. Soon it also emerged that Kissinger had chastised Ambassador Popper for bringing up human rights with Chilean defense officials. Kissinger's terse admonition in the margins of the cable—"Tell Popper to cut out the political science lectures"—has become the stuff of legend. The quote was widely repeated, though it is unclear if it was leaked by human rights advocates (who may have wanted Kissinger's private sentiments laid bare) or by Kissinger himself (who may have wanted his position to be clear to Pinochet and the foreign service). Either way, the statement belied his claim that the United States was privately discussing human rights issues with the Chileans. "I find it outrageous—incredible," said Donald Fraser. "I'm beginning to wonder how long the secretary's usefulness to his country will continue."[76] When Congress halted military aid for six months, Kissinger decried activists' double standard. Congressional liberals "won't rest until we have left wing governments in power everywhere," he complained. "I think it's a disaster."[77]

Two interesting details emerge from Kissinger's now-declassified private conversations. First, he comes across as virulently anticommunist behind closed doors. If his conservative critics had seen this side of him, they might have been much more willing to accept his détente goals with Moscow. Second, he saw Chile as a test of wills for his entire foreign policy. Early in Nixon's presidency, Kissinger had been so uninterested in South America that he dismissed Chile as "a dagger pointed at the heart of Antarctica." But Allende's accession had changed his mind, and even after Pinochet's coup he continued to fear a leftward tilt in the region. Kissinger sought to hold the line against congressional and foreign meddling, even if it meant ignoring Pinochet's autocratic policies, and he warned his staff that Chile was the tip of the spear in Congress's attack on presidential foreign policy. If the administration capitulated, Congress would cut support to a succession of allies and America would lose its reputation as a trustworthy ally. "There isn't going to be any end to it," he told his staff. "It is a problem of the whole foreign policy that is being pulled apart, pulling out thread by thread, under one pretext or another."[78] In hindsight, Pinochet's Chile seems a strange place for Kissinger to have stood on principle. It might have been easier for him to justify support to a less oppressive government, or one more important to American interests. But he believed that executive foreign policy and his own reputation were being undone from all sides, with liberals assailing him as an apologist for right-wing dictators and conservatives attacking him for treating with communists in Moscow and Beijing.

In 1975 and 1976, the Ford administration was confronted with a combination of growing congressional activism, Pinochet's intransigence, and a severe downturn in the Chilean economy. Wanting to maintain relations while also deflecting congressional and NGO attention, the administration applied more pressure on Chile. Unfortunately, the Pinochet government was its own worst enemy in the battle for global opinion. Pinochet brooked no outside interference, even declaring in June 1975 that there would be no elections during his tenure or in that of his successor. (That his statement was consistently misquoted as "no elections during my lifetime or in the lifetime of my successor" did not help his image.) He also refused entry to U.N. inspectors. Ambassador Popper, who was otherwise somewhat sympathetic, told Kissinger that the regime "must have some kind of a death wish" to cancel the inspection. This prompted Kissinger to ask why Chile had been singled out for an investigation. "Why doesn't [Ugandan dictator Idi] Amin receive a human rights commission? What about some of the other African countries where people are executed in the public square? There has to be some limit to this screaming hypocrisy."[79]

In light of the problems the Ford administration was facing in Congress, Kissinger candidly explained in a letter to Foreign Minister Patricio Carvajal that the president's ability to aid Chile was directly influenced by Chile's human rights posture. The decision to prevent entry to the United Nations, for example, could convince Congress to restrict aid and arms sales. "Openness, and a demonstrated intention to move toward restoration of traditional Chilean legal rights," wrote Kissinger, "make it easier for us to help you." These were not Kissinger's personal sentiments, of course, but political realities that he only halfheartedly reported to Santiago. One month later he told Carvajal in person not to take the letter too seriously, and added that he decried activists' interference in Chilean affairs as "a total injustice." But he also emphasized that the domestic political problem was real. "We understand the problem," he said. "The solution has to be a Chilean one."[80]

Neither Congress nor the executive branch was unified on Chile. Some legislators preferred close relations for ideological or economic reasons, while others hoped to use tough policies to force reforms. Ford and Kissinger resisted congressional restrictions, but many advisers and FSOs wanted to distance the United States from repressive states. One faction in the State Department argued that the administration's chief interest was preventing a government hostile to the United States; even some who disliked the Pinochet regime believed that tougher policies would not improve Chile's performance. Still others countered that close ties to Pinochet were hurting American national interests and the Chilean people. "In the minds of the world at large," noted an American diplomat privately, "we are closely associated with this junta, ergo with fascists and torturers."[81]

Kissinger then began to use public rhetoric as a means of deflecting criticism. When he traveled to Chile to attend the opening of the Organization of American States assembly in June 1976, his opponents' misgivings were offset by his strong support of human rights in his speech, a stance so powerful that a South African activist proclaimed it to be among the major declarations that "ought to be taken as the 'Magna Carta' of the human rights movement." The State Department's James M. Wilson noted sardonically of this reaction that Kissinger then told his staff "that he did not want all he had said publicly applied too literally in practice."[82] Indeed, when the speech was being drafted, Kissinger had called the human rights statement "ridiculous." "Human rights make me love the State Department," he said to his aides. "Am I supposed to make a revolution in Chile? . . . Why is it that only now when terrorists are being killed is action being proposed? What about earlier when the terrorists were doing the killing? Why wasn't there any action then?"[83]

While in Santiago, Kissinger had a long, friendly conversation with Pinochet. Kissinger was clearly uncomfortable with broaching domestic matters, and only did so to explain that Chilean policies affected bilateral relations. After Pinochet repeated several times that he had always fought against communism, Kissinger promised President Ford's continued support and explained the seriousness of opposition in the United States. Chilean domestic matters had become a major complication to business as usual, he said, and Ford wanted to respect Chilean sovereignty while also preventing new American laws that would hurt the relationship. "You are a victim of all left-wing groups around the world," said Kissinger. "Your greatest sin was that you overthrew a government which was going communist."[84]

The final nail in the coffin of the U.S.-Chile relationship was the September 1976 car bombing murder of Orlando Letelier in Washington. Because Letelier had served as a diplomat under the Allende regime, much of the American and Chilean public immediately suspected Pinochet's secret police—suspicions that were amplified by Pinochet's foot-dragging in investigating the killing. This crime would be a burr in the bilateral saddle for years, and the Pinochet regime would remain in Congress's crosshairs until the end of the 1980s. Yet although there is evidence that the Chileans took American criticism seriously, especially in 1975–1976, congressional actions and executive persuasion ultimately proved rather fruitless in encouraging them to liberalize or democratize.[85] In time, Pinochet realized that American support was unnecessary for his regime's survival. Even during the Carter years, when the president and Congress were much more in lockstep on human rights, Chile's reforms were limited. Most U.S. support was halted by the end of 1976, but Pinochet remained firmly entrenched in power for seventeen years, making him one of the era's longest-reigning autocrats. Washington's arms embargo and aid cuts led Chile to build up its domestic production and to seek arms from South Africa, Israel, and Europe. American votes against Chile in multilateral development banks were largely symbolic, and since Congress did not limit private lending, American banks loaned billions to the Chilean government and its citizens. In a sense, then, Henry Kissinger was correct in arguing that congressional sanctions were misguided. The anti-Pinochet drumbeat in Congress may have pleased activists, but it hurt U.S. trade and did little for the Chilean people.

The Limits of Multilateralism: Human Rights Treaties and the Helsinki Accords

Congressional efforts made the United States a world leader in bilateral human rights laws, but the U.S. government made little headway in the direction of a multilateral policy.[86] Despite the groundswell of congressional activism, the traditional American aversion to multilateralism prevented the United States from ratifying most of the U.N. human rights instruments. The United States played a leading role in drafting these postwar covenants, but the Senate tabled them in the fifties and sixties as a result of anticommunism, isolationism, and domestic political conflicts. Consequently, when Richard Nixon entered the White House the United States was a signatory to only two of the eighteen human rights treaties: the Supplementary Slavery Convention of 1952 and the 1967 Refugee Protocol.

Of all the multilateral human rights instruments, none was more controversial than the Genocide Convention. President Truman enthusiastically signed the convention and the SFRC took it up for discussion in 1950, but senators tabled it for the next twenty years, and it was not until 1986 that the Senate finally ratified it. The convention languished for many reasons. For starters, it was difficult to garner a two-thirds Senate majority for *any* treaty. Congressional rules also granted individual senators tremendous power to prevent debates and votes, a procedural privilege that allowed opponents like Senators Sam J. Ervin (D-NC) and Russell Long (D-LA) to keep the convention off the agenda for years. And although several presidents supported the convention, it was never a top priority for any of them. Finally, the relatively small, active constituency that favored ratification was more than matched by the persistent, effective campaigns of opponents. Opposition ran the gamut from the mainstream conservatism of the American Bar Association to the far-right agendas of the Liberty Lobby and the John Birch Society.

Opponents of the genocide treaty feared a loss of America's sovereignty and the expansion of "world government." They also worried that anti-American governments would subject American citizens to international penal tribunals. These fears were particularly resonant during the Vietnam era, when opponents worried that enemies would prosecute soldiers and politicians for crimes against the Vietnamese. ("Genocide" accusations against the United States began almost as soon as President Johnson sent American troops to Southeast Asia.) Also at issue was the exclusion of "political groups" from the treaty's list of potential genocide victims, an oversight that seemed to exonerate communist regimes' liquidation of political opponents.[87] Contemporary racial issues amplified the debate, as it became somewhat fashionable for radical organizations to charge the United States with "genocidal" policies against African Americans. In 1970, the Black Panther Party sent a petition to the United Nations charging that this "genocide" was being carried out through the denial of jobs, food, and money. Others adapted the term to fit a wide variety of charges, such as "educational genocide," "psychological genocide," and "institutional genocide."[88] Such claims fed opponents' fears and fueled opposition campaigns.

The treaty's advocates supported it with a combination of moral and legal arguments, giving particular attention to America's international reputation. Former Supreme Court justice Arthur Goldberg argued that nonratification had become a diplomatic embarrassment, while Chief Justice

Earl Warren averred, "We as a nation should have been the first to ratify the Genocide Convention. . . . Instead we may well be the last." In response to questions about the convention's legality, supporters hoped to persuade through common sense. "If our country can protect the lives of seals and migratory birds through agreements with other nations," said one advocate, "it should be able to prevent mass murder of human beings."[89] Senator William Proxmire (D-WI) was so disturbed by the Senate's inaction that he pledged to deliver a speech on the Senate floor every day until it was ratified. He ultimately gave 3,211 such speeches over a twenty-year period.[90]

An apparent turning point in the Genocide Convention's fortunes came in February 1970, when President Nixon sent the treaty to the Senate for advice and consent. Although this decision seemed out of character, in reality Nixon had few qualms about ceding human rights issues to the United Nations. He supported the convention as a means of improving America's (and his own) international image, and likely hoped to win over a few liberal voters in the process. The SFRC then took up the convention for the first time in twenty years and reported it out favorably, but the congressional session ended before a vote could be called. A few months later, the committee once again voted for ratification. "We find no substantial merit," their report concluded, "in the arguments against the convention. Indeed, there is a note of fear behind most arguments . . . as if we as a people don't trust ourselves and our society."[91] Yet the full Senate did not take up the convention for debate because opponents were able to prevent its introduction. A few senators could block a vote or a debate, and a single senator could deny unanimous consent. When Senator Mike Mansfield (D-MT) introduced it for debate in October 1972, Senator Sam Ervin was able to prevent it simply by stating, "Madam President, with reluctance I object." This effectively killed the matter until the next congressional session.[92] The SFRC voted the treaty out favorably again in February 1973, prompting the Liberty Lobby, the John Birch Society, and the American Legion to mount a campaign in which letters to senators ran fifty-to-one against ratification. When Senator Mansfield brought the treaty up on the floor of the Senate in February 1974, Senator James B. Allen (D-AL) led a bloc of Southern Democrats and conservative Republicans in a filibuster to prevent a vote. Cloture motions were then defeated on two consecutive days. Once again the convention was relegated to the backburner, and would not gather any serious momentum again for a decade.[93]

Coming as it did alongside the congressional human rights push, the Senate's rejection of the Genocide Convention in the 1970s seems an aberration. But it is easily explained. In addition to the procedural difficulties of treaty ratification in a democracy, multilateral human rights treaties were seen as more symbolic than cutting military aid to an abusive regime. There was no statistically significant correlation between ratification of treaties and respect for human rights.[94] And of all the multilateral instruments, accession to the genocide treaty was seen as particularly likely to lead to entrapment of American citizens by communist nations and their allies. More than anything else, the Senate's inaction reflected the traditional American fear of multilateralism and the specter of diminished sovereignty.

One multilateral arrangement that did become a surprisingly important link in the international human rights chain was the 1975 Helsinki Final Act. This agreement was intended to address several territorial and political problems that had hampered European interstate relations since 1945. Because there had been no comprehensive post–World War II peace treaty, Soviet leaders had long sought an agreement that would legitimize their wartime annexation of the Baltic states and their extension of their borders, while other European states hoped to ensure peace and maintain their own sovereignty. The NATO nations rejected talks in the 1950s and 1960s, but by the early 1970s the environment was more congenial for negotiations. With the United States and Canada also insisting on a place at the table, Europeans and North Americans began the negotiating process at the 1973 Conference on Security and Cooperation in Europe (CSCE) and finished two years later with the comprehensive agreement. The Final Act favored several Soviet interests, including territorial sovereignty, "inviolability" of borders, and noninterference in internal affairs.[95]

But although the Soviets considered the Helsinki Accords a guarantee of the status quo, in the long run the agreement undermined the Kremlin's authority. It was the accords' human rights and humanitarian measures that would bring about the most unexpected outcomes. The two sections' rather anodyne titles—Principle VII, "Respect for Human Rights and Fundamental Freedoms," and Section Three (known as "Basket Three"), "Cooperation in Humanitarian and Other Fields"—masked their potentially transformative effects. They proclaimed that signatories would "respect human rights and fundamental freedoms, including the freedom of thought, conscience, religion or belief," protect national minorities, and "promote and encourage the effective exercise of civil, political, economic, social, cultural and other rights and freedoms." Western Europeans had taken the lead in adding these safeguards. Not only did Europeans place more faith in multilateral agreements, but they had also been adjudicating human rights disputes for several years via intra-European commissions and courts. The human rights language in the Helsinki Accords generally reflected specific European concerns, such as family reunification and visitation, freedom of movement, and expanded press freedom.

Some in the West hoped that Helsinki would herald a new era. Because the inviolability clause also applied to Eastern European states, the agreement prohibited Soviet intervention in these nations' affairs. And because the accords allowed for borders to change by mutual consent, there was a possibility of future alterations. The most optimistic supporters argued that the humanitarian provisions held out the possibility of liberalization in the Eastern Bloc. As for the Kremlin, they hoped to impress the Soviet people with the boundary agreements while downplaying the humanitarian issues, but the accords' publication in *Pravda* gave the latter the appearance of official sanction. Conditions for dissidents did not change overnight, wrote Soviet Ambassador Anatoly Dobrynin years later, "but they were definitely encouraged by this historic document. . . . It gradually became a manifesto of the dissident and liberal movement, a development totally beyond the imagination of the Soviet leadership."[96] Now armed with an international legal compact through which they could challenge their governments to free political prisoners and allow religious freedom, dissidents began to establish "Helsinki Commissions" to monitor the agreement's implementation.

But the positive long-term outcomes were unforeseeable in 1975, and many Western observers were harsh in their appraisals. American conservatives and ethnics saw Helsinki as a sellout of Eastern Europe, some even calling it "the new Yalta." "I am against it," said Ronald Reagan, "and I think all Americans should be against it." In response to President Ford's decision to sign the document, the *Wall Street Journal* implored, "Jerry Don't Go." Aleksandr Solzhenitsyn (now residing in the United States) stated that Ford was going to affirm "the betrayal of Eastern Europe, to acknowledge officially its slavery forever."[97] Even those who appreciated the humanitarian provisions noted that the accords included no enforcement mechanism.

Despite these objections, Ford had many reasons for making the trip. Since every European state but Albania and Andorra was planning to sign,

American inaction would have seemed callous and unilateral. And although the United States had not taken the lead in pushing for the agreement, neither did the administration want it to be a source of conflict with the Europeans or the Soviets. An agreement on European boundaries could foster stability without necessarily signaling acceptance of Soviet domination in the East. The borders had been set years earlier, argued Kissinger, and the rest of the document was not unfavorable to American interests.[98] Indeed, Kissinger believed the agreement was so superfluous that he privately called the accords "a bunch of crappy issues" and assured Soviet Foreign Minister Andrei Gromyko that Basket Three was far more important to the Europeans than to the United States.[99] Ford hoped that his signature would help build a positive environment for the SALT II arms limitation talks while also preventing NGOs and Congress from pressing for new human rights laws.[100] He invoked traditional Western liberal language in Helsinki, saying of the agreement's human rights provisions, "To my country, they are not clichés or empty phrases. We take this work and these words very seriously." He concluded with a poetic flourish: "History will judge this conference . . . not by the promises we make, but by the promises we keep."[101]

Notwithstanding this rhetorical artistry, few Americans were convinced that the agreement would have much of an impact on Eastern Europe. The skepticism seemed justified in the short run, as Helsinki monitoring groups in the Eastern Bloc were harassed and arrested. But the accords' human rights provisions gave dissidents more ammunition to press their leaders, and in the long run these monitoring groups would play a major role in Eastern European affairs. Yuri Orlov, Anatoly Shcharansky, and nine others formed the Moscow Helsinki group in 1976, while in Czechoslovakia a dissident statement signed by over two hundred intellectuals set in motion the Charter 77 reform movement. These signatories claimed to have no political agenda, but as John Prados has pointed out, promoting freedom of expression was a fundamentally political act in a totalitarian state.[102] As dissidents stepped up their activity, the Soviet authorities began to see them as "subversives"—as *Pravda* had it, "a pitiful handful of characters with anti-Soviet sentiments who are slandering their own homeland"—trying to forge links with "anti-Soviet" elements in the West. The KGB blamed the West's "special and propaganda services" for creating "the appearance of the existence in the Soviet Union of a so-called 'internal opposition'" and for supporting "those inspiring antisocial trends."[103] In reality, Western support for such groups was meager at first, though it would grow in the years to come.

Helsinki had some significance to U.S. human rights policies. As Eastern Bloc activists more vigorously pursued reforms based on Helsinki provisions, American legislators and ethnics became more amenable to the accords.[104] The initial ambivalence gave way to greater support as the U.S. government joined with its European counterparts in establishing Helsinki commissions. Sarah B. Snyder notes that although American delegates followed the European lead in the initial CSCE negotiations, the United States played a much more active role in the follow-up meetings in Belgrade (1977–1978), Madrid (1980–1983), and Vienna (1986–1989). Moreover, the administration of Jimmy Carter took the CSCE process seriously enough that the United States became the major advocate for compliance at Belgrade.[105] Yet the CSCE follow-ups were not at the center of the overall story of human rights in American foreign policy. The fact that East and West were gathering to discuss such issues was an innovation, but East/West sniping in multilateral settings had been a hallmark of the Cold War from the very beginning. In the case of the United Nations' human rights bodies, multilateral discussions had engendered no notable improvements in the East. Indeed, American misgivings about multilateralism owed nearly as much to these forums' inherent weaknesses as they did to neo-isolationism and to conservatives' fears of diminished sovereignty. From the perspective of the 1970s, it remained to be seen whether Helsinki would improve human rights after all.

The Ethnic Influence on Human Rights Policymaking

American human rights policies developed in concert with a phenomenon that contemporary observers called the "ethnic movement," or the "ethnic revival." This revival, which began in the sixties and accelerated in the seventies, was characterized by a profound reawakening of ethnic and ethnoreligious pride and activism. Inspired by long-term social transformations, Americans of a variety of lineages entered the public arena to assert their identities and to influence political and diplomatic outcomes. The revival was germane to human rights policymaking in two ways. First, ethnic lobbies and voters petitioned the U.S. government to address violations in their respective ancestral homelands. Second, the political establishment gave extraordinary attention to their concerns because of the revival's apparent profundity and because the Cold War thaw had made the geopolitical environment more flexible. The congenial political climate of the détente era led ethnics and other ordinary Americans to create NGOs and to lobby in Washington. Members of Congress responded by crafting laws and publicizing the plight of specific dissidents overseas.

Ethnic influence was only one among several spurs to human rights diplomacy, and attention to international human rights was only one of the ethnic movement's many consequences. Ethnics' primary political concerns—employment, housing, busing, education—were domestic in nature. It is also difficult to pin down the real significance of the revival. It now seems that ethnic "consciousness" was increasing while demographic trends were making European ethnics less prominent. The ethnic trend gradually waned after reaching peak strength in the mid-1970s. Yet despite the revival's short-lived momentum, ethnic interest groups did play a significant role in many of this period's major human rights efforts. Some ethnic human rights campaigning was much in the tradition of anticommunist, "captive nations" rhetoric and lobbying, but other campaigns emphasized individual liberties more than anticommunism. Moreover, some ethnic campaigns addressed noncommunist polities like Cyprus, South Africa, and Northern Ireland. Within the realm of international relations, the revival embodied a strange paradox: it influenced the East/West détente, but it was also an irritant to the statesmen who used the détente process to minimize the Cold War's effects. Ethnic activism also begged the question of whether a narrow interest in the well-being of one's own kin group could be considered a true "human rights" cause rather than a parochial interest.

Ethnic influence in American foreign policy paralleled the growth in interest groups and the development of political pluralism, and with greater pluralism came much broader definitions of the "national interest." Increased congressional oversight of foreign policy further fueled interest groups' influence in diplomacy because such groups were often concentrated in powerful legislators' districts. Of all of this period's interest groups, the ethnic organizations were among the most plentiful and influential. Some, like the Polish-American Congress (founded 1944) and the America-Israel Political Action Committee (1953), had formed a generation earlier, but many more were created in the midst of the 1970s revival, such as the Irish National Caucus (1974), TransAfrica Forum (1977), and the Cuban-American National Foundation (1981). As these NGOs grew in size and influence, they also established overseas connections.

Not everyone was smitten with this changing political dynamic. The historian David Farber has noted that such "identity politics"—in which organized groups challenged the notion of a common national purpose and instead worked for their own interests—became both commonplace and highly controversial in the 1970s.[106] Some observers worried that the ethnic NGOs were more concerned with their distant "kin" than they were with American interests. Senator Charles Mathias (R-MD) blamed ethnic influence for spurring "the loss of cohesion in our foreign policy."[107] But others perceived a democratizing trend that contrasted with the exclusivity of traditional diplomacy. "American foreign policy at times has been an elitist operation," stated Congressman Lee Hamilton, "and it needs the counterbalance that ethnic groups can often give."[108]

Ethnic interest groups responded to the era's opportunities by fighting on behalf of their coethnics or coreligionists in a variety of nations. Christians and Jews fought for religious freedom in communist countries, Irish Americans and Slavic Americans for civil liberties in Europe, Cuban Americans for political prisoners in Cuba, and African Americans for blacks in South Africa. In Matthew Frye Jacobson's words, issues ranging from the suffering in Northern Ireland to the workers' movements in Poland "captured the attention and sympathy of overseas ethnic compatriots, whose diasporic cultures had invested Old World nationalist causes with a kind of mantric power." Indeed, the groups that were the most dedicated to "rights" causes tended to be conservative political organizations that grew out of a renewed commitment to the overseas "homeland," such as the controversial Irish Northern Aid Committee, which was formed by Irish Americans in 1970.[109] The trend toward authoritarianism in Eastern Europe and Latin America further galvanized American ethnics to act.

Several cases illuminate the role that the ethnic revival played in the human rights movement and in the Cold War. One example was Greek Americans' influence on the U.S. arms embargo against Turkey. This conflict began in 1974 when the Greek military junta backed a coup in Cyprus, which had long had a Greek majority and a Turkish minority. Turkey responded by invading the island, ostensibly to protect ethnic Turks, and this facilitated a de facto partition of Cyprus into Greek and Turkish zones.

The invasion was widely criticized as a violation of Cypriot sovereignty, and Turkey was further accused of dividing families, detaining innocent civilians, mistreating detainees, and expelling the Greek-Cypriot population from occupied territory. The European Commission of Human Rights concluded that most of these allegations had merit, as did some atrocity allegations against ethnic Greeks.[110] Eventually over a hundred thousand Turkish nationals would leave mainland Turkey and settle in occupied Cyprus. In later years people would term this process "ethnic cleansing," but it had no name in the 1970s.

Given the U.S. interest in maintaining the Atlantic alliance and limiting Soviet influence, the prospect of a war between two NATO members troubled Washington. Security strategists sought to prevent the outbreak of a Greece-Turkey conflict, while others sought to punish Turkey for using American arms in breach of U.S. law. After considering several solutions, Congress voted in October 1974 to cut off military aid and soon thereafter also embargoed arms sales. President Ford, who had spent over two decades on Capitol Hill, called the cutoff "the worst decision I have seen in my time in Congress."[111] The administration's fears were confirmed by a predictable diplomatic backlash and Ankara's closing of over two dozen NATO and American military installations. "Turkey is not going to change its Cyprus policy under the pressure of the American Congress's position," stated the foreign minister.[112]

Legislators supported these decisions for several reasons. The primary rationale was that the Turks had used American weapons in the invasion and occupation. Some also saw the crisis as an opportunity to limit presidential power or to cut military aid spending. Yet it is also possible that some legislators supported it because lobbyists convinced them that the Turks were abusing Greek Cypriots. There had never been much of a "Greek lobby" in America, but the three million Greek Americans found a common interest in challenging what they perceived as Turkish oppression. They utilized two existing networks—the Greek Orthodox Church and AHEPA, the largest Greek fraternal organization—and formed two new organizations, the United Hellenic American Congress and the American Hellenic Institute. Activists were careful to construct their position as an American one, not a Greek one, especially by tying the struggle of Greek Cypriots to universal human rights principles and American values.[113] Absent a substantial Turkish community in America, President Ford's support for continued aid was an unpopular stand. "There is no way that any

Greek American can vote for Ford as president," argued the head of one
NGO.[114] The activists were particularly angry at Henry Kissinger, whom
they vilified as personally responsible for Greek suffering. Characteristically
unimpressed, Kissinger complained to the Greek foreign minister that
Greeks and Greek Americans alike were calling him "a murderer and a
liar."[115]

Some members of Congress were none too sympathetic to the ethnic
lobbyists. "I can only give my loyalty to one country," Senate Majority
Leader Mike Mansfield proclaimed to reporters. "My father and mother
were immigrants from Ireland, but my loyalty isn't to Ireland, it is to this
country, no question." Others downplayed ethnic influence, emphasizing
instead that Greek-American interests were consistent with the national
interest. Congressman Henry Waxman (D-CA) noted of the arms embargo,
"If the so-called Greek lobby were wrong in terms of American interests,
they would not have gotten 223 votes in the House."[116] This debate illustrated the difficulties of making foreign policy in an open, pluralistic society. America's liberal tradition gave cover to those who cited human rights
motives in Cyprus, while the increasing acceptance of interest-group pluralism gave cover to ethnic activists who were, after all, standing up for the
citizens of another country. Legislators like Senator Mansfield could perhaps be excused for thinking that their colleagues were casting their votes
for short-term political gain.

Although it is difficult to pinpoint the exact influence of the Greek-
American community in the passage of this legislation, some scholars have
concluded that ethnic politics played a key role. "It was the vigorous, inces-
sant, forceful pressure from the ethnic groups that set the other groups in
motion, focused attention on the issue and gave it high priority," wrote
Göran Rystad.[117] John Lewis Gaddis similarly asserted that "a vociferous
Greek-American lobby managed to impose an arms embargo" over the
opposition of Ford and Kissinger.[118] These scholars overstate Greek power
somewhat, though it is certainly plausible that activists' promotion of the
human rights dimension swayed at least some legislators. Zinovia Lialiouti
and Philip E. Muehlenbeck are closer to the mark in suggesting that the
most significant factor was broad congressional and public dissatisfaction
with Kissingerian foreign policy. They are also correct in noting that Greek
Americans' commitment to their Cypriot confreres drove a wedge between
the United States and Turkey while also giving Moscow the opportunity to
become Turkey's major military benefactor for a brief period. Meanwhile,

Greek and Greek American nationalism (and earlier U.S. support to the Greek junta) weakened Greece's devotion to NATO, fueled anti-Americanism, and damaged America's regional position.[119] The Greece/Cyprus quandary showed that debates over ethnic politics, human rights advocacy, and realpolitik were more than just philosophical. U.S. Ambassador Rodger Davies was killed by Greek Cypriot gunmen during a demonstration at the U.S. embassy in Nicosia in August 1974, and the Marxist terrorist organization 17 November killed the CIA station chief in Athens the following year. All the while, the Turkish occupation continued.

Because the Cold War thaw gave ethnic activists some ability to influence policy, President Nixon's geopolitical and domestic interests put him into a difficult position. He pursued détente as a means of preventing nuclear war and containing Soviet ambitions, and he muted human rights rhetoric in order to maintain détente. He also hoped to move Warsaw Pact states away from planned economies and coax them from the Soviet orbit, all while wooing ethnic voters into the Republican fold. In his 1970 and 1971 foreign policy reports, he argued that the United States considered the countries of Eastern Europe to be "sovereign, not as parts of a monolith," and he expressed an interest in gradual normalization of relations. In a nod to ethnics and conservatives, he similarly spoke of the "cruel and unnatural division of Europe," which was "no longer accepted as inevitable or permanent." Because détente's goals included expanded intra-European contact and cooperation, the United States recognized every nation's right to develop its own policies in light of its own interests.[120] Although the administration suggested that détente was contributing to a gradual liberalization in the East, Nixon remained a realist. As he stated in his second inaugural address (perhaps with the growing human rights trend in mind), "The time has passed when America will make every other nation's conflict our own, or presume to tell the people of other nations how to manage their own affairs."[121]

Americans of Eastern European descent were divided on the goals and benefits of détente. Some wanted the United States to avoid any engagement with Eastern Bloc governments (thus keeping them economically weak and denying them international legitimacy), while others sought constructive ties (thus encouraging liberalization and higher living standards). Virtually all wanted the United States to condemn Soviet domination and stand up for basic liberties. Even Nixon's supporters could be critical. "We strongly disagree with your policy of coexisting with the communist countries," wrote a spokesman for Americans to Free Captive Nations. "By not interfering in internal matters you are actually condoning the persecution of the Captive Nations under the domination of Russian imperialism."[122]

Nixon was able to win over some of his critics by promoting mild liberalization in the East and building bridges to Poland, Yugoslavia, and Romania. Just as in China, the staunchly anticommunist Nixon was one of the few political figures who could pull off such a feat. Although his overtures to Romania and Yugoslavia were not chiefly aimed at winning votes—after all, these nationalities comprised a tiny percentage of the American electorate—they appealed to many ethnic constituents. The Assembly of Captive European Nations declared that his 1969 trip to Bucharest had had "a tremendous impact on the Romanian people and the other nations in communist-dominated Europe," whose peoples now knew that they were "not forgotten by the United States."[123] There was, however, a clear conflict between the goals of a realist-oriented détente, which defined the world in terms of interstate rivalry and cooperation, and the goals of a humanitarianism that prioritized the rights of individuals. Nixon's 1970 visit to Yugoslavia was clearly rooted in the former, as it was an unmistakable confirmation of his desire to keep Josip Broz Tito outside of the Soviet orbit. This approach angered some émigrés. One Croatian American warned Nixon, "The cause and purpose of your trip is not worth the humiliation you will be going through when shaking hands with a murderer who is responsible for so many deaths, suffering and sorrow."[124] But Nixon defended American ties to Yugoslavia as integral to the national interest. When Tito visited Washington in October 1971, Nixon toasted him as "the man who stands for the right of every country in the world to choose its own way," and their joint statement touted "adherence to the principles of independence, mutual respect and the full equality of sovereign states."[125] Some ethnics protested, but neither Congress nor human rights NGOs made a major issue of Yugoslavia's human rights record. This had much to do with Tito's independence, as well as the lack of a powerful Yugoslavian immigrant bloc.

Poland was of even more interest to Nixon and the American public than were Yugoslavia and Romania. Nixon's Poland policy grew out of geostrategic considerations and domestic politics. Recognizing that Poland was in a dangerous region and had long been the victim of historical circumstances shaped by its powerful neighbors, Nixon wanted to show Poles that they were part of the East/West bargaining process. The Republican Party also hoped that closer relations would have domestic political benefits. Because the nine million Americans of Polish descent had considerable political clout in a few large states, Nixon repeatedly placed Polish and Catholic organizations at the top of his agenda when he visited the Midwest.[126] The Polish American Congress (PAC) supported Nixon's negotiations and policies as long as they benefited the Polish people through economic support, Radio Free Europe (RFE) funding, and substantial trade credits. On the strategic front, the PAC argued that if Nixon acquiesced to the Soviets' call for noninterference, it would cement the "political subjugation" of the Warsaw Pact nations. If the Soviets wanted the United States to stay out of their affairs, said the PAC, then Moscow would have to stay out of Poland.[127]

Because Nixon's summer 1972 visit to Moscow raised some eyebrows among Polish Americans and among his regional partners, he tried to dispel these fears by scheduling a stopover in Warsaw.[128] The ostensible purpose of consulting with Poland's new, reform-minded leader Edward Gierek was to seek out areas of mutual interest in trade and travel, but the administration also hoped to show that the United States did not accept Soviet domination. Domestic political considerations played a part as well. A party insider advised that the visit would be an opportunity to "break up the virtual monopoly which the Democrats have enjoyed over the Polish vote," especially since the "congenitally anticommunist" Polish Americans did not trust Democratic doves.[129] But while Nixon did have an interest in publicly reiterating Polish sovereignty, human rights were otherwise not on the agenda. Secretary of State Rogers even advised Nixon to avoid public statements about sensitive matters like RFE and Polish elections. RFE had grown out of the Western belief in freedom of information, but it was a product of the early Cold War, not the human rights era. (When the Polish foreign minister told Rogers that RFE broadcast titles like "The Daily Hell of Communism" poisoned bilateral relations and imperiled détente, Rogers reminded him that American politicians were far more frequently attacked in the press back home.)[130]

In the Nixon-Gierek meeting, the Poles clarified their interest in economic concessions, trade credits, and technology, while Nixon promised Gierek that the United States would not make superpower arrangements at the expense of Poland.[131] Their joint communiqué emphasized greater cooperation, and it included an affirmation of "territorial integrity" and "non-interference in internal affairs"—clear allusions to greater independence from the Soviet Union. The two leaders also acknowledged that Polish Americans maintained "an interest in the country of their ancestors" and that the two sides recognized this interest as "a valuable contribution" to bilateral relations. When Nixon returned home, most Polish American leaders applauded his efforts, as did many voters. In another shrewd move, during the week of the 1972 election the administration released a large sum in Export-Import (Ex-Im) Bank credits to Poland, and the U.S. government opened an American trade information center in Warsaw, the first of its kind in the communist world.

The net effect of these developments was that Poland and "Polonia" (the diaspora) grew closer through trade, tourism, and cultural exchanges. With the strengthening of these bonds in the 1970s, Polish Americans became more aware of the plight of Poles and more insistent that the U.S. government act on their behalf. True, Nixon and Gierek did not discuss any controversial human rights matters, in part because of Nixon's realist philosophy and in part because no single Polish rights issue had yet captured the American public's imagination. But as Polish internal affairs became more tumultuous in the late seventies and eighties, the Polish American connection to the human rights movement became more profound.[132] The United States increasingly rewarded acts of independence from Moscow and punished Warsaw for limiting the Polish people's freedom. As Tony Smith has demonstrated, Polish nationalism complicated Soviet political life, and the Polish American community had a very real influence on Warsaw and Washington.[133]

In retrospect, then, Nixon deserves credit for laying the groundwork for a fruitful relationship that held the potential for later liberalization, much as he did in China and the Soviet Union. Although he did not say or do much about Warsaw's human rights record, his policy was popular in Poland and among Polish Americans. Indeed, Eastern European governments and citizens alike were baffled by the Watergate fiasco and Nixon's fall from grace. "Mr. Nixon's popularity may be at its lowest point in the United States," wrote a visiting American journalist in 1973, "but throughout Eastern Europe he is regarded as a great president whose vision and courage in foreign policy ended the Cold War."[134]

The Soviet Jewry Movement

Persecuted Soviet Jews were at the center of a major human rights dilemma. Western criticism of Soviet anti-Semitism had few positive effects in the

1960s, but after 1970 a new cause dramatically altered U.S.-Soviet relations. Unable to practice their religion freely, and subjected to a variety of indignities, many Soviet Jews sought to emigrate to Israel or the West. But because the Kremlin prohibited open emigration, they were forced to remain in the country as second-class citizens. As their predicament became widely publicized in the West, the ensuing Soviet Jewry movement grew into the most prominent international human rights movement of the era, connecting Soviet domestic policies, American domestic interest groups, and the Cold War power struggle in Eastern Europe and the Middle East. It would be hard to overstate the role of this movement in American, Soviet, and Israeli affairs. As Gal Beckerman has suggested, the same Soviet Jews who were largely ignored in Washington in the sixties found themselves at the center of superpower relations in the seventies and eighties. And among American Jews the cause of Soviet Jewry arguably became more prominent than even the cause of Israel.[135] The movement galvanized support from across the American political spectrum, and it served as a model for many other transnational rights struggles. The emigration problem also proved to be one of the most nettlesome foreign policy issues for presidential administrations *and* the Kremlin throughout this period. "Probably no other single question did more to sour the atmosphere of détente than the question of Jewish emigration," recalled Soviet Ambassador Dobrynin.[136]

The Soviet state always had its dissenters. Nationalists, dissidents, and religious minorities were dealt with harshly under Lenin and Stalin, somewhat less so during the Khrushchev "thaw" (1956–1964), and harshly again during the Brezhnev era (1964–1982).[137] A crackdown on dissident activity began in 1966, when the Kremlin staged a show trial of two satirists. They were charged with "anti-Soviet agitation and propaganda," an accusation that would become a catch-all to punish many brands of dissent in the ensuing years. Demonstrations for greater freedom were then met with mass arrests and harsh sentences, and Jews and Baptists found themselves the target of renewed persecution. By the decade's end, a nascent dissident phenomenon was clearly afoot. The U.S. State Department noted that "a spate of petitions, appeals, and protests" had "confound[ed] the regime," while on the Soviet side the KGB suggested that dissent could comprise a new propaganda problem.[138] Kremlin authorities saw human rights activism as anti-Soviet activity generated by Western governments. According to the KGB, the nuclear physicist Andrei Sakharov's "politically harmful activities" were "fomented by the enemy's special services and are actively

used in the West for anti-Soviet and anti-Communist propaganda." Western journalists were increasing their contacts with dissidents so that "propaganda agencies of the leading capitalist countries, the U.S.A. first of all,"
could carry out "a slanderous anti-Soviet campaign."[139]

This dissident activism did not begin as a rejection of socialism, but as
a demand for the state to live up to its civil obligations.[140] The Soviet critics
of the 1960s did not press the authorities based on international law or
"universal" human rights principles, but rather on the terms of the 1936
Soviet constitution, which officially allowed certain liberties, such as freedom of religion, press, and assembly. These early dissidents appealed to
domestic law first, but within a few years they would cite international
covenants like the Universal Declaration and the Helsinki Accords. Meanwhile, the authorities counterargued that citizens' rights emanated from the
state, which was meeting their economic and social needs. The Kremlin's
position—that citizens had a right to be critical, but not anti-Soviet—
allowed Soviet leaders to interpret dissidence as alignment with foreign,
"anti-socialist" interests.[141]

As suppression of speech and writing increased, *samizdat* (illegal, self-
published literature) became more widespread. Dissent also began to take
a more organized form. In 1968, anonymous authors began cataloguing
Soviet abuses in a publication called the *Chronicle of Current Events*. The
following year, the biologist Sergei Kovalev formed the first Soviet human
rights association, and shortly thereafter Andrei Sakharov cofounded the
Moscow Human Rights Committee. The authorities' mistreatment of Sakharov and the writer Aleksandr Solzhenitsyn was highly publicized in the
West, while countless others dissented in obscurity. The crackdown on dissent was accompanied by a revival of state-sponsored anti-Semitism, which
was itself part of a long-term Soviet reaction to "dangerous" nationalism.
The Soviet Union's "nationalities problem" had been a source of concern
since 1917, and it intensified in the détente era. In a tacit acknowledgment
that the system had neither thoroughly Russified the republics nor eradicated nationalism and religious faith, the Kremlin feared that nationalism
in the republics and in Eastern Europe could spur the dissolution of the
Soviet empire.[142] These fears had a profound influence on Soviet reactions
to American human rights activism in the years to come. Because ethnic
and ethno-religious issues were potentially damaging to the state's integrity,
Soviet authorities quashed nationalism and religious fervor within the
Soviet republics and the Eastern European states.[143]

Among all of the Soviet Union's ethnic and religious minorities, its three million Jews were among the most persecuted. Restrictions on religious and cultural expression had inhibited the maintenance of Jewish identity, yet Soviet Jews were not allowed to assimilate or emigrate, either. Those prevented from emigrating came to be known as refuseniks. Of course, anti-Semitism had been a problem in Russia for centuries, but its official sanction in this period grew directly from the surge in Zionism following the 1967 Arab-Israeli Six-Day War. Jews in the Soviet Union and elsewhere experienced a wave of pride following the Israeli victory, and this enthusiasm led the Kremlin to embark on a repressive campaign that equated Zionism with fascism and racism. The anti-Zionist campaign was also motivated by Moscow's Middle East interests, which led the Kremlin to break relations with Israel and strengthen relations with key Arab regimes.[144]

The Six-Day War also precipitated an increase in American Jewish activism. There had been little contact between American and Soviet Jews before 1967, but that changed abruptly with Israel's victory. One scholar has identified this as the moment that Israel launched its successful effort "to convert American-Jewish identity into Israeli nationalism."[145] As Jacob Heilbrunn has shown, the war made Israel a more prominent cause among American Jews and helped create the pro-Israel, anticommunist, neoconservative movement.[146] There was also a radical side to this transformation, as evidenced by the Jewish Defense League's bombing of several targets in the early 1970s, including the New York office of the Soviet airline Aeroflot.[147]

The anti-Semitism campaign and the rise in ethnic feeling would have meant little to American policymakers had it not been for the emigration issue. Eastern European Jews had been leaving the region for a century (over one million entered the United States before 1924), but Soviet authorities used a variety of laws to prevent a mass migration. Although visa applications for Israel increased exponentially after the 1967 war, only four thousand people of all faiths left the Soviet Union in the 1960s. An unusual event in 1970 then brought Soviet Jews' plight to international attention. Mark Dymshits and Eduard Kuznetsov were sentenced to death after attempting to hijack a civilian plane to Sweden, and the publicity surrounding their trial and sentence caused an international outcry. The authorities eventually commuted the death sentences and increased the emigration quota, but because this higher quota led to a "brain drain" of

educated Jews, the Kremlin imposed an exit fee, or "diploma tax," on grad-
uates of Soviet universities. It applied to fewer than 10 percent of prospective émigrés, but the high fee was out of reach for most applicants. These
events touched off the Soviet Jewry movement.

The emigration issue had a clear appeal in the United States. Soviet
policies were a casus belli for American Jewish activists, who felt a deep
sympathy for their coreligionists.[148] They formed NGOs like the National
Conference on Soviet Jewry and focused on the emigration cause with
unparalleled vigor. The issue also appealed to civil libertarians, who supported freedom of migration, freedom of worship, and maintenance of cultural integrity. Conservatives further embraced the cause of Soviet Jewry as
a means of attacking Soviet communism and détente. American interest
also grew out of the close diplomatic and economic relationship that was
developing between the United States and Israel. The American side of the
movement was characterized by publicity campaigns, fund-raising, lobbying, and frequent demonstrations at the Soviet embassy.

The Soviets defended their policies by invoking ideology and their
nation's tumultuous history. A mass exodus, they believed, would weaken
the state on several fronts. Émigrés could spread state secrets or scientific
information, and the flight of university-educated citizens would diminish
the nation's intellectual capital. An exodus would also demonstrate the
regime's inability to control its population, and would perhaps suggest that
the state had bent to international pressure. Ambassador Dobrynin wryly
argued that the most important reason was simply the Kremlin's fear that
"an escape hatch from the happy land of socialism" would lead to far more
substantial, destabilizing demands for liberalization.[149]

It would be an understatement to say that the Nixon administration did
not welcome the emigration issue. Nixon and Kissinger's top priority in
East/West matters was improved superpower relations, not individual
rights. Indeed, as Noam Kochavi has argued, the reluctant Nixon administration only addressed the issue because Soviet anti-Semitism was so conspicuous and because American domestic concern was so extensive.[150] As
we have seen, Nixon believed that if such issues were to be addressed at all,
they were the concern of the United Nations, the State Department, and
private citizens. He allowed his U.N. representatives to mention Soviet
Jews' plight on a few occasions, but he argued that high-level inquiries
would only invoke a sharp reaction, which would in turn imperil any possibility of better relations. Although Nixon had little choice but to publicly

support the émigrés' cause, he argued that quiet diplomacy was the best way to achieve a mutually agreeable détente that would benefit all American and Soviet citizens. As the political debate continued, there was no denying the dramatic rise in emigration after 1970. Around sixty thousand left for Israel from 1971 to 1973, including thirty-two thousand in 1972 alone.[151] Activists claimed credit for these concessions, while the Nixon administration cited private diplomatic efforts. Alongside Western pressure, a major factor was the Kremlin's desire to attract trade and placate Western critics while exporting "troublesome" citizens.

Before the May 1972 U.S.-Soviet summit in Moscow, Nixon was flooded with letters from citizens, NGOs, and members of Congress asking him to broach emigration. His aides stated that he would do so, but he left it to his deputies.[152] It is clear that his priorities were elsewhere. "We are meeting here not because of sentiment," he said to Brezhnev, "but because we are pragmatic men [who] . . . have learned the lessons of history and will not allow ourselves to be dragged into conflict in areas peripheral to our interests." Brezhnev, who also did not want this issue to hamper the summit, even temporarily jailed several dissidents to keep them away from the meeting site. In an earlier era this decision might have gone unnoticed, but in this age of expanding international activist networks, it became front page news in America.[153] Another sign of the times was that Secretary of State Rogers briefly discussed Soviet Jewry with Foreign Minister Gromyko, and even gave him a list of seventy people who wanted to join their relatives in the United States. Divided families were a traditional subject for low-level diplomacy, but raising such matters at this level was unprecedented. After the summit, the State Department instructed its officers to deliver an ambiguous line to the press regarding Soviet Jewry: "I have good reason to believe that this issue was properly taken care of during the president's visit to the U.S.S.R."[154] But Nixon stood by his guns, telling a group of Jewish leaders in New York that he would not engage in "harsh confrontations" with the Soviets. His press secretary added, "The way to deal with this is not to engage in public confrontation or inject it into the political arena."[155] Even Rogers's quiet diplomacy was aimed at educating Gromyko about the strictures of the American political system; it was not intended to challenge Kremlin policies or change Soviet society.

Nixon's true feelings on the subject are open to debate. His apparent indifference to Soviet Jews' plight stemmed from his belief in realpolitik and his unwillingness to complicate an already difficult détente, as well as his conviction that private diplomacy was bearing fruit.[156] But it is also true that he had a troubled relationship with Jews whom he considered left-leaning members of the East Coast establishment.[157] Henry Kissinger—himself a Jewish refugee from Nazi Germany—sympathized with the cause, though he joined Nixon in defending détente. When Israeli Prime Minister Golda Meir asked Nixon and Kissinger to exert more pressure on the Kremlin, Kissinger privately suggested to Nixon that emigration may be a humanitarian concern, but added that it would not be an American foreign policy objective even if the Soviets were murdering their own citizens. Nixon agreed: "We can't blow up the world because of it."[158]

Nixon and Kissinger's bête noire in the emigration matter was Senator Henry M. Jackson. At a time when the cause of Soviet Jewry and the broader human rights movement needed political sponsors, the hawkish senator latched onto the emigration issue with a passion. Jackson was not Nixon's political opposite—Nixon even considered nominating him as his secretary of defense in 1968—but he was a Democrat and an outspoken critic of détente. To Jackson, the Cold War thaw had merely altered the Kremlin's tactics. "The Soviets have not changed," he declared. "[They] are like a burglar going down a hotel corridor, trying all the doors. When they find one that's unlocked, they go in."[159] In 1972, he joined with other Democratic hawks and neoconservatives and formed the Coalition for a Democratic Majority to promote a military buildup in the name of "peace through strength." Jackson's long-standing support for Israel and Jewish causes was inspired in part by his visit to the liberated Buchenwald concentration camp in 1945, but he also saw potential political benefits in the emigration cause. Indeed, his embrace of the émigrés seemed motivated in equal parts by his disdain for détente, his desire for political aggrandizement (for a potential presidential bid), and his belief in human rights. Complicating relations with Moscow also served his interest in maintaining a certain level of bilateral tension, thus strengthening the defense industry and its many contractors in his home state.[160]

As it happened, trade laws would be the congressional mechanism of choice. Before 1970, only about 1 percent of the Soviet Union's trade was with the United States, but the thaw gave trade much more potential, and in fact offered tremendous economic benefits to the United States. American exports to the Soviet Union rose from $160 million in 1971 to $546 million in 1972, with a favorable balance for the United States.[161] In October 1972, as the two countries came closer to inking an agreement that would oblige the United States to extend most-favored-nation (MFN) status, a Jackson bill declared that Congress would not approve the package unless the Soviets repealed the exit tax. The following spring, Jackson and Congressman Charles Vanik (D-OH) engineered an amendment to the trade bill that denied MFN to countries with nonmarket economies that also restricted emigration or imposed inordinate exit fees. The Jackson-Vanik amendment did not specify the Soviet Union or its Jewish minority, but the target was obvious. The amendment not only became the most visible American political effort in support of free emigration, but also impacted East/West relations even beyond the Cold War's end. "It is important that the Russians understand," said Jackson, "that they are dealing not only with the administration but also with Congress."[162] Some in Congress did not back the amendment, including majorities in the Senate Finance Committee and the Commerce Committee. But the overall trend was undeniable: Congress would not approve MFN or trade credits without Soviet concessions on emigration, even though these were not required by the Nixon-Brezhnev agreement. In the years to come, the Soviets found that even their occasional concessions, such as rescinding the exit tax, did not convince Congress to overturn the amendment. Bilateral trade would remain bound to Soviet emigration policies by statute.

It was quite clear that Jackson was targeting Nixon's foreign policy as much as he was supporting Soviet Jewry. Jackson's vision for an American human rights policy fell somewhere between the goals of congressional liberals and realists. "We are asked to believe," he quipped, "that the prospects for peace are enhanced by the flow of Pepsi-Cola to the Soviet Union and the flow of vodka to the United States. I say that we will move much further along the road to stable peace when we see the flow of people and ideas across the barriers that divide East from West."[163] Jackson called for a "human détente" that emphasized individual liberty, especially the right to emigrate. "Of human rights," he wrote in the *New York Times*, "free emigration is first among equals." He went on to assert that the argument was "between those who recognize that a genuine era of international accommodation must be based on progress toward individual liberty and those who choose to pretend otherwise."[164] From an activist's standpoint, it was strange to call free emigration the "first" right. Surely most observers would have agreed that torture and extrajudicial execution were worse than a high fee for exit visas. But from a political standpoint Jackson's position made perfect sense. The Jackson-Vanik amendment united Jewish activists and labor unions with liberals and conservatives in what William Bundy called "a broad and almost unique coalition."[165] Liberals appreciated it in principle and as a challenge to Nixon; the AFL-CIO saw it as a means of protecting American jobs; and conservatives saw it as a way to keep Nixon from getting too close to the Kremlin.

While the central human rights cause of Jackson-Vanik appealed to liberals and activists, such antitrade measures also appealed to American conservatives who wanted to weaken the Soviets by avoiding trade and summits altogether.[166] Many of Jackson's supporters in this latter camp were more anticommunist than pro–human rights. "Your positions on defense against this rising communist threat continue to have our support," wrote one Californian. "To be blunt about it," wrote an Arizonan, "no other previous administration has done so much to *save* [the] Soviet Union and Red China as much as [the] Nixon administration has done." Jackson's replies combined anti-Sovietism with activist language, as when he assured supporters of his "continued best efforts on behalf of Soviet citizens who are denied their fundamental human right to emigrate." Some letter writers invoked the struggles of other ethnic groups, a few going so far as to criticize the focus on Soviet Jews. As one Lithuanian American pointed out, Soviet oppression "transcends the impediments imposed upon the Jewish minority," and encompassed dozens of religious and ethnic groups.[167] Some of these sentiments may have been motivated by anti-Semitism, but the question was a logical one. If the U.S. government was going to give this much official attention to a suffering minority in a single foreign country, why not also act on behalf of suffering minorities in every country? Where should Washington draw the line? There would be no consensus answer to these questions in the human rights era.

Of course, Nixon and Kissinger did not believe that they had a moral duty, or even much practical ability, to change the Soviet Union. "We have an insane situation now when people here want to cut the defense budget and at the same time they want to change Soviet society," Kissinger told the West German foreign minister. "They think the latter is possible for some amount of trade."[168] Kissinger went on a diplomatic offensive to reassure his Soviet counterparts, and the administration worked with Jackson to dilute his amendments. But Jackson continued to be a gadfly even after the Soviets made concessions. Early in 1973, Nixon's emissary convinced the Kremlin to lift the exit tax, but this was not enough for Jackson, who demanded further concessions, such as allowing a watchdog organization to monitor emigration levels. Jackson, Congress, and activists knew that the amendment gave them leverage and that the granting of MFN and credits would take this leverage away.[169] The administration then worked to gain support from several groups in America—businesses, Jewish groups, congressional moderates—and worked with the Kremlin to seek some minor concessions that would placate Congress. Kissinger gave the Soviets two lists of refuseniks in Moscow in May 1973, and he advised Nixon that he should clarify the importance of further Soviet reforms: "Remark that . . . you raise the matter not to argue the principle but because Soviet practices affect chances of achieving a common goal: MFN and credits in acceptable form."[170] The House passed Jackson-Vanik with a veto-proof majority in December 1973.

These events coincided with the growing Watergate crisis, and when Nixon's long, downward spiral began, his opponents smelled blood. Jackson began demanding a minimum number of exit visas, and he insisted that other ethnic groups be included in emigration deals. In March 1974, Kissinger assailed the growing congressional pressure: "These bastards on the hill ignore the fact that 400 Jews were leaving the Soviet Union in 1969 and now say that 30,000 a year is inconsequential."[171] While Nixon was fighting for his political life in June 1974, he mounted a vigorous public defense of his foreign policy and raised some of the central human rights questions of the age. "What is our capability to change the domestic structure of other nations?" he asked in his commencement address at the Naval Academy. "What price, in terms of renewed conflict, are we willing to pay to bring pressure to bear for humane causes? Not by our choice, but by our capability, our primary concern in foreign policy must be to help influence the international conduct of nations in the world arena. . . . We cannot gear our foreign policy to transformation of other societies. . . . Peace between nations with totally different systems is also a high moral objective."[172] Kissinger, too, emphasized Americans' inability to force internal changes in foreign countries. Knowing these limits, he argued, was a "recognition of the necessity of peace—not moral callousness. . . . We cannot demand that the Soviet Union, in effect, suddenly reverse five decades of Soviet, and centuries of Russian, history."[173]

After Nixon resigned in August 1974 and Gerald Ford entered the White House, the Soviets made a verbal guarantee that they would allow fifty thousand émigrés per annum. When Ford sent a confidential letter on the proposal to select senators, Jackson publicized the deal and upped the figure to sixty thousand—a move that prompted Ford to mutter that Jackson had "behaved like a swine." A compromise bill allowed the president to grant short-term MFN status, but it also drastically curtailed trade credits. Stung by this rebuke, early in 1975 the Soviets nullified the trade agreement on the grounds that the U.S. government was meddling in its internal affairs.[174] When Brezhnev asked why the United States had granted MFN to other nations but not the Soviet Union, Kissinger argued that Congress, and especially Jackson, was now gunning for more power in foreign affairs. "[Jackson] doesn't only claim he has defeated the Soviet Union," said Kissinger. "He claims he has defeated *me*." He added, tongue in cheek, that he would be glad to arrange for Jackson's emigration. President Ford promised to seek new legislation, but he pointed out to Brezhnev that both American political parties were unlikely to act without further signs of cooperation from Moscow. But Brezhnev refused, and the Soviets only got tougher in the months to come. They even rejected American lists of prospective émigrés and flatly stated that "a list of persons said to desire to leave the U.S.S.R. for Israel has no bearing on U.S.-U.S.S.R. relations."[175]

American and Soviet proponents of détente were convinced that Senator Jackson was an opportunist who had his eye on a presidential bid. Shortly before resigning, Nixon suggested to Ambassador Dobrynin that "Jackson is just playing 1976 politics."[176] Kissinger later wrote that Jackson "sought to appeal to a Jewish constituency for his Presidential ambitions—a not unworthy motive for a public figure fortunate enough to be a native-born citizen of the United States." (The German-born Kissinger was ineligible for the presidency.) He added that Jackson was often as interested in the symbolism of the confrontation as in the result, and that the prevailing public mood would not allow anyone in Congress to risk appearing to be soft on emigration.[177] The State Department's James M. Wilson similarly found that many in the Jackson camp were "more interested in gigging the Russians or cutting back on trade than they were about actually getting more Soviet Jews out of Russia."[178] Scholars' conclusions have been mixed. The historian Noam Kochavi concludes that Jackson was "inflexible" and that both Jackson and Kissinger were unable to subordinate their personal ambitions to the goal of a workable solution to the émigré problem.[179] But Jackson biographer Robert G. Kaufman offers a more forgiving appraisal. Since the Soviets had always acted evasively on emigration, a good case can be made that Jackson-Vanik created a strong incentive for the Soviets to relax their restrictions. Moreover, writes Kaufman, Jackson's blend of geopolitics, Judeo-Christian morals, and prodemocracy principles "offered the best practicable framework for a remarkably successful American foreign policy during the Cold War era."[180]

In retrospect, few of the major political actors involved were helped to any great degree by their efforts. Nixon resigned for unrelated reasons, and Ford and Kissinger were turned out of office. Jackson was reelected to the Senate but never won the presidential nomination, due in large measure to the waning appeal of his brand of prodefense liberalism. However, it is now clear that Jackson was an important transitional figure in the neoconservative movement that challenged the Nixon-Kissinger foreign policy and eventually helped bring Ronald Reagan to the White House. As Kaufman has noted, many of the "Reagan Democrats" of 1980 had started out as "Jackson Democrats."[181]

Two additional questions are worth considering: Who really won out in this political/diplomatic conflict, and what did the United States gain from the movement? There is no doubt that Soviet policies changed. Although observers disagree as to whether congressional action, private bilateral diplomacy, Soviet domestic politics, or negative publicity was the most important factor, over two hundred thousand Jews left the Soviet Union in the 1970s.[182] But while this was a fortunate outcome for émigrés, what did it mean for America? And considering that so many people suffered human rights violations in the Soviet Union and in dozens of other nations, why did American policymakers focus so strongly on the plight of Soviet Jews? In attempting to use trade policy to help prospective émigrés, Congress weakened détente, thus hurting the U.S. economy by limiting trade and perhaps also preventing U.S.-Soviet breakthroughs in other important areas. The American political conflict arguably made emigration more difficult at times. As Congress became more assertive, the Soviets closed ranks and allowed only twenty-one thousand émigrés in 1974, thirteen thousand in 1975, and fourteen thousand in 1976.[183] (The numbers would rise again at the end of the decade, and then again at the very end of the 1980s.) For Soviet leaders, these were matters of principle. As we have seen, they simply pulled out of the trade agreement rather than accept interference in their internal policies. But perhaps this standoffishness illuminated the most salient point of all: Soviet leaders recognized that emigration and dissidence were points of vulnerability, and they believed that giving an inch on either one could cause the entire Soviet system to unravel. From this perspective, the exodus that began in the early seventies was the first substantial step toward the system's ultimate dissolution years later.

Irrespective of the debate between Congress and the administration, the emigration issue had lasting significance for the human rights movement. While some supporters of détente saw this activism as a threat, ironically these activities would not have been possible without the improvement in superpower relations. Emigration was one of the clearest cases of a connection between the burgeoning ethnic movement and the development of human rights interest in diplomatic circles. Moreover, it demonstrated how an effective coalition could be cobbled together from disparate elements. Conservatives, liberals, and moderates found common ground in the fight for freedom of religion and emigration, and American Jews' domestic activism helped convince many other Americans that the U.S. government should act. This movement inspired the work of countless activists in the 1970s and 1980s.

Détente on Trial: The 1976 Election

The 1976 election was a perfect storm of debate over détente, ethnic concerns, and morality in foreign policy. While Congress was pursuing human rights matters, the ethnic revival was at its apex and the détente process was as controversial as ever. All of the major presidential candidates made appeals to ethnic voters, who in turn lobbied on behalf of their overseas compatriots. In this way, ethnic anticommunism became even more overtly expressed in the language of human rights for Eastern Europeans.

Given the general public dissatisfaction with political leaders in the Watergate era, morality in politics and diplomacy also became a central theme of the campaign. All of the major candidates promoted a "moral" vision for America. Jimmy Carter, a devout Southern Baptist and former one-term governor of Georgia, promised to restore America's reputation as the world's preeminent democracy. As a Washington outsider, he benefited from the post-Watergate rejection of inside-the-Beltway politics. His political style—he was both a rational problem solver and a Wilsonian idealist—reflected his religious convictions and his training as an engineer. Carter's overt moralism did not appeal to everyone, but many Americans appreciated his religiosity, and he entered the national scene when evangelical

Christians were becoming more politically active.[184] A Ford operative went so far as to assert that "the morality issue . . . created Jimmy Carter."[185]

Senator Henry Jackson, the early Democratic frontrunner, was less moralistic but did argue that the election would be a referendum on leadership and national will. "We seem to lack, at the highest levels of government," he asserted, "the willpower and conviction to take a strong stand. Détente has become a one-way street on which advantages pass to the Soviets."[186] Conservative Republicans' standard-bearer, Ronald Reagan, also used moral rhetoric to assail the Ford-Kissinger foreign policy. Attacking Kissinger's alleged statement that "the dynamics of history" were on the Soviets' side, Reagan asked, "Is this why Mr. Ford refused to invite Aleksandr Solzhenitsyn to the White House . . . [and signed] the Helsinki Pact, putting our stamp of approval on Russia's enslavement of the captive nations?"[187] Because détente was losing favor with middle America, Ford dropped the term from his campaign, arguing that the word was "inconsequential" next to the very real need to minimize superpower conflicts.[188]

Considering Jimmy Carter's image as a human rights advocate, in reality he came rather late to the cause. He called for greater attention to moral principles and humanitarianism, but he remained vague for most of the campaign. He then more openly embraced human rights after the party platform was written. Several factors contributed to Carter's embrace of human rights and moral diplomacy. His religious faith and his experiences in the segregated South played a part, as did his personal commitment to humanitarianism. At the same time, Carter gathered from the public mood that human rights rhetoric could constitute an effective oppositional tool in the campaign. Polling data and the new human rights legislation suggested profound public and congressional dissatisfaction with American complicity in rights abuses. As one journalist concluded before the election, "The evidence suggests that large numbers of American citizens are demanding that their government no longer look the other way as the Pinochets and Park Chung Hees crowd their prisons with the innocent."[189] Zbigniew Brzezinski acknowledged that Carter's prioritization of human rights reflected both his personal beliefs and his political acumen, since he could use the issue to draw a strong contrast between himself and his opponents.[190]

By the time of the October presidential debates, Carter was combining traditional anticommunist rhetoric with liberal internationalism to attack executive secrecy, détente, support for undemocratic regimes, and general immorality in foreign policy. He argued that Americans had lost "what we were formally so proud of . . . the strength of our country, its moral integrity." This language appealed to many Americans, but Carter was unable to offer many practical alternatives. When asked whether he was willing to risk an oil embargo to promote human rights in Iran and Saudi Arabia, or whether he would withhold grain shipments to the Soviet Union, he avoided the question. He found that it was much easier to emphasize values and criticize the incumbent's record than to outline superior policies. President Ford countered by defending quiet diplomacy, his overtures to South Korea, and his success in preserving peace with Moscow. "What is more moral than peace?" he asked. "And the United States is at peace today."[191]

The political parties' unusual interest in moral concerns and human rights paralleled their efforts to win the support of ethnic voters. Some ethnics were growing disillusioned with the Democratic Party, but they were reluctant to embrace President Ford's foreign policy or the Helsinki agreement. Ethnics were especially critical of what came to be called the "Sonnenfeldt Doctrine," named for Kissinger's deputy, who was alleged to have said that the Soviet sphere in Eastern Europe was a fixed reality. (Ford denied that such a doctrine existed.) Ford reiterated his support for Eastern European aspirations, promised to visit the region, and assured ethnic representatives that the Helsinki agreement would break down barriers and increase contacts.[192] Jimmy Carter and the Democrats also courted the ethnics. Carter's campaign staged photo-op walking tours of ethnic neighborhoods, and Carter participated in "family days" in working-class districts. "It's time we had leaders who will speak up for freedom in Eastern Europe," he said to a group of Chicagoans. "There has to be access to those who live in Poland from the free world."[193]

Indeed, Eastern Europe received the lion's share of the candidates' human-rights-cum-anticommunist attention. So strong was the Cold War tone of the Carter/Ford contest that one reporter quipped, "Sometimes it has seemed as if Ronald Reagan were debating Ronald Reagan."[194] Ethnic politics made headlines during one of these debates. President Ford committed one of the most serious errors of his presidency when he declared, "There is no Soviet domination of Eastern Europe and there never will be under a Ford administration." Carter rose to the bait by combining appeals to ethnic pride and human rights with a sharp attack on his opponent's phrasing: "I would like to see Mr. Ford convince the Polish Americans and the Czech Americans and the Hungarian Americans in this country that those countries don't live under the domination and supervision of the Soviet Union behind the Iron Curtain."[195] Ford's reluctance to retract his remark hurt his candidacy. "There are no free countries in Eastern Europe," stated the chairman of the Captive Nations Committee, "and the president should be the first to know that." Stanley Makowski, the mayor of (heavily Polish) Buffalo, said of the city's electorate, "Many were undecided. Sometimes it takes one thing that pushes them over the brink. This looks like it."[196]

In reality, Ford's opponents had turned a molehill into a mountain. He had clearly misspoken, for the "no Soviet domination" statement was entirely inconsistent with his long-standing beliefs. To paraphrase one contemporary journalist, no one could reasonably question Ford's anticommunist credentials or expect that the United States would liberate Eastern Europe.[197] Ford finally apologized to a group of ethnic leaders, but his misstatement may have turned the tide of opinion in key districts. More importantly for the human rights story, Carter eked out a close electoral victory to become the thirty-ninth president.

Chapter 3

The Carter Human Rights Policy

Jimmy Carter holds a place in the public imagination as the "human rights president" because he pursued a high-profile policy. Indeed, the 1976 presidential campaign and the Carter presidency were arguably the high-water mark for human rights optimism in Washington. Sensing the popular demand for a new brand of politics, Carter embraced human rights as an oppositional campaign strategy and promised a foreign policy antidote to eight years of Nixon, Kissinger, and Ford. He believed that the United States should promote democracy and humanitarianism, engage with the developing world, strengthen its partnerships with Europe and Japan, and rethink its obsession with the Soviet Union. In Latin America especially, Carter claimed that he would cultivate mutually beneficial partnerships that transcended the narrow paternalism of Cold War anticommunism.

True to his promises, his first six months in office saw a great deal of activity in the humanitarian realm. He cut military aid to some regimes, spoke out on behalf of dissidents, and appointed energetic bureaucrats to handle human rights issues for the State Department and the National Security Council (NSC). He laid the groundwork for a variety of representations, from the carrot of positive inducements to the stick of economic sanctions. In addition to his public statements, his administration frequently used private diplomacy, and Carter authorized his representatives to make critical statements in multilateral forums with unprecedented frequency. By the end of his presidency, the Carter administration had altered relations with several nations—mostly in Latin America—and had won the release of thousands of political prisoners and émigrés.

Although Carter did more for human rights than any of his predecessors, and even most of his successors, his reputation as a "moralist" has been largely exaggerated by supporters and opponents alike.[1] Much to the chagrin of activists and ethnics, he generally prioritized security, sanctioned relatively few governments, and even worked around Congress in order to strengthen relations with some authoritarian rulers. His administration was defined by a conflict between the career officers of the State and Defense Departments, who saw humanitarianism as a distant national priority, and the new human rights bureaucrats, who routinely clashed with American and foreign officials. The latter tried, largely unsuccessfully, to swim upstream against the tradition of "clientism" that had long defined the State Department and its geographic bureaus.[2] In time, Carter realized the difficulties that a moral posture posed to his overall foreign policy. He had a hard time providing a broad vision, and he found that "human rights" had limits as a unifying principle, even within his own party. More specifically, he was unable to pull together the Democrats' liberal and neoconservative wings—the former wanted a foreign policy that distanced America from unsavory regimes of the right, while the latter wanted a strong stand against communism.[3] Carter never entirely abandoned his early activism, but his priorities changed in response to several unexpected events in the second half of his presidency, including runaway inflation, the energy crisis, the Nicaraguan Revolution, the Soviet invasion of Afghanistan, and the Iran hostage crisis.

Most early interpretations of Jimmy Carter's human rights policy were quite critical. Scholars and pundits alike generally considered his efforts to have been naïve, quixotic, inimical to broader national interests, and even dangerous.[4] Those writing in the post–Cold War era have been somewhat more willing to give Carter credit for trying to move the United States beyond anticommunism and realpolitik. Some have even been effusive in their praise of his human rights efforts and his overall foreign policy.[5] I argue that the effort to score Carter's policy either an outright "success" or an unmitigated "failure" obscures more fundamental questions about the purposes of a human rights policy. In this sense, I agree with those who suggest that Carter never adequately expressed to the American people what, exactly, the U.S. government was trying to accomplish. I also contend that interpretations of his policy's effectiveness have invariably been filtered through scholars' ideologically tinted glasses. The truth is that his policy was not as groundbreaking as his supporters have insisted, nor was it as inept or as "dangerous" as his detractors maintained. By the end of his presidency, he could list many genuine humanitarian accomplishments, few of which came at great cost to the American people. But unfortunately for Carter, even his successes paid him few political dividends.

The Carter Administration's Early Measures

President Carter had several reasons for pursuing a vigorous policy. For starters, Democratic polling experts found that human rights rhetoric during the campaign appealed to a wide demographic.[6] "Human rights had become the central theme of our foreign policy in the minds of the press and public," Carter wrote in his memoir. "It seemed that a spark had been ignited, and I had no inclination to douse the growing flames."[7] Second, in light of the divisive 1968 and 1972 elections, he hoped to unify the Democratic Party's conservative and liberal wings. Third, such initiatives were consistent with the prevailing belief in limits to American power. Most of the U.S. government's prior human rights activity—public pronouncements, nonbinding "sense of the Congress" resolutions, cuts in aid, and private diplomacy—had been relatively painless to Americans, and Carter was willing to exploit these lower public expectations. "We have learned," he said in his inaugural address, "that even our great nation has its recognized limits, and that we can neither answer all questions nor solve all problems."[8] Finally, a human rights policy was consistent with Carter's personal moral compass and his liberal internationalist goals. The Cold War thaw allowed him to continue his predecessors' relationships with the Eastern Bloc states while also giving him some cover to experiment in the Third World. He hoped that a robust policy would improve America's international image and restore its reputation as the world's foremost champion of liberal democracy. As he explained his motivations early in his presidency, "We've been through some sordid and embarrassing years recently with Vietnam and Cambodia and Watergate and the CIA revelations, and I felt like it was time for our country to hold a beacon light of something pure and decent and right and proper that would rally our citizens to a cause."[9]

In order to promote diverse views within his administration, he appointed a veteran of the Kennedy/Johnson years, Cyrus Vance, as secretary of state and a Poland-born academic and staunch cold warrior, Zbigniew Brzezinski, as his national security adviser. Vance and Brzezinski agreed on most foreign policy issues, but they often diverged on détente and human rights. Vance saw détente as a means to promote arms control and peaceful East/West relations, which meant using quiet diplomacy instead of what he called "strident or polemical" public criticisms.[10] Brzezinski, on the other hand, preferred to combine a tough anti-Soviet stance with greater attention to the rights of Eastern Europeans. Yet Brzezinski, too, knew that diplomacy required nuance and that human rights were generally outside his purview as national security adviser. Carter also built up the human rights bureaucracy with several Washington outsiders, including a microbiologist, Jessica Tuchman, who became director of global issues at the NSC, and a civil rights activist, Patricia Derian, who became his human rights coordinator in the State Department. The twenty officers and staffers working under Derian kept tabs on violations, produced country reports, and weighed in on foreign aid decisions. Carter also tasked his deputy secretary of state, Warren Christopher, with heading an interagency group (the "Christopher Group") intended to ensure human rights consideration in the allocation of export licenses and foreign aid.

Carter opened his presidency with a flurry of activity. After asserting in his inaugural address that "our commitment to human rights must be absolute"—read by critical observers as a troublingly ambiguous, open-ended pledge—he worked with Congress to trim military aid to Ethiopia, the Philippines, and several regimes in South America. Carter also convinced Congress to repeal the Byrd Amendment, which had allowed Rhodesian chrome imports. Unlike his predecessors, he challenged the Soviets right off the bat. He publicly protested the persecution of the Charter 77 group in Czechoslovakia; published an open letter to Andrei Sakharov; issued public statements on the Aleksandr Ginzburg and Yuri Orlov arrests; met with the exiled dissident Vladimir Bukovsky; and stated that he would continue to speak out despite the risk to arms control negotiations. Some in the administration believed that the Kremlin would understand the domestic sources of Carter's boldness. "Surely the Soviets are sophisticated enough," suggested Press Secretary Jody Powell, "to understand that the domestic political flexibility we need to make progress in other areas is enhanced by your position on human rights."[11] But the experts were more skeptical. The U.S. ambassador in Moscow, Malcolm Toon, perceived that the human rights issue stirred "deep emotions" and could become "a major stumbling block" in U.S.-Soviet relations.[12]

As it turned out, Toon was largely correct. Although legislators and activists had assailed Soviet internal policies in the détente era, criticisms

from a sitting president were new. Predictably, the Kremlin responded harshly to his public entreaties by stressing the "noninterference" principle.
Ambassador Dobrynin told his American counterparts that U.S. embassy
meetings with Sakharov, for example, "aroused the utmost bewilderment"
in Moscow, and that such "categorically unacceptable" efforts would only
complicate relations.[13] The Kremlin similarly warned Carter that "matters
of internal development, reflecting differences in ideology and sociopoliti-
cal systems, should not be made a subject of dealings between states."[14]
Ideological perceptions were central to this reaction. The Kremlin understood the nature of propaganda, but not high-level human rights intercession. One month into Carter's presidency, KGB head Yuri Andropov
reported to the Politburo that the "anti-Soviet campaign" was no longer
the work of journalists and activists: "Now diplomats and other U.S. representatives, appropriately instructed and actively aided by the CIA and DIA,
are working purposefully with the so-called 'democratic movement,' with
Jewish '*refuseniks*,' and with nationalists." Andropov did not credit Carter
or Congress with creating this campaign, but considered them to be stooges
of "ideological centers and Zionist organizations." Soviet propagandists
responded by ramping up their own efforts. *Pravda* charged that American
militarists and conservatives were using the "smoke screen of the 'defense
of human rights'" to launch a "campaign of slander and provocations . . .
over imaginary violations."[15]

Early bilateral meetings were correspondingly harsh. The Soviets set the
tone for Secretary Vance's first visit to Moscow by arresting the dissident
Anatoly Shcharansky and charging him with spying for the United States.
When Vance arrived in March 1977, Brezhnev berated him for America's
violations of earlier agreements, and the two sides made no progress on
arms control. Vance later acknowledged that Carter's human rights efforts
had negatively influenced "the general atmosphere" of the talks.[16] In June
the Kremlin sent yet another message by arresting and expelling an American journalist who had interviewed Shcharansky, and even forcing him to
sign a confession that he had accepted secrets from the dissident. That same
month, Carter clarified that there was no relationship between human
rights and the SALT negotiations, yet he also admitted that he was taken
aback by the Soviets' anger about "a routine and normal commitment to
human rights." Carter had hoped that his humanitarian goals would not
imperil progress in bilateral relations, arguing instead that "the period of
debate, disagreement, probing, and negotiation was inevitable."[17] But given

the long-standing Soviet posture on such matters, as well as his Sovietologists' warnings, perhaps Carter should not have been so surprised.

He raised human rights in his initial correspondence with the Kremlin, and also told Ambassador Dobrynin that statements of support for dissidents and White House visits with émigrés were not intended to embarrass Moscow. An incredulous Dobrynin, who well understood his superiors' state of mind, was bewildered that Carter believed he could separate these public acts from other bilateral concerns.[18] Soviet Premier Leonid Brezhnev was even more forthright when Carter broached the dissident question in his opening letter. In reply to Carter's assertion that "we cannot be indifferent to the fate of freedom and individual human rights," Brezhnev offered a curt reminder of the noninterference principle. Carter reiterated that he did not want to create problems, but he also admitted that his administration would have to "express publicly on occasion the sincere and deep feelings of myself and our people." This touched a nerve with Brezhnev, who asked why Carter was corresponding with an "apostate" (Sakharov) who had "proclaimed himself the enemy of the Soviet state." Regarding the "so-called question of human rights," Brezhnev assured him that the Soviets would not accept this kind of interference, "whatever pseudo-humanitarian slogans are used to present it."[19] Carter often claimed that his policy applied to all countries equally and that he did not seek to revive the Cold War. Nevertheless, the level of Soviet resistance eventually led him to drop human rights references from his letters to Brezhnev and at the Geneva arms control talks. (His administration would later raise these matters via other bilateral channels and during the 1979 Vienna Summit.)

Due in part to the harsh Soviet reaction and the surfeit of public and journalistic queries, the administration clarified the human rights policy's parameters in a series of statements during Carter's first six months in office. Less than two weeks after Carter's inaugural claim for an "absolute" commitment, Secretary Vance clarified that the administration would comment when it was "constructive to do so" on a case-by-case basis.[20] In a March 1977 address at the United Nations, Carter expressed support for multilateral sanctions against Rhodesia and majority rule through peaceful means in South Africa. In recognition of the world's contempt for U.S. unilateralism, he acknowledged that America could help other peoples resolve their differences but could not do so "by imposing our own particular solutions."[21] One month later, Secretary Vance clarified the administration's definition of a "human right" with three categories drawn from the

Universal Declaration: integrity of the person (freedom from torture and arbitrary arrest), fulfillment of "vital needs" (food, shelter, health care), and civil and political liberties (freedom of speech, movement, and political participation). Vance promised that the administration would view each case individually, with due consideration to the nature of the abuses, the nation's importance to the United States, and the prospects for effective action. "We are embarked on a long journey," he proclaimed. "We can nourish no illusions that a call to the banner of human rights will bring sudden transformations in authoritarian societies."[22] President Carter then spoke in broad terms about his policy's practicality. Because the United States was now free from the "inordinate fear of communism," it no longer needed to dogmatically support anticommunist dictators. He assured his listeners that he understood "the limits of moral suasion" and had no illusion that changes would be easy or rapid. He would not practice foreign policy by rigid moral standards; nevertheless, he said, Americans should not undervalue the power of words and ideas. The world, he asserted, expected Americans to take a leading role in the modern democratic revolution.[23]

It was not until February 1978 that the administration finally consolidated all previous iterations into a presidential directive. The human rights policy was to apply globally, but with due consideration to other U.S. interests and the unique cultural, political, and historical characteristics of each nation. The administration would prioritize integrity of the person and civil and political liberties, while economic and social advances would be only "a continuing U.S. objective." Carter would use the full range of diplomatic methods, with a preference for the carrot over the stick.[24] That same month, Carter sent four international covenants to the Senate—covering civil and political rights, economic/social/cultural rights, the elimination of race and sex discrimination, and rights in the inter-American region.

These speeches and directives were groundbreaking articulations of American human rights policy thinking, and they demonstrated that the Carter administration was hardly naïve about the complex tasks they faced.[25] Yet one also gets the sense here that the administration was feeling the burden of its cause. For while human rights rhetoric had some popularity at home, such a policy commitment created a host of new problems, not the least of which was having to explain to Americans and the world what, exactly, Carter stood for. If he had downplayed these issues early on, he might have made more progress with autocratic regimes in private. But this would have given the impression that he was reneging on his promises.

As it was, his early enthusiasm required him to explain and re-explain his goals to supporters and opponents alike. Carter's team clarified the high points—they sought a serious, effective policy that would also take other national interests into account—but this selective posture was bound to make Carter appear inconsistent.

To activists, the Carter administration's early goals were erratically pursued. Because a president has a primary responsibility to maintain key security and trade relationships, Carter often clashed with congressional liberals who found his human rights posture lacking in vigor. Particularly divisive was legislation that brought human rights considerations into military aid and arms sales decisions. In order to maintain maximum flexibility, the administration often narrowly interpreted the law's definition of "consistent pattern" and "gross violation," and they routinely erred on the side of certification in order to encourage sales. Of the nearly seventy states that were potential recipients of U.S. security assistance or arms sales, the administration was reluctant to charge most offenders with engaging in a consistent pattern of abuse. Fourteen violators fell within the narrow definitions of the law at different times during Carter's presidency: Guatemala, El Salvador, Haiti, Nicaragua, Paraguay, Uruguay, Argentina, Bolivia, the Philippines, South Korea, Indonesia, Iran, Ethiopia, and Zaire. And even with these nations Carter routinely invoked the "extraordinary circumstances" clause.[26] Indonesia, South Korea, and the Philippines were strategic allies; Iran was a strategic ally and a supplier of oil. Even Zaire was granted an exception because it was the chief supplier of cobalt, a vital material in the production of turbine blades and jet engines. Ultimately, then, aid was reduced or terminated to only eight Latin American nations, and even in many of these cases the administration allowed substantial trade and loans.

A close look at the Christopher Group's records gives us a sense of just how complex human rights policymaking was at the bureau level.[27] The group, which included representatives from several federal agencies and executive departments, was charged with deciding whether allegations of a government's abuses were serious enough to warrant a "no" decision on arms sales, trade, and loans. This work involved many layers of bureaucracy. A staff-level working group screened all military and economic aid, multilateral development bank (MDB) loans, food aid, arms export licenses, and export credits to see if they met human rights requirements. In each case, they considered the severity of violations, the nation's stage of economic and political maturity, whether or not funds would help the needy, and overall U.S. interests. The working group recommended approval of the vast majority, either because the government in question was improving or because the loan or aid would meet another U.S. interest. If the working group decided that a government's record was bad enough to warrant further review, the Christopher Group reviewed it and, in most cases, recommended approval. Of the more than five hundred MDB loans they considered between April 1977 and April 1978, for example, the United States voted against only ten (Argentina, Chile, Paraguay, Uruguay, and South Yemen) and abstained from seventeen on human rights grounds.[28]

These votes invariably angered the would-be recipient without halting the loan or improving human rights. The World Bank granted nearly $3 billion to fifteen of the world's worst abusers in 1979 alone. Four erstwhile democracies—Uruguay, Argentina, the Philippines, and Chile—saw their World Bank loans increase from an average of $90 million per annum to $664 million in the 1970s, mainly because their governments were willing to impose austerity measures on their economies.[29] The Christopher Group and the human rights bureau saw their influence wane after Carter's first year as several other agencies and departments received exemptions from their oversight. The Department of Defense was able to exempt military assistance, the Treasury Department was able to exempt the International Monetary Fund, and the Agriculture Department and USAID exempted food and development aid to the poorest nations.[30]

As Carter settled into the presidency after his first year, his human rights policy faced a wide array of criticism. Critics called it moralistic, selective, confusing, and everything in between. Conservatives thought he was ignoring communists and targeting anticommunists, while liberals believed the opposite. Activists thought he was doing too little altogether. Others pointed out that such a policy created new and unexpected burdens. "Is Mr. Carter aware of the problems he is creating for American foreign policy by his damn-the-torpedoes approach on this question?" asked the *Washington Post* in 1977. "Whether other governments find us intrusive and arrogant (as they do) is not so important as that we have diminished our power to deal effectively with them."[31] Internal reviews found mixed results. A CIA assessment midway through 1978 suggested that American attention had contributed to greater global sensitivity, though disregard of human rights remained "a depressing fixture of the world scene."[32] By the end of 1978, the administration was touting results throughout Latin America, including the release of political prisoners (Peru, Argentina, Chile, Paraguay), announcement of democratic transition plans (Argentina, Bolivia, Peru, Ecuador, Chile), and new due process measures (Argentina, Bolivia, Colombia). But although Latin American citizens may have been more appreciative of American foreign policy under Carter, it is not so clear that American policies influenced all of these outcomes. By and large, the most significant factors were local.

Much like the Nixon-Ford years, the new policies elicited some resistance from the foreign policy bureaucracy.[33] Foreign service officers (FSOs) continued to worry that the administration's enthusiasm would hurt bilateral relationships, and many complained that the new human rights requirements created much more work for bureaucrats. One Christopher Group participant lamented that so many people were spending hours agonizing over mundane matters such as "whether some road in an AID project would benefit poor people." Another assailed the "broad-brush moralism" of the "uppity" new bureaucrats.[34] A high-ranking State Department official accused the administration of using South America simply to "show what they can do in human rights" because they saw little economic, strategic, or political importance in the region.[35]

The State Department human rights bureau was the source of much of this friction. On those frequent occasions when the bureau disagreed with an aid decision, it nearly always locked horns with the regional bureaus or members of Congress. Patricia Derian was a particularly tough advocate. "She was very clear about her views," one aide said of Derian's work in Argentina, "even to the point of being undiplomatic."[36] Activists and many scholars have found much to admire in Derian's zeal. But while she deserves credit for making human rights more visible, and even for saving lives and freeing prisoners in places like Argentina and Romania, it is worth asking whether her tactics were sometimes counterproductive. Because she lacked prior experience in foreign affairs, diplomatic language was not her strong suit, and she took an almost religious, all-or-nothing approach to human rights matters. One FSO asserted that Derian and her colleagues seemed to regard reasonable criticism of the human rights policy "as bordering on immorality or disloyalty to the administration. It is difficult to have a serious discussion with someone who thinks you are immoral." Similarly unimpressed was Assistant Secretary of State Terence Todman, a defender of realpolitik who broke with protocol by stating that the United States "must avoid holding entire countries up to public ridicule and embarrassment."[37] Many observers saw this open criticism as proof that the U.S. government was divided. Paraguayan dictator Alfredo Stroessner was jubilant, saying privately, "We survived John Foster Dulles telling us we should kill all our communists, and now we can survive Jimmy Carter telling us we should let them all go free."[38] (Todman was reassigned as ambassador to Spain.)

One of the most common criticisms was the charge of inconsistency, as some regimes were the target of close scrutiny while others were largely ignored. In reality, though, "consistency" was an impossible standard. Old friendships with undemocratic regimes could not be disregarded so easily, nor could Carter simply abandon newer relationships with regimes of the left. There was also disagreement within the administration as to which regions deserved the most attention. Jessica Tuchman of the NSC asserted that the human rights policy's bottom line was its "seriousness vis-à-vis the Soviet Union."[39] It soon became clear, though, that Latin American governments bore the brunt of Carter's attention and American aid cuts. Meanwhile, Carter had virtually nothing to say about abuses in China, Yugoslavia, and Romania. He was pursuing normalization of relations with China, and he wanted to showcase Yugoslavia and Romania as courageous opponents of Soviet domination.

Carter backed some humanitarian initiatives in Africa, and even became the first American president to pay a state visit to the sub-Saharan region. But his administration generally ignored the continent's worst regimes, in part because these nations were not vital to American interests and in part because Carter sought better relations with the developing world and the African American community.[40] His opposition to economic sanctions against Idi Amin's Uganda led Congress to embargo trade to that country in 1978. In North Africa and the Middle East, energy and security consistently took precedence over human rights in Saudi Arabia, Egypt, and pre-revolutionary Iran. The administration's major exceptions were the white-minority-led regimes in South Africa, Rhodesia/Zimbabwe, and South-West Africa (Namibia). Carter backed the United Nations' 1977 mandatory arms embargo against South Africa, called for a negotiated end to apartheid, and prohibited American enterprises from selling goods or weapons to the South African military and police. However, Carter did not support economic sanctions or a withdrawal of trade and investment, as these policies would have had a considerable economic impact in America. (His successor, Ronald Reagan, would be similarly opposed.) For the remainder of the 1970s and 1980s, most such pressure on South Africa would come from Congress or activists working in concert with the business community. In 1977, a board member of General Motors, Reverend Leon Sullivan, drafted a set of rules for American entities doing business in South Africa. Many companies voluntarily followed these "Sullivan Principles" with respect to issues like equal treatment and equal pay for black South African employees. The following year, Congress required the State Department to certify that these principles were being followed before it would approve credits for U.S.-South Africa trade.[41] But a major U.S. antiapartheid effort would have to wait until the 1980s.

These differing regional priorities gave Carter's policy an image of incoherence. Depending on one's ideological stance, the administration paid either too much attention to Latin America and too little to the Soviet Union, or vice versa. A critical observer commented that the president was essentially dividing the world into two categories: "countries unimportant enough to be hectored about human rights and countries important enough to get away with murder."[42] Carter might have been more successful in these early endeavors if he had clarified to the American public that consistency was impossible. But then, this might have sent the wrong signal to autocratic regimes, and it may have been more honesty than voters wanted.

American Hypocrisy? Carter and the Dictators

America's long-standing friendships with dozens of dictatorial regimes made Carter's pursuit more difficult. In Eastern Europe, he got mixed results in his early attempts to achieve a balance between his domestic political interests, East/West security requirements, and human rights concerns. Like his predecessors, he sought to build bridges to Poland, Romania, Hungary, and Yugoslavia in order to make the détente process more inclusive while showing American ethnics that he supported liberalization. As Zbigniew Brzezinski stated early in 1977, "We wanted to show that the road to Eastern Europe did not necessarily lead through Moscow."[43] But unlike Nixon and Ford, the Carter administration would sometimes reward states that improved their human rights records.[44]

The U.S.-Poland relationship demonstrated Carter's difficult balancing act. Poles already enjoyed the most religious freedom and property ownership of anyone in the Eastern Bloc, and Polish American NGOs lobbied both capitals for liberal reforms, more family contacts, and economic aid for the Polish people.[45] The Gierek regime in Warsaw, meanwhile, faced economic problems and public demands for higher living standards. The regime wanted to meet these needs while also calming Soviet fears by keeping reforms within narrow limits.[46] Since the nearly ten million Polish Americans constituted an important Democratic constituency, Carter hoped to please these voters while also cultivating a special relationship with the people of Poland. Consequently, during his December 1977 visit to Warsaw he proposed closer economic ties and suggested more social and economic reforms. As a result of Carter's visit, Gierek granted some concessions on emigration, and his government even broadcast the Carter-Gierek press conference in its entirety. Beyond these small steps, though, Carter could do little to change Poles' living conditions. He was also in the unenviable position of having to justify his scoring of President Ford over "Soviet domination." When an American reporter in Warsaw asked him if this domination might someday end, Carter gave a pro forma response emphasizing Poland's strong religious traditions and stated that "the will of the Polish people for complete preservation and enhancement of human rights" was "the same as our own." When asked whether he was denying Soviet domination, Carter refused to comment.[47] It had been much easier for him to condemn his opponent during the election than it was to bring substantive changes to Eastern Europe as a sitting president.

In East Asia, he had to balance his humanitarian goals with other interests in relations with South Korea, the Philippines, and Indonesia. He would have some successes, but ultimately he would side squarely with long-standing American economic and security interests. Indonesia's President Suharto was still holding twenty thousand political prisoners, and NGOs accused his military of brutal measures in the occupation of East Timor. Carter pursued a dual policy of strengthening relations and securing freedom for political prisoners through grants of U.S. arms and aircraft sales. But he largely ignored the violence in East Timor, as well as East Timorese claims to independence, despite mounting evidence of atrocities. And in justifying the arms sales to Congress, the administration obscured the fact that these weapons would likely be used in the occupied province. The administration also voted against U.N. resolutions that condemned the occupation, and they downplayed Indonesian forces' use of violence.[48] Carter continued to support aid and weapons sales under the guise of an "improving" situation in Indonesia, not East Timor.[49] When Assistant

Secretary of State Richard Holbrooke met with Suharto in 1977, he did not broach the atrocity allegations, and he accepted at face value Suharto's statement that his government "does not seek to hide anything." (Journalists and NGOs were barred from entering the country at the time.)[50] Congressional activists pushed the administration to alter its policies, but they were unable to stem the growth in military aid and weapons sales.

U.S.-Indonesia relations improved under Carter, and the administration did win the release of many prisoners. But this relationship came at a cost. Brad Simpson has argued that the administration's inattention to the East Timorese independence struggle enabled a "near-genocidal assault" on the breakaway province. Simpson rightly argues that many Western activists did not accept self-determination as a clear "right," though he and others downplay Indonesia's security concerns and Jakarta's ability to act without the blessing of the United States.[51] Since the United States was Indonesia's major benefactor, the violence in East Timor might have been considered a reason for Washington to halt arms sales, but Jakarta would surely have found other willing merchants.

South Korea was even more important to America as a result of the nations' long-standing special relationship, the proximity of a dangerous regime in North Korea, and the presence of forty thousand American troops. South Korea was authoritarian for most of its first forty years, during which the United States generally tolerated its undemocratic character while privately suggesting reforms. General Park Chung-hee, who had acceded to the presidency in 1961, maintained some vestiges of representative government, but his rule was otherwise heavy-handed and illiberal. Yet although he did not build a functioning democracy, he did oversee robust economic growth. Between 1968 and 1977, per capita income increased by a factor of four, leading one Western journalist to call South Korea "a nation with microwave ovens but little democracy."[52] The country was beginning to emerge as a modern economy alongside the other "Asian tigers" Hong Kong, Taiwan, and Singapore.

Overt U.S. concern for human rights in South Korea was rare before the Carter presidency. Above all, American policymakers wanted a strong, viable South Korea that could withstand the pressures of its neighbors. Most in Washington would have preferred a functioning liberal democracy, but the existential threat led the United States to downplay problems like political imprisonment and restrictions on political rights. As we have seen, the Nixon and Ford administrations had prioritized realpolitik and had tended to believe that Seoul was moving in the right direction, albeit slowly. American embassy officials met regularly with opposition figures and offered them quiet encouragement beginning in the mid-1970s, but the United States almost never publicly criticized Seoul. When Carter came to office, he followed Secretary Vance's recommendation for a quiet, high-level initiative on Korean human rights issues, and he announced that he would begin withdrawing American troops because Koreans had grown more self-reliant.[53] The United States had been considering a withdrawal since the sixties, but the North Korean threat and the misgivings of South Korean and Japanese leaders had always prevented it. In response to Carter's announcement, a veritable "Korea lobby" of American legislators, military commanders, and intelligence officers challenged the decision. Nevertheless, the first brigade withdrew on schedule.

As for human rights, Carter was polite but firm in his early dealings with President Park. He promised to maintain America's commitment, increase military equipment loans, and stay out of Korea's internal affairs. But he also emphasized that Congress, journalists, and the American public were paying close attention, and that Park's "sensitivity" to these issues would allow policymakers to justify a strong relationship. "Just as we intend to defend our relationships with your country," wrote Carter, "I request that you give consideration to what can be done in the human rights area in Korea."[54] He similarly told Foreign Minister Pak Tong-chin that the political prisoner problem was inhibiting American support, and that even small, "properly publicized" gestures from Seoul could "pay rich dividends in changing U.S. public attitudes." Pak emphasized the security situation and Asian exceptionalism. Korea's experience with democracy was relatively new, he pointed out, and its "assimilation of foreign concepts and ideas" was slow. Koreans "must be allowed to choose which problem among the many they face should be dealt with first." He insisted that Western-style individualism did not rank high on Koreans' list. In turn, Carter pointed out Americans' waning support for the relationship (only one in sixteen agreed that the United States should defend South Korea if it was attacked), and he suggested that in the absence of concrete reforms, such concerns would be "a cancer eating at the core of our relationship."[55]

Although Park did not want to make these concessions, the South Korean public widely supported expansion of personal and political rights. Park seemed to recognize that easing controls and releasing prisoners would help the bilateral relationship, but, wrote the U.S. ambassador, "I continue to be depressed about Park's inability to grasp realities of American politics after all these years of dealing with us."[56] Relations improved after Carter's first year, and it seems that the human rights policy got some results in 1977–1978. The CIA detected some "lingering resentment" over American interference, but also noted that Seoul had released some prisoners and eased up on surveillance of dissidents. In May 1978, Carter deferred two-thirds of the first troop withdrawal phase. He claimed that the decision was unrelated to South Korea's internal affairs, but he also told Park directly that he was gratified with the relaxations on political expression. An interagency study found that South Korea had done the most of any Asian government to improve its record, largely because of Park's sensitivity to external scrutiny and U.S. pressure.[57]

Carter's three-day visit to Seoul in summer 1979 was tense at first but ended amicably. In response to the ongoing security threat and Park's promises of further reforms, Carter agreed to pare down the troop withdrawal. (He would soon cancel it outright after only 3,600 were sent home.) Nevertheless, he was forthright in his public toast, pointing out the "growing consensus among the international community about the fundamental value of human rights, individual dignity, political freedom, freedom of the press, and the rule of law."[58] Seoul soon released eighty-six prisoners and implemented additional reforms, but a major crackdown on dissent halted this momentum for the rest of 1979–1980. Park's expulsion of an opposition party leader from the National Assembly spurred a violent political crisis and led Carter to briefly recall the ambassador. In Carter's last missive to reach Park before the latter was assassinated in October 1979, he cautioned that these events were damaging Park's support in America.[59]

Carter's forthrightness with South Korean leaders is very telling. Anyone seeking evidence that he was serious about human rights and that he understood the political difficulties posed by congressional activism need look no further than his conversations with Seoul. For although the political turmoil that followed Park's assassination caused the United States to ease up on its pressure, Carter continued to speak frankly with the Korean leadership. When Chun Doo-hwan emerged as the military strongman at the end of 1979 and assumed the presidency in August 1980, Carter informed him that Americans were greatly troubled by the crackdown on political rights and the trial of the opposition politician Kim Dae-jung. "We regard free political institutions as essential to sustaining a sound relationship," wrote Carter. "I urge you privately to take whatever steps are necessary to avoid having the issue of fair treatment erode your nation's relations with the United States."[60] As to whether he was emphasizing the power of Congress and public opinion as a means of pressuring Seoul to act, or if Congress and public opinion really were vital to improved relations, the answer lies somewhere in between. Carter may also have decided to continue pressuring Seoul during his final year in office because he was tilting to the right in South America and Europe. Either way, he consistently addressed Seoul's human rights record throughout his entire presidency, though security concerns led him to temper his comments with increased military support. Since he guaranteed the security commitment, South Korean leaders saw no need to make human rights a priority. In the bigger picture, neither the ongoing dictatorship nor the 1979–1980 crackdown led Washington to sanction Seoul.

There was some truth to conservatives' charge that Carter was focusing too much attention on nominal allies. The administration and congressional liberals paid far more attention to violations in South Korea, for example, than they did the far more egregious violations in the North. And of course, the dictatorships of Latin America received the lion's share of Carter's attention. Moderate and conservative Democrats—many of whom had only grudgingly backed Carter in 1976—joined with Republicans in criticizing these priorities. "If the foreign service prevails," wrote Senator Moynihan, "the secretary of state will soothe the Soviet Union and only challenge Ecuador."[61] In a widely read 1979 essay, the political scientist Jeane Kirkpatrick contrasted the "authoritarian" tendencies of right-wing regimes with the more extreme "totalitarian" tendencies of left-wing regimes. The former, she argued, were worth supporting because they offered their people more liberties and were able to change through democratic processes.[62] This "Kirkpatrick Doctrine" essentially encapsulated the neoconservative criticism of liberal human rights efforts. (Ronald Reagan was such a fan of Kirkpatrick's ideas that he would later appoint her as his U.N. ambassador.) Carter defended himself by pointing out that "world condemnation and our influence" were much more effective against right-wing regimes than against communist countries, "where repression was so complete that it could not be easily observed or rooted out."[63] Furthermore, policymakers expected more from a nation like Chile because of its democratic traditions, whereas a developing nation like Uganda had no comparable pedigree.

Carter's activism put him in a bind. He cared about human rights, but he also had to maintain national security and key relationships—a dual posture that many took as hypocritical. Realists like Nixon and Kissinger bore no such stigma because they did not acknowledge human rights as a proper subject for bilateral consultation. Activists accused them of callousness, not double standards. By contrast, since Carter had so inflated expectations during his campaign and at the outset of his presidency, activists were consistently disappointed with his record. His public diplomacy added fuel to the critics' fire. He gave a warm welcome to the Romanian and Yugoslavian dictators Nicolae Ceauşescu and Josip Broz Tito in 1978, and he won approval for a congressional renewal of most-favored-nation status for Romania. These actions made sense from the standpoint of geostrategy: he was pulling two communist states further outside Moscow's orbit, thus continuing long-standing policies. Tito and Ceauşescu were also considered important intermediaries to nonaligned states. Yet it was also clear that Carter was welcoming autocrats who granted their citizens few liberties. His May 1977 introductory missive to the eighty-five-year-old Tito could very well have come from any postwar American presidential administration. Referring to Tito's long-standing split with Moscow, he called the leader a symbol of Yugoslavia's "fierce spirit of independence" and noted that America and Yugoslavia had a "mutual commitment to the principle of undiluted sovereignty and the right of every nation to chart its own path." The United States, he promised, would continue to respect Tito's nonalignment and support Yugoslavia's independence. This was pure realpolitik, without a hint of humanitarian language.[64] Some ethnics and conservatives in America were unhappy that their president was hobnobbing with the likes of these dictators, but the policy remained intact without major congressional opposition.

Other state visits to Washington angered the political left. When Augusto Pinochet arrived in September 1977 to attend the Panama Canal treaty ceremony, Carter decided that a face-to-face meeting was the best way to let him know the feelings of the U.S. government. Yet although Carter succeeded in winning some concessions, such as allowing international observers to enter Chile, activists were livid. At a Lafayette Park rally, one demonstrator complained, "From now on, Jimmy Carter, you have given us the signal of what our attitude must be towards your administration. This administration is all lip, all words." Another called the visiting dictators of Paraguay, Uruguay, and Bolivia "the most motley collection of butchers ever assembled," akin to inviting "Franco, Hitler, and Mussolini."[65] Activists echoed these sentiments when Carter invited hundreds of NGO members to the White House the following year. "The

Carter administration," griped an Amnesty International board member, "has given human rights more public visibility but it still has relegated it to the status of a footnote to policy."[66] Considering Carter's unprecedented attention to abuses in Latin America, these evaluations were a bit unfair, yet they spoke volumes about activists' perceptions.

Some of Carter's other sins of omission incensed activists of both the left and right. He did not criticize the Khmer Rouge of Cambodia until April 1978, a full three years after the regime had begun its campaign of genocide. This was understandable from a political standpoint: his administration had no leverage in Cambodia, and the American public would not tolerate new adventures in Southeast Asia. Still, Carter's silence surprised activists, as did his later tilt toward the Khmer Rouge. Although in 1978 he was willing to call the Cambodian government "the worst violator of human rights in the world today," for reasons of geostrategy his administration gave verbal support to the regime after Vietnam invaded Cambodia in 1979. Because the United States was normalizing relations with China, Carter was willing to accept Chinese plans to arm Cambodia against Vietnam and the Soviet Union, and he did not dissuade the Chinese from invading Vietnam and setting off the Third Indochina War.[67] He went on to support U.N. recognition of Pol Pot's government, despite opposition from the State Department human rights bureau. This U.N. vote was an unmistakable sign that the administration was siding with China and Cambodia—strange bedfellows, indeed.

Carter's relationship with the Shah of Iran caused him the most trouble of all. By the mid-seventies Iran was no longer receiving U.S. military assistance, but the Shah was using his huge oil receipts to purchase over $1 billion in high-tech weapons per annum—roughly half of America's annual foreign military sales. Congress began criticizing Iran's arms buildup and human rights abuses during the Nixon and Ford years, but the nation's oil wealth prevented congressional activists from using economic muscle to encourage reforms. Carter's election spurred the Shah to pass some judicial reforms and allow human rights NGOs to enter the country. But although Carter wanted to limit arms sales and improve Iranian human rights, he essentially followed his predecessors' lead, emphasizing security and economic interests over Iran's internal policies.

The Shah was a difficult ally. The CIA concluded that he wanted to improve his global image and avoid problems in Washington, but he was also defensive and increasingly fatalistic. In an attempt to goad Washington into maintaining support, he went on a public offensive against America's "loss of will," its moralism, and its double standards. Why, he asked, was Iran being singled out? "There has been enough of this preaching, moralizing, telling others that they are trash," he told an interviewer. Carter's first letter to the Shah expressed hope for a continuing friendship, though he also presciently noted that there were "bound to be challenges to our common objectives."[68] When Secretary of State Vance visited Iran in May 1977 to discuss arms sales, he denied that Iran was being singled out, and he noted that the administration was encouraged by Iran's recent steps. In response to his Western critics, the Shah fell back on the cultural argument that his society could only handle very gradual changes. He also asserted that his country was threatened by "communists and assorted fellow travelers"—like all allies, he assumed that this was what the Americans wanted to hear. When Ambassador William Sullivan and the Shah had a frank discussion, the latter expounded what Sullivan called "a rather sardonic exegesis on the 'liberal' approach to human rights" before pointing out that he had halted torture and implemented further judicial reforms. He was doing these things for Iranians, he said; he was not "looking for favor from foreigners." President Carter tried to mend fences by pushing the sale of seven airborne-warning aircraft through Congress, but the eventual approval was a Pyrrhic victory, as the congressional debate further exposed the Shah's humanitarian shortcomings.[69]

By the time of the Shah's November 1977 visit to Washington, the administration believed that Carter's policy had had a positive impact in Iran, but they also foresaw negative pressures that might damage American interests. "Old habits die hard," wrote a Carter adviser. "The Shah tends to be both defensive and defiant on the subject of human rights." Vance advised the president to clarify the administration's seriousness, but he also admitted that there were few real options beyond recognizing positive developments. The crux of the relationship was strategic and economic, not humanitarian.[70] As it turned out, the Shah's Washington visit was a turning point, but not in the way that he or Carter had hoped. The two leaders saw eye-to-eye on most issues in private, but this restoration of amity was overshadowed by the riot that greeted the Shah's arrival.

When Carter visited Teheran a month later, he was more willing to speak out. "The interests of our nations are built on the interests of individuals," he asserted at the welcoming ceremony. "And in all of our discussions, both public and private, we emphasize guaranteeing our citizens the fullest economic and political human rights." That evening he toasted the Shah for making Iran "an island of stability" in a troubled region, and he stretched the truth somewhat by adding that the human rights cause "is one that also is shared deeply by our people and by the leaders of our two nations."[71]   Although   such   toasts   are   always   occasions   for   polite platitudes—especially in this case, because Carter was a political neophyte while the Shah had spent thirty-seven years on the Peacock Throne— activists and the global left bristled at what seemed a blatant *volte-face*. The French Communist Party newspaper *L'Humanité* asked how Carter could have "presented himself as the apostle of human rights" in Poland while remaining silent about the Shah's "torture and murder of opponents."[72] But more neutral observers noted that Iran's record had, indeed, improved and that the records of several other nations on Carter's itinerary were worse than Iran's.

Carter justified his fêting of the Shah by pointing out Iran's liberaliza- tion efforts, but his administration was still divided over U.S. support. At the end of 1978, with Iran on the verge of revolution, the administration stuck by the Shah. When Iran sought to purchase tear gas grenades for use against demonstrators, the NSC and the State Department judged that to do otherwise would anger the Iranian government, which would simply buy them from someone else. After Carter approved the sale, one disillu- sioned bureaucrat invoked Stephen Decatur, saying, "The White House attitude was very close to 'our Shah, right or wrong.'" Carter himself suc- cinctly explained to a group of activists the inherent dilemmas of human rights diplomacy: "Seldom do circumstances permit me or you to take actions that are wholly satisfactory to everyone."[73] His backing of the Shah would come back to haunt him when the Iranian revolutionaries took American hostages in November 1979.

The historian John Dumbrell is more or less correct in asking whether a change in policy could really have produced a different outcome. The security relationship was the first priority, and Carter did not press the Shah much on human rights. But Carter's appearance on the scene did encourage Iranian liberals and other opposition figures, and as the Shah's legitimacy slipped Washington did not know how to react.[74] However, whether American human rights policies had much to do with the opposition's boldness is not entirely clear. Cyrus Vance suggests that the human rights policy caused much less bilateral discord than some suggested and that the Shah's problems were of his own making. With too many competing interests to balance, he was unable to placate his critics with reforms and unable to restore order by force.[75] In retrospect, it is clear that Iranian revolutionaries were motivated by far more than a desire for individual liberties, as the nation's post-Shah implementation of an authoritarian, theocratic republic made abundantly clear.

China, too, largely avoided American criticism. Although Carter privately promised during the 1976 campaign that he would not "ass-kiss" the Chinese, he ultimately followed a Nixonesque policy of playing China against the Soviet Union and advancing normalization of relations.[76] China remained peripheral to his overall foreign policy, and Chinese human rights were barely a blip on his radar screen compared with violations in Latin America and Eastern Europe. Activists had little concrete information on abuses there, and the lack of full diplomatic relations during Carter's first two years limited his leverage. An NSC official summarized this problem regarding reports of Chinese labor camps: "Let us look forward to the day when our diplomatic relations with China are such that we can begin to raise this issue, and the Chinese will have a sufficient stake in their relationship with us that they will simply have to respond."[77] The administration argued that full relations would give the United States more influence, but to critics normalization looked like a major concession to an autocratic state. An August 1977 NSC review noted that normalization would "place some strain on the credibility of our human rights policy" because Carter was clearly prioritizing other considerations.[78] But Carter expressed optimism about China and its post-Mao economic reforms. A classified CIA report called China the most prominent case of a "poor-but-improving" record and argued that Chinese rhetoric showed "a new and noteworthy recognition . . . that such concepts matter to countries the PRC now finds it in its interest to cultivate."[79]

The apparent liberalization trend was evidenced in the Democracy Wall movement of 1978–1979, in which thousands gathered in major cities to hang posters critical of the government. Because Carter was still negotiating normalization, he did not publicly support the demonstrators, but instead noted that "there are public and apparently permitted demands or requests for more democratic government policies."[80] When Beijing cracked down on the movement and arrested its leaders in 1979, including the prominent democracy advocate Wei Jingsheng, the administration offered no protest. The political scholar James Mann has argued that Carter's actions in the Democracy Wall case undercut the moral foundation of his policy while also establishing a double standard in his approach to Soviet and Chinese dissidents.[81] On this point Mann is half right. Absent a "China human rights lobby" in America—or even an indignant NGO community and news media—there was only a minor American outcry against Beijing's practices. Moreover, considering Sino-American relations in the long term, it is worth asking what American interest would have been met by pressuring Beijing or halting the nascent engagement. Virtually every Asian government was authoritarian, and thus to some degree at odds with external human rights pressure. Perhaps most important of all, there was a general feeling in the Carter administration, in Washington, and even in the NGO community that East Asian societies could not be judged by the same standard as Greece or Argentina. A 1978 State Department study noted that although American pressure had elicited some changes among American allies in Asia, "The basic, underlying features of authoritarian rule generally remain intact."[82] For all of these reasons, American anticommunism did not translate into pro–human rights fervor in China as easily as it did in Eastern Europe, at least not until the Tiananmen Square massacre of 1989.

Nevertheless, the Sino-American normalization process proved tricky. The Carter administration was split between the Brzezinski camp, which tilted toward China as a means of countering Soviet power in Asia, and the Vance camp, which feared offending Moscow while the SALT II talks were in progress. Carter could also count on opposition from some pro-Taiwan congressional conservatives, and he hoped to avoid alienating moderates and pro-China conservatives. Much more was at stake than simply offending sensibilities, of course; normalization would facilitate substantial trade and arms sales. When the United States finally granted formal diplomatic recognition in January 1979, China was not required to alter its domestic practices. Carter even proposed, and Congress accepted, conditional most-favored-nation (MFN) status for China but *not* for the Soviet Union. Carter had first opposed MFN for both countries (Jackson-Vanik was aimed at the Soviet Union, but also applied to China), but he switched to a pro-China policy as part of his tougher anti-Soviet stand. Carter also revoked the U.S.-Taiwan defense treaty, sparking an unsuccessful legal challenge from some congressional conservatives and a backlash from Taiwan. Two weeks after the decision, a mob in Taipei attacked visiting Undersecretary of State Warren Christopher's car as he traveled into the city.[83]

Carter was essentially choosing expediency over idealism. By accepting that Beijing was ruling over nearly one billion Chinese, he was continuing a normalization process that had begun under Richard Nixon. He was also acknowledging that China's fabled market potential, which had enticed Western traders for centuries, seemed poised for development in the post-Mao era. Removing Jackson-Vanik restrictions and granting MFN status would most certainly stimulate trade. Moreover, conservative opponents of Carter's decision were generally still operating from the older, ideological position—they were far more pro-Taiwan than pro-Chinese-human-rights.[84] There was also the practical inapplicability of the emigration issue. When Vice Premier Deng Xiaoping visited Washington in January 1979, he insisted that his nation was cautiously liberalizing and that its internal issues could not be compared to those of the Soviet Union. Jackson-Vanik "really has nothing to do with China," he insisted to Carter. "Would you like to import ten million Chinese?"[85] This logic was good enough to win an MFN waiver and support from Senator Jackson himself, who believed that the chief danger to the United States was the Soviet Union. "Basic Soviet policies constitute a real threat to our interests and those of our allies," stated Jackson. "Basic Chinese policies do not."[86] In fact, Deng flatly refused to discuss human rights matters. Referring to the Chinese democracy movement, he simply said that this kind of thing would happen from time to time. Meanwhile, Carter went no further than a brief, fruitless intercession regarding Western journalists' freedom to operate in China without censorship. Even if Deng had been open to a discussion, internal documents make it clear that Chinese human rights were not a high Carter administration priority. The White House acted much as Richard Nixon had acted in 1972, stressing that China was changing for the better and that Carter's human rights commitment had to be considered in the context of his overall foreign policy.[87]

The Soviets were unhappy with discriminatory trade treatment, but Sino-American normalization turned out to be popular with most Americans. The diminutive Deng carried out a public relations coup during his cross-country trip, once even delighting onlookers by donning a ten-gallon cowboy hat at a Texas rodeo. Under Deng, Beijing was beginning to embrace the market reforms that would transform China into a manufacturing and trading powerhouse. After the Senate finally accepted MFN in January 1980, Sino-American trade doubled to $5 billion in one year.[88] Seven years after his visit with Carter, *Time* named Deng its "Man of the Year."

Carter's Activism in Latin America

By the end of Carter's first year in office, he was focusing most of his human rights attention on Latin America, especially South America. There were several reasons for this orientation. Washington had more leverage with these regimes than it had with the world's communist states, and in the late 1970s fewer Americans worried that Latin American nations would fall to Castroesque revolutionaries, though leftist activity did worry conservatives. There was also the profound nature of the region's violations. Military governments and state-sponsored violence were endemic. Uruguay had the world's highest ratio of political prisoners, leading Amnesty International to call it the "torture chamber of Latin America." Others were not far behind on the list of the world's most egregious offenders. The Carter administration directly sanctioned Brazil, the Central American states of Guatemala and El Salvador, and the states of the Southern Cone (Argentina, Chile, Paraguay, and Uruguay).

Carter's actions won him acclaim among activists throughout the hemisphere, but relations with most South American governments suffered considerably. Several responded to aid cuts by finding other sources of loans, aid, and weapons. Many Americans were similarly troubled by Carter's focus on the Western Hemisphere. The Republicans' nationalities division decried "the switch in the thrust of the human rights issue from the [Eastern European] captive nations to Latin America."[89] Likewise, conservatives attacked Carter's policy as "the new Big Stick" in Latin America and declared it a strategic cop-out that ignored near-civil-war conditions in the region.[90]

Nicaragua became an unexpected trouble spot for the administration. Anastasio Somoza had long kept a firm grip on power and distributed his impoverished nation's spoils to its landed elites. Opposition to his rule arose in the 1960s and 1970s, most notably in the form of the left-wing FSLN Sandinistas. In the interest of preventing another Cuba-like revolution, the United States had granted Somoza millions in military aid, training, and economic assistance, and in return Somoza had ensured stability and a congenial business climate for foreign investors and U.S.-based fruit growers. The Carter administration faced a difficult quandary.[91] Somoza was not democratically elected, and his National Guard was widely accused of violence against civilians in the name of counterterrorism. Yet he was

also a long-standing, anticommunist ally. In response to Democratic legislators' calls for military aid cuts, Carter mildly rebuked Somoza by temporarily withholding some military assistance, though he acquiesced in
allowing U.S. loans. But stability in Nicaragua was hard to come by, and in
1978–1979 Somoza's fate paralleled that of the Shah of Iran. In response to
riots and a general strike, a reluctant Somoza freed some political prisoners
and announced that he would allow an IACHR investigation. As conditions
worsened, the Cuba-backed Sandinistas ramped up their efforts and succeeded in seizing the congress building and taking fifteen hundred hostages.
The regime's heavy-handed response targeted many innocent civilians, thus
strengthening sympathy for the rebels.

American policymakers were divided between Somoza supporters and
those who wanted him replaced by the moderate FAO (Broad Opposition
Front). Carter decided to back Somoza for the time being while also promoting a plan to have Central American nations negotiate a settlement. Both
Somoza and the Sandinistas rejected the plan, as well as a later proposal for
a national plebiscite on Somoza's rule. Yet despite Somoza's obstinacy, Carter
continued economic aid in order to placate congressional conservatives. This
apparent inconsistency made Carter appear indifferent to human rights in
Nicaragua, though in reality he was focused on two other regional issues:
ratification of the Panama Canal treaties and Marxist revolutionaries' coup
on the island nation of Grenada. He was also distracted by the U.S.-Soviet
SALT talks and the events in Iran. Congressman Charlie Wilson (D-TX)
emerged as a prominent defender of the Somoza regime and an equally
prominent critic of the human rights bureaucrats. Upon visiting Managua at
the end of 1978, he argued that Somoza's fall would precipitate "three or
four more Cubas" in the hemisphere. He further assailed the "adolescent
anarchists" and "extreme left-wing ideologues" in the State Department's
human rights bureau for their indifference to Nicaragua's fate. Wilson threatened a tough fight on foreign aid and the Panama Canal treaties if Carter did
not defend the status quo in Central America.[92]

By summer 1979, with Somoza clearly on the way out, the administration was still divided. Carter backed Brzezinski's proposal of a coalition
government and the entry into Nicaragua of a transitional, inter-American
"peacekeeping force." But the moderate FAO did not have enough support
to assume power, while the Sandinistas had gained the most legitimacy by
waging a long-term struggle against the regime. Since the Sandinistas would
need economic support anyway, Secretary Vance argued that some U.S.

assistance would help Washington maintain leverage and avoid repeating the mistakes of 1959–1960, when American animosity encouraged Fidel Castro to tilt toward Moscow. Somoza fled the country on July 17, 1979, and a Sandinista-dominated coalition assumed power in Managua. Carter then proposed $75 million in economic aid as a means of locking out the Cubans and Soviets. Congressional conservatives blocked the aid until Carter could certify that the new government was not supporting guerrillas in nearby El Salvador. Carter did so, and the aid went through, prompting him to invite the Sandinista leadership to the White House in September 1979. But although the new government accepted the aid, it also kept Washington at arm's length. The junta then took a more radical turn and began to marginalize Nicaraguan democrats and crack down on dissent.

Conservatives like Ronald Reagan charged Carter with "losing" Nicaragua, much as the previous generation had said of Truman and Eisenhower with respect to China and Cuba. They claimed that Carter had fiddled while Moscow and Havana had established a beachhead in Central America, and they (inaccurately) assailed him for choosing human rights over anticommunism. In a biting critique, Jeane Kirkpatrick asserted that Carter had not simply "lost" Nicaragua, but that he had actually "brought down the Somoza regime." Carter was so committed to repudiating America's "hegemonic past" in the region, argued Kirkpatrick, that he removed ideology from his foreign policy and erected an impossible human rights standard that punished America's friends.[93] But in reality Carter's ability to influence events in Nicaragua had always been minimal. The Nicaraguan Revolution succeeded because the Somoza regime had mismanaged the country for decades, not because the United States had failed to shore up a vital ally. Carter might have prevented Somoza's fall with an immense infusion of money and arms, but this would have made him responsible for bloodshed on a mass scale. Still, Carter does deserve at least some blame for steering an ineffective middle course. Believing that Somoza was a major obstacle to a centrist democracy, his administration withheld aid, condemned him for human rights abuses, and eventually called for his resignation. As Scott Kaufman has argued, Carter's combination of "nonintervention with intervention" and "support for human rights with support for a repressive government" was inherently contradictory.[94] In the Reagan years, conservatives would take the Nicaraguan lesson to heart and would offer huge amounts of aid to the anti-Sandinista contras and the governments of El Salvador and Honduras.

Among the many troubled states of Latin America, Argentina was the target of the most U.S. scrutiny during the Carter presidency. The Argentine government's legitimacy was undermined in the mid-1970s by political and economic turmoil, triple-digit inflation, high unemployment, and left-wing extremists' killing and kidnapping of hundreds of soldiers, police, and civilians. In response to these problems, a March 1976 coup brought the military junta of General Jorge Rafael Videla to power. In what came to be known as the Guerra Sucia (Dirty War), the Videla regime incarcerated, tortured, and even killed thousands of suspects in the name of counterterrorism. The term *desaparecido* (disappeared) entered the lexicon to describe those whom the junta detained in secret locales or killed without trial. Between ten thousand and thirty thousand were secretly killed from 1976 to 1983, though the junta pled ignorance. General Videla once even gave a memorably disturbing, ambiguous response to questions about the *desaparecidos*: "The 'disappeared' are just that—disappeared. They are neither alive nor dead; they are disappeared."[95] A group of women began to hold regular vigils in front of the Casa Rosada in Buenos Aires demanding to know the whereabouts of their children. These "mothers of the disappeared" soon became a fixture of Argentine political life and the international human rights movement.

The Argentine junta received mixed signals from Washington. The U.S.-Argentina relationship had been defined by consistent U.S. support for anticommunist measures, millions in military aid and training, and development loans. The Department of Defense, in particular, had a close relationship with the Argentine military via the U.S.-based School of the Americas. When the coup took place in March 1976, there was some hope in Washington that it would mean greater stability, but these hopes turned to disappointment as the junta increased the level of repression in the name of counterinsurgency. In the waning months of the Ford presidency, U.S. Ambassador Robert C. Hill worked to free American citizens who had been arrested, and was even able to secure the release of some Argentines. But Ford was distracted by the presidential campaign, and Secretary of State Kissinger was unsympathetic to Hill's reports on extrajudicial violence. "Our basic attitude," Kissinger told the Argentine foreign minister, "is that we would like you to succeed [against left-wing terrorists]. I have an old-fashioned view that friends ought to be supported." The message of noninterference was clear. "Kissinger gave the Argentines the green light," said Ambassador Hill privately upon his exit from Buenos Aires.[96] In fairness to

Kissinger, it would have been more accurate to say simply that the secretary of state promised not to intervene; Kissinger did not need to "green-light" repression that was already taking place.

Jimmy Carter entered the White House ten months after the coup, and his early actions were consistent with his promises. He hoped to strengthen relations, but he also continued the congressional sanctions trend. In its early dealings with the Argentines, the Carter administration politely explained that the junta's actions were harming congressional opinion, while the Argentines defended their policies as proper responses to terrorism. With Carter's approval, Congress cut military aid from $48 million to $15 million in 1977. Carter went on to deny hundreds of millions in nonmilitary U.S. exports and Ex-Im Bank credits, and on several occasions he instructed his MDB representatives to abstain or to vote no.[97] (In four years, they would cast three nay votes against Argentina and would abstain twenty-five times.) But Carter still had to balance his human rights goals with America's security and commercial interests. When the Argentine junta sought to purchase $200 million in weapons and support during 1977–1978, Senator Edward Kennedy sponsored a bill calling for termination of military aid. Hoping to keep policy in the executive's hands, the White House convinced Congress to delay a cutoff. Then, over the opposition of the State Department's human rights bureau, the administration approved $120 million in nonlethal military hardware, the most ever allotted to Argentina. The junta's leaders began to believe that American support would continue, irrespective of the internal U.S. debate over human rights.[98]

Not only did Patricia Derian's human rights bureau face a difficult task in convincing the junta that the United States was serious, but she also had to persuade the State Department, the Defense Department, and ultimately the president to take her reports seriously. When she made her first trip to Argentina, she understood the terrorism problem but also surmised that American defense and intelligence agencies were subverting Carter's efforts and encouraging the junta. On a second visit in August 1977, she warned the interior minister and navy commander that Argentina was becoming "the next Chile" in the eyes of the world. After listing a litany of abuses (she later claimed to have confronted them on tortures taking place in that very building), her hosts responded that their sole interest was to restore stability and protect their people against terrorism.[99]

When General Videla met with Carter in Washington in September 1977, the three main sticking points were political prisoners, accounting for the disappeared, and the desirability of international inspection. Videla predictably emphasized the insurgency problem, though he did agree to address the disappearances and to release many of the four thousand political prisoners in exchange for Carter's support of arms sales. Carter was confident that further human rights progress would undercut terrorists' propaganda abilities, but progress was so slow that congressional sanctions continued.[100] By May 1978, Carter suggested that if the IACHR were allowed to visit, the administration would permit military training and would consider further concessions. Videla agreed to free more prisoners, but it became increasingly clear that the administration had few options to influence his behavior.[101]

The junta's record came into focus once again as a result of the massive Yacyretá hydroelectric dam project on the Argentina/Paraguay border. The Yacyretá story illustrates the dilemmas that a human rights policy posed in light of other national interests. The Carter administration rarely used trade sanctions to promote human rights, but this case was unique. When the dam was first planned, Argentina awarded U.S.-based Allis-Chalmers a $500 million turbine installation and support contract. Chalmers naturally sought Ex-Im Bank export financing, but the chief South American firm on the project was owned by the Argentine Navy, which activists accused of torturing internees. When the U.S. embassy sent this information to Washington, the Christopher Group and the State Department voted against financing. This was the first case of the U.S. government stopping nonmilitary trade for human rights reasons.[102] Chalmers, the Argentine government, and other potential contractors lobbied heavily for two months, but Warren Christopher defended the decision, telling a Chalmers executive that Argentina had not given them "even the most modest basis" for deciding otherwise. Furious with the decision, the Argentines charged that America's attitude amounted to "intervention" in the affairs of a nation under siege by terrorists. "It is sad to see that the sacrifices and hardships which the Argentine people have passed through . . . are so overlooked in such a flagrant manner," said the foreign minister.[103]

The administration faced a stark choice. If they denied the funding, U.S. exports would be reduced by $500 million, the trade deficit would rise, and Argentina would probably buy the equipment elsewhere. Worse yet, the funding denial was unlikely to soften the junta's domestic policies. "We get the worst of both worlds," an NSC adviser concluded. "Good policy avoids these no-win situations."[104] The administration then made it clear that if the junta invited the IACHR and freed some detainees, the funding decision would be reversed—terms to which Videla readily agreed. The journalist Iain Guest has suggested that the Argentines won out because the administration wanted the huge contract to go through. Not only was the junta making only a mild concession in allowing the IACHR visit, but they then delayed the commission's arrival long enough to clean up some evidence and they prohibited the visitors from seeing army bases. Still, the investigation uncovered so much evidence of abuse that the December 1979 final report included damning documentation of brutal prison conditions and over five thousand allegations of disappearances.[105]

By 1979, the evidence of torture and murder against the junta was overwhelming. "There is no longer any doubt that Argentina has the worst human rights record in South America," advised Patricia Derian. Still, it was hard for the Carter administration to win Argentine concessions or score domestic political points with its policy. Virtually every success was followed by a setback. After the IACHR completed its inspection, disappearances increased. And after Congress passed the arms embargo, the United States lost key leverage, and European companies were more than happy to fill Argentine orders. In a time of unprecedented trade deficits, American businesses lost an estimated $800 million in Argentine contracts.[106]

The Crises of 1979–1980 and the End of Détente

While Carter's attention to Latin America pleased at least some activists, his policies toward the Soviet Union seemed to please no one. As we have seen, after campaigning on a platform of tough talk against Soviet violations and Kissingerian diplomacy, he wavered between confrontation and quiet diplomatic efforts, and this vacillation led to accusations of incoherence. In time, Carter grew more vocal about the Soviets' foreign policy actions, not their internal policies. By mid-1978, he was accusing the Kremlin of using détente to continue an "aggressive struggle for political advantage and increased influence," and the Soviets were countering that the human rights policy had closed the door to other potential breakthroughs.[107] But while the Soviets consistently assailed outside interference, they also implemented a more liberal emigration policy, in part to alleviate domestic unrest and to facilitate trade.

Although Carter had cut back on his criticisms, in summer 1978 it became clear that a new crackdown was afoot. The State Department noted a "draconian effort" by the Kremlin to kill the dissident movement through public trials, harsh sentences, and new internal restrictions.[108] The trials and long sentences of Anatoly Shcharansky, Aleksandr Ginzburg, and Viktoras Petkus caused an outcry in the West and led Carter to restrict computer and oil drilling equipment sales—the first executive sanctions against the Soviet Union since the start of détente. The sanctions might have had more of an effect if not for the comments of Carter's U.N. Ambassador, Andrew Young, who told a French newspaper that there were "hundreds, perhaps even thousands" of political prisoners in America. The White House issued a public correction and a private reprimand, but the misstatement remained great fodder for Eastern Bloc propaganda. *Izvestia* asserted that Young's remarks constituted "an official admission of widespread political persecutions in the United States."[109]

After the dissident trials, U.S.-Soviet relations were dominated by the SALT II negotiations. Humanitarian issues were not a part of the arms talks, and they were only peripheral at the June 1979 Vienna Summit. In their only one-on-one meeting in Vienna, a visibly ill Brezhnev surprised Carter by raising human rights first. Reading from prepared notes, he argued that there could be no progress if trade was tied to human rights, and he assailed the "attempts to exploit [internal matters] in the relations between states." After all, he pointed out, the Soviet Union did not relate trade to America's unemployment rate or its racial discrimination. The two sides should concentrate instead on "safeguarding the right of people throughout the world to live without war." Carter acknowledged the Soviets' more open emigration policy, but he stood his ground on the appropriateness of his cause. Americans took human rights seriously, he suggested, and the Soviet Union had willingly signed the Helsinki Accords.[110]

But no agreements came of this brief chat, and Carter would have no luck with Brezhnev in the months to come, either. Their exchange in Vienna demonstrated the standard East/West divergence of views. Whereas many American policymakers considered Soviet human rights concessions essential prerequisites to a better relationship, Soviet leaders countered that American "interference" was, itself, the chief obstacle to détente. Nixon and Ford had only reluctantly raised such issues in order to highlight congressional obstruction, but Carter was the first to defend human rights principles directly with a general secretary. Brezhnev was reflecting not only

a long-standing Soviet negotiating principle, but also a genuine bewilderment as to why dissidents mattered. The Kremlin could not understand
why the Americans would imperil relations over Shcharansky, who was, in
Andrei Gromyko's words, merely "a microscopic dot on the landscape."[111]
The dissidents themselves soon learned that the Vienna Summit would not
meet their high hopes for major concessions and freeing of political prisoners. Instead, as Raymond Garthoff has argued, the summit only temporarily
interrupted the decline in détente.[112] Bilateral trust had been waning for a
few years, and a combination of rising conservatism in America and continuing human rights accusations (albeit not from Carter) had kept the Kremlin on the defensive. The July 1979 decision to grant MFN status to China
further angered the Soviets because they had hoped to win the same
through a more liberal emigration policy.

The human rights policy was already wavering midway through Carter's
presidency as a result of public criticism, international difficulties, and
intra-administration conflicts. The final straw came with the international
crises of 1979–1980—the Soviet invasion of Afghanistan, the Iran hostage
crisis, and the Nicaraguan Revolution. As Red Army tanks were heading
toward Kabul in the final days of 1979, a terse *Washington Post* headline
said it all: "Détente Is Dead." Worse yet from the standpoint of human
rights, this tectonic strategic shift was accompanied by new East/West animosity and a major crackdown on dissent in the Soviet Union.[113] Dozens
were arrested, and Andrei Sakharov was sent into internal exile following
the KGB charge that he had taken measures "to build a unified block of
anti-Soviet elements inside the country." The U.S. embassy in Moscow
called the crackdown "possibly the most severe and sustained action in the
recent history of the Soviet human rights movement."[114] In response to
Soviet and Iranian belligerence, as well as double-digit inflation at home
and a formidable election-year challenge from within his own party, President Carter shed the vagaries of moral appeals in favor of the pre-Vietnam
certainties of overt anticommunism. He never abandoned his principles
altogether, but he became convinced that the only appropriate strategy for
his foreign policy—and for his reelection—was the Cold War reorientation
advocated by Zbigniew Brzezinski.[115]

The Carter administration's rhetoric and policies shifted from liberal
internationalist goals such as human rights and arms control to security
and defense. Carter also muted moral rhetoric during his final year, much
as President Ford had done with respect to the term "détente" during *his*

final year. Brzezinski later wrote that human rights "tended to overshadow the pressing requirements of strategic reality" early on. Consequently, in 1979–1980 the administration "had to make up for lost time, giving a higher priority to more fundamental interests of national security." Not everyone appreciated this sweeping shift. Patricia Derian later wrote that Brzezinski "tried to cut the throat of everyone who stood in the path of his power and strategic principle."[116] Secretary of State Vance, who found himself increasingly marginalized, resigned following the failed April 1980 hostage rescue attempt in Iran. America's European allies felt threatened by what they considered Carter's revival of hostilities with Moscow.[117] Congressional liberals also challenged Carter's right turn. Senator Edward Kennedy entered the presidential race as a liberal alternative to Carter and mounted a serious challenge all the way to the Democratic convention in August 1980.

Several domestic factors contributed to Carter's turnabout. First, his promises during the 1976 election and early in his term led to inflated expectations and later public perceptions of failure. In light of these expectations, writes Jack Donnelly, it was perhaps inevitable that many observers would judge American actions as "heartless and inconsistent."[118] After Carter left the presidency, even he acknowledged that he had not fully grasped all of the policy's ramifications.[119] A second reason for his change in priorities was that work on behalf of dissidents and political prisoners paid few political dividends. Ethnic interest groups certainly influenced Carter's embrace of the dissident cause, but he could never placate all of these constituents. He had a limited ability to influence the internal policies of the Eastern Bloc, and he had even fewer electoral motives to help dissidents in places like South Korea and Uruguay.

Third, and perhaps most important, the human rights policy did not unite the American public as the administration had hoped. The apparent political consensus in 1976 had been largely anti-Washington in nature; once the Nixon/Ford administrations were out of the picture it was much harder to unite people under the human rights banner. In a Council on Foreign Relations poll two years into Carter's presidency, respondents ranked promoting and defending human rights tenth out of thirteen foreign policy goals, and only 1 percent mentioned human rights as an important foreign policy problem.[120] Another poll showed that the American public agreed with U.S. human rights pressure, but not when it undercut other national interests. Fewer than 10 percent thought that condemning Soviet treatment of Jewish dissidents was more important than SALT II.[121]

A human rights policy could not build consensus in the way that anti-communism had in the 1950s and 1960s. The Cold War struggle against communism had united Americans behind domestic and international crusades, including everything from expansion of the defense industry to construction of the interstate highway system. This national unity grew, in part, from the fear of communist incursions into North America and other regions of vital interest. But because human rights policies were aimed at foreign governments' treatment of faraway people, rights issues did not have the same resonance. As David Skidmore has argued, anticommunism justified containment and interventions under the guise of a direct threat to the United States, while human rights merely called for altruism in response to largely unseen, faraway abuses.[122] The drop in congressional support also influenced Carter's policy shift. Many congressional activists were ousted in the 1978 midterm election, including Donald Fraser. These losses stemmed primarily from the conservative voting trend and the majority party's traditional difficulties during midterms. Nevertheless, the results hindered the movement in Congress.

As Carter tilted back to a more traditional anti-Soviet posture, he began to shore up relations with authoritarian states like Pakistan, Somalia, and China. By his final year, 75 percent of America's total Africa aid was going to the Horn of Africa, where Somalians were fighting a proxy war against the Soviet-backed Mengistu regime of Ethiopia. The administration also lobbied Beijing and Pakistan to assist anti-Soviet forces in Afghanistan in exchange for American communications equipment, helicopters, and radar systems. The State Department's human rights reports were only mildly critical of China.[123] Carter also changed course in Latin America. Stung by international rebukes and American policies, the Argentine junta had begun selling tons of grain to the Soviet Union in exchange for support in multilateral forums. In response, the Carter administration stretched the definition of an "improved" human rights record and approved nearly $80 million in credits to Buenos Aires while also lobbying them to join the grain embargo against the Soviets.[124] Military aid stayed off the table, but arms sales to some South American governments resumed. This is not to say that the administration stopped pressing Argentina on human rights in 1980. Carter continued to call for due process for the accused, political prisoner releases, acceptance of international investigations, and an end to torture and disappearances. By May, the junta had limited its grain sales to the Soviets and joined the Olympic boycott. But the message to Latin American governments was clear. If they threatened to engage with Moscow, then Washington would respond by offering more aid and weapons.

Carter's outlook on Central America changed significantly in summer and fall 1979, when the Sandinistas took power in Nicaragua and a military/civilian junta gained control in El Salvador. Amid the bloody civil war that broke out in El Salvador, the administration supported the ruling coalition in the hope of cultivating moderates and preventing a revolution. But because this was a civil war and not a simple case of state oppression, American policymakers were unable to develop a coordinated effort on the political or human rights side. Early in 1980, over activists' objections, Carter agreed to a nominal $5 million, nonlethal military assistance package. In March, the outspoken Archbishop Óscar Romero was killed by members of a progovernment death squad while celebrating mass. Nevertheless, the administration went forward with plans to supply another $5 million, this time to provide weapons and counterinsurgency training. Carter cut military and economic aid in response to the brutal killing of four American nuns, but he soon resumed it after junta moderates promised reforms and a murder investigation. In December 1980, the civilian José Napoleón Duarte became the junta's leader, and Washington received intelligence that Cuba and Nicaragua were funneling troops and weapons into El Salvador. When the left-wing FMLN began a full-scale attack on the Salvadoran government and military in January 1981, it seemed to confirm these reports. Carter approved the release of lethal military aid to the Salvadoran junta, and he cut the remaining economic aid that was apportioned for Nicaragua.[125]

The Carter Legacy

Scholars and pundits still debate several questions about Carter's human rights policy. Did it improve human rights practices? Was it good for America? How influential was Carter in the larger human rights story, and how influential were Congress, NGOs, and global events? If Carter had never been elected, would human rights practices (or American foreign policy) have suffered, improved, or remained much the same? Activists find much to admire in the Carter administration's record in international human rights. He took a fledgling movement and helped to institutionalize it. His presidency lent more visibility to the cause and gave hope to the persecuted. Indeed, many dissidents welcomed the support of the American government, even if this was often only rhetorical. When Andrei Sakharov was asked in 1977 if Carter's position had led the Soviets to increase pressure on dissidents, he answered, "Categorically—no! Repressions are our daily life."[126] Carter's policy helped restore America's democratic reputation, and it boosted the morale of activists worldwide.

With respect to Latin America, Carter made a difference in South America but had little effect in Guatemala and El Salvador. "Perhaps nowhere in the world," concludes Kathryn Sikkink, "was Carter's human rights policy more forcefully implemented than toward the countries of Latin America's Southern Cone."[127] Deeply ingrained anticommunism and the State Department's inertia inhibited the policy's effectiveness, but as a result of his vigilance—in conjunction with congressional actions and the State Department country reports—various forms of assistance were cut to Chile, Argentina, Brazil, Uruguay, and Paraguay. American military aid to the region fell from $233.5 million to $54 million between 1976 and 1979. Perhaps more important, disappearances in Argentina and torture in Uruguay and Paraguay declined through a combination of those nations' changing domestic situations, U.S. policies, and increased international attention.[128] In Chile, U.S. pressure played a role in the reduction of torture, disappearances, and political imprisonment. Not only did the Carter administration pressure General Pinochet to release political prisoners, but Chile dissolved the state security apparatus following a visit from Assistant Secretary Todman in 1977. The U.S. embassy also increased its contacts with opposition groups.[129]

Carter's supporters could point to Paraguay as a place where the human rights policy got clear results. The long-reigning dictator Alfredo Stroessner, who had ruled his country for more than two decades, was a pariah in Washington. Under Robert White's ambassadorship, the United States formed contacts with the opposition and intervened to free some dissidents. When Stroessner arrested leaders of Paraguay's fledgling labor movement, pressure from Washington and international NGOs freed them within two months. Carter also convinced Stroessner to allow a visit from the IACHR, and he expressed willingness to support IADB loans if the dictator showed more signs of restraint.[130] Nevertheless, Stroessner remained firmly entrenched in power, and the dictatorships in nearby Argentina, Chile, and Brazil made it easier for him to justify his autocratic methods. Carter's

critics were at least partially correct in arguing that he was tough on Paraguay because the United States had few interests in the small, landlocked
nation. And although neither Paraguay nor Chile would receive much U.S.
support throughout the Carter and Reagan presidencies, both dictatorships
would last until the very end of the 1980s.

Cuba gives us another good example of the human rights policy's lack
of political dividends.[131] Carter's efforts to forge a détente with Cuba were
frustrated by a combination of Cuban Americans' opposition and Fidel
Castro's international adventures. (By the end of the seventies, Cuba had
forty thousand troops in a dozen countries.) Despite the lack of leverage,
the administration's secret negotiations won the release of three thousand
political prisoners and facilitated the visits of eighty thousand Cuban
Americans to Cuba. But even though Castro admitted that Carter's policy
was one factor in his decision to release prisoners, these results did little for
Carter politically because few Americans were aware of the negotiations. As
an NSC adviser wrote in a classified memo, the prisoner release "represents
one of Carter's best human rights achievements and an acknowledgement
by Castro of political persecution," but the administration had failed to
take credit.[132] Indeed, Carter actually looked worse in the eyes of Cuban
Americans and the world because the bureaucratic machinery in Washington was slow to process refugees from the 1980 Mariel refugee boatlift.
What seemed at first to be an American victory over a repressive regime
turned into a political loss for Carter during the 1980 election season, for
Castro not only sought to rid his country of troublesome citizens, including
some criminals and mental patients, but also hoped to expose Carter's false
bravado on human rights.[133] Conservatives and Cuban exiles welcomed the
exodus, but many other Americans falsely perceived that Castro had simply
emptied his prisons onto American shores.

On a more positive note, the Carter administration succeeded in publicizing the plight of, and even saving the lives of, many individual dissidents
and prisoners. Patricia Derian was particularly active in Argentina, where
her reputation reached far beyond the halls of government. The Argentine
news editor and erstwhile political prisoner Jacobo Timerman, who was
released because of outside intercession, stated, "I know positively how
many lives were saved because Patt Derian was making a great scandal."
Although U.S. human rights policies would not change governments,
argued Timerman, they had a value that outweighed their inherent limitations: "What a human rights foreign policy does is save lives. And Jimmy

Carter's policy did."[134] American pressure freed prisoners in other regions as well. The Soviet Union freed or exiled some dissidents and increased its emigration allowance, though the émigré numbers fell rapidly after the Afghanistan invasion. Romania, too, increased its emigration numbers in response to efforts by the Carter administration and the West German government.[135] Patricia Derian convinced the governments of Bangladesh and Pakistan, among others, to free hundreds of political prisoners after making personal visits to their capitals.[136]

The Carter administration's human rights policy also had considerable weaknesses. It could not overcome the perception of its internal contradictions or the impossibility of evenhandedness. His tough campaign rhetoric paid off in the 1976 election because these matters were a point of vulnerability for President Ford, but by inflating expectations Carter limited his own freedom of movement. It is difficult to avoid the conclusion that he made a mistake in pushing human rights so hard during the campaign and in his first year. It was not the case that the American public accepted Carter's liberalism and moralism only to abandon both as the global situation intensified in 1979–1980. It is more accurate to say that he never had much of a moral mandate to begin with. He was barely elected in one of the closest races in U.S. history, and when activists complained that he was not doing enough, they really meant that he was not doing as much as they wanted or expected. They could not really accuse him of being "against" human rights.

Carter often wavered when dealing with undemocratic regimes, and this combination of sanctions and support usually hurt relations while not necessarily improving human rights. It also hurt him domestically, because the denial of credits and funding meant the loss of millions in contracts. "If we stop arms sales to a dictator and France steps into the void," concluded a Carter cabinet member, "it is not clear that we advance anything except our moral purity."[137] Just as conservatives criticized interference in commerce, liberal activists decried Washington's tendency to rubber-stamp arms sales. As one group of NGOs put it, the administration's justifications on national security grounds were "so broad and diffuse that U.S. support for human rights can amount to little more than a series of statements of concern."[138] The State Department country reports further symbolized the executive branch's ambiguity. When the first few sets were released to the public in 1978 and 1979, activists criticized them for their brevity and their tolerance of allies' abuses. Some asked why the U.S. government needed to apply more layers of bureaucracy rather than obtain this information from non-governmental sources. Even Patricia Derian doubted that the reports would improve human rights. More likely, she argued, the State Department would have to "spend months assuring everyone that we do not feel that we are better than all other nations."[139]

The administration's awkward bifurcation was also clear in the U.S.-Soviet relationship. When Carter worked to maintain détente while also making humanitarianism a subject of bilateral discussion, the Soviets predictably closed ranks. Ambassador Anatoly Dobrynin concluded that Carter's human rights policy, while sometimes well intentioned, was also "a convenient propaganda weapon" for the Kremlin that did more harm than good to relations and even to human rights in the Soviet Union. When Carter invited dissidents to the White House to show support for individual freedom, the Kremlin saw only provocation.[140] His concrete successes—freed political prisoners and increased emigration numbers—were the work of painstaking private diplomacy, and might have been achieved without the public rhetoric, or even by another presidential administration if Carter had never been elected.

Since human rights possibilities were sharply reduced as Cold War tensions returned in 1980, it is also worth asking whether Carter overreacted to the Soviet invasion of Afghanistan. His tough reaction was justifiable if, as Zbigniew Brzezinski argued, the invasion was the culmination of years of Soviet provocation and growing American anxiety over Soviet intentions. In this scenario, a tough response was necessary to shore up America's regional interests and to inform the Kremlin that America would not accept their expansionism. But Carter's response now appears to have been largely political. Public opinion favored a strong anti-Soviet stand, and in an election year Carter may have felt obligated to roll with the tide. Either way, during his final year the United States lost its leverage over Moscow, citizens in the Eastern Bloc experienced renewed repression, and Carter reembraced right-wing dictators in the developing world. Human rights suffered because of the renewed Cold War.

As for parallel developments in Iran, it is difficult to gauge the extent to which Carter's foreign policy was responsible for the revolution, the Shah's fall, the hostage crisis, and the creation of an Islamic theocracy. But his efforts and those of the international community likely played a part in the Shah's mild liberalization efforts, which in turn provoked further public assertiveness in Iran. Carter's repeated public backing of the Shah and his continuation of billions in arms sales tied the United States to the Shah in the minds of many Iranians. The administration's actions in the Philippines had a similar effect. The United States tripled military aid in order to maintain the U.S.-Filipino military base agreements, but this may have hurt the United States in the long run by tying it more closely to the authoritarian regime of Ferdinand Marcos. (The long-term consequences were clearly direr in Iran, which became an anti-American state.)[141]

Even in Latin America, Kathryn Sikkink has shown that Carter could not showcase any dramatic "success story." At the end of his term, El Salvador and Guatemala were devolving into terrible civil violence and the Southern Cone states were still under repressive regimes.[142] True, the administration won freedom for some Argentine political prisoners, but the policy's broader effects on Argentina are debatable. The administration allowed the junta to buy an unprecedented amount of military hardware before finally terminating arms sales. And although the junta improved its behavior somewhat after the cutoff, the generals simply purchased weapons from other countries. The administration's nay votes and abstentions in MDBs were fundamentally symbolic. Moreover, the junta was able to secure millions of dollars in private loans from American investors.[143] Ultimately, Carter had a limited ability to prevent Argentines from oppressing Argentines. The "Dirty War" was a quasi–civil war, and the Argentine junta was willing to use violence to counter what it considered a serious internal threat. It was far less willing to heed the threats of activists in Washington.

Carter's multilateral efforts were also largely unsuccessful. His inability to secure Senate ratification of the human rights covenants symbolized the deeply rooted American fear of multilateralism. Nonratification was also a consequence of the low priority Carter accorded these treaties. He had to choose his political battles. Because he focused his human rights energies on high-profile cases in Eastern Europe and Latin America, items like the Genocide Convention fell by the wayside. As for his relations with the Senate, he spent the bulk of his political capital pushing for ratification of the Panama Canal Treaty and SALT II. Powerful senators like Strom Thurmond (R-SC), Jesse Helms (R-NC), and Robert Byrd (D-WV) disliked all of the human rights treaties in principle, as did many conservative voters. Thus the administration tabled the genocide pact during the canal negotiations because Carter did not want to give his antagonists another rallying point.[144]

Considering Carter's prominence among the political actors of this era, it is easy to overstate his influence on the human rights story.[145] A counterfactual question is worth considering. Would the American human rights policymaking narrative have been decidedly different if Jimmy Carter had lost the 1976 election to Gerald Ford (as he nearly did)? We cannot know the answer, of course, but it is not hard to imagine a scenario in which a reelected President Ford would have placated his party's ascendant conservative wing by jettisoning Henry Kissinger and forging a path that reflected his own moderate political beliefs. If he had attempted to move the party to the right or to continue Nixonian realpolitik, this would surely have emboldened the Democrat-dominated Congress to further restrict presidential power through new human rights requirements. In this scenario, then, the human rights cause would have moved forward, albeit in a slightly different form, even without Jimmy Carter.

But this is just conjecture. If we take a close look at Carter's record, it is hard to deny that his policies had at least some effect on global events. In the short term, he showed the world—especially South Americans—that mere anticommunism would not be enough to ensure American support. This turnabout helped convince some governments to adjust their practices. Carter was not too far from the mark when he said to the Organization of American States after losing his reelection bid, "Today no government in this hemisphere can expect silent assent from its neighbors if it tramples on the rights of its own citizens. The costs of repression have increased, but so have the benefits of respecting human rights."[146] Despite some activists' disappointment, those who understood the complexities of the policymaking process were more forgiving. In the words of AIUSA director David Hawk, "Anyone who worked in the field of human rights before Carter became president can appreciate the difference he makes."[147]

It is difficult to define Carter's role in the democratization trend that swept the world in the late 1970s and 1980s—a period that saw democratically elected governments replace undemocratic ones worldwide. Nor can we gauge the precise extent to which he contributed to the weakening of communism in Eastern Europe. Yet although it was the peoples of Eastern Europe who would overturn their governments a decade later, we must credit Carter with giving a shot in the arm to the dissident cause and the Helsinki follow-up process.[148] Moreover, his human rights policy further developed the language and the tools with which the incoming Reagan administration could hammer at the Soviet Union in the 1980s. In the final analysis, whatever weaknesses Jimmy Carter had as president, he did as much as any major political actor in the world to further the cause of international human rights.

Chapter 4

Ronald Reagan and the New Conservative Internationalism

Never, perhaps, in the postwar decades was the situation in the world as explosive and hence, more difficult and unfavorable, as in the first half of the 1980s.
　　　—Mikhail Gorbachev

President Gorbachev's assessment is rather surprising to the twenty-first-century reader, not only because the postwar era was so often fraught with international tension, but also because popular memory of the 1980s is dominated by sanguine images of the decade's endpoint—the Reagan-Gorbachev summits, glasnost, and jubilant crowds celebrating the fall of the Berlin Wall. Yet Gorbachev's judgment is accurate. The hardening of Moscow's internal policies and the corresponding U.S. military buildup brought U.S.-Soviet relations to their lowest point in at least two decades. Following the Afghanistan invasion, the Kremlin exiled the prominent dissident Andrei Sakharov, broke up the various Helsinki groups, and cut emigration to a trickle. Other Eastern Bloc governments also imposed harsh measures, the most notorious of which was Polish authorities' declaration of martial law in 1981. "Not since Stalin's time has the Soviet Union been engaged in such a severe and unrelenting crackdown on dissenters of all kinds," concluded Helsinki Watch.[1]

In exploring the human rights story during Reagan's first term, this chapter makes three broad claims. First, human rights debates and policies were filtered through the first Reagan administration's obsession with events in Central America (especially Nicaragua and El Salvador) and Eastern Europe (especially the Soviet Union and Poland). Second, the administration did not ignore human rights altogether, but rather interpreted human rights goals to coincide with the narrow interests of Cold War anticommunism. In practice, this meant improving relations with the authoritarian, right-wing regimes of East Asia and Latin America while castigating the human rights records of the Soviet Union, Cuba, and Nicaragua. This controversial posture fueled fierce domestic debates. As Robert M. Collins astutely observes, "Reagan's Cold War abounded in the sort of moral compromises Americans found troubling."[2] Indeed, Congress challenged the administration's approach from the start, as evidenced by the struggle over his Central America policy. Third, U.S.-Soviet tensions limited Washington's ability to influence internal policies in Eastern Europe and in the developing world, and it encouraged the administration to improve relations with China. But perhaps the most significant development of Reagan's first term came at its endpoint, when the administration began to shift its policies to the center and even began to apply pressure to long-standing allies.

The Reagan Foreign Policy Record

The image of Ronald Reagan so dominated American politics in the 1980s that it is easy to forget just how unlikely his presidency really was. Although the political establishment of the 1970s considered the former actor and two-term California governor too extreme for the voting public, he mounted a remarkable comeback in 1980. He entered the White House hoping to revive the nation's prestige, strengthen its military, and reorient foreign policy to the ideological simplicity of the 1950s. Not only was this approach consistent with his image as a conservative anticommunist, but it was also a continuation of Jimmy Carter's tough turn. Reagan went even further than his predecessor in reenergizing the containment doctrine. He believed that Carter's failure to project national strength had emboldened the Soviets and the revolutionaries in Iran and Nicaragua. Reagan, by contrast, promised to challenge Soviet aggression and support anticommunists in the developing world. During his first few years as president, he expounded a Manichean worldview of communism and capitalism, regularly accusing Soviet leaders of crushing individualism in the Soviet Union and using regional proxies to foment Third-World revolutions.[3]

Reagan's personality drove his policies. He had an unimpeachable faith in individual liberty, free market economics, and the power of religion. When it came to policymaking, he was no technocrat. He had so little interest in the minutiae of arms negotiations or economic indices that his advisers limited their memos to only a few pages. Gorbachev later wrote that Reagan "preferred discussing general politics" rather than complicated technical issues.[4] His relatively uncomplicated outlook was reflected in his penchant for personal diplomacy and pragmatic solutions. Despite his reputation as an inflexible conservative, he would happily meet with his political rivals if it meant the possibility of an understanding. Even his opponents marveled at his personal political style and his ability—developed through his years as an actor and advertising pitchman—to reach audiences through anecdotes, jokes, and homespun wisdom.

Ronald Reagan did not embrace Nixonian realism, nor did he overturn the new human rights laws, but human rights were definitely a low administration priority early in his presidency. The Kirkpatrick Doctrine became the foundation of his approach. The administration would challenge communist states and support friendly, right-wing governments, often to the point of overlooking blatant transgressions. Reagan created or extended security agreements with these governments and increased aid on ideological grounds, a policy that was especially controversial in war-torn Central America, where government security forces were responsible for torturing and murdering thousands. In Eastern Europe, he stridently embraced the dissident cause, and he became the first president to hold an annual signing ceremony for Captive Nations Week. He also sent a message by nominating a critic of liberal human rights diplomacy, Ernest Lefever, as his assistant secretary of state for human rights. As Stefan-Ludwig Hoffmann has aptly noted, the administration's embrace of containment was a way to reclaim political power from the liberal internationalists by assisting anticommunist movements and shoring up traditional alliances.[5]

The administration's foreign policy changed considerably after these first few years. One of the singular political stories of the era was Reagan's transition from a dogmatic hard-liner to a more open-minded, creative executive from 1984 until the end of his tenure in 1989. This "second-term shift" spawned several policy innovations, including a surprising turnabout on democracy promotion and U.S. ratification of international covenants. Reagan pursued a détente with his Soviet counterpart, Mikhail Gorbachev, and the two men successfully defused bilateral tensions and shaped agreements on arms control and regional issues. But unlike Richard Nixon's détente with Leonid Brezhnev, the Reagan-Gorbachev détente was not predicated on the president's silence on human rights matters. Reagan had long used moral rhetoric against the Soviets, and he went on to debate human rights with Gorbachev during every superpower summit. He was especially drawn to individual stories of suffering families and dissidents. He broached freedom of religion and emigration, and he regularly handed Gorbachev lists of separated families and political prisoners. His administration also became more active in multilateral forums such as the UNHRC in Geneva and the Conference on Security and Cooperation in Europe (CSCE) follow-up in Vienna (1986–1989). Reagan's surprising activism on this front proved to be a fundamental source of U.S.-Soviet disagreement. Whereas the Reagan administration saw Soviet reforms as integral foundations for a working relationship, the Soviets argued the opposite. To Gorbachev and the Politburo, Western human rights demands *prevented* an improvement in relations. The Kremlin repeatedly called for mutual relations on the basis of "equality and noninterference" in each nation's internal affairs. Even in the final days of Reagan's presidency, the two leaders never saw eye-to-eye on these issues.

Reagan's turnabout went beyond East/West relations. He also proved willing to criticize the policies of the nonaligned nations and anticommunist allies, and his administration began to pursue a democracy promotion policy in several countries. Some of this period's human rights causes were driven by congressional pressure, as when the Reagan administration somewhat reluctantly offered support to indigenous democracy movements in the Philippines and Haiti. In perhaps the clearest example of Congress taking the lead, legislators pushed antiapartheid policies as a means of challenging the Reagan administration's passive approach to South Africa.

Although the first Reagan administration would prove to be circumspect in its pursuit of international human rights goals, Reagan himself was particularly concerned about religious persecution throughout his entire presidency. In his 1980 nomination speech, he improvised a conclusion that placed the Cold War struggle within the context of the Puritan legacy. "Can we doubt," he declared, "that only a Divine Providence placed this land, this island of freedom, here as a refuge for all those people in the world who yearn to breathe freely: Jews and Christians enduring persecution behind the Iron Curtain, the boat people of Southeast Asia, of Cuba

and Haiti."[6] He found the official atheism of the communist world especially troubling. Midway through his presidency, he began peppering his
annual Human Rights Day addresses with references to religious persecution, and he placed religious freedom high on the agenda during the U.S.-
Soviet summits. Skeptics could argue that religious liberty and democracy
were rather painless causes for an American president—nice fodder for
speeches, perhaps, but unlikely to alter other nations' internal policies. But
there is little doubt that Reagan sincerely believed in both. His faith, writes
Andrew Preston, "was eclectic rather than systematic, lived rather than
learned"; yet this faith was genuine. Religious conservatives found much to
like in both his anticommunism and his enthusiasm for religious
freedom—causes for which these voters found President Carter's efforts
lacking.[7]

Despite the more ecumenical approach to the world during his second
term, neither the Reagan administration nor Congress applied human
rights policies equally on a global scale at any time in the 1980s. The lion's
share of American political attention was on the Soviet Union and Central
America, with a few other regions and nations occasionally coming into
focus. Some of the worst offenders—especially those in the Middle East,
Africa, and Asia—received scant attention from American policymakers.
There were exceptions, but the prevailing belief in Washington was that
these regions could not be judged by the same standard as Western societies. China was virtually absent from human rights discussions in Washington until the Tiananmen Square massacre of 1989.

The Reagan Administration and Human Rights, 1980–1983

The 1980 election took place against an unusually tense international backdrop. The Soviet Union was occupying Afghanistan, fifty-two Americans
were being held hostage in Iran, a left-wing coalition was ruling Nicaragua,
and Saddam Hussein's Iraq was fighting for control of Iran's oil fields. With
the return of the Cold War, the rhetoric of the 1980 election resembled that
of the early 1950s, when each party tried to outdo the other in proving its
anticommunist credentials. Meanwhile, President Carter had to defend his
human rights policy against the barbs of his main challengers, Senator
Edward Kennedy and Ronald Reagan. Kennedy, who ran on a domestic
"social justice" platform, applauded Carter's human rights efforts but also

criticized his turn toward anti-Soviet containment. Reagan was far less willing to admit any Carter successes, choosing instead to align traditional anticommunist sentiments with the new human rights terminology. Consequently, the 1980 campaign became a turning point in conservatives' melding of Cold War ideology with the liberal human rights language of the seventies.

Although Reagan did not announce his candidacy until November 1979, he had been campaigning, formally and informally, since completing his term as governor of California four years earlier. His strong showing in the 1976 Republican primaries heartened party conservatives, and he continued to lambaste the Democrats through public appearances and his weekly radio editorials. Between 1975 and 1979, he delivered over a thousand radio commentaries in which he assailed communism, liberal social policies, the Democrat-dominated Congress, and President Carter. On foreign policy, Reagan attacked Carter's human rights efforts as inconsistent, too weak on the communists, and too strong on America's allies. "If we deplore alleged violations of human rights in Chile, Argentina, and Brazil," he said, "can we ignore them in Panama? . . . [Can we] carry on a constant drumbeat of criticism toward South Africa and Rhodesia at the same time we talk of recognizing a regime in Cambodia that has butchered as much as a third of its population?"[8] According to Reagan, Carter marginalized the Shah of Iran merely because he "didn't meet exactly our standards of human rights," but he hypocritically maintained a détente "with the one nation in the world where there are no human rights at all—the Soviet Union."[9]

The Reagan campaign laid out a pragmatic approach that would place international human rights alongside other interests. The new policy would reject the notion of a "universal standard," instead defining America's national interests narrowly and differentiating between governments of the right and left. In the words of a campaign memo, there was "nothing morally wrong" with "aligning ourselves with less than 'perfect' nations (human rights wise) for national security reasons."[10] The Reagan campaign also continued the Nixonian strategy of bringing blue-collar ethnics into the Republican fold. Reagan even cribbed his campaign slogan—"Work, Family, Neighborhood, Peace Through Strength"—from the theologian and ethnic specialist Michael Novak. Observers began to use the term "Reagan Democrat" to describe disaffected working-class voters whose loyalties were shifting to the right. Ethnic voters were most interested in domestic issues, but many appreciated Reagan's statements on Soviet repression in Eastern Europe, the decline in Jewish emigration, and the 120,000 Cuban boatlift refugees. By design, Reagan's human rights platform generally paralleled the interests of Eastern European ethnics. In campaign letters to ethnic newspapers, he applauded the ethnics for serving as the "national conscience" on the reality of Soviet tyranny, and he charged that "Mr. Carter's is not a human rights policy worthy of the United States. . . . We should respond to the Helsinki Accords with a vigorous and consistent policy so that both ally and adversary alike will know that our human rights intentions are true and our policy substantive."[11]

The growing crisis in Poland gave each candidate a chance to stake his claim as the more serious defender of the Polish people. In August 1980, striking shipyard workers in the Baltic coastal city of Gdańsk formed the Solidarność (Solidarity) trade union and began negotiating with the Polish government. As the first independent trade union in a communist country, Solidarność was a unique threat: a dissident organization created and run by workers. Their leader, Lech Walesa, became the international face of the movement. But with the Carter administration unwilling to exacerbate the situation for fear of provoking a crackdown from Warsaw or a violent intervention from Moscow, it was the Republicans' turn to use the human rights "stick" to attack the president. Said Congressman Edward Derwinski, the Carter administration "[is] interested in placating the Soviets. They're not concerned for the welfare of Polish workers."[12] Reagan took advantage of his opposition candidacy to remind Polish Americans of Carter's earlier claim that "our concept of human rights is preserved in Poland." Reagan rejoined, "The Polish workers obviously do not believe him. They want free speech and free trade unions."[13] In a nod to blue-collar patriotism, Reagan made a public appearance alongside Lech Walesa's father, Stanley, on Labor Day 1980 in the shadow of the Statue of Liberty. Carter responded by emphasizing his policies' effects in Eastern Europe and his support for Polish trade credits. Speaking before a group of Polish Americans in Philadelphia (also with Stanley Walesa in tow), he turned conservatives' longstanding criticisms to his advantage. "They seem to think it's naïve for America to stand up for freedom and to stand up for democracy," he argued. "What should we stand for? . . . Just ask the Polish workers."[14]

The 1980 party platforms clearly connected anticommunism, ethnic interests, and human rights.[15] The Republicans accused Carter of sowing "chaos, confusion, and failure" and making the United States seem "vacillating and reactive." Carter had turned his back on America's friends, but a Republican president would continue to support "genuine independence" for Cuba, Eastern Europe, and the repressed in the developing world. The Democrats countered with their own combination of toughness and humanitarianism. At first glance, their platform offered a more Wilsonian vision than the Republican statement. It called on American policymakers to pursue moral objectives and "make clear our support for the aspirations of mankind." These statements grew from the efforts of the party's liberal activists and their standard-bearer, Senator Kennedy, who did not officially end his candidacy until the second night of the Democratic convention. Yet notwithstanding these allusions to global melioration, the Democrats' anti-Soviet human rights stance was virtually indistinguishable from the Republicans'. Human rights considerations, the platform stated, should be "a permanent feature of U.S.-Soviet relations," and Democrats stood with the oppressed Helsinki monitoring groups, Soviet Jews, and dissidents. President Carter defended his policy at the convention, though his message was more anticommunist than pro–human rights. "Just what do [Republicans] think we should stand up for? Ask the former political prisoners. . . . Ask the dissidents in the Soviet Union. . . . Ask the millions who've fled tyranny if America should stop speaking out for human principles."[16]

But the political winds had shifted since 1976. In 1980, there were few differences between the Democrats' and Republicans' anti-Soviet messages, and the American public was concerned with more pressing domestic matters like inflation, unemployment, and high gas prices. Carter seems to have sensed that devotion to his policy would not put him over the top: in a fifty-three-minute nomination speech, he dedicated about one minute to human rights. On November 4, Ronald Reagan carried forty-four out of fifty states. Reagan's campaign managers were astute in recognizing that patriotism and anticommunism were still popular. And by defining "human rights" as essentially "anti-Soviet" and "anti-communist," Reagan was setting himself up for an easier time as president. Unlike Carter, Reagan would not have to decide the extent to which the United States should sanction its allies. Moreover, although Reagan talked tough, few would expect him to actually *do* anything related to human rights while in office. After all, he could not possibly change the Soviet Union.

Once Reagan was in office, his administration set about reversing many of Carter's policies. In the name of security and Cold War concerns, they began to reset relations with regimes that had been ostracized in Washington. Most of these were in Latin America and the Caribbean, with a few others scattered throughout the world. Reagan would offer these leaders a warm welcome in Washington, and would seek congressional reinstatement of security assistance and multilateral loans. To many such leaders, it seemed that American meddling would now decrease. A leaked State Department memo implied that the ambassadors to El Salvador and Nicaragua, Robert White and Lawrence Pezzulo, were being replaced because they were acting more like liberal social reformers than ambassadors. Whether or not the claim was true, Central American leaders seem to have believed it. In the words of the Haitian dissident Michele Montas, the region's autocrats "thought human rights was over."[17] Reagan's cabinet nominations further confirmed activists' suspicions. Several were cold warriors who had criticized liberal human rights efforts, including General Alexander Haig (secretary of state), Richard Perle (assistant secretary of defense and arms negotiator), Jeane Kirkpatrick (U.N. ambassador), and Ernest Lefever (assistant secretary of state for human rights). Reagan's priorities were also reflected in his refugee policy. His administration interpreted the very unideological Refugee Act of 1980 in such a way that the United States would admit more from communist countries.[18]

Unsurprisingly, Reagan's early moves prompted a congressional and NGO backlash. The combination of the administration's apparent intransigence and the growing violence in Central America led the founders of Helsinki Watch to expand their purview into the Western Hemisphere by creating Americas Watch in 1981. Helsinki Watch also challenged the administration's adherence to the Kirkpatrick Doctrine. "It damages the United States to side with oppressive governments that happen to be anti-Soviet," they wrote, "for if we aid and abet torturers and murderers, the United States will be seen as a torturer and murderer."[19] In the long run, Americas Watch enhanced the Watch organizations' claims to evenhandedness. By establishing a watchdog organization to root out violations in the Americas, the organizers shielded themselves from Soviet accusations of propagandism. At the same time, Helsinki Watch earned conservatives' respect by publicizing communist states' violations.[20] (They would add Asia, Africa, and the Middle East to their ledger in the second half of the 1980s and would formally adopt the name Human Rights Watch in 1988.) This early conflict between activists and Reaganites shows the central role of ideology in human rights debates. As Helsinki Watch cofounder Aryeh Neier has noted, the first Reagan administration did not argue that human rights were unimportant, but rather that U.S.-aligned states had better records than America's opponents.[21] This position would require many obfuscations, distortions, and leaps of logic in the years to come.

Secretary of State Haig announced in his first press conference that international terrorism would replace human rights as a top White House concern. The administration would use private diplomacy when necessary, but would not go abroad in search of monsters to destroy.[22] Haig also personally opposed "report cards"—a clear reference to the State Department country reports. In response to some vocal critics, he modified this position a few months later by clarifying that such rights were "an integral element of the American approach, at home and abroad." But even this clarification was cautious. Echoing Richard Nixon, Haig asserted that foreign policymaking "must be rooted in the world of reality" and that the U.S. government had "neither the power nor the desire to remake the world in our own image." Undemocratic governments were not ideal allies, argued Haig, but noncommunist states rarely threatened their neighbors or the international order. The new administration would be pragmatic in opposing communism and in encouraging "the evolution of authoritarian regimes toward a more humane society."[23] For the time being, then, the Kirkpatrick binary remained intact. In private, the Reaganites retained the Nixon/Kissinger belief that every nation had its own traditions and unique economic and security needs. "Shrill and public denunciation of foreign governments," wrote a National Security Council (NSC) adviser, "has in the recent past very often proved counterproductive."[24]

These became the early Reagan administration's guidelines. Its human rights pursuits would cohere with its other foreign policy objectives. The Soviet Union would be the prime target, but the administration would try not to jeopardize U.S.-Soviet progress in other areas. In order to bridge this divide, the administration planned to air public criticisms and broach specific human rights issues privately—a twin trick that Jimmy Carter had never quite pulled off. Reagan, too, would soon find that this approach bore little fruit because the overall U.S.-Soviet relationship was so antagonistic. Moreover, Reagan could not overcome Moscow's tendency to see Western human rights activity as state-directed propaganda rather than the legitimate interest of non-state actors. It is clear from Soviet documents that high-ranking Kremlin figures sincerely believed that activism on behalf of dissidents was, at its root, simply anti-Soviet agitation.[25] This misperception was based, in large part, on Soviet leaders' inexperience with liberal societies, though these leaders were also correct in asserting that anti-Soviet sentiment melded fairly seamlessly with prodissident and pro–human rights activity in the West.

Reagan tested out his brand of personal diplomacy shortly after his inauguration. In a handwritten note to Soviet Premier Brezhnev, he pled for Anatoly Shcharansky's freedom, promising that "if you could find it in your heart to do this the matter would be strictly between us." Reagan also brought up two Pentecostal families—the Vashchenkos and the Chmykhalovs, known to activists as "The Siberian Seven"—who had sought asylum in the U.S. embassy in 1978. The Kremlin had refused to allow them to emigrate, so they remained residents of the embassy. Reagan promised secrecy if Brezhnev allowed them to leave, and added that such an action would surely establish a positive tone for future bilateral negotiations.[26] But because the two leaders had no real relationship, the Soviets did not accept his promise of discretion. Nothing came of this opening, and the administration soon learned that it was unable to achieve much in the humanitarian realm during Reagan's first two years in office.

Reagan's nomination of Ernest W. Lefever to replace Patricia Derian as assistant secretary of state for human rights proved to be another early administration setback. Lefever was a controversial choice for several reasons. As a senior researcher at the Brookings Institution and founder of the conservative Ethics and Public Policy Center, he had been an outspoken critic of Carter's human rights efforts and liberal internationalism in general. He touted private diplomacy, a narrow definition of the national interest, a tough stand against communist regimes, and noninterference in the internal affairs of strategic allies. Upon Jimmy Carter's accession to the White House, Lefever argued in the *New York Times* that "it has become chic to talk of morality and foreign policy, but there is little awareness of the pitfalls in these noble words."[27] He elaborated on these ideas when he told a congressional subcommittee, "We cannot export human rights [to] Third World countries. Their foreign policy behavior should be the determining factor, not their domestic practices."[28]

These attitudes hurt Lefever when he was brought before the Republican-majority Senate Foreign Relations Committee (SFRC) for his confirmation hearings. He had the support of many conservative organizations, as well as his ideological compatriots from the academic and policy-making worlds, but his dismissal of the new human rights requirements disturbed many others. As expected, Democrats were skeptical. Senator Claiborne Pell acknowledged Lefever's humanistic and academic credentials, and admitted that there was merit to the differentiation between totalitarian and authoritarian governments. But he concluded that Lefever's own ideas imperiled his nomination. At a symbolic level, stated Pell, putting Lefever into this position was like "putting . . . the fox in the chicken coop"—it would suggest to the world that America's interest in human rights had weakened. Senator Alan Cranston (D-CA) tore into Lefever, calling him "a man who has made a career out of promoting a diminished, muted role for American human rights advocacy" and who "generally displayed a blindness towards human rights violations by right-wing dictatorships." In a question about whether the human rights bureau was even necessary, Lefever was unenthusiastic. "[It] was established by the wisdom of Congress, and I accept that fact," he said. "The bureau now exists."[29] More significant, perhaps, were the tough questions from fellow Republicans and the lobbying work of NGOs. Helsinki Watch met with nearly every committee member—access that signified activists' growing influence in Washington. Senator Pell even brought the Argentine dissident Jacobo Timerman into the hearing room, where he received a standing ovation.[30]

In a surprising result, the SFRC rejected Lefever by a vote of thirteen to four, with all eight Democrats and five of nine Republicans voting against. It was the first time in thirty-one years that a Senate committee had rejected a presidential nominee. A few factors played a part in this vote, including the revelation that corporate donations might have created a conflict of interest for Lefever's policy magazine. But his thinly veiled hostility toward human rights laws was the major factor. On this point, his own writings were his Achilles' heel. He had produced so much scholarship that his opponents had no trouble finding evidence against him. Rather than face another fight in front of the entire Senate, Lefever withdrew his name, citing his opponents' use of "suspicion and character assassination" to challenge his integrity.[31]

The case showed that Congress was unwilling to allow a rollback of the previous decade's legislative accomplishments. As David Forsythe has written, the SFRC made it clear to Reagan that he could not turn America's human rights policy into one of mere anticommunism.[32] He would have to take the new movement seriously. The activist Aryeh Neier went so far as to call Lefever's defeat the turning point in establishing the human rights cause in foreign policy, as it seemed to settle the question of whether these concerns belonged in American diplomacy.[33] Considering the strong case that could be made for Lefever's credentials in the vein of the Kirkpatrick

Doctrine, it is perhaps more accurate to say that his defeat was a triumph of the left/liberal vision of human rights policymaking, including the belief that the head of the human rights bureau must be an advocate, not a neo-conservative ideologue or an ineffectual bureaucrat.

Stung by the Senate rebuke, Reagan dragged his feet on making a new appointment. He also stayed on the offensive by changing multilateral development bank voting policy to support loans to authoritarian allies in South America, and his deputy secretary of state casually admitted that the administration might seek to dismantle the human rights bureau.[34] After more than four months, Reagan finally nominated Elliott Abrams, who had earlier served as an aide to Senators Henry Jackson and Daniel Patrick Moynihan. Abrams had few difficulties in winning Senate approval, in part because he was more polished and polite, but also because he was a more credible human rights advocate. Under Abrams, the human rights bureau's work would generally be consistent with the administration's anticommunist interests.[35] Yet although some scholars have interpreted this work as mere anticommunist "propaganda," the bureau's efforts were more complex.[36] Inspired by the philosophies of Jackson and Moynihan, Abrams laid out a "two-track" policy. At first, this generally meant supporting rightists while fighting leftists, but in the long run it became a much more nuanced approach centered on the promotion of reforms in allied states.

The Lefever melee also showed the administration that inaction could invite congressional interference in other areas. Having taken this lesson to heart, the administration purposely leaked a State Department memo that described a more moderate stand. Because a human rights policy meant making hard choices, it read, the administration would have to speak honestly about America's allies or risk the appearance of simply "coddling friends and criticizing foes." If any nation curtailed freedom, "we should acknowledge it, stating that we regret and oppose it." On a more practical level, the appearance of inconsistency could disrupt key foreign policy initiatives. The memo did not signal a complete reversal, but it did demonstrate that Reagan might be more flexible than many observers had expected.[37] It is also possible to read the memo's release as a cynical cover for what was, in essence, an ideologically conservative policy. The administration's neoconservatives had adopted the idealistic rhetoric of the human rights movement and used it to redefine the Cold War as a human rights struggle. The administration would prove to be more active in the long run, but it would also consistently conjoin human rights with its broader anticommunist goals and limit its definition to democracy and the most basic of individual liberties.

Poland became a testing ground for the administration during Reagan's first year. Shortly after the 1980 election, with the Solidarity movement challenging Polish trade union regulations, the outgoing Carter administration and the incoming Reaganites rewarded the Polish government's restraint by promising food aid and a rescheduling of debt. The Reagan administration's chief goals were to prevent a Soviet intervention and to help Poland strike a "middle way" between East and West—"a regime not intolerable to the Russians and yet capable of further development toward democracy," in the words of a classified memo. The United States would offer economic aid in exchange for Polish reforms, but a Soviet invasion or a Polish government crackdown would halt the flow.[38] Due in part to Moscow's threats, General Wojciech Jaruzelski imposed martial law in December 1981, abolished Solidarność, and imprisoned its members. When they came for Lech Walesa, he said to the arresting agents, "This is the moment of your defeat. These are the last nails in the coffin of communism."[39]

The Reagan administration responded with measures aimed primarily at Moscow, though they also punished Warsaw. Reagan sanctioned both countries, halted negotiations on a U.S.-Soviet grain deal, canceled renewal of trade credits, banned Aeroflot and LOT flights, and suspended shipments of some U.S. products. This was a rare instance in which Congress, a Republican president, and American labor unions worked together for a common cause. He accompanied the sanctions with several proclamations, including designating the one-year anniversary of the crackdown as a Day of Prayer for Poland and Solidarity with the Polish People. But the United States found it difficult to entice European allies, who feared losing out on trade and energy agreements. Reagan privately called European leaders "chicken littles" and suggested punishing them for their obduracy, but his administration also restrained its sanctions because of European concerns.[40] Europeans used the Helsinki Accords to argue that the Soviets should stay out of Poland, but some also accepted martial law as an internal Polish affair.[41]

The Polish government slowly eased its controls in 1982–1983. They released Walesa, lifted martial law, and even accepted a papal visit. But as Gregory Domber has shown, there is little evidence that Western human rights criticism played a major part in spurring these actions. Domestic politics and economic needs were more important. One exception was the

Reagan administration's May 1983 offer to allow LOT flights and renewed scientific-technical cooperation in exchange for eleven dissident prisoners.[42] But such concessions were rare. After announcing that it was releasing nearly all of the seven hundred remaining political prisoners in 1984, the regime renewed its crackdown and rearrested many of them, and soon thereafter the pro-Solidarity Father Jerzy Popieluszko was murdered by state security forces. Due in part to these actions, the sanctions remained intact.[43] In the mid-1980s, Poland remained a major focus of the administration's anticommunism and its human rights efforts, and private citizens in the United States and elsewhere continued to send aid to the Polish people.

Central America's Civil Wars

Of far more significance to the early Reagan presidency were the growing crises in Central America and the Caribbean. Not only would this region prove to be a top foreign policy priority throughout the entire decade, but it would also be a major source of conflict in Washington over security and human rights concerns. The administration's support to various factions spurred public and congressional misgivings about American involvement in other nations' civil struggles. Indeed, there was a powerful domestic fear that Central America was a potential quagmire, as evidenced by the popular bumper sticker slogan, "El Salvador is Spanish for Vietnam." This domestic political conflict developed alongside these nations' ever-changing political and military situations. The solutions were never simple. As Secretary of State George Shultz later wrote, "Trying to forge policy [in Central America] was like walking through a swamp."[44]

President Reagan viewed Latin America through the lens of the Cold War. His hawkish Central America policy was heavily influenced by his first administration's conservative wing, which included men like CIA director William Casey, Chief of Staff Donald Regan, and NSC director John Poindexter. Convinced by the Nicaraguan Revolution that the Soviets and Cubans wanted to expand their influence in the region, these men sought to bolster security and combat leftist insurgents by supporting moderate and rightist governments. Reagan increased security assistance to El Salvador, Honduras, Guatemala, and Costa Rica, and he supported the Nicaraguan contra rebels in their fight against Daniel Ortega's Sandinista government. As we will see, he continued to follow these principles during the Reagan-Gorbachev détente of 1985–1989, even to the point of clashing with Congress and nearly losing his presidency to a scandal.

Cuba was another major source of anxiety. Fidel Castro was burnishing his reputation as the leader of Third-World Marxism by sending soldiers to participate in "wars of national liberation" in Africa and South America. Meanwhile, the Soviet Union increased its aid to Cuba, sending over $2 billion per annum in the form of loans, development aid, and sugar subsidies.[45] In language reminiscent of the Kennedy years, CIA director Casey advised that Castro was "promoting revolution on our doorstep" and that there was a "real danger of another Cuba spreading over three or four countries in Central America."[46] Castro also appeared to be cultivating a close relationship with Maurice Bishop, who had taken power on the Caribbean island of Grenada in 1979. Reagan, who feared that Havana and Moscow would use Grenada and Nicaragua as footholds in the hemisphere, sought to reverse what he considered President Carter's weak Cuba policy. Along these lines, Reagan formed a strong bond with Cuban-American hard-liners. Encouraged by National Security Adviser Richard Allen, exiles formed the Cuban American National Foundation (CANF) in 1981. The CANF not only lobbied to maintain a united front against Castro, but also pushed for a tough stand in Central America and Southern Africa, where Cuban troops and advisers were stationed. Exiles raised funds for the contras, voted overwhelmingly for Reagan, and supported nearly all of his positions in Latin America. The administration responded favorably by creating Radio Martí in 1985 and granting funds to the CANF to publicize Cuban human rights abuses.[47] The CANF was anti-Castro and anticommunist first, and only secondarily "pro–human rights," but its close ties to the administration demonstrated the fine line between anticommunism and rights activism in the 1980s.

A central question defined Washington's interest in Central America: To what extent were the region's conflicts fueled by external sources—namely, the Soviet Union and Cuba? While liberals and moderates generally saw these conflicts rooted in domestic social problems that could be alleviated with a combination of land reform, education, and economic assistance, Reagan and his allies saw extensive Soviet and Cuban involvement alongside homegrown leftist terrorism. Greg Grandin has noted that Central America became the primary locale for conservatives to recast the Cold War as a moral struggle between good and evil.[48] The Reaganites downplayed, though did not entirely discount, right-wing violence and the endemic problems of poverty and political mismanagement, and they marshaled evidence that Moscow and Havana were supporting rebels and exploiting the anger of the impoverished. They made much, for example, of the Soviets' grain purchases and their granting of scholarships to Latin American students, but in reality the Kremlin recognized America's sensitivity to outsiders in the hemisphere. American policymakers could also generally assume that Latin American publics were largely unreceptive to communism. At issue, then, was the extent to which the Soviets and Cubans were willing to support indigenous struggles.[49]

The human rights situation in Latin America differed from that of Eastern Europe. Whereas repressive Eastern European governments ruled relatively stable societies (Poland during the martial law crisis was an exception), Central America was plagued by violent civil wars, long-simmering class animosities, roving death squads, and terrorism against civilians and governments. Violations clearly went beyond freedom of conscience. Central America also differed from Eastern Europe in that its plight was not publicized in the United States by ethnic immigrant groups, though there were vocal advocates in the Catholic Church and the Cuban-American community.

Nicaragua was a specter that haunted all of the administration's regional interests. The Reaganites argued that the Sandinistas were abusive, undemocratic, and so unpopular that their survival relied on the support of Moscow, Havana, and radical Arabs. The administration further asserted that the contras were a legitimate insurgency composed of peasant farmers, former Somoza regime members, and democrats who had formed independently and had only resorted to violence because of Sandinista repression. The administration also noted that America's regional allies in El Salvador, Costa Rica, and Honduras wanted Washington to back the contras. American conservatives tended to see a Sandinista-Cuba connection at every turn. Upon entering the White House, Reagan suspended loan payments to Nicaragua and cut off the remaining $15 million in economic aid in response to Sandinista involvement in El Salvador's civil war. He left open the possibility of resumed aid because he did not want to push the Sandinistas further into the Soviet camp, but as the political negotiations in Nicaragua fell apart in 1981, Reagan declared his support for the contras. In May 1982, Moscow agreed to grant Managua nearly $170 million in aid over five years, a move that many in Washington considered both a Soviet provocation and a Sandinista repudiation of the United States. The Nicaraguan government then grew even bolder, publicly advocating and privately supporting revolutionary activity in El Salvador.

As the ideological battle lines hardened, each side castigated the other's powerful benefactors and publicized their human rights violations. Objectively speaking, the Sandinista record was poor. During Nicaragua's postrevolutionary transition, many former Somoza supporters were targeted for arrest, abuse, imprisonment, and even extrajudicial reprisal killings, including Anastasio Somoza himself, whom Sandinista commandos killed in Paraguay. The government maintained a state of emergency for much of the 1980s, which allowed them to suspend freedom of expression and hold prisoners indefinitely. They censored radio transmissions and the independent newspaper *La Prensa*, and they arrested some human rights monitors. The Inter-American Press Association concluded that Nicaragua had the most egregious record of censorship in the Americas.[50] The Nicaraguans' forced relocation of 8,500 Miskito Indians helped make this group a popular activist cause across the political spectrum. Consistent with contemporary legislation and political trends, American conservatives pressed to apply tough human rights standards to Nicaragua.

But the Sandinistas were not as brutal as the Reagan administration claimed. As Greg Grandin has suggested, even in the darkest days of the contra war the Sandinistas' violations never reached the level of Somoza's. The Sandinistas' spotty record was also arguably better than the records of many other Latin American governments, especially considering their ongoing struggle against an armed insurgency. Meanwhile, even many Sandinista opponents were disturbed by the contras' corruption and occasional cruelty. One adviser to the Joint Chiefs of Staff called them the "strangest national liberation organization in the world, just a bunch of killers."[51] This debate over which side was more abusive highlighted the problem of American involvement in another nation's civil war. Choosing a side meant having to defend or downplay that side's legal and moral transgressions. Reagan publicized Sandinista abuses in order to build sympathy for the contra cause, but it became increasingly clear that the contras, too, were guilty of atrocities. Given the large number of NGO and press accounts of these abuses, Reagan had to perform acrobatic leaps of obfuscation to justify declaring them "democratic" and "freedom fighters." The contras' method of undermining the Sandinista regime by targeting economic enterprises and farm cooperatives meant that many of their victims were civilians. When an attack on a cattle cooperative killed several children, the

Reagan administration dismissed the deaths as collateral damage. "It is not the policy of the resistance to attack civilian targets," said a State Department spokesman—a statement that Americas Watch declared "would do credit to George Orwell's Ministry of Truth."[52] In its defense of the contras, the Reagan administration proved even more likely than Jimmy Carter to cloak U.S. national interests in moral rhetoric, and they continued to do so even after public and congressional support for anticommunist forces in Central America had dwindled.

Congress was far from unified on Central America. Many legislators had misgivings about American involvement, but virtually none wanted to take responsibility for a disengagement that might facilitate a friendly regime's fall. And unlike the faraway struggles in Angola, the Horn of Africa, and Afghanistan, the Reaganites could make a more credible case that the Central America/Caribbean region was a vital national interest. Nevertheless, Reagan had a hard time convincing Congress and the public, and U.S. aid to the contras was a tough sell throughout his entire presidency. He chalked up American indifference to the propaganda campaigns of Central American leftists, and he assailed American observers who had come back from Nicaragua "bamboozled by the Potemkin villages and the Sandinistas' disinformation machine."[53] Late in 1982, Congressman Edward Boland (D-MA) authored an amendment that prohibited U.S. military aid to the contras. Because Americans feared being dragged into another unwinnable jungle war, the administration was unable to block the proposal. The Boland Amendment would nettle Reagan for years, and his attempts to circumvent it would later cause a scandal that threatened to undo his presidency.

The administration's other top regional priority was El Salvador, which was in the throes of a brutal civil war. President Reagan was a staunch supporter of the anticommunist ruling junta in their fight against leftist rebels, and he did his best to boost military and economic aid. But in order to secure this support, he had to convince Congress and the public that vital interests were at stake and that the government in San Salvador was worth supporting. Unfortunately for Reagan, not only were Americans generally uncomfortable with choosing sides in a full-scale civil war, but Salvadoran security forces and death squads were widely accused of atrocities. International relations expert Thomas Carothers neatly summarized the zeitgeist: the American public was wary of "anticommunist crusades in obscure countries where the United States was defending a government of dubious character." With NGOs, church groups, and congressional liberals opposing U.S. support, the administration became more active in promoting democracy and some human rights reforms as a fig leaf for aid to the regime. The tragic level of violence and the fierce funding debates in Washington led Secretary of State Shultz to call El Salvador "the hot spot of the hemisphere."[54]

Reagan and his allies saw El Salvador as a test case of its Central America policy. In a classified memo, former ambassador James D. Theberge argued that "it is of the utmost importance to our national security [that a] communist takeover is prevented in El Salvador."[55] The Reaganites were clearly very serious about the endeavor. Military aid soared from $6 million to $82 million during Reagan's first two years in office before reaching a peak of nearly $200 million in 1984. It would total nearly a billion dollars in the eighties. Economic aid nearly tripled to $200 million in 1982–1983 and hovered between $300 and $500 million for the rest of the decade. For much of the eighties, El Salvador was the second-highest per capita recipient of American aid after Israel, and these amounts had an overwhelming effect in such a small nation.[56] Ambassador Robert White later asserted that the Reaganites "wanted to demonstrate an ability to crush revolutions. They wanted to say in El Salvador, this is what we could have done in Vietnam, had we not been saddled by reporters, by columnists—all those liberals."[57]

The clear problem was that the administration had to justify American support in the face of tremendous civil violence and reports of atrocities. They generally argued, often in the face of contrary evidence, that the perpetrators' identities were unknown and that violence was a part of Salvadoran culture. One year into Reagan's presidency, the State Department recommended that the administration avoid harsh human rights criticisms because El Salvador was a traditionally violent society in a state of civil war. The country's "tangled web of attack and vengeance, traditional criminal violence and political mayhem" meant that the killers were "the true phantoms" of the struggle. The report concluded that the combination of the war and a tradition of violence had led to "a descent into ad-hoc summary justice and unimaginable savagery." Gradual improvement was possible, but violence was "too engrained in this society to expect more."[58]

As in Nicaragua, then, human rights were central to Washington's debate over El Salvador. Congress would only release aid funds if the State Department could certify that San Salvador was meeting the Foreign Assistance Act's human rights standards. This biannual requirement was a clear sign of the politicization of human rights. In the words of Ambassador Deane Hinton, the procedure was also a political cop-out from legislators who did not have the stomach to endorse or deny aid. The requirement was a way for Congress to "dump the hard decisions back on the president."[59] Irrespective of its origins, certification set off a series of clashes between the administration and its adversaries. Reagan hoped to pull off the twin trick of supporting the Salvadoran regime's counterinsurgency efforts while at the same time undermining the Nicaraguan regime's similar efforts against the contras. But because the Salvadoran security forces and nongovernmental death squads were responsible for so many killings, the administration could not simply rubber-stamp a certification form. They had to show evidence of progress and convince Congress that they were urging the Salvadorans to rein in the killers and implement reforms.[60] Much as in Nicaragua, the administration had to be remarkably optimistic in its assessments and highly flexible in its definition of "progress."

When the administration's January 1982 certification noted a slight reduction in violence and asserted that San Salvador was making a "concerted and significant effort" to comply with international standards, Democrats countered that the regime of José Napoleón Duarte was using its security forces against innocent civilians. They cited reports from the ACLU and Americas Watch that the Salvadoran military had carried out a massacre in the village of El Mozote in December 1981. Administration officials declared that these reports were based on "dubious" and "partisan" sources, but later investigations would show that the Salvadoran army killed as many as nine hundred civilians, making this one of the worst massacres in modern Latin American history.[61] The Reagan administration continued to doubt the veracity of reporting on El Mozote, but more and more policymakers were questioning the ethics of further grants to San Salvador.

Most NGOs worked against certification, or at least hoped to convince Congress to pressure the administration. After reviewing hundreds of detailed accounts, Amnesty International concluded in January 1982 that "a gross and consistent pattern" of abuses had occurred on a massive scale and that torture, disappearance, and extrajudicial executions were rampant. There were abuses on all sides, but the evidence suggested that the government and rightist paramilitaries were responsible for most of it. The State Department's Elliott Abrams acknowledged the dire situation, but also argued that responsibility was shared by terrorists of the left and the right. He cited steps the junta had already taken, including removing officers from their posts, abolishing the paramilitary organization ORDEN, and instituting a military code of conduct.[62] After the administration increased pressure on the Salvadorans to hold elections, the national assembly named a prominent banker, Álvaro Alfredo Magaña, as the provisional president in May 1982. The White House had wanted more concrete measures, but they were at least satisfied that the Salvadorans had chosen a civilian instead of the Nationalist Republican Alliance (ARENA) and its candidate, Roberto D'Aubuisson, who was widely perceived as an organizer of death squads. (U.S. embassy personnel called him "Blowtorch Bob" due to his alleged predilection for using the device during interrogations.)[63]

By the end of Reagan's second year, his advisers increasingly suspected that the Salvadoran government and its military were resisting reforms. When certification came up for renewal in June 1982 and January 1983, the administration qualified its approval. In the latter instance, Secretary of State Shultz stated that although El Salvador was meeting the statutory criteria for certification, it had fallen short of "broad and sustained progress." He singled out several areas of concern, including the security forces' brutal tactics and the slow investigation of murder cases.[64] Even this heavily qualified certification elicited criticism in Washington, with opponents suggesting that the administration's focus on elections was coming at the expense of civilians' right to life and liberty. Many more questioned the huge sums being shipped off to such a small country, the insufficient means of tracking their use, and the possibility that U.S. aid was exacerbating the war. Insurgent leader Guillermo M. Ungo argued that U.S. military aid was strengthening the militarists who opposed dialogue, and he charged that the administration was responsible for "the continuation, intensification, and regionalization of the war."[65] These critics were not simply questioning the Reagan administration's version of events, but were offering a competing vision of America's approach to Central America. Fifty-five members of Congress signed a letter of protest calling American support to Salvadoran forces who were killing civilians both "morally wrong and counterproductive."[66] The moderate Congressman Jim Leach (R-IA) said of the drop in noncombatant deaths from twelve thousand in 1981 to eight thousand in 1982, "That is good progress, but it is like closing Buchenwald and keeping Auschwitz open."[67]

The Reagan administration was not entirely unified. Speaking to the American Chamber of Commerce in San Salvador late in 1982, Ambassador Hinton asserted that the Salvadoran legal system was "rotten" and that the right-wing "mafia" had to be stopped. Few killers had been brought to justice, he noted, though around thirty thousand people had been murdered. "Is it any wonder that much of the world is predisposed to believe the worst of a system which almost never brings to justice either those who perpetrate these acts or those who order them?" A dozen members of his audience walked out, and the chamber later called the speech "a slap in the wounded and bloodied face of our country." Hinton claimed his words had been cleared in Washington, but the White House denied it.[68] Despite the controversy over increasing aid, Reagan himself was adamant that El Salvador remain noncommunist as a matter of American national security. He wrote to one of his ambassadors that there was "a sense of 'déjà vu' in this chorus over El Salvador with the same voices that gave us Cuba and Nicaragua."[69] But despite the continuation of military aid, Salvadoran leaders could not deny that more and more Americans were asking tough questions about who was doing the killing and whether the United States was indirectly contributing to the violence. As one contemporary scholar noted, the debate was no longer over whether human rights mattered, but over the extent of abuses—and America's ability to end them.[70]

A flurry of activity late in 1983 put even more pressure on San Salvador. Following violent opposition to land reform, the administration began to differentiate between the "legitimate right," which operated within the political system, and the "violent right," which did not. The administration also clarified that its four central goals were strengthening democratic groups and processes, supporting the land reform and improving economic conditions, opposing the violent right and violent left, and supporting dialogue to facilitate a political solution.[71] Defense Secretary Caspar Weinberger, Vice President George H. W. Bush, and the U.S. ambassador all spoke openly on these points when they addressed officials in San Salvador. Bush went so far as to proclaim that "these cowardly death squad terrorists are just as repugnant to me, to President Reagan, to the U.S. Congress, and to the American people as the terrorists of the left." He warned that if the killings continued, San Salvador would lose the support of the American people. Reagan then pressured President Magaña to remove officers who may have been involved in death squads, and Secretary Shultz announced to the candidates in the upcoming Salvadoran election, "Death squads and terror have no place in a democracy, and I mince no words in saying it here or anywhere else."[72]

At the same time, Reagan worked to continue military aid in order to show consistent support to the government's efforts against extremists of the left and right. His zeal on this point had much to do with his concern over Nicaragua, of course, but it also grew out of events in Grenada, where a Marxist regime had been bolstering its strength with Soviet and Cuban support. In October 1983, a U.S./Caribbean coalition mounted an invasion and deposed the regime, thus ending the fledgling Moscow-Havana-Grenada relationship. The successful ouster led the Reagan administration to believe it was stemming the tide of Soviet advances in the region. The following year, José Napoleón Duarte defeated Roberto D'Aubuisson in a close Salvadoran election. Believing that a hard-right victory would imperil Reagan's ability to provide aid, the U.S. embassy had clarified to Salvadoran leaders that they wanted Duarte to win, and the CIA channeled upward of $3 million to his campaign.[73] The Salvadoran military still retained a great deal of power, and the civil war continued, but the election was widely considered the nation's fairest since the 1930s. The administration continued to defend the regime publicly, even to the point of denying San Salvador's responsibility for blatant human rights violations. But in reality the administration neither fully supported nor fully abandoned San Salvador. They demonstrated public support but also pressed for reforms—as long as these did not threaten noncommunist rule. Washington's certification requirements improved human rights in El Salvador, but only to a point. The Salvadoran government knew that the administration was on its side, but also realized that it had to convince Congress to continue sending funds. This gave them at least some incentive to rein in violent extremists.

Argentina offered the Reagan administration another certification challenge and another set of security and human rights concerns. The U.S.-Argentina relationship was still recovering from the tensions of the Carter years, when Washington's sanctions had estranged the two governments while doing little to change the junta's practices. Carter had rekindled the relationship somewhat during his last year, and Reagan sought to build on this momentum. To the extent that Reagan even had a South America policy, it was largely aimed at strengthening relations with the military rulers of Chile, Argentina, and Brazil in order to gain their support for the Salvadoran government and Nicaraguan contras. He also wanted closer military cooperation and a united hemispheric front against potential Soviet incursions into the South Atlantic sea lanes. In contrast to Carter, the early Reagan administration shifted American attention away from human rights in South America and toward violations in Eastern Europe. And as in

Central America, the Reaganites tended to publicly applaud, and overstate, the South Americans' minor reform efforts.

In an effort to pull the Argentines back from their Soviet tilt and prevent European contractors from cornering the arms market, the administration lobbied Congress to amend or repeal the 1978 arms sales ban. In turn, Argentine leaders pledged their verbal support for Reagan's Central America policy. When the incoming president, General Roberto Viola, visited Washington in March 1981, both sides wanted better relations. Reagan's advisers considered Viola a pro-U.S. moderate who favored a return to civilian rule. "Argentina sees your administration as being more sympathetic toward Argentine concerns over terrorism and less inclined to 'interfere' in its internal affairs with accusations of human rights violations," advised Secretary of State Haig. But given the climate in Congress, the administration knew they had to encourage reforms, even if only to placate legislators. "In our efforts to improve relations," wrote Haig, the administration must "*impress Viola with the importance of further progress on human rights.*"[74]

Lobbying from the administration and American business leaders led Congress to repeal the arms sales ban, but a new law required certification that Argentina had made progress in human rights and that new weapons sales or aid would be in America's interest. The administration continued privately to encourage reforms, but it also whitewashed Argentina's record. Unfortunately for Reagan, Buenos Aires was not in lockstep with American interests. The Argentines had already refused to join the Carter-led grain embargo against the Soviet Union, and they had sided with the Soviets on some U.N. votes in exchange for political support on human rights matters. U.S.-Argentina relations then hardened when Reagan offered mild support to Britain during the April to June 1982 Falklands War.

The following year, the administration debated Argentina's certification, which would allow for the allocation of military aid and defense equipment sales. Supporters of certification noted that elections were scheduled and that the Argentines would simply acquire equipment elsewhere if the United States refused to sell.[75] The administration certified Argentina in December 1983, and the civilian Raúl Alfonsín was elected president two days later. Vice President Bush met with Alfonsín at his inauguration, and the administration invited him to Washington to demonstrate support for the emerging democracy and to get Argentina on board with Reagan's Central America policy. But the new leader had little interest in American support. Anti-American feeling in Argentina was strong, due in part to Carter-era policies and Reagan's eleventh-hour tilt toward London in the Falklands conflict. Moreover, the United States had played only a minor role in the Argentine democratization process. More significant to this process was domestic pressure, which was possible in large measure because international attention afforded Argentine activists some protection.[76] Thus the new Argentine leadership kept Washington at arm's length and pursued an independent path while moving beyond junta rule. In a sign of their caution, the Alfonsín visit to the United States was postponed until March 1985. He did address a joint session of Congress with the full support of the Reagan administration, but otherwise democratization in Argentina paid Reagan few dividends.

Reagan's lack of success in forging an entente with South American governments had much to do with differing threat perceptions. Argentina and Brazil saw significant internal threats in the form of insurgencies and economic stagnation, but they did not perceive a major Soviet or Cuban threat. Nor did they want to invest heavily in Central America just to satisfy the Americans. After the failed rapprochement of Reagan's first two years, his administration adopted a lower-profile course of mild diplomatic support for democracy, a policy that Thomas Carothers called "democracy by applause." Argentina's democratic transition fit into a regional trend. In 1982, Bolivia transitioned to civilian rule and Brazil held legislative elections; three years later Brazil's military passed power to a civilian president. Uruguay transitioned to democracy in 1984. In most of these cases, the United States played only a minor role by offering some diplomatic and public support for the elected governments and some funds for democracy assistance.[77] Later in the decade, the administration would take a much more active role in promoting democracy in Augusto Pinochet's Chile.

East Asian Predicaments: China and South Korea

The first Reagan administration also faced dilemmas in East Asia. Reagan tried to balance support for regional allies with encouragement for democratic reforms, but his Asia policy was based primarily on strategic concerns. Because his administration sought to maintain the strategic balance and protect America's regional interests, human rights were not central to their thinking during his first term. Each nation in the region had a unique value to America: Japan was a powerful economic player, while South Korea and the Philippines were strategic allies and hosts to thousands of U.S. troops. Taiwan was a long-standing partner and a potential irritant between Beijing and Washington. Indonesia was yet another anticommunist ally. Washington had long accepted these regimes' authoritarian tendencies in light of their internal threats and their proximity to communist regimes in North Korea, China, Vietnam, and Cambodia.

Sino-American relations in the first Reagan administration turned on security and trade matters, not China's internal policies. Consistent with his predecessors, Reagan considered China a potential partner against the far more dangerous Soviet Union, and he was enticed by its market potential. A national security specialist summarized the security priority: "We have found in the PRC a leadership that shares our apprehensions and those of most Asian countries about the threat of Soviet expansionism."[78] Few Americans brought Chinese human rights to public attention, and there was no Chinese parallel to the issue of Soviet emigration. As James Mann has written, "Human rights was considered a suitable subject for high-level American diplomacy with the Soviet Union, but not with China."[79] The administration did voice some concerns behind closed doors, but in public they touted China's economic reforms, expanding trade and student exchanges, and Sino-American cooperation in Southeast Asia and Afghanistan.

Reagan's decision to sell advanced weapons to Taiwan did hinder relations with China during his first year. But Secretary of State Haig and Vice President Bush—both of whom had spent considerable time in China—soon convinced Reagan that a closer relationship could counter Soviet ambitions. In June 1981, Reagan sent Haig to Beijing to rekindle relations, and soon thereafter the administration lifted the ban on lethal weapons sales to China (a decision that was also intended to send a message to Moscow to stay out of Poland). Reagan then renewed a Jackson-Vanik waiver for trade with China, Hungary, and Romania, citing continued improvements in their emigration policies. U.S. immigration laws, he pointed out, were doing much more to prevent the entry of Chinese immigrants than were the exit laws of China.[80] Arms sales to Taiwan remained a sticking point, but the two sides finally had a breakthrough in the summer of 1982. In a joint communiqué, the administration reaffirmed acceptance of the "one China" policy, and it pledged that the United States would gradually reduce its sales to Taipei. Reagan believed this was consistent with the normalization process that had begun a decade earlier, and he noted that the Chinese had promised to resolve the Taiwan issue peacefully.[81]

The Sino-American relationship proceeded apace with nary a mention of human rights, though there were a few bumps in the road. In addition to some tensions over Taiwan and the Korean Peninsula, China criticized America's policies in Central America and the Middle East. There were also some embarrassing humanitarian episodes, as when the Chinese tennis player Hu Na requested asylum while on tour in California in July 1982. Despite Beijing's request that she be returned, the U.S. government allowed her to stay until federal agencies had fully assessed her case. After eight months, during which Hu became a popular cause with the American public, the Justice Department decided in her favor. Beijing responded by cutting bilateral cultural ties, but the administration worked to paper over the differences, even releasing a cautiously optimistic human rights report that noted a "longer-term positive trend" in China with "gradual movement toward a more open society."[82]

Congress was largely compliant with the overall approach. Liberals rarely publicized Chinese abuses, and hawks like Senator Henry Jackson generally saw China as a strategic counterweight to Moscow. Some conservatives, though, criticized the administration's trade and security decisions. When Reagan once again waived restrictions on MFN treatment for China, Romania, and Hungary in 1983, Senator Jesse Helms asked what concessions China was willing to grant in exchange for advanced weapons. After all, he reasoned, China appeared to be supporting some insurgencies in Africa and Asia, and it was not altogether clear what China would do with advanced technologies. "What Free World country would Red China most resemble should a significant relaxation of export controls be implemented?" asked Helms. "Great Britain? Yugoslavia? India?"[83] Some observers pointed out the lack of liberal and political reforms to match China's economic reforms, but conservatives were unable or unwilling to maintain much attention on China as a strategic threat or as a chronic human rights abuser.

Four months after Chinese Premier Zhao Ziyang visited Washington in January 1984, Reagan paid a personal visit to Beijing. Although Reagan had visited China as Nixon's personal representative in 1971, this was his first presidential trip to a communist country. He fended off his fellow conservatives' criticisms by touting China's new generation of reformers. "They are not the leaders who carried on the killings and persecution of their people," he asserted. "China is embarked on economic changes that in many ways are beginning to look like our own free enterprise."[84] Speaking in the Great Hall of the People, he contrasted China's economic reforms and the improvement in Sino-American relations with the military expansionism of the Soviet Union. Rather than castigate China's leaders, he touted the strength of Western liberalism, individualism, and democracy, calling the American Revolution "the first great uprising for human rights and independence" and quoting Abraham Lincoln: "No man is good enough to govern another man without that other's consent." He closed by imploring his listeners to "trust the people."

The provocative nature of these remarks was immediately clear. When the speech was broadcast in China, the authorities deleted the references to democracy, capitalism, and religion. The Reagan administration registered its regrets, but also diplomatically referred to this decision as "an internal matter for the Chinese to decide." Upon Reagan's return to the United States, he spoke glowingly of Chinese reform efforts and even referred to "this so-called Communist China."[85] Reagan's tilt toward Beijing was clearly intended to give him a stronger hand in his dealings with Moscow. As a sign of the budding relationship, each side not only expanded trade and student exchanges, but the United States also allowed China to purchase defensive goods and services. The Chinese refused to join the Soviet-led boycott of the 1984 Los Angeles Olympics, and Chinese President Li Xiannian returned Reagan's favor and visited the United States in 1985. Reagan's second term then saw the most productive Sino-American relationship of the entire 1949–1989 era.[86]

The Reagan administration's approach to the Korean Peninsula was motivated by a different set of principles. The United States had maintained its security commitment during the Carter years, though a potent combination of South Korean authoritarianism, the U.S. troop withdrawal plan, and American human rights rhetoric had hindered the relationship. The government in Seoul had passed some reforms, but the assassination of Park Chung-hee and the accession of General Chun Doo-hwan heralded the Korean military's reassertion of control over the state. Reagan's first-term approach to Korea stressed continuity. The United States would offer mild enticements for human rights progress, but would also prioritize South Korea's security needs.

Reagan was confronted with a South Korean human rights problem only days after his election. General Chun's government had imprisoned the opposition politician Kim Dae-jung and several other dissidents in 1980 following antigovernment demonstrations. Kim was then sentenced to death in a trial that was heavily criticized by human rights NGOs and foreign governments, and the Carter administration was unsuccessful in its efforts to have the sentence overturned. President-Elect Reagan, who privately asserted that Kim's execution would be "a moral and political disaster," asked his new national security adviser, Richard Allen, to negotiate on his behalf. In the tough meetings that followed, Allen told his Korean counterparts that America's reaction to Kim's execution would be "like a lightning bolt from heaven striking you."[87] The South Koreans then suggested that they might change the sentence if the United States invited President Chun to Washington. Reagan agreed, but only if Kim's safety was ensured and the entire deal was kept secret. Chun then commuted the sentence to life in prison and headed to Washington.

Chun's February 1981 visit to Washington set off protests near the White House and outside his quarters at Blair House. The Soviet news service Tass rather creatively noted that "the warm welcome accorded by official Washington to the stranglers of freedom in South Korea sparked off a vigorous protest by the American public."[88] Truth be told, official Washington *did* set out the red carpet. Reagan's work on Kim's behalf did not mean that he was against the South Korean leaders. To the contrary, he personally affirmed America's commitment to the mutual defense treaty, promised not to withdraw any U.S. troops, and pledged that he would not make a public issue of South Korean human rights. He understood that Korea was in a precarious position and that its security needs trumped all other concerns. Reagan had also been briefed that cultural barriers would not allow for a simple transition to American-style liberal democracy. (In Alexander Haig's words, Chun's style of governance was "Confucian and authoritarian," and the Koreans expected "less gratuitous public advice on internal affairs" from Reagan, though the administration could still "encourage internal trends toward moderation and greater freedom.")[89] President Chun agreed that South Korea had had only partial success in "transplant[ing] American democracy across the Pacific," but added that past American policies had confused Seoul. Reagan concurred that the two nations must consider the human rights issue "in the proper manner"—that is, in private.[90]

In marked contrast to the Carter years, the State Department was very clear that the Reagan administration did not intend to weigh in on South

Korea's internal affairs. Administration officials expressed hope that Seoul would eventually achieve democracy, and they were careful not to over-praise the South Korean leaders—after all, these men had taken power in a coup. But the administration's support was unmistakable. Following Chun's visit, Richard Allen wrote to Reagan that "human rights survives as a concept [in bilateral relations], but in a broadened context."[91] In the next two years, activists pressured the administration not to sell security equipment that could be used against civilians, while legislators joined the U.S. embassy in pressuring President Chun to reduce Kim's sentence and exile him to the United States. Reagan was heartened by Kim's eventual release, but he was unwilling to meet with him out of respect for the South Korean government.

By 1983 the administration was more forthright in pushing for democracy. They were increasingly aware that overt support for the regime was spurring anti-Americanism in Korea, and they felt a growing sense that authoritarianism was undermining Korean national strength. Thus although South Korean security remained the primary bilateral goal, the administration shifted to arguing that a more democratic society would better ensure that security.[92] In its private consultations with Seoul, the administration pressed harder for democratic reforms and the freeing of political prisoners, though crackdowns on press freedom and student activism remained common. During the spring 1983 visit of foreign minister Bum Suk Lee, Reagan expressed satisfaction with recent moves toward a more participatory system. When Reagan visited South Korea six months later, the administration sought to clarify further its belief that "the open and representative governmental process provides the truest basis for security." As Secretary Shultz advised the president, "We need to signal our strong interest in further progress."[93] In Seoul, Reagan indicated a slight adjustment in his support, politely pressing his hosts to work toward democratic procedures and privately maintaining that "the soul of democracy is freedom under law." Speaking before the National Assembly, he surprised many Koreans with his directness. While acknowledging the need for strength to deter aggression, he asserted that the development of democratic political institutions was "the surest means to build the national consensus that is the foundation of true security."[94] These encouragements continued into his second term.

The Reagan administration's approach to South Korea and China was a study in contrasts. Internal documents show very little interest in China's human rights situation but a great deal of interest in Korea's. This reflected Washington's vested interest in Korean stability and strength, as well as its relative ability to get results there. But it also demonstrated the legacy of the 1970s human rights push and the fact that activists and legislators tended to fixate on the abuses of America's allies. Reagan would have preferred not to make an issue of South Korea's internal policies, but he did worry about South Korea's stability, and he had to show Congress that Seoul was "making progress" toward a more democratic society. (The more flagrant violations in North Korea meant comparatively little to democracy advocates and dissidents.) The administration did not effect a democratic transition during Reagan's first term, but their private encouragement got some results. After Reagan's 1983 visit, the regime restored civil rights to several hundred opposition politicians, freed nearly all political prisoners, withdrew security forces from campuses, and allowed over one thousand university students to return to school. These reforms grew from many factors, but Washington's pressure was among the most important.

The Second-Term Shift and the Promotion of Democracy

One of the most notable aspects of Reagan's presidency was his substantial change in outlook and policies from late in 1983 until the end of his tenure. This second-term shift saw the Reagan administration become much more active on the humanitarian front, including not only the promotion of democracy and support for the Genocide Convention, but also a much greater willingness to criticize America's allies. Meanwhile, the State Department country reports improved dramatically, even winning praise from activists and congressional liberals.[95] President Reagan himself also underwent a considerable change in attitude toward nuclear disarmament, and he was adamant about broaching human rights issues with the Soviets. He was able to get results in both arenas because of the improvement in U.S.-Soviet relations and the remarkable working relationship that he forged with Mikhail Gorbachev.

Several factors contributed to this shift. For starters, the strengthening of America's defense posture gave Reagan a stronger negotiating hand, while his 1984 reelection freed him from some partisan and ideological constraints. Moreover, Reagan was never as doctrinaire as his opponents (and many supporters) supposed. Despite his tough public persona, he was always troubled by the prospect of nuclear war and the lack of a viable missile defense. This is one reason why he clung so tenaciously to the Strategic Defense Initiative, also known as "Star Wars," which he presented to the public in March 1983. He never accepted the doctrine of mutually assured destruction, which posited that the superpowers would remain at peace as long as they held arsenals large enough to destroy each other. The burgeoning nuclear freeze movement likely influenced his direction as well, though it is clear that his interest in reducing nuclear arsenals predated his presidency.[96] Reagan's advisers and cabinet appointees may also have played a role. His original advisers were traditional cold warriors, but several later appointees were known for their political moderation, including Secretary of State George Shultz, National Security Adviser Robert "Bud" McFarlane, ambassador and Eastern Europe specialist Jack Matlock, and Assistant Secretary of State for Human Rights Richard Schifter. Shultz, who replaced Haig in July 1982, deserves perhaps the most credit. As a former economics professor and secretary of labor and the treasury, his credentials as a free market economist were undeniable, but few could have known that he would also master the realm of diplomacy.

Reagan had a minor breakthrough with the Soviets early in 1983 following a private tête-à-tête with Ambassador Anatoly Dobrynin. Although this was two years into his presidency, it was his first lengthy meeting with a senior Soviet representative. In addition to strategic and regional issues, Reagan brought up human rights matters like the Pentecostals in the U.S. embassy, divided families, and the plight of Soviet Jews. Dobrynin later wrote of his surprise that the president addressed the Pentecostals "as if it were the most important issue between us," but Reagan had been adamant about their cause since taking office. Moreover, this gambit was intended to test the waters. A few months later, the Politburo allowed the Pentecostals to leave the Soviet Union, and shortly thereafter the two nations reached a satisfactory grain trade deal. This turned out to be Reagan's first diplomatic success with Moscow. It established a measure of trust between the two sides, and it helped to change his attitude about what could be accomplished in the human rights arena. He would continue to make public pronouncements on the evils of communism, but he realized that quiet diplomacy with Moscow could be used to settle delicate humanitarian matters.[97]

Although Secretary Shultz got little traction when he broached human rights issues with Ambassador Dobrynin in 1982–1983, he did recognize that the Soviets were willing to adjust their demands somewhat in order to improve the relationship. In a detailed March 1983 memo, he laid out the four major areas of consultation that would define U.S.-Soviet relations for the remainder of the decade. The United States would negotiate with the Kremlin on arms control, bilateral issues (trade, aviation, exchanges), regional issues (Afghanistan, Eastern Europe, Central America), and human rights. The Soviets resisted the inclusion of human rights, of course, but they eventually accepted some of these overtures in order to win concessions in other areas. Testifying before the SFRC, Shultz made it clear that human rights were not, as Soviet Foreign Minister Andrei Gromyko had once said, "a tenth-rate question" in bilateral relations. "Our Soviet interlocutors . . . seek to dismiss human rights," stated Shultz, but "we have made it clear that human rights cannot be relegated to the margins of international politics."[98] Such talk was surely intended, in part, to placate Congress, but it also accurately reflected the administration's new position.

Reagan's second-term shift began in earnest later in 1983, when a string of events indicated to him that the threat of an accidental nuclear war was altogether too real.[99] The first was in September, when a Soviet pilot shot down a Korean passenger jet that had strayed into Soviet airspace, killing all 269 people onboard. The incident led to worldwide condemnation and a harsh diplomatic reaction from Washington. Behind the scenes, though, it became clear that the incident was the tragic result of human errors rather than a provocation. The second event was Reagan's viewing of the antinuclear television movie *The Day After*, which graphically depicted a fictional nuclear strike. Such a screening might otherwise warrant little scholarly attention, but Reagan was a man who responded to human stories more than theoretical explanations. He wrote in his diary that the film was "very effective and left me greatly depressed. . . . My own reaction: we have to do all we can to have a deterrent and to see there is never a nuclear war."[100] A few weeks later, he attended his first Pentagon briefing on the Single Integrated Operational Plan for nuclear war. He was strongly affected by the suggestion that so many civilians would be wiped out on both sides. He later wrote that the description was a "scenario for a sequence of events that could lead to the end of civilization as we knew it." Those at the Pentagon who claimed that a nuclear war was winnable were simply "crazy," he concluded.[101] The fourth important event was the NATO military exercise known as Able Archer 83, which took place over nine days in November. Soviet intelligence agencies—already on edge, and believing that Reagan was the "madman" president of their nightmares—were alarmed at its scope. The Kremlin placed their forces on high alert in the fear that Able Archer was the prelude to an offensive strike carried out under the pretext of a faux planned exercise. When American intelligence passed along word of the misunderstanding, Reagan was shocked that the two countries had nearly gone to war. With the exception of the Cuban Missile Crisis, this may have been the closest the world came to a nuclear exchange at any time in the Cold War era.[102]

Reagan was so moved by these events that he set out to improve the relationship in order to reduce the possibility of war. He tasked his National Security Planning Group with charting an opening to the Kremlin, and he showed a slight change of attitude in his December 1983 Human Rights Day speech. The Soviet Union was still at the center of his critique, but he was also willing to invoke the struggles of black South Africans and Iranian Baha'is. And in a clear message to the authoritarian governments of Central America, he decried the activities of the death squads.[103] Then in January 1984, Reagan delivered a speech that was like none of his previous statements. He announced that the United States sought to engage the Soviets in a constructive dialogue in order to promote peace, reduce arms levels, and build a working relationship. He maintained his anticommunist bona fides, acknowledging that the United States was competing with a government "that does not share our notions of individual liberties at home and peaceful change abroad," but he also expressed his "dream" of seeing the eventual abolition of nuclear weapons. The major innovation was his insistence that human rights form an integral part of the dialogue and that progress on emigration and political imprisonment would lead to breakthroughs elsewhere. "Respecting the rights of individual citizens bolsters the relationship," he asserted. "Sealing off one's people from the rest of the world reduces it." He concluded with a self-penned anecdote about a fictional Russian "Ivan and Anya" and an American "Jim and Sally." If such ordinary people met, suggested Reagan, they would not debate political systems, but would engage in more human concerns like work and family, and they would agree that "people don't make wars."[104]

Unfortunately for Reagan, his Soviet counterpart, Yuri Andropov, died three weeks later. Nevertheless, the administration remained cautiously optimistic. Reagan's advisers were divided on arms control and regional matters, but there was basic agreement that it was worth pressing for Soviet internal reforms. This may have been due to the relative painlessness of such overtures when compared with security matters, but irrespective of the motive Reagan was now fully rekindling earlier activists' arguments that Soviet concessions would open up opportunities for breakthroughs elsewhere. In a conversation with Ambassador Dobrynin, Reagan once again promised to keep their agreements private if the Soviets eased up on dissidents, and in a letter to the new premier, Konstantin Chernenko, he asserted that humanitarian gestures would be taken seriously in Washington.[105] He noted that the Pentecostal episode had shown that "quiet and sincere efforts could solve even the most sensitive problems in our relationship." But rather than take the bait, Chernenko assailed the United States and NATO for placing Pershing and cruise missiles near the Soviet border, and he added that "the introduction into relations between our two states of solely domestic affairs . . . does not serve the purpose of improving these relations if this is our goal. I wish that questions of such nature do not burden our correspondence."[106]

Hopes for a détente faded even further with the Soviets' announcement that they would boycott the 1984 Summer Olympics in Los Angeles. Moscow cited security concerns and American "politicization" of the games, but a more credible explanation lay in the generally poor state of relations and the Kremlin's desire to avenge the U.S. boycott of the 1980 Moscow Olympics. Human rights criticisms were also a part of this conflict. Not only were some émigrés encouraging Eastern Bloc athlete defections, but Reagan had long supported the Baltic peoples' national aspirations and had even hosted émigré groups in the White House.[107] Even after the Olympics, Reagan's overtures were largely fruitless. His September 1984 meeting with Foreign Minister Andrei Gromyko—his only session with a high-ranking Moscow official in his entire first term—ended with no substantive agreements.

While a U.S.-Soviet détente seemed out of reach, the Reagan administration pursued a separate policy of democracy promotion in the developing world. In doing so, they were latching onto one of the most significant international trends of the era. Around sixty nations underwent democratic transitions between 1974 and 1994, a multicausal phenomenon that the political scientist Samuel Huntington dubbed the "third wave of democratization."[108] The Reagan administration and Congress responded to this trend and at times even contributed to it, though Reagan's approach was generally cautious. He emphasized gradual change but also occasionally took more concrete actions to encourage democratization in troubled states. As we will see, after Reagan's reelection democracy and human rights promotion became integral to American policies toward the Philippines, Haiti, Chile, and South Africa.

We can trace the origins of the democracy promotion policy to Reagan's June 1982 speech to the British Parliament, in which he implored the Western world to assist the campaign for democracy in the belief that "freedom is not the sole prerogative of a lucky few, but the inalienable and universal right of all human beings." He also embraced the Wilsonian view that the world's parliamentary states should foster the "infrastructure of democracy"—a free press, labor unions, universities, and political parties.[109] The message was very Reaganesque in its simplicity, and critics dismissed it as simple pandering to the Anglo-American audience. In light of the considerable European antinuclear movement then afoot, it is possible that the speech was meant to soften Reagan's image as a right-wing "warmonger" and to demonstrate support for something besides anticommunism. Whatever his motive, the speech would have been quickly forgotten if his administration had not gone on to devise concrete policies.

The democracy promotion principle became more of a policy in 1983–1984. Congress turned down the administration's $65 million request for an initiative called Project Democracy, but it did fund the new National Endowment for Democracy (NED), a nonprofit, private foundation intended to promote democratic institutions worldwide through grants and publications. The government also created the National Democratic Institute and the International Republican Institute as NED-funded organizations with unique regional and program mandates. The NED had its critics, both among conservative budget hawks and in the human rights activist community. Much like America's foreign aid projects, the democracy programs would be geared in large measure toward American interests rather than simply reflecting a philosophical or humanitarian affinity for democracy. The NED budgets of the 1980s show that funding was generally consistent with Reagan and Bush administration priorities. There was also speculation that the NED was taking up the slack for the statutory limits on the CIA's involvement in overseas politics. And those who supported a bold American democracy-promotion effort noted the modesty of the annual congressional NED appropriation.[110]

But considering U.S. democracy promotion activities in the long run, one cannot help but be struck by their breadth. For while it was true that the lion's share of funds went toward programs that were acceptable to the

Reagan and Bush administrations, the NED's nongovernmental status gave it the ability to support democratic institutions in controversial places like Chile, Poland, and the Philippines. Congress also had influence over the allocation of funds and the planning of programs. As democracy promotion became more central to American foreign policy in the late 1980s and 1990s, the budgets increased considerably. There were many valid criticisms of the programs' aims and execution, but the U.S. government's activism was undeniable. With democracy promotion as a policy, the Reagan administration pressured longtime allies like Ferdinand Marcos and Jean-Claude Duvalier to legitimize their rule by strengthening parliamentary procedures. All of Reagan's successors were committed to the principle.[111]

This activity raises questions about the motives of the administration and members of Congress. Why did they promote democracy? Was it in America's interest because it encouraged stability? Or was democracy something to be pursued irrespective of its effect on American interests? Reagan's personal beliefs surely had something to do with his embrace of this goal: there is much evidence that he believed political democracy and religious freedom to be the two most basic rights. Reagan's conservatism was very "American" in the sense that he had an unimpeachable faith (his critics would say naïveté) in the basic goodness of people. Just as his worldview influenced his domestic political philosophy—that is, less government, freeing people to follow their own desires—it also influenced his global ideology of fighting communism, promoting liberty, and freeing people to choose their own governments. Another reason for the democracy push was that the Nicaraguan Sandinistas seemed to be following the Castroist governance model that "the revolution has no time for elections." By promoting the democratic process in Central America, Reagan could assert U.S. allies' superiority to the Sandinistas. El Salvador's 1982 and 1984 elections were hardly flawless, but they arguably laid the groundwork for a more stable political system, and they certainly made for good public relations in Washington.

Critics of the administration's approach argued that the policy was intended to undercut those who questioned aid to undemocratic regimes. These critics believed that Reagan was using democracy promotion as the "sugar" that would make the "medicine" of military aid to anticommunists more palatable. Reagan's critics also noted that his definition of democracy was narrowly based on the American experience, and that the administration was largely concerned with the outward trappings of democracy, particularly multiparty elections. Even those opponents who supported political rights and representative government pointed out that democracy did not always equal human rights. In the name of urging friends to reform politically, the administration could, if it desired, do very little of substance while continuing aid to a repressive regime. There was also the question of national sovereignty. Although Americans generally admired democracy promotion proposals, in part because these did not involve painful military operations or expensive nation-building efforts, other governments considered them an intrusion into their internal affairs. Democracy programs could veer uncomfortably close to direct financial support for a nation's political parties and candidates.

In a fine critical study of Reagan's efforts in Latin America, the former State Department officer Thomas Carothers confirmed that the policy was not simply a cynical cover for realpolitik. Within the administration, there was a high degree of genuine interest in democracy and its associated institutions and liberties. But this interest easily and regularly grew into political interference, and too many American policymakers knew too little about the societies they sought to change. Just as significant, other administration goals and American national interests—anticommunism, trade and economic development, peace settlements—were subsumed under the "democracy promotion" umbrella. The administration invoked the term so frequently and indiscriminately, writes Carothers, that "it took on the quality of a refrain one often hears but rarely listens to."[112] Meanwhile, activists were divided over democracy and human rights promotion. Some saw a close connection between the two, but many reacted negatively to initiatives that promoted free market economics and support for anticommunist governments with poor human rights records. Some NGOs worried that democracy promotion would privilege elections while ignoring other civil and political rights and obscuring the focus on violators. These criticisms had some merit, but they also reflected activists' political affiliations and ideologies. Because much of the human rights activist community was left/liberal in persuasion, it was natural that they would be suspicious of Reagan administration policies. And since their work was advocacy and lobbying, activists generally hoped to disassociate human rights from America's other foreign policy interests.[113]

Yet another sign of Reagan's changing attitude was his support for ratification of the Genocide Convention. This was a surprising turnabout, because he had refused to endorse the convention early in his presidency.

When the SFRC held hearings on it in 1981, no one from the Reagan administration even showed up to testify. But by 1984, he was willing to ask his advisers to study all of the U.N. human rights instruments. When the Democrats included a Genocide Convention ratification pledge in their platform, Reagan moved to undercut their moral authority by supporting the convention. Speaking before the International Convention of B'nai B'rith in September, he declared that his administration would use the convention in its efforts to fight human rights abuses worldwide: "Like you, I say in a forthright voice, 'Never again!'"[114] It was a public relations coup that was easy to understand from a political standpoint. Not only had B'nai B'rith long fought for ratification, but because the Senate would be in session for only three more weeks, Reagan could score political points without fear that the convention would be brought up for a vote before the presidential election.

Advocates for ratification were thrilled, but opponents chalked up the decision to electoral politics. Activist groups on the right were especially angry. A Liberty Lobby statement charged that Reagan was "bowing to the pressures of an election year" and "placating the internationalist lobby by dragging out this old treaty, which none of his predecessors has been able to persuade the Senate to ratify."[115] Despite these criticisms, Reagan's public support brought along many conservatives. In October 1984, the SFRC voted unanimously to approve ratification, and the entire Senate later voted eighty-seven to two for a resolution approving the treaty's principles and pledging quick action at the next legislative session.

Reagan's changing attitude toward humanitarian policies was important, but the real push for ratification came in the wake of an unexpected controversy during his trip to Europe the following spring. When his advisers planned a wreath-laying ceremony at a military cemetery in Bitburg, West Germany, in May 1985, they did not realize that forty-nine members of the Waffen SS were buried there. Reagan's refusal to cancel the trip touched off a firestorm of criticism among Jewish and veterans' groups. The American Jewish Committee stated that it would be "morally obscene" for the president to place the wreath, while the head of the Polish American Congress asserted that Polish Americans were dismayed by Reagan's decision to memorialize German soldiers "while declining to pay tribute to the countless victims of the Nazi-German Holocaust."[116] The decision also became ammunition for Soviet propagandists. *Izvestia* alleged that Reagan's "reconciliation with fascism" was consistent with

Washington's justification of "the crimes of the American Rangers in Korea and Vietnam [and] the subversive activity of the Somocista contras." (This prompted Reagan to pen an angry response in his diary: "Forty years after the Holocaust, the Soviets are the only ones officially practicing anti-Semitism.")[117] Rather than cancel the cemetery visit, Reagan defended the trip as a gesture of goodwill toward America's former enemy, and he agreed to visit a concentration camp. When he returned to Washington, his administration pushed the Genocide Convention as a means of mending fences. With Reagan's full backing, the Senate finally ratified the convention early in 1986.

Reagan's growing amenability to human rights and democracy would last throughout his second term. His administration developed a two-tiered policy of opposing violations whenever action was feasible—even the violations of long-standing allies—and addressing the long-range need to build stronger institutions and political systems. Many motives were involved, but the official explanation for this second track was that respect for human rights was more likely under a democratic form of government.[118] This policy shift was not without its controversies. Activists and legislators would challenge the administration's view of events in Central America and South Africa, while conservatives and allied foreign governments would insist that Cold War security concerns were still central to America's global interests. Reagan's December 1984 Human Rights Day speech signaled his willingness to accommodate both sides of this debate in his second term. With Andrei Sakharov's son-in-law and Anatoly Shcharansky's wife at his side, he accused the Soviet Union of religious persecution, suppression of individual liberty, systematic anti-Semitism, and forced psychiatric confinement. But for the first time, his primary message was not a harsh attack on Moscow, but rather an enthusiastic endorsement of the world democracy trend.[119]

Chapter 5

Global Human Rights, Democracy, and the Cold War's End

Three hours after the death of Konstantin Chernenko on March 10, 1985, the Soviet Politburo named Mikhail Gorbachev to the post of general secretary. It would be hard to overstate this decision's effect on the Soviet Union, East-West relations, and the development of individual rights in Central and Eastern Europe. If the Politburo had chosen someone else, or if Gorbachev had been a more doctrinaire leader, then the history of this region would surely have been very different. Western policymakers and activists had achieved only limited results with Brezhnev, Andropov, and Chernenko, but Gorbachev seemed to offer something new. At a time when the Soviet ship of state was being steered by the elderly, the fifty-four-year-old Gorbachev infused new ideas into the Kremlin. He later wrote of his accession, "There was a sense, an intuition, that an era was coming to a close. . . . The very system was dying away; its sluggish senile blood no longer contained any vital juices."[1]

Gorbachev's pedigree suggested that he might be a different kind of leader. He was a student of law and economics, and his travels throughout Europe had given him a firsthand look at wealthier, more liberal societies. His reformist instincts were matched by a modern political style that impressed British Prime Minister Margaret Thatcher, who later wrote of their first meeting, "His personality could not have been more different from the wooden ventriloquism of the average Soviet *apparatchik*. He smiled, laughed, used his hands for emphasis. . . . I found myself liking him."[2] Gorbachev and his foreign minister, Eduard Shevardnadze, would dominate Soviet foreign policy decisions between 1985 and 1991, and Gorbachev would become a domestic reformer nonpareil with his unprecedented economic and political restructuring programs, perestroika and glasnost. In a way that few could have predicted, Gorbachev and Ronald Reagan would transform all facets of U.S.-Soviet relations by hammering out groundbreaking agreements at summits in Geneva (1985), Reykjavik (1986), Washington (1987), Moscow (May 1988), and New York (December 1988).

Yet although Cold War postmortems present an image of the Reagan/Gorbachev relationship as one of amiability, pragmatism, and even friendship, in reality their interactions were fraught with disagreement. Gorbachev was a committed socialist and Reagan a fervent anticommunist; whenever they met, they differed on nearly every substantive issue. Indeed, it was a major leap of faith for the two men even to meet. The confidential diplomatic channels so painstakingly established in the 1960s and 1970s were neglected during Reagan's first term as a result of the Soviets' provocative global moves and Reagan's anti-Soviet rhetoric and military buildup. "One is constantly struck," writes the historian Fraser J. Harbutt, "by the great difficulty these two great systems of power had in even considering the possibility of fundamental change."[3] Nevertheless, these leaders managed to look past their differing worldviews and political systems to forge the most fruitful détente of the entire Cold War era. Their working relationship contributed mightily to transforming the human rights situation in Eastern Europe.

This chapter highlights human rights in American foreign policy from 1985 to 1991. When compared with the ideological rigidity of the decade's first half, this period saw a striking transformation in Washington's outlook on democracy and human rights. The combination of new leadership in Moscow and the Reagan administration's more open-minded attitude brought the two nations into a complicated but fruitful détente that fostered new possibilities in arms control, regional issues, and civil freedoms. Congress and the Reagan administration also exerted various forms of pressure to encourage democratic transitions in the Philippines, Haiti, and Chile, and Congress took the lead in fighting apartheid in South Africa. With the decade's conclusion came the end of Soviet domination of Eastern Europe, as well as democratic transitions that speeded the Cold War's end. But these developments also fostered unforeseen problems. While the liberalizing trend was spreading through Eastern Europe and the Soviet Union, the George H. W. Bush administration faced an unexpected humanitarian crisis in China and potentially explosive national independence struggles in the Soviet republics. Central America, too, remained a contentious region in Washington throughout the 1985–1991 time frame.

Gorbachev, Perestroika, and the Reagan Turnaround

When Mikhail Gorbachev arrived on the scene, Reagan administration officials noted his energy and his style, but they had mixed expectations on substance. The U.S. embassy in Moscow warned the administration that Gorbachev was likely to be much like his predecessors. "Most of the indications are that he is a clone [of the older leaders]," said an official.[4] Vice President Bush and Secretary of State Shultz came to a different conclusion after meeting him. Their appraisals were tempered with caution, but their clear impression was that they were dealing with a unique figure. Shultz told reporters that Gorbachev was "totally different from any Soviet leader I've met."[5] Bush was even more effusive, noting that Gorbachev had a disarming personality and "an engaging way of making an unpleasant point and then bouncing back to establish real communication with his interlocutors." When Bush raised human rights matters, Gorbachev struck back with charges of American violations, but he also suggested an ongoing dialogue. Even Gorbachev's personal appearance was untraditional. "This Gucci Comrade," wrote Bush, "beats the hell out of the Penney's basement look that some of his predecessors projected."[6]

The initial Reagan-Gorbachev dialogue was not very promising. In a pair of cautiously optimistic introductory letters, Reagan emphasized his interest in eliminating nuclear weapons, and added that American interest in humanitarian progress "remains as strong as ever." He assured his counterpart that the issue was important to all Americans, and he expressed hope that the two sides could resolve some specific problems. Gorbachev replied that he, too, wanted better relations, but he also asserted that nations had the right to choose their destiny without interference. "There should be no misunderstanding," he wrote, "concerning the fact that we do not intend and will not conduct any negotiations relating to human rights in the Soviet Union." Reagan then tied human rights to other bilateral concerns. He wanted more trade, but added that a fundamental change in trade relations was unlikely "without parallel improvements in other aspects," including emigration, persecution of Christians and Jews, and Soviet involvement in Latin America. In a defensive reply, Gorbachev once again rejected American involvement in his nation's domestic affairs, though he did leave the door open for continued arms talks and a super-power summit.[7]

As a result of these arguments and the apparent worsening of conditions for Soviet dissidents, the administration developed a low opinion of Gorbachev's reformist potential. Not only had the authorities wiped out the nascent human rights movement in the Soviet Union, but they had also stepped up oppression of religious and ethnic minorities. Gorbachev even went on the offensive and ordered his advisers to raise "our own banner of human rights" in order to prevent the West from winning the propaganda battle. The State Department concluded that Gorbachev "seems determined that the U.S.S.R. will not be put in the position of apologizing for its policies."[8]

It is clear from these early exchanges that the fundamental disagreement remained in place. The Americans argued that Soviet internal policies limited bilateral possibilities, while the Soviets countered that American demands were the limiting factor. Moreover, while Reagan was broaching human rights and arms control in his letters to Gorbachev, he was also publicly applauding Soviet dissidents and assailing the Kremlin's record of treaty compliance.[9] He saw no contradiction in mixing firm public language with conciliatory private missives, but these mixed signals confused and angered the Kremlin. Vice President Bush counseled Ambassador Dobrynin not to take Reagan's rhetoric too seriously, but Dobrynin concluded that Reagan did not realize, or did not care, that his "loose anti-Soviet rhetoric" damaged relations. "All those things combined incomprehensibly yet harmoniously in his mind," mused the ambassador.[10]

On the tenth anniversary of the 1975 Helsinki Final Act, there was a general feeling of disappointment in the West. Emigration numbers had dropped and Helsinki monitoring groups had been dismantled. Despite the Final Act's value as a standard of conduct, stated Secretary Shultz, "the most important promises of a decade ago have not been kept."[11] Nevertheless, the agreement had at least created a forum in which East and West could speak face to face. The Ottawa Experts' Meeting of May and June 1985 was the first Conference on Security and Cooperation in Europe (CSCE) meeting dedicated entirely to the Final Act's human rights provisions, and five months later the Budapest Cultural Forum became the first to deal exclusively with the act's cultural content. "At least the Soviets come to talk," said Jeri Laber of Helsinki Watch, "and sometimes it's the only forum where East/West relations are raised and they have taken a lot of abuse without walking out."[12]

It remained to be seen whether Reagan and Gorbachev, too, would be able to hash out their differences in a scheduled exploratory summit in Geneva, Switzerland. This promised to be a unique meeting, for although American and Soviet trade and arms control specialists had been negotiating for years, the two leaders had not developed a relationship. So while arms reductions and conflict prevention would remain primary goals, each side hoped that the Geneva Summit would establish a personal rapport and lay the groundwork for future agreements. The Soviets reluctantly agreed to include human rights matters as one of the four major items for summit discussion alongside arms control, bilateral issues, and regional issues. In stark contrast to the Nixon/Ford détente a decade earlier, the Reagan administration began to embrace the argument that a government that did not respect its citizens' rights and live up to its international human rights commitments would not be trustworthy in other areas. Reagan's advisers suggested that his "key message" should be that "respect for the individual and the rule of law is as fundamental to peace as arms control."[13] Shultz and National Security Adviser McFarlane also tried to convince their Soviet counterparts that there were practical reasons for improvement. They claimed, for example, that Moscow's internal policies were road blocks to better relations because America was a nation of immigrants who took these issues very seriously. Shultz suggested an informal reciprocity: if the Soviets released a few high-profile dissidents, increased emigration, or even took up some dual citizenship and divided spouse cases, then the Americans could offer trade incentives and energy development contracts. He promised that the administration would take no credit if the Kremlin decided to act.[14]

Before the summit, Shultz also gave Gorbachev an impromptu lecture on the free market, the link between personal freedom and economic freedom, and the likelihood that a more liberal Soviet Union would also be more prosperous. The world was changing rapidly, he told Gorbachev— business, information, and technology developed from the freedom of individual innovators, and "closed and compartmented" societies were bound to fall behind. "People must be free to express themselves," said Shultz; "move around, emigrate and travel if they want to, challenge accepted ways without fear." Shultz expected a defensive response, but because Gorbachev knew firsthand the endemic weaknesses of the Soviet economy, he was surprisingly amenable. "You should take over the planning office here in Moscow," he quipped, "because you have more ideas than they have."[15] Over the next few years, Shultz would reprise his professorial role and give Gorbachev several informal economic "seminars." But Gorbachev and Shevardnadze's openness had its limits. They wanted a stronger, more prosperous nation, and they worried that human rights concessions would look like a surrender to the West. They also wondered why the Americans cared about Soviet citizens, though in time the Kremlin would use this American interest to their advantage, and would garner concessions in exchange for minor reforms.

In the buildup to Geneva, each side was willing to use goodwill gestures to improve the bilateral environment. The Soviet authorities resolved some divided family cases and the Politburo allowed Andrei Sakharov's wife, Yelena Bonner, to travel to the United States for medical treatment. She had long been Sakharov's intermediary with the West and, to the dismay of the authorities, also a frequent visitor to the U.S. embassy. Her efforts had so angered the Politburo that one member even called her "a beast in a skirt, an imperialist plant." Wanting to appear magnanimous, they freed her but maintained that the decision was "purely our internal matter" and that Bonner had to pledge not to speak to journalists. Reagan administration officials also assumed a more moderate posture, and Reagan himself told a reporter that he saw no need for the two countries to point accusing fingers at each other.[16]

The November 1985 Geneva Summit was a breakthrough. Since it had been more than six years since the previous summit, most of the agenda was aimed at creating trust and sounding out areas of mutual agreement. Neither side planned to grant any major concessions.[17] After a day of talks on arms control, Strategic Defense Initiative (SDI), and each nation's military industry, Reagan decided to broach human rights with Gorbachev on the second morning with only the interpreters present. In a seventy-minute chat (it was scheduled for only fifteen minutes), he explained the nuances of the American political system and stressed that Congress, powerful lobbies, and ethnic and religious groups took human rights very seriously. He suggested that as long as NGOs and immigrant groups perceived oppression, the two governments would not be able to do much. Shortly before the summit, for example, the entire Senate had sent him a letter encouraging him to discuss such matters in Geneva. He insisted that the two leaders would be able to accomplish much more if the Kremlin freed more dissidents or loosened other restrictions. He then handed Gorbachev a list of people who sought to emigrate or reunite with family members, and he pledged that he "would never boast that the Soviet side had given in," citing the Pentecostal precedent as proof of his good intentions. Gorbachev responded by stressing two things. First, an "atmosphere of goodwill" was impossible as long as American agitators politicized Soviet affairs. The bilateral relationship must improve before humanitarian issues could be fully addressed. Second, not only were there many injustices in America, but Gorbachev did not agree that the president was "so dependent on the opinion of small groups." Surely he could follow whatever path he desired—a sentiment that led Reagan to exclaim, "You sure are wrong about an American president's power!"[18]

Although they agreed on nothing, the conversation was significant not only for its candidness, but also because Reagan chose to have it. Activists in Congress and the public may have influenced his decision to do so, but he was also acting on his own principles. When the two men and their respective entourages met again that afternoon, Gorbachev noted a general agreement on the principle of arms reductions, but he clearly feared SDI. He proclaimed that the Soviet Union would dramatically reduce its offensive weapons as long as neither side opened "an arms race in space," and Reagan once again linked "trust" in arms agreements to Soviet human rights.[19] In their final meeting, both men admitted that there had not been much concrete progress at the summit, but they agreed that it was good to be talking. The postsummit statement was steeped in sanguine language concerning each side's desire to continue negotiating on everything from civil aviation agreements and exchange initiatives to nuclear nonproliferation. The document included nothing on human rights, save for their agreement "on the importance of resolving humanitarian cases in the spirit of cooperation."[20]

In the final analysis of Geneva, each leader recognized that the other was committed to his worldview. Gorbachev later wrote that Reagan's human rights charges were nothing new, though he admitted in his memoir that he fended off accusations "even though I was not always convinced that these were not justified." Yet he was steadfast that the United States had no right to impose its standards on other countries. He told his colleagues that Reagan was not merely a conservative; he was a "dinosaur"— "so loaded with stereotypes that it was difficult for him to accept reason."

Reagan similarly came away with the impression that Gorbachev "believed propaganda about us that he had probably heard all his life." When Gorbachev read the minutes of their first meeting many years later, he was surprised by the "extremely ideological" stands they had taken, concluding that they read "like the 'Number One Communist' and the 'Number One Imperialist' trying to out-argue each other." Tempers flared hottest when they discussed human rights, SDI, and the conflicts in Afghanistan and Central America. Nevertheless, they were thick-skinned enough to acknowledge that a frank working relationship was far better than isolation. "The human factor," wrote Gorbachev, "had quietly come into action."[21] As for Reagan, he enjoyed the one-on-one meetings, and he was particularly intrigued that Gorbachev had twice invoked God's name and had even cited a Bible verse. "After almost five years," Reagan wrote in his memoir, "I'd finally met a Soviet leader I could talk to."[22]

The public and the press scored the summit a great success for Reagan, whose approval rating reached 84 percent, the highest of his presidency. Some criticized him for not achieving more, but most understood that there were limits to what could be accomplished in a first meeting. When asked why the joint communiqué disregarded humanitarian issues, Reagan replied that nothing could be achieved by "pushing the Soviets into a corner."[23] But he also reiterated in his postsummit address that "those countries which respect the rights of their own people tend, inevitably, to respect the rights of their neighbors." Human rights, then, was not "an abstract moral issue," but rather "a peace issue."[24] The response from Congress was overwhelmingly positive. As Reagan wrote in his diary, "I haven't gotten such a reception since I was shot."[25]

Once Geneva had set the right mood, a rather surprising thing happened. The Reagan administration implemented major changes to its global human rights policy, while Gorbachev embarked upon the most sweeping Soviet liberalization program since the Khrushchev era. Neither leader could have known that this combination would contribute to the fall of the Berlin Wall, the democratization of Eastern Europe, and the dissolution of the Soviet empire. Given the high degree of East/West animosity, these breakthroughs were not yet clear to contemporary observers. Arms talks stalled, due in part to American nuclear tests in Nevada, U.S. airstrikes on Libya, and the April 1986 explosion at the Chernobyl nuclear plant. In the summer and fall, a few minor diplomatic incidents spun into a crisis that culminated in the arrest and deportation of several diplomats. The bilateral

friction extended into the human rights arena. The administration continued to press the Soviets on human rights, and Gorbachev continued to
call these "domestic" matters. Shortly after Geneva, Reagan suggested to
Gorbachev that action on human rights and a withdrawal from Afghanistan
would show the world that the Soviets were serious about peace and progress. "The political importance of resolving such well known cases as the
Sakharovs, Shcharansky, and Yuri Orlov cannot be overestimated," he
wrote, while the status quo would "only hold us back." Gorbachev
responded much as he had the previous year. The relationship was not
imperiled by Soviet inaction, he argued, but by the "continuing attempts
by the American side to tie up trade and economic relations with questions
of a different nature." Soviet emigration laws, he insisted, were not a matter
for bilateral consultation.[26] Despite this friction, they were able to harness
enough of the Geneva momentum to arrange a summit in the neutral site
of Reykjavik, Iceland.

Much of this energy was sustained by Mikhail Gorbachev's broad-
minded worldview and his drive for domestic reform. Gorbachev's reputation as a reformer stems from his far-reaching liberalization program,
widely remembered in the West through the terms *glasnost* ("publicity,"
"openness") and *perestroika* ("restructuring," economic reform). Simply
put, he believed that his nation needed fundamental institutional changes
to engender improvements in productivity, the quality of life, and national
strength. Gorbachev may have believed that the West would give him some
credit if he implemented these reforms—indeed, he grew increasingly interested in the Soviet Union's integration into Europe—but his primary interests were domestic. He did not promote these policies in order to conciliate
Americans.

Perestroika was his first project. The Soviet economy was so sclerotic
that Gorbachev famously told his wife the night before he was elected general secretary, "We can't go on living like this."[27] In April 1985 he proposed
reforms that encouraged decentralization and economic incentives. More
significant to the international human right story was his elucidation, the
following year, of the need for major changes in political and social policies.
Glasnost, he told the 1986 Party Congress, was the necessary catalyst for
"the political creativity of the masses."[28] In Gorbachev's eyes, the slow pace
of economic change required glasnost to accompany perestroika. This did
not mean an overnight embrace of Western-style liberalism, as neither Gorbachev nor his more conservative adversaries wanted change to come too

rapidly. But the policy did initiate a gradual liberalization in the production of news, literature, and entertainment, and it facilitated an unprecedented opening of the public sphere. This trend accelerated considerably toward the end of the decade, spreading even beyond the Soviet Union's borders to influence events in Eastern Europe and China. (By decade's end the trend would become too strong for Gorbachev to manage.)

While Gorbachev and his reformist comrades were implementing major changes in the Soviet Union, the Reagan administration's human rights posture was also undergoing a profound change. The combination of Reagan's evolving attitude, Gorbachev's rise to power, and the global democracy trend made the administration more willing to promote democracy and criticize allies like South Korea, South Africa, and El Salvador. Reagan's December 1985 Human Rights Day speech anticipated this shift. Although he detailed communist nations' abuses, he did not dwell on the Soviet Union for fear of damaging the still-fragile détente. More significantly, he implied that his administration would no longer give allied governments a pass. "The American people cannot close their eyes to abuses of human rights and injustice," he said, "whether they occur among friend or adversary or even on our own shores." He called on South Africa to take steps toward ending apartheid, and he pointed out Chile and the Philippines as two places where the United States had shown its strong concern "when our friends deviate from established democratic traditions."[29] Two months later, Reagan tasked Secretary of State Shultz with conducting a major effort for achieving U.S. human rights objectives with the Soviet Union.[30]

Cautious Democracy Promotion: Haiti and the Philippines

Haiti and the Philippines were two major tests for Reagan's policy shift. In both cases, the administration showed a willingness to cut ties with friendly governments when these leaders lost the support of their people. However, Reagan and his advisers were also quite cautious. They responded to events far more than they intervened to shape outcomes, and they refrained from major efforts until it seemed that the governments in question were no longer tenable. With respect to the Philippines, Congress arguably played as important a role as did the executive in applying pressure to the regime. American actions in these two states also contrasted sharply with Reagan's continuing support of right-wing dictators—Indonesia's Suharto, for example—who maintained a firm grip on power.[31]

Haiti's endemic poverty and political mismanagement had long troubled Washington.[32] The John F. Kennedy administration had cut aid to the dictatorial government of François "Papa Doc" Duvalier, but later administrations were more willing to accept Duvalier and his son, Jean-Claude "Baby Doc" Duvalier, as regional anticommunist allies. During Reagan's first term, the younger Duvalier's authoritarianism did not stop the administration from continuing aid allocations. But trouble in Haiti led twenty-five thousand refugees to flee to Florida. The Congressional Black Caucus sought higher refugee numbers and more attention to Haitian suffering, while most Floridians wanted to curb the refugee influx. In 1982, Congressman Dan Mica (D-FL) authored an amendment that made U.S. assistance conditional upon Haitian cooperation in halting emigration, as well as "concerted and significant" democratic reforms within Haiti. Mica's amendment was a means of addressing the refugee problem while also pressuring the Reagan administration and formally rebuking the dictatorship.

In the next three years, the administration sent mixed messages on Haiti's compliance. Reagan continued to support aid to Duvalier, but the State Department's annual country reports included detailed criticisms. As late as October 1985, Secretary Shultz was reporting to Congress that the Haitian government was "making progress toward implementing political reforms," but by the end of the year the administration had concluded that Duvalier's repressive policies all but forced the United States to terminate assistance. In response to strikes and widespread rioting, the administration announced in January 1986 that it would not certify Haiti. Secretary Shultz went even further, stating in a television interview that the administration wanted to see a democratically elected government.[33] The isolated Duvalier fled Haiti for France on February 7, and the administration recertified Haiti shortly thereafter. In the aftermath of Duvalier's departure, even Reagan's opponents credited him with taking a firm stand against a dictatorship.

The administration had practical and humanitarian reasons to encourage democracy in Haiti, including curbing the influx of émigrés. But in the end, the administration gave up on Duvalier because he had lost the support of the Haitian public. The decision to suspend aid and convince Duvalier to abdicate was almost purely pragmatic—in Thomas Carothers's words, "a quick and sensible reaction to a crisis, not the implementation of a premeditated policy." Unfortunately for the administration, despite the high economic costs to the United States (aid nearly doubled to $101 million by 1987), the democratic transition failed. Duvalier's successor, Lieutenant General Henri Namphy, proved unwilling to give up power, and General Prosper Avril, who toppled Namphy in 1988, ruled with an iron fist for the next two years. Carothers accurately concludes that the administration's chief fault in Haiti was that it established a goal that it could not achieve and gave Namphy diplomatic and financial backing before observing his performance. The United States could not easily enforce a smooth transition in this troubled nation, but it could have distanced itself from the new autocrats while saving tens of millions of dollars.[34] Given the prevailing social conditions, Haiti was not a good laboratory for an experiment in democracy promotion.

The Reagan administration faced a similar predicament in the Philippines, where President Ferdinand Marcos had long practiced a brand of political control that observers described as constitutional authoritarianism mixed with "crony capitalism." Elected president in 1966, Marcos took an authoritarian turn six years later in the face of internal threats and dissolved the legislature, censored the news media, carried out mass arrests, and wrote a new constitution. He lifted martial law in 1981, but continued to limit political participation and crack down on dissent. Yet the staunchly anticommunist Marcos was friendly to American business and security interests, including the presence of two of America's largest Pacific military installations, Clark Air Base and the Subic Bay Naval Complex. Moreover, the United States had a special bond with the Philippines as a result of former colonial ties, the struggle against Japan in World War II, and shared regional security concerns. There were fifty thousand American civilians in the Philippines and eight hundred thousand Filipinos in America.

Reagan sought to strengthen the relationship for security reasons and because of his long-standing friendship with the Marcos family. Consequently, military aid and U.S. payments for base leases increased during Reagan's first two years. When Reagan welcomed Marcos to Washington in 1982, he praised the Philippines' economic development and the joint security relationship.[35] But the sheer magnitude of problems facing the Philippines made close U.S. ties awkward. Not only was Marcos an autocrat, but the country was plagued by high unemployment and an insurgent coalition led by the Marxist New People's Army (NPA). At the center of all this was Marcos himself, whose nepotism and lavish lifestyle angered many. There were widespread rumors that he had chiseled billions from his impoverished nation's citizens and from U.S. aid grants, and much was made of his wife Imelda's three thousand pairs of shoes. In the face of the NPA insurgency and a weak economy, his regime increased political detentions and was accused of heavy-handed anti-insurgent tactics, including torture and extrajudicial killings of civilians. When his political opponent, Benigno Aquino, was killed in August 1983, many Filipinos held Marcos responsible. Filipino liberals, the Catholic Church, and the middle class began to join with human rights activists to oppose his rule.

This was a dire combination for Marcos's long-term legitimacy. Between 1983 and 1986, there was a growing feeling in Washington that Marcos was unable to hold together his nation's disparate elements. The historian David Schmitz has noted that the Philippines posed a dilemma for Reagan much like Jimmy Carter had faced in Iran and Nicaragua: a U.S.-backed dictator was being weakened by economic trouble, a military insurgency, middle-class opposition, and global ostracism. Having learned from Carter's mistakes, Reagan did not want to abandon an old friend simply to have something worse take his place. While Reagan himself stood firm in his backing of Marcos, the State Department and the U.S. embassy wanted to pressure Marcos to reform in the interest of fending off the insurgency and maintaining order.[36] It is worth noting that this strategy originated for reasons of security rather than humanitarianism, though in time the desire for liberal reforms and representative government would become more attractive to American policymakers.

The administration's new approach to the Philippines developed within the context of Reagan's democracy promotion policy. The Reagan-Marcos correspondence shows a marked upswing in talk of democratic procedures from 1983 onward, much of it in the form of a Reagan-proffered quid pro quo arrangement. In exchange for Marcos taking steps toward democratic reforms, Reagan would work to supply more development aid, loan restructuring, and a higher share of the U.S. sugar quota. It is clear from this correspondence that Marcos took American concerns seriously. He was confident of Reagan's personal support, but the mild rebukes expressed in the 1983 and 1984 State Department country reports showed that he was facing more scrutiny in Washington. When Reagan politely asked Marcos to follow democratic procedures in the scheduled May 1984 legislative assembly elections, Marcos personally assured him of "objectivity and fairness" and "the widest possible participation" of political parties. Through a set of new reforms, his government was "bending over backwards to allow the opposition to express itself and to obtain every possible chance of winning."[37]

Publicly, Reagan defended Marcos in black-and-white terms, arguing that if the United States did not stand by him then the Philippines could fall to the NPA. In his October 1984 presidential debate with Walter Mondale, Reagan laid out the prospect of "losing" the Philippines: "I know there are things there in the Philippines that do not look good to us from the standpoint right now of democratic rights, but what is the alternative? It is a large communist movement to take over the Philippines." The United States would be better off, he argued, maintaining the friendship and encouraging reforms "rather than throwing them to the wolves." Mondale retorted that Reagan was simply tying the United States to yet another dictatorship at a time when "we need to make it clear we're for human liberty."[38] After Reagan's reelection, the administration became more active in nudging Marcos toward reforms and elections. A secret national security directive concluded that the Philippines' weaknesses threatened American interests, and it laid out a program to strengthen democratic institutions with the ultimate goal of facilitating a peaceful, democratic transition. The administration would maintain contact with leaders from various institutions and communities, would continue to link financial aid to economic and political liberalization, and would seek market reforms that curbed cronyism, encouraged responsible military leadership, and promoted political reforms. They saw Marcos as "part of the problem," but "also necessarily part of the solution"—that is, the administration preferred a democratic system with or without Marcos. Since it was possible that he would try to use the United States to remain in power, Washington would have to avoid "being made hostage to Marcos' political fortunes" or being saddled with responsibility for defeating the insurgency. After Reagan summed up some of these conclusions in a letter to Marcos, the State Department leaked the secret directive in March 1985, ostensibly to let Filipinos know where the administration stood.[39]

Assistant Secretary of State Paul Wolfowitz and Assistant Secretary of Defense Richard Armitage became particularly vocal about the need for democracy. Wolfowitz met with several leaders of the Manila political opposition in January 1985, and upon his return to the United States he publicly identified the major problems. True to the administration's public line, he stressed the communist threat and noted "considerable" progress in political reforms. But he also called for more substantial changes in Filipino

military operations, especially with respect to abuse of civilians. "The communist insurgency cannot be combated effectively without also addressing
the political and economic problems that the communists exploit," stated
Wolfowitz. "The best antidote to communism is democracy." (This was a
noteworthy conclusion, since mainstream conservatives had long argued
that the best antidote to communist insurgents was military force.)[40] By the
end of the year, Marcos's rule came under increasing public scrutiny in
America, and Congress became much more active. Not only was the Filipino military reluctant to reprimand its worst charges, but U.S. defense
officials grumbled that they were not a strong fighting force. The administration's public position matched its private one: it sought more security
assistance from Congress while it also pressed Marcos hard for reforms.
Testifying before the SFRC in October 1985, Wolfowitz threw a bone to
Senate conservatives by emphasizing the security motives behind the reforms. America would continue to stand by its ally to prevent a communist
takeover, but the administration wanted to see revitalization of democratic
institutions, the free market, and military professionalism. On this point,
Wolfowitz saw no conflict between U.S. interests and democracy: "We are
not afraid of democratic change. To the contrary, we believe that reform is
essential to prevent a communist victory."[41]

Reagan followed the State Department's suggestion of urging reforms,
but he also wanted Marcos to remain in power, and he wanted to maintain
control over U.S. policy. When he asked Marcos whether he could hold off
the insurgency, Marcos replied in a long, handwritten letter that he was
"crestfallen" that Reagan was influenced by the dire predictions. "We are
not another South Vietnam," he declared.[42] Reagan may have been primarily interested in fending off the insurgency, but Congress was more interested in a democratic transition. A Senate intelligence report blamed the
Marxist NPA's growth on endemic poverty, Marcos's policies, the military's
abuse of civilians, and the regime's loss of credibility after the Aquino killing. Meanwhile, congressional hearings exposed Marcos's acquisition of
American real estate through laundering and secret investments, a revelation that undermined his credibility in both countries. When a subcommittee voted unanimously to halt military aid, it was another message to
Marcos and Filipino citizens that he did not have America's full support.[43]

Following more American expressions of concern, in November 1985
Marcos made a surprise announcement that the presidential election
planned for late in 1987 would now take place in February 1986. It seems

that Marcos believed his opponents were too disorganized to win, but events would prove him wrong. Immediately following the February 7, 1986, contest between Marcos and the opposition coalition's consensus candidate, Corazón Aquino, Marcos declared victory, while international and American observers found evidence of vote rigging and intimidation. The observers also generally concluded that Aquino had won. Reagan, who believed that a Marcos victory was in America's interest, suggested that there were irregularities on all sides—a claim that Congressman Stephen Solarz (D-NY) called "proof positive that they are smoking marijuana in the White House."[44] As thousands poured into the streets of Manila and the provincial capitals, Reagan was faced with a tough decision: support a long-standing American ally or withdraw support and let the chips fall where they may. If he chose the latter, the United States could improve its image by aligning itself with the popular will, though the Philippines could also devolve into chaos, civil war, and a Marxist grab for power. Members of Congress and NGOs then went on the offensive. Senator Sam Nunn (D-GA) crystallized congressional opposition when he argued that Marcos had lost legitimacy with the majority of Filipinos. "If we are not perceived as being unalterably opposed to this election fraud," said Nunn, "the United States itself will become a target of the hostility of the Philippine people." America's business and military presence, he argued, were useful only "if the people want us there."[45] This was a rather traditional "national interests and anticommunism" argument, but it melded well with democracy and human rights promotion. The Senate then overwhelmingly passed a resolution that Marcos had stolen the election. Nevertheless, calling the election fraudulent and telling Marcos that he must step down arguably meant that Americans were taking a side in another nation's very close election. After all, many Filipinos still supported Marcos.

Two weeks after the election, Reagan's National Security Planning Group hammered out a potential solution. Having concluded that the election was seriously flawed and that the ongoing unrest threatened to spill over into "massive bloodshed," the group considered a different tack. Much of the military had joined the opposition, as had two of Marcos's cabinet members—one even admitting that he had participated in the election fraud. Yet international observers still feared that Marcos might use force to keep himself in power. Deputy CIA director Robert Gates's argument won the day. Because the Filipino public believed that Aquino had won, the United States had to see her into office and give Marcos a dignified way out. "Let's be realistic, not legalistic," said Gates. "Aquino in, Marcos out." Shultz, Gates, and Philip Habib then convinced a reluctant Reagan that this was the best option. Reagan alerted Marcos that the United States would protect him and his family, and the administration issued a statement calling on him to step down. Reagan's friend, Senator Paul Laxalt (R-NV), made a phone call to Marcos on February 24 and told him that he no longer had U.S. support. "I think you should cut and cut cleanly," said Laxalt. "I think the time has come." The United States flew Marcos and his family to Hawaii, and his place was taken by Corazón Aquino, whom the United States recognized immediately. There was very little bloodshed.[46]

The Philippines story hardly highlights Reagan as a democratic visionary. In essence, the United States stopped backing Marcos out of self-interest rather than to "support democracy." The Philippine president had been losing legitimacy for several years, and his weakness imperiled the American interest in stability and security. If he had been able to provide his people with a better living standard, domestic peace, and basic democratic procedures, Washington would have looked the other way indefinitely. But the unrest got Americans' attention, as did the apparent ascendance of communist insurgents. Since both the right and left in America wanted a friendly leader who had popular support, Reagan had little choice but to act because of the two countries' special relationship and because the election was major news in the United States. While the administration was cautious throughout, Marcos found that he had fewer and fewer friends in America. In the end, Reagan recognized that he could grant him asylum without facing repercussions as Carter had faced for helping the Shah of Iran. (Having absconded with millions of dollars, Marcos could still live a lavish lifestyle.) But it is also true that the Reagan administration had begun encouraging democratic reforms at least three years earlier, and had also stepped up pressure after Reagan was reelected. When Corazón Aquino took power, even Reagan's opponents applauded him. The following September, Aquino thanked the United States in front of a joint session of Congress, and legislators lubricated the transition by voting up a $200 million aid package.

The Reagan administration quickly built on the legacies of Haiti and the Philippines with several new steps in March 1986 alone. In its first condemnation of Chile in the UNHRC, the United States called on General Augusto Pinochet to rein in his security forces, stop torture, and implement democratic reforms. The administration also came out in favor of majority rule in South Africa, and Reagan delivered a groundbreaking message to Congress in which he asserted that his administration would oppose *all* dictatorships. In the worldwide democratic revolution, he declared, "there can be no doubt where America stands. The American people . . . oppose tyranny in whatever form, whether of the left or the right. We use our influence to encourage democratic change."[47] Reagan had several motives here. The anti-dictatorial message fit in with his long-standing support for democratic transitions, and he could not help but notice that Americans had reacted positively to the events in Haiti and the Philippines. With Congress debating aid to the Nicaraguan contras, he hoped that "democracy promotion" would offset legislators' opposition. And since several other nations had democratized in the eighties, including nine in the Western Hemisphere alone, it was now less dangerous to oppose dictatorships. When Marcos and Duvalier lost their legitimacy, Reagan could argue that human rights (vaguely defined as a dictator's ouster) were now in America's national interest. Whatever the reasons, the shift was clear. "It is rare indeed," wrote the journalist Tamar Jacoby, "that an American president reverses his position on a major issue. Yet Ronald Reagan seems to have done just that, picking up the pieces of a human rights policy he tried very hard to dismantle in his first days as president."[48] This transition surely had as much to do with public opinion and Reagan's political instincts as with international developments and his personal beliefs.

Meanwhile, Central America remained the clearest example of Washington's politicization of the human rights cause. The administration continued to make a political choice to ignore or downplay friendly regimes' violations while publicizing those of the Nicaraguan Sandinistas, the Cubans, and various left-wing insurgency groups. Reagan held up Honduras, Guatemala, and El Salvador as successes in progress, though even the most optimistic observers admitted that the latter two were hobbling toward peace and democracy at a snail's pace. While these societies were in flux, the administration continued to condemn the Sandinistas as a regional aberration. As part of Reagan's case to Congress, the State Department issued detailed reports with titles like "Persecution of the Catholic Church in Nicaragua" and "Crackdown on Freedom in Nicaragua." A report titled "Broken Promises: Sandinista Repression of Human Rights" portrayed a climate of fear and a regime devoted to arbitrary arrest, torture, political killings, and disappearances.[49] In order to counter Soviet aid, Reagan pushed a trade embargo through Congress in May 1985, and in 1986 he asked Congress for $100 million in contra aid. "You can't defend yourself against Soviet helicopter gunships with bedrolls," he declared. He called the contras "the moral equivalent of our Founding Fathers" and privately lamented the sophistication of the "pro-Sandinista lobby on the Hill. . . . Nicaragua is nothing but a Soviet-Cuban base on our mainland."[50]

Some of the administration's Sandinista criticisms were valid, or at least seemed to be, given the Nicaraguans' poor public relations decisions. Shortly before Sandinista leader Daniel Ortega addressed the United Nations in October 1985, his government implemented a state of emergency and cracked down on civil liberties amid the contra guerrilla threat. The *New York Times* called these restrictions "the Sandinista road to Stalinism," and argued that the Nicaraguan Revolution's pluralistic promises had been "hopelessly betrayed."[51] Ortega also raised American hackles when he pursued closer ties to the Soviet Union and Cuba for financial and security reasons. The Reagan administration contrasted these events in Nicaragua with "positive" steps in El Salvador, while also making much of the threat posed by Salvadoran FMLN guerrillas. There was some truth to this charge as well. In June 1985, Salvadoran guerrillas kidnapped President Duarte's daughter and killed several locals and Americans in an attack on the Zona Rosa nightclub. At the end of 1985, the administration once again certified that El Salvador had made significant progress in reducing political violence, improving the justice system, and working toward democracy with its latest election. But congressional liberals and NGOs asserted that the administration was overstating its case. Americas Watch agreed that the Sandinistas were guilty of abusing prisoners and suspending press freedoms, but the group reserved its sharpest criticism for the contras. It concluded that in 1986 "violations of the laws of armed conflict by the contras cause great suffering to the Nicaraguan people" and that "disregard for the rights of civilians has become a de facto policy of the contra forces."[52]

Reagan's attention to Nicaragua created a scandal that threw his Central America policy into disarray and nearly ended his presidency. The Iran-contra affair began when Iran made a back-channel request to buy U.S. weapons for the Iran-Iraq War. Iran was no American ally, but Reagan hoped the sale would win the release of Americans who were being held hostage by Iranian-backed terrorists in Lebanon. Despite divisions among his top advisers, the existence of an arms embargo, and Reagan's own promise that America "does not negotiate with terrorists," the missile sale went through. The sale did not solve the hostage problem, but it provided seemingly untraceable funds that enterprising NSC officials diverted to the contras in violation of the Boland Amendment. When the Iran-contra story was leaked, Reagan first denied that any such operation had taken place, and then stated that he had no knowledge of it. Nine days after the 1986 election, the White House admitted that the United States had sold arms to Iran, and two weeks later they admitted that funds had been channeled to the contras. A congressional inquiry concluded that Reagan was ultimately responsible as the chief executive, while the Reagan-appointed Tower Commission exonerated Reagan but was otherwise very critical of the whole affair. Although Reagan was never directly linked to the Iran-contra decisions, his presidency was seriously weakened for nearly a year in 1986–1987. But the scandal did not bring down his presidency, nor did it interrupt the long-term trend in human rights policymaking or the U.S.-Soviet détente.

The Perils of "Constructive Engagement": South African Apartheid

While insurgencies in Central America were giving Reagan headaches, South Africa was becoming yet another testing ground for the administration's human rights posture.[53] Despite the long-standing global criticism of apartheid, during the 1970s and early 1980s antiapartheid activism in America was the purview of a relatively small number of student activists and civil rights groups. Then, between 1984 and 1986 the cause developed quite rapidly into a broad-based global movement and a front-burner issue in America. Unlike with Eastern Europe and Nicaragua, President Reagan was not at the forefront of calls for change in South Africa. His administration did make some moves to encourage South African reforms, but many Americans were under the (often flawed) impression that Reagan sought to preserve the status quo. The ongoing violence and injustice led Congress to take the lead in establishing the parameters of American policy.

The debate in America was not between supporters and opponents of apartheid, as virtually no one in Washington supported this system. Rather, the debate was defined by three central conflicts. The first was between Cold War hawks, who perceived South Africa in a geostrategic context, and those who rejected the Cold War framework as outmoded or irrelevant to South Africa's social and political problems. The second was between supporters of gradual evolution, who hoped to see apartheid peacefully dismantled over time, and proponents of rapid change. The third conflict was between isolationists, who believed America had no role to play in South Africa, and interventionists, who believed the United States should play a central role. In the first two conflicts, President Reagan was in the former camp. He considered the Southern Africa region—Angola, Zambia, South Africa, South West Africa (Namibia), Mozambique, and Rhodesia/Zimbabwe—a Cold War battleground, and he hoped to see South Africa evolve slowly toward majority rule. In the third conflict, he fell somewhere in the middle. He disagreed with apartheid in principle, but was far more concerned with Eastern Europe and Central America than Africa. During his first term, he was generally swayed by those advisers who emphasized South Africa's economic and strategic importance.

Meanwhile, the Congressional Black Caucus, TransAfrica, and liberal Democrats generally rejected the Cold War geopolitical analysis in favor of a U.S.-led effort to bring rapid changes to South Africa. The Reagan administration was divided, as were congressional Republicans. Conservatives generally ran the gamut from those who had little interest in South Africa to those who supported close relations with the Afrikaners out of fear that South Africa could otherwise be a future "loss" for America, à la Nicaragua, Iran, and Cuba. Conservative Republicans clashed with the State Department, party moderates, and more liberal party members like Richard Lugar and Lowell Weicker.

Two developments are central to this story: the Cold War, and the general Western rejection of racial supremacist ideologies and racial separatism. That is to say, the antiapartheid cause would have had considerably less impact in America had it not been for the waning of the Cold War after 1985 and the discrediting of racism in American culture. Indeed, the antiapartheid movement and its accompanying economic and diplomatic outcomes—withdrawal of trade and investment ("disinvestment"), sanctions, and Pretoria's political isolation—comprise perhaps the clearest case of the human rights movement as an outward expression of America's own troubled evolution. Americans had only recently come to grips with their own racial issues, and the fight against apartheid was a way for them to show how much they had advanced. By the 1980s, racism had been so thoroughly discredited in polite circles that antiracism had become a part of American national identity. The scholar David L. Hostetter has aptly suggested that American antiapartheid activism had the most impact when it defined South African conflict in terms that were familiar to Americans.[54] The solutions—social equality, democracy, and civil liberties—also seemed simple. Antiapartheid activists' promotion of their cause as a straightforward *moral* struggle gave it more resonance than did complex strategic explanations.

This activism had a downside. Few Americans understood the complexities of South African society, its political divides, or its ideological conflicts. Most saw it as a simple matter of proapartheid versus antiapartheid, racists versus antiracists, or even righteous blacks versus sinister whites. Fewer still understood the regional political and military situation or the extent of Cuban and Soviet influence in Southern Africa. Some scholars have all but ignored the Cold War ideological basis of American political decision making, preferring instead to paint a picture of morally upstanding activists undercut by apartheid apologists.[55] In regard to outsiders' sanctimony, Assistant Secretary of State Chester Crocker wrote in 1989 that the Southern African region had become "a moralist's theme park" because it featured "almost every form of odious human behavior," from Marxism and authoritarianism to racism and terrorist violence.[56] Still, from the standpoint of liberal, Western societies, it was hard to deny South Africa's systemic inequalities. The formal implementation of *apartheid* (Afrikaans for "apartness") in 1948 clarified that full citizenship was only held by the nation's whites, not its three other racial classifications: "blacks," "Asians," and "coloreds." Technically, blacks were citizens of ethnic homelands created by the government in Pretoria. Not only were nonwhites denied the political rights of South African citizenship, such as voting and officeholding, but the apartheid philosophy also necessitated an all-encompassing range of laws that denied social and legal equality to nonwhites well into the 1980s.

When Ronald Reagan entered the White House, his administration's holistic approach placed apartheid alongside several other Southern African problems. The low priority they accorded apartheid was natural for an administration that was lukewarm about changing noncommunist societies but fully dedicated to challenging Soviet and Marxist influence in the developing world. Reagan hoped to reestablish U.S. influence in order to push the Soviets and Cubans out of Angola and Mozambique, decrease violence between South African forces and neighboring guerrillas, achieve independence for Namibia, and encourage South Africa's political evolution. A more stable region, his experts hoped, could weaken Soviet influence and relieve the pressure exerted on South Africa by its neighbors—pressure that had long reinforced white South Africans' siege mentality. These goals necessitated working with vastly different governments, liberation movements, militaries, and Western allies.[57]

Reagan had long been critical of apartheid, and upon taking office he maintained the existing antiapartheid resolutions and laws. But he also sought to strengthen relations, arguing that engagement would help Washington promote reforms. Most American businesses were already following the Sullivan nondiscrimination principles, and Reagan believed that sanctions and disinvestment would hurt black South Africans while reducing American leverage. The administration surely had other considerations in mind as well. Americans had nearly $10 billion in business and investments in South Africa, and annual bilateral trade was nearly $4 billion. South Africa also produced a substantial share of vital raw materials like platinum and chrome—commodities that were otherwise plentiful only in the Soviet Union. There were also strategic considerations. South Africa stood as a gateway between the Atlantic and Indian Oceans, and the anticommunist Pretoria government was fighting Soviet- and Cuban-backed forces in neighboring countries. Just as Reagan had sought to strengthen ties with other anticommunist states during his first year in office, he put out feelers to South African leaders.[58]

The administration eventually adopted a policy of "constructive engagement," which was intended to combine private diplomacy and positive incentives to pull South Africa out of its isolation and encourage peaceful steps toward multiparty democracy. The policy was the handiwork of Assistant Secretary Crocker, who sought a middle course between the neglect of the Nixon/Ford years and the antagonistic approach of President Carter. A regional outlook was central to this posture. The United States would work with European and African governments to end the region's cross-border fighting and facilitate stability that would allow for negotiated solutions in South Africa and elsewhere. Ideally, the policy would undercut the violent separatism of the most militant Afrikaners and blacks. "Although we may continue to differ on apartheid and cannot condone a system of institutionalized racial differentiation," Crocker advised the president, "we can cooperate with a society undergoing constructive change." The administration would maintain the arms embargo, but would also avoid trade and investment sanctions. The two nations began exchanging intelligence on Cuban activities in Africa, and the United States vetoed

Security Council resolutions against Pretoria. If America was willing to negotiate with the Russians, argued Reagan, then it should also do so with South Africa.[59]

Though there is little evidence that Reagan's policy was a cynical ploy to keep apartheid intact, critics charged that constructive engagement demonstrated his administration's disdain for human rights standards. Trade and security cooperation were geared toward the American national interest, while promoting human rights and a peaceful democratic transition were only secondary concerns. Perhaps the chief problem with constructive engagement was that it was predicated on substantial reform efforts within South Africa. On this count, the government of Prime Minister (later President) P. W. Botha fell far short of expectations. Despite Pretoria's steps toward "modernizing" apartheid, they did not appear to be pursuing a multiracial democracy. Yet the Reagan administration proved highly tolerant of this position, and did not demand concrete reforms in exchange for U.S. concessions.[60]

This lack of visible progress was exacerbated by Reagan's failure to build effective domestic support for constructive engagement. The administration did a poor job of publicizing its broader goals, though it was also true that the American public had little patience for complex explanations and regional solutions. While the administration insisted that its policies were bearing fruit, congressional liberals and moderates assailed the lack of results. It appeared to many apartheid opponents that Reagan was defending a regime that refused to enact true reforms. It did not help Reagan's cause that the most vocal South African opposition leaders also disapproved of constructive engagement. Bishop Desmond Tutu called the Reagan administration's "support and collaboration" with the South African government "immoral, evil, and totally un-Christian."[61] When Pretoria introduced a new constitution in 1984, Reagan approved the move as a step in the right direction. But most South Africans opposed it because it granted legislative reforms only for "Asians" and "coloreds," not the nation's twenty-two million blacks.

Events in South Africa then brought the issue onto the American legislative agenda. A series of violent township uprisings began in August 1984 and continued for several years. As images of violence and police reprisals were broadcast with greater frequency in America, opinion polls showed that apartheid was unpopular in America, though few had a firm grasp on South African realities, and fewer still had a clear idea of what the U.S.

government should do.⁶² Activists targeted the constructive engagement policy, which, while it did not cause South Africa's violence, was clearly not alleviating it. The Reagan administration's obligations in South Africa were debatable, but there was no denying that Reagan's policy had not engendered substantial changes.

Between 1984 and 1986, the apartheid issue pitted Congress and NGOs against the Reagan administration in America's first major national conversation about Africa policy. Meanwhile, the antiapartheid crusade became the biggest international human rights campaign since the Soviet Jewry movement of the 1970s. NGOs and national legislatures joined to condemn South African abuses and Reagan's apparent indifference, and they pressured American and European corporations to change their practices or to withdraw their operations. Even best-selling musicians got into the act. The 1985 "Sun City" protest record included a cross-section of the world's most famous recording artists. In the United States, where the campaign was called the Free South Africa Movement, longtime activists marveled at this upsurge in attention. As a Chicago organizer stated in 1985, "In my twenty years of working on this [cause], I have never seen such a groundswell as we are currently seeing." By this time, thirteen state governments, eleven city governments, and over one hundred colleges and universities in the United States had dropped their South African investments.⁶³

Owing to the apparent lack of progress, Congress threatened to take control of South Africa policy. Legislators deliberated bills that would restrict bilateral trade, limit the importation of South African currency, and make the Sullivan Principles mandatory for U.S. businesses. Fearing a legislative coup, Reagan decided to get ahead of the curve. In the summer of 1985, the White House affirmed the need for "basic reforms moving away from apartheid, which system we consider to be repugnant and largely responsible for the current violence." The administration was careful not to indict the government too harshly, but behind the scenes they were tougher. Classified memos argued that Pretoria's "half-hearted reforms" and "continuing failure to demonstrate a real commitment to black advancement" had created the present tragedy. The administration hoped to join with its European allies to put "maximum pressure" on South Africa to introduce "meaningful and speedy reforms with the clear intent of eliminating the policy of apartheid." Assistant Secretary Crocker laid out the fundamental proposition that apartheid was abhorrent and the violence had to stop ("any status quo that excludes 73 percent of the population . . .

affronts our fundamental values"), but he added that the U.S. approach could not be insulated from concerns for regional stability, security, or the competition with Moscow.[64]

By 1985–1986, the administration could point to a few successes that may have been influenced by American initiatives. South Africa and Mozambique had signed a nonaggression pact, South Africa had withdrawn many of its troops from Angola, and there had been progress in the Namibian independence process. South Africa now allowed black voting in local elections, limited power sharing with "Asians" and "coloreds," and free black trade unions. The government also desegregated workplaces and private schools, repealed antimiscegenation laws, and abolished forced resettlement. In January 1986, President Botha committed to equality of education and restoration of citizenship to blacks. Three months later, the government repealed the humiliating system of internal passports known as the "pass laws." But the township uprisings focused American attention on the violence rather than the steps that had been gradually eroding apartheid. Moreover, few Americans considered the apartheid issue as one among many regional problems; rather, they perceived the issue as a unique, straightforward case of an undemocratic government oppressing its subjects. Thus the debate in America became a simple one of "constructive engagement" versus "sanctions," with other regional issues largely ignored. Sanctions became the default position of "doing something" about apartheid.[65] In light of the opposition, the Reagan administration then got more specific with the potential economic ramifications of sanctions. A Commerce Department study estimated that termination of U.S. investment would cost the United States $400 million in direct exports, 14,000 jobs, and $7.2 billion in the market value of corporate assets.[66]

As it became clear in 1985 that Congress, including many Republicans, was no longer willing to accept constructive engagement, conservatives ramped up their fight. For interested Americans, South Africa became an ideological battleground much like Nicaragua and El Salvador, with each side cherry-picking information that helped its cause. Conservatives emphasized a combination of domestic and international ideological connections, arguing that many antiapartheid factions were radicals.[67] In response to the Western news media increasingly suggesting that the African National Congress (ANC) was the legitimate majority party, conservatives pointed out its ties to Cuba, the Soviet Union, South African communists, and terrorist organizations. They also highlighted the ANC's acts of violence against other blacks and their terror bombings against the general population. While Nelson Mandela's refusal to renounce violence in exchange for amnesty made him a hero to many, it made him a pariah to others. "There is no alternative to taking up arms," he said from his prison cell in 1985. "There is no room for peaceful struggle."[68] White House staffer Phil Nicolaides privately argued that most Americans were unaware of the multiple voices of black aspiration because public opinion was being molded by groups "dominated by left-wing ideology," especially TransAfrica, which sought to replace the South African government with the "Soviet-controlled African National Congress."[69]

Some South Africans asserted that Americans were ignorant of this far-away nation's affairs. One moderate argued that Americans seemed "unable to grasp the complexity of race relations in South Africa: eleven major languages, four races, twelve major religions, vast disparities in income and education—the world in microcosm." Many black South Africans were against sanctions and disinvestment, including Gatsha Buthelezi, the chief of six million Zulus. Lucy Mvubelo, a director of the nation's largest trade union, argued that South Africans who sought disinvestment and boycotts "are simply a small fringe of desperate revolutionaries. They realize the basic condition from which revolution can rise does not exist, thus the world must create it. Who will suffer? Clearly the greatest hardship would fall on my people, the black people."[70] Terrorists bombed Mvubelo's home in 1984. There were also uncomfortable questions about the dismal human rights records of other African nations that received less attention from activists. Still others asked whether South Africa deserved so much censure considering it had the strongest economy on the continent. In the 1970s, the House subcommittee on Africa held over seventy public hearings on the three white-controlled countries in Africa—South Africa, Rhodesia, and Namibia—and none on other African states, even though many of these states were plagued by violence and autocracy. Fully 85 percent of black Africans were effectively disfranchised because of military coups, suspension of constitutions, one-party rule, or outright dictatorship.[71] None of this is to suggest that apartheid was a just system. But critics of the American antiapartheid movement could legitimately ask why injustice in relatively prosperous South Africa was worthy of U.S. government intercession while Washington ignored undemocratic, and often murderous, regimes elsewhere on the continent. As the scholar Ryan M. Irwin has asked, given the many crises of this period, why did apartheid engender such a powerful global response? The antiapartheid movement, writes Irwin, "flattened human rights discourse and hardened binaries of power resistance" in such a way that the experiences of real South Africans were oversimplified.[72]

Late in 1985, Reagan issued an executive order that banned new loans, imports of South African military equipment, and exports of American computer products. In an attempt to win over realists, he declared that South African policies constituted "an unusual and extraordinary threat to the foreign policy and economy of the United States." He then added an unmistakable moral condemnation: apartheid meant "deliberate, systematic, institutionalized racial discrimination, denying the black majority their God-given rights. . . . We condemn it, and we're united in hoping for the day when apartheid will be no more." But he tempered the tough message with an appeal for moderation. America's influence was limited, he argued, and unlike many African and Eastern European states, South Africa was "not a totalitarian society." The United States should support peaceful opponents of apartheid, oppose those who used violence, and avoid sanctions that would harm "the very people we're trying to help."[73] This gambit bought him some time, but because the executive order was more moderate than most of the legislative proposals, his opponents kept South Africa on the congressional agenda. As a substantial antiapartheid act worked its way through Congress, the administration worked to maintain control over American policy.

Reagan's policy statements did little to remedy the perception that his administration was unfocused. His July 1986 speech to the World Affairs Council and the Foreign Policy Association illustrated the intra-administration divides. The State Department's Africa Bureau hoped that this speech would help Reagan reclaim the moral authority to shape policy while also giving the American people a sense of where apartheid and bilateral relations were heading. But they underestimated his continuing adherence to a Cold War model of world affairs. In the speech, Reagan reiterated that apartheid was "morally wrong and politically unacceptable" and was the root cause of South Africa's troubles, and he criticized the heavy-handed tactics of the South African police. But he offered little in the way of a blueprint for further progress. In a provocative demonstration of his geopolitical views (and a sign that administration conservatives had helped draft the speech), he assailed the "calculated terror" wielded by "the Soviet-armed guerrillas of the African National Congress." Reagan's opponents were incensed that he seemed to be blaming the ANC for South Africa's ills. Desmond Tutu found the speech "nauseating," adding that Reagan "sits there like the great big white chief of old" who "tells us black people that we don't know what is good for us." In Assistant Secretary Crocker's view, this speech lost Reagan the sanctions debate because it gave his congressional allies nothing to work with.[74]

Congress then took the reins in August and September 1986. Overwhelming majorities passed a far-reaching sanctions package, the Comprehensive Anti-Apartheid Act (CAAA), which went much further than Reagan's executive order. The act effectively declared that the establishment of a nonracial democracy in South Africa was the U.S. government's central goal. The legislation increased the list of banned imports and exports, halted importation of vital raw materials, prohibited bilateral military cooperation, terminated flights, and cut trade assistance to companies that violated the Sullivan Principles. It also laid out specific steps that Pretoria should take, including releasing Mandela and setting a timetable for elimination of apartheid laws. Considering the Republicans' slim fifty-three to forty-seven Senate majority, a veto override was impossible without Republican support. Unfortunately for Reagan, Democrats would soon win a fifty-five to forty-five Senate majority in the 1986 election. Worse yet, many Republicans not only signed onto the CAAA, but up-and-coming congressmen like Newt Gingrich and John McCain even helped craft the language. These defections grew from contemporary events: Reagan's policies had not curbed the violence, and Congress was more willing to challenge the executive in Reagan's second term. The CAAA was also palatable to Republicans because they had added amendments banning U.S. assistance to the ANC until the organization had expelled communists and renounced violence. The most important factor, though, was that institutionalized racism was perceived as the root of the problem in South Africa. Americans who understood almost nothing about South Africa at least understood that there was official racism. Thus legislators who did not act appeared immoral.

Both houses overrode Reagan's veto—the first time since the 1973 War Powers Act that Congress superseded a presidential veto on foreign policy legislation. Alongside similar sanctions from the British Commonwealth and the European Community, the CAAA dealt a powerful blow to Pretoria and placed a heavy burden on South African and American businesses. Much like the Soviet Jewry movement, this was a human rights case in which activists and the news media publicized the cause and then found a great deal of sympathy in a Congress that was wary of presidential indifference. As Chester

Crocker argued, the fundamental struggle in Washington was not over apartheid, but rather over control of America's South Africa policy.[75] Yet the sanctions package put Reagan's opponents into a difficult position. They had to persuade Americans that they were obliged to change South African *society*, not just effect a transition to democracy. Human rights activists were faced with the hard reality that South Africa was not Argentina or South Korea. It was a multiracial state with inequalities and animosities that had been built up over centuries. Was it America's job to change such a society?

The administration agreed to enforce the law—a sign, perhaps, of its own exasperation with the Pretoria government—and it employed tougher rhetoric while enhancing opposition contacts and promising increased aid for "black empowerment." Reagan's new appointee, Ambassador Edward J. Perkins, who was the first African American to hold the position, became an energetic advocate for change. Over a hundred American companies sold their South Africa subsidiaries in 1986–1987, and the majority of the remaining two hundred subscribed to the Sullivan Principles. In the next two years, conditions within South Africa got worse before they got better. The township unrest and the state of emergency continued, and the nation's economy flagged as a result of disinvestment, sanctions, and domestic violence. President Botha continued some reforms but would not negotiate with banned organizations like the ANC until they renounced violence. Meanwhile, with the Kremlin now less willing to support insurgents in the global South, there was a growing acceptance in Washington that Moscow did not have major designs on the region. Afrikaners' claims that they were standing firm against a combination of the "red menace" and the "black threat" rang increasingly hollow.[76]

In September 1987, Secretary of State Shultz gave a landmark speech that laid out specific goals regarding equal rights and a democratic constitution. The administration still opposed sanctions, and Shultz acknowledged that no outside nation could impose a solution, but he declared that the United States would support moderates' efforts to create a "new constitutional order" that included multiparty elections and that guaranteed political and social rights for all.[77] Thus much like the administration's approach to El Salvador earlier in the decade, they openly aligned with moderates of all races against white and black extremists. It is unclear whether Reagan was pushed in this direction by the congressional sanctions, changing geopolitical realities, the domestic movement, or some other factor. But in the final years of his presidency and in the first few years of George H. W.

Bush's, the U.S. government became an open, though cautious, supporter of a fully democratic South Africa. Lasting changes would come in the wake of the 1989 election of the reformist F. W. de Klerk as president. Within months of his accession, he lifted the state of emergency, legalized banned parties, and freed political prisoners, including Mandela. Through a set of tough negotiations in the next few years, South Africans embarked on a dramatic transition to the postapartheid era.

Back in the U.S.S.R.: Glasnost, the Summits, and the New Détente

Reagan's handling of Eastern European dissident issues in 1986 showed that he was careful not to provoke the Kremlin. After the Soviets freed Anatoly Shcharansky in a prisoner exchange, he made a triumphal visit to the United States that included an address in the Capitol and a private visit with the president. Shcharansky's release was widely seen as a Reagan victory, but the president walked a fine line to preserve the burgeoning détente. With the administration negotiating for the release of Andrei Sakharov, Reagan chose not to meet with his wife, Yelena Bonner. There was no doubt that he sympathized with Bonner's cause, but the minor "snub" led critics to recall President Ford's rebuff of Aleksandr Solzhenitsyn a decade earlier. Reagan responded by declaring Andrei Sakharov Day and publicly criticizing "the overall grim human rights situation" in the Soviet Union.[78]

The dissident issue then became entwined with a series of incidents that posed a major threat to the Washington-Moscow thaw. In August, the FBI arrested a Soviet scientist, Gennadi Zakharov, who was caught selling technical information to an undercover agent. The Soviets retaliated by arresting American journalist Nicholas Daniloff in Moscow on trumped-up espionage charges. The Reagan administration made Daniloff's release one of their chief conditions for continued U.S.-Soviet talks, and they added a list of twenty-five Soviet dissidents to the negotiations. The Soviets freed Daniloff late in September, and shortly thereafter the Americans freed Zakharov in exchange for Yuri and Irina Orlov and two other dissidents. (Zakharov had pled nolo contendere to the charge of selling documents.) Administration officials denied that this was a quid pro quo exchange, but the truth was unmistakable. The day that Zakharov was released, Shultz announced that the dissidents would also be released and that a U.S.-Soviet summit would soon take place in Reykjavik, Iceland.[79] The Zakharov-Daniloff episode was only the fourth such spy exchange in the entire Cold War era, and it was doubly significant in that the administration went out of its way to put the Orlovs on the agenda. The Zakharov arrest also set relations on a downward spiral that included tit-for-tat arrests, expulsions of diplomats and alleged spies, a Kremlin halt to grain purchases, and Soviet complaints that they had found listening devices in their new Washington embassy. Gorbachev sent an angry letter to Reagan decrying the "massive hostile campaign" against the Soviet Union, and he fumed to the Politburo that the Americans "behave like bandits."[80] This conflict formed the backdrop to the October 1986 Reykjavik Summit.

Each side had very different goals in Reykjavik. Secretary Shultz counseled Reagan that arms control and human rights were the two issues that demanded the most progress. "Gorbachev must go home," said Shultz, "with a clear sense that Moscow's continuing insensitivity to the humanitarian dimension" was hindering other breakthroughs. Despite some progress on dissident cases, the State Department noted that prospects for Soviet Jewry were bleak and that emigration levels were at their lowest point since the 1960s. This drop-off had led many Americans to question the efficacy of private diplomacy. Others in the administration suspected that Moscow's occasional freeing of a few dissidents had prevented them from enacting a more liberal emigration policy. Gorbachev, by contrast, planned to make big offers at Reykjavik. He would press a 50 percent reduction in nuclear weapons and would pledge further cuts, but he would give no ground on human rights. He even promised the Politburo that he would go on the offensive and point out America's many social ills. "We should continue in the assertive spirit," he told the group—even, if possible, enticing émigrés to return to the Soviet Union. "Get the return flow in motion," he implored. "We need to be more upbeat about these things, more upbeat!"[81]

When Reagan and Gorbachev met, they reprised their roles from the Geneva Summit. Reagan continued to argue that liberal reforms would help establish mutual trust, while Gorbachev continued to counter that these were internal matters. Their meetings were characterized by ideological sniping and accusations that each side misunderstood the other nation.[82] Regarding nuclear weapons, Reagan agreed that avoiding war was the most important bilateral issue, but he also connected arms control to humanitarian issues. Once again he highlighted American public opinion and familial ties to the Eastern Bloc, arguing that bilateral agreements would be easier if the public were not aroused by injustices in their ancestral homelands. "If the Soviets loosened up, we would not exploit it," he promised. "We would simply express our appreciation." He also handed Gorbachev a list of twelve hundred Jews who wanted to emigrate.[83] Gorbachev countered that each nation had the right to organize its society according to its own terms, and he lashed out at Reagan's earlier comment that socialism needed to be relegated to "the ash heap of history." The Soviet public was equally concerned about human rights in America, he assured Reagan. He then attempted an unusual cultural bargain. He proposed an end to jamming of Voice of America if the United States would accept Soviet broadcasts, and he asked why so many American films were shown in the supposedly "undemocratic" Soviet Union but virtually no Soviet films were shown in "democratic" America. Reagan, who knew a bit about the film industry, countered that the difference was a function of the market; if Gorbachev visited the United States, he would see that people really could express their beliefs. In the end, the two men brokered no film or radio deals.

The Reykjavik Summit would be remembered not for human rights breakthroughs, but for the way in which the two leaders snatched defeat from the jaws of victory over nuclear weapons and SDI. In their final meeting, they came to a remarkable verbal agreement that each side would reduce, and eventually destroy, its nuclear arsenal. But Gorbachev's condition was the abandonment of SDI, a suggestion that Reagan would not consider. Less than two months later, Reagan's annual Human Rights Day speech began with an optimistic recounting of recent democratic trends, but he added a scathing critique of the communist states' intransigence. With the recently freed dissidents Yuri Orlov and Anatoly Shcharansky at his side, he assailed the Soviets' "posturing" and their restrictions on emigration, dissent, and religious activity. "These realities remain unacceptable," he asserted, "and we will continue . . . to bring our moral and diplomatic weight to bear on behalf of those brave souls who speak out within the Soviet bloc."[84]

Despite the grandstanding and the apparent setback, the two sides were willing to move forward. In a way, they had no choice but to soldier on. Not only were they committed to reducing arms and decreasing the possibility of war, but they were further goaded on by international democratization and human rights trends. In 1987, the Pinochet government in Chile legalized political parties and scheduled a plebiscite on the general's rule. South Koreans held their first democratic presidential elections since 1971

and ushered in a political transition that paralleled their impressive economic growth. In both cases American pressure played a significant role,
though not necessarily a determinative one.[85] The Vienna round of the
CSCE, which began in November 1986 and would carry on until 1989, was
already being hailed for its productivity. Back in the Soviet Union, the
Kremlin quietly granted exit visas to dozens of the people on Reagan's lists.
The Politburo also released most of the remaining political prisoners,
decriminalized some previously banned literature, announced higher emigration visa numbers, and stopped jamming Voice of America broadcasts.
In a striking move, the Soviets then freed Andrei Sakharov from internal
exile. Since the authorities had long considered him to be among the most
symbolic of dissidents, his liberation was a clear sign to the West that the
reformers meant business. Many in Congress and the administration now
believed that Gorbachev's desire for internal liberalization was genuine,
though conservatives had misgivings about Soviet expansionism and the
still-deadly conflicts in Central America, Afghanistan, the Horn of Africa,
and Southern Africa.

U.S.-Poland relations and Polish human rights practices also improved
considerably as Warsaw tilted toward the West to escape its economic troubles. In 1986, the Europeans were willing to join the United States in taking
a much stronger human rights stand, and this transatlantic unity brought
significant changes to Poland. A joint U.S.–European Economic Community threat to withhold credits or to maintain sanctions indefinitely led
Warsaw to release all of its political prisoners.[86] When the State Department's John Whitehead visited Warsaw in February 1987, the authorities
told him that he could not meet with Lech Walesa because the activist had
"used all of his vacation days." Whitehead's threat to skip his meeting with
President Jaruzelski then convinced the Poles to deliver Walesa to the U.S.
ambassador's residence. During Whitehead's tense meeting with Jaruzelski,
his comments about the regime's domestic repression elicited the customary objection to outside "interference," and this in turn prompted Whitehead to note that the United States preferred to choose friends who treated
their citizens with respect. He went on to propose a quid pro quo in which
the United States would grant trade and investment concessions in response
to Polish advances in personal freedom. The United States would move
"just as fast as you are willing to go," he said.[87]

In response to some Polish moves, the Reagan administration lifted
economic sanctions in 1987 and restored MFN status. In September, Vice

President Bush traveled to Warsaw to further mend fences and to cast himself in the role of statesman for the 1988 presidential election. He brought a promise that the United States would reschedule much of Poland's foreign debt, and he offered further assistance if Poland moved toward political pluralism. He also pointedly met with leaders of the Catholic Church and Solidarność. The regime made the unprecedented decision to broadcast Bush's address on live television. "It is not for me to try to tell you what road to take," he told his audience. "But I can tell you what has worked in our country and in many other countries. It is respect for human rights. It is the right to form independent and self-governing organizations. . . . It is an economic system that encourages people to reach their full potential."[88] A wave of strikes the following year would force the Polish government to recognize Solidarność for the first time, and this recognition would be the beginning of the end for Polish communism. The Polish people were the driving force behind their nation's political changes, but Aryeh Neier of Helsinki Watch has made a compelling argument that the Reagan administration's steady, managerial approach to sanctions also played a part. In contrast to earlier all-or-nothing ultimatums, the sanctions worked because they were based on measurable, incremental steps that the Polish government could meet. Once the regime allowed dissent, it had to negotiate with Polish citizens who sought to transform the system, not work within it. Poland was thus one of the Reagan administration's clear successes.[89]

U.S.-Soviet relations also improved during 1987–1988. The two sides made great leaps in arms control negotiations, and the administration became somewhat less aggressive in its human rights demands because perestroika and glasnost were changing Soviet society. Secretary Shultz's working relationship with Gorbachev and Shevardnadze also became much more productive, due in part to the Soviets' respect for Shultz. In elaborating on the connection between individual rights and free market economics, Shultz emphasized that significant action on these fronts would advance the Soviet economy and that "the gap will widen between nations that adapt to the information age and those that do not."[90] Sticking points remained, of course. While in Moscow, Shultz attended a Passover Seder with several refuseniks at the U.S. ambassador's residence. And it was in June 1987 that Reagan stood at Berlin's Brandenburg Gate and demanded that Gorbachev tear down the Berlin Wall.

But the Soviets were willing to show restraint because they were becoming convinced that SDI was years from completion. By September 1987, the

Kremlin's posture had changed considerably. Gorbachev sent a conciliatory letter to Washington in which he hinted that he would make bold concessions on arms control and regional conflicts, and Shevardnadze indicated that Moscow wanted to clear up all dissident and divided family issues. "Give me your lists," he told Shultz, "we'll be glad to look at them." Within one year of Shultz's Passover Seder, all of the refuseniks in attendance had been allowed to emigrate.[91] These changes were significant because Gorbachev had consistently maintained the Brezhnev position that the Soviet Union would not be pressured, and he had always rejected American interference in his nation's affairs, often to the point of defending blatant violations. But he became more open to these conversations, in part because he sought further liberalization and in part because he hoped that such concessions would enable victories in other areas. He had taken the reformist path in order to strengthen his nation, and now he sought to preserve this domestic agenda and win more Western concessions.

Still, there was the danger that perestroika and glasnost would spin out of control if implemented too quickly—a reality that was lost on many Americans. In August 1987, demonstrations broke out in the Baltic republics of Latvia, Lithuania, and Estonia on the anniversary of the Molotov-Ribbentrop pact. The authorities' decision not to crack down galvanized nationalists throughout the Soviet Union, especially in republics with strong ethnic identities, like Ukraine and Armenia. The following year, tens of thousands gathered to demonstrate on the same anniversary, and Estonians created a national independence party. These developments made it clear to Gorbachev that the new reforms could foster dangerous nationalist and separatist tendencies. Although he wanted to liberalize socialism, he was committed to maintaining the Soviet Union and the Warsaw Pact. He had no tolerance for separatists, in part because their activities could encourage Soviet conservatives to suspend perestroika. There is also evidence that Gorbachev believed the Baltic states could not survive on their own, and thus would not ultimately declare independence. Events would prove him wrong on both fronts.[92]

The December 1987 superpower summit in Washington turned out to be the breakthrough meeting. Now beginning his final year in office, and with his popularity beginning to recover from the Iran-contra scandal, Reagan was more open to an agreement than ever. Gorbachev, too, was at the height of his popularity. Glasnost and perestroika were in full swing, and large crowds turned out to greet him wherever he went. More importantly, the two men had learned to trust one another, and they pulled off a major arms-control pact. Yet even with these breakthroughs, they continued to lock horns over human rights. At their first meeting, Gorbachev was conciliatory on the humanitarian front. When Reagan introduced a list of divided family cases (about which a Soviet aide later wrote, Reagan "had to show off in front of his own people"), Gorbachev noted the Soviet Union's multiethnic character and its various levels of autonomy, and he assured Reagan that protecting this diverse population's rights was always on the Kremlin's agenda. The "occasional roadblocks" on domestic freedoms and emigration would be solved. But when Reagan continued to press him on religious freedom, Gorbachev stressed that he "would not sit as the accused before a prosecutor." He also challenged Reagan's rosy interpretation of life in America and lashed out at America's immigration policies, noting that the U.S.-Mexico border was guarded with fences and guns. "What kind of democracy is this?" he asked.[93]

At a later meeting, Gorbachev acknowledged that his reforms were causing him difficulties at home. He had yet to impress Soviet conservatives and much of the public, and he had to be careful not to overpromise or act too quickly. He wanted the Americans to ease up on their criticisms so that he could continue to fight those "who sought to shackle people in dogma" and "adventurists" who wanted to forge ahead haphazardly. When he met with members of the U.S. Congress, he argued once again that it was "unacceptable for one side to assume the role of a prosecutor and the other side that of the accused." He then turned the tables on his interlocutors, pointing out that America, too, had its problems, and he defended the traditional Soviet emphasis on economic and social rights: "We believe our human rights are better than your human rights. . . . We believe in the right to a decent standard of living of every human being, of every individual's right to security. . . . Examine your own record."[94]

Despite the disagreements, both sides considered the summit a success. They signed the Intermediate-Range Nuclear Forces (INF) treaty, which was the first ever agreement to reduce nuclear arsenals rather than merely limit weapon production. Their joint statement was the first to acknowledge human rights as a subject of bilateral concern, and there was much more openness behind the scenes. The State Department's summary concluded that "our discussion has become systematized. We talk about everything: names, lists of cases, Soviet laws." Gorbachev's Politburo briefing spoke volumes about the momentous changes in the relationship. The discussion was constructive, he said, and Reagan was no longer "blaming us for the crises of the modern world. . . . This is bigger than Geneva or Reykjavik."[95]

Although the U.S. side was cautiously supportive of Gorbachev's reforms, most policymakers underestimated his willingness to move quickly on arms reductions, nuclear abolition, and, ultimately, ending the Cold War. While the Americans pushed for more rapid social and political changes, Gorbachev asked his Washington counterparts why Reagan seemed so hesitant on arms control. Was it because of congressional conservatives? The defense industry? Why, he asked Shultz, was the administration "still operating under the assumption that there's a real threat of communist aggression"?[96] The perception went beyond Reagan himself. State Department analysts were largely unwilling to believe that Gorbachev wanted to transcend the Cold War. They advised instead that his primary foreign policy objective was to achieve stability in Soviet foreign relations in order to create breathing room for domestic economic reforms. Meanwhile, some in the Soviet Union were still persecuted.[97] Moreover, although Reagan dealt with the Soviet leaders directly, he continued to support anticommunist insurgencies in places like Nicaragua and Afghanistan. "Reagan changed his image of the Kremlin," writes Beth Fischer, "but he did not revise his assessment of communism."[98] All the while, Gorbachev faced mounting difficulties at home. In February 1988, anti-Armenian violence in Soviet Azerbaijan claimed three dozen lives and signaled a new era of open ethnic conflict in the Caucasus region. The world was witnessing a harbinger of the ethnic violence that was to plague the Caucasus and the Balkan Peninsula in the years to come.

Before the ink was dry on the Washington Summit agreements, the two sides scheduled a summit in Moscow. The Reagan administration saw this as a mostly ceremonial occasion for the outgoing president to meet Soviet citizens and encourage Gorbachev to maintain his course. In an internal directive, Reagan stated that progress in human rights would be his first objective for the summit.[99] Meanwhile, the Soviets wanted to tackle serious arms control and regional matters, and Gorbachev hoped to use Reagan's visit to bolster his own domestic support. In preliminary meetings with Secretary Shultz, Eduard Shevardnadze expressed satisfaction that the dialogues had become a "two-way street" and that both sides seemed to accept that progress in human rights was tied to progress elsewhere. Shultz was similarly impressed, and soon adopted as his working mantra the Russian phrase *bolshe dyela, menshe slov*—more action, fewer words. The U.S. government had allowed Soviet doctors to visit the convicted murderer, American Indian activist Leonard Peltier, but similar U.S. requests to visit Soviet prisoners had been denied. Nor had the Soviets acted on a carefully prepared list of seventeen refuseniks. Shultz was especially puzzled by the Soviet CSCE delegation's apparent independence from Gorbachev's foreign policy. Shevardnadze was somewhat sympathetic, but he also took up the Kremlin's new line of counterarguments: the United States should ratify the human rights covenants, adhere to the ones it had signed, be honest about its social problems, and take seriously the Soviets' list of American "political prisoners."[100]

The May 1988 Moscow Summit was remarkable for several reasons. Not only was it the first such meeting in Moscow in fourteen years, but the fact that it took place only five months after the Washington Summit demonstrated the strength of the relationship and the optimism in both capitals. As a sign of this progress, the U.S. Senate and the Supreme Soviet ratified the INF treaty just days before Reagan's arrival. The symbolism was equally noteworthy. The world's preeminent anticommunist leader strolled through Red Square and later stood at a Moscow University podium under the watchful gaze of V. I. Lenin's bust and extolled the virtues of the free market and the information revolution. But from a policy standpoint, one of the most remarkable things about the Moscow Summit was the prominent role of human rights throughout the entire proceedings. Not only did Reagan broach these issues with Gorbachev, but Richard Schifter and his State Department human rights bureau held four lengthy meetings with political leaders and groups suffering discrimination.[101]

Just as in the earlier summits, among the most interesting aspects of the Moscow gathering was Reagan and Gorbachev's open, philosophical discussions about individual rights. At their first meeting, they agreed that they had accomplished a great deal and that their personal relationship had benefited both countries.[102] Yet even at this late juncture, with the Kremlin having implemented sweeping domestic reforms, human rights questions put Gorbachev on the defensive. When Reagan handed him the customary list of a dozen prospective émigrés, the Soviet leader promised to take the request seriously but once again emphasized that he would not be backed into a corner. He admitted that the Soviet standard of living was lower, but argued that his country had nothing like America's huge disparity in wealth and education, and most likely nothing like its racial problems. Reagan acknowledged that there was a history of prejudice in the United States, and he pointed out that discrimination was now illegal. He then broached religion, arguing that if the Kremlin made religious freedom one of the Soviet people's rights, the emigration problem would dissipate and much anti-Soviet feeling would disappear "like water in the hot sun."[103] Gorbachev denied that religion was a major problem or that people were not free to believe as they chose. He himself had been baptized, he pointed out, though he was not a believer. When he further charged that nonbelievers were persecuted in America, Reagan clarified the separation of church and state and mentioned that even his own son was an atheist.

In their last one-on-one meeting, Gorbachev lambasted the Jackson-Vanik amendment and asked how Americans would feel if the Soviets started talking about the rights of Hispanics or the treatment of American Indians. Or what if they commented on American states the way Americans had passed judgment on the Baltics and Ukraine? These Cold War attitudes, said Gorbachev, called for "shock therapy." Reagan differentiated between stifling religious freedom and solving social problems like those Gorbachev had mentioned. Indians could live as they wished; some stayed on the reservations, and others left. As for Hispanics, illegal immigration was a problem because there was a limit to how many people the United States could absorb. Gorbachev complained that Reagan "was unwilling to accept criticism."[104] On the subject of Soviet reform efforts, Gorbachev asserted that his country needed to expand individual enterprise in order to develop socialism, not to emulate Western capitalism. The country did not want big gaps between rich and poor, he said, but better workers and scientists should be paid more. Indeed, it seems that Reagan's idealism about the promises of liberal democracy was matched by Gorbachev's idealism regarding the promises of reformed socialism. As the latter said in his toast at the state dinner, "We see ourselves even more convinced that our socialist choice was correct, and we cannot conceive of our country developing without socialism. . . . Our goal is maximum freedom for man, for the individual, and for society."[105]

Ronald Reagan was never more in his element than when he was speaking about human freedom, and he had a special opportunity to do so when he met with dissidents in the U.S. ambassador's residence. He and his audience seem to have been equally moved by each other's presence. "Coming here, being with you, looking into your faces," he said, "I have to believe that the history of this troubled century will indeed be redeemed in the eyes of God and man, and that freedom will truly come to all." In a sign of the times, Soviet military and KGB agents actually assisted in bringing guests into the embassy compound. Reagan's contact with ordinary Russians was perhaps the singular achievement of this summit. While standing in Red Square, he disavowed his "evil empire" charge and expressed confidence in the new reforms. When he spoke at Moscow State University that evening, he heralded the information revolution and the importance of technological advancement—progress that could only come about with freedom of thought, information, and communication.[106] One month after the summit, the Supreme Soviet passed the era's most liberal regulations on travel and emigration.

Gorbachev returned the favor and traveled to New York in December 1988 to attend his last summit with Reagan and to meet with the newly elected George H. W. Bush. True to the established protocol, Reagan brought up human rights at their final meeting and handed Gorbachev a small list of names, prompting the latter to joke that Reagan could now tell the press that he had done so.[107] As for Reagan, his long-term turnabout on human rights remained one of his most important legacies. His early criticism of liberal activism had earned him a reputation for indifference in the NGO community, and his adherence to the Kirkpatrick Doctrine had even led to accusations of complicity in allied nations' abuses. Reagan's Central America policy, in particular, was the subject of fierce criticism. But as his foreign policy evolved in the mid-1980s into a more pragmatic, cautious embrace of democracy promotion and human rights, activists took notice. He had always spoken up for dissidents and refuseniks in Eastern Europe, and during his second term his administration was far more willing to press allied governments to implement reforms. By the end of his presidency, his administration had accepted that human rights and democracy promotion were worthwhile pursuits for the U.S. government.

George H. W. Bush and the Events of 1989

The year 1989 began with a new president in Washington and more steps toward liberalization in the East. But notwithstanding the tremendous strides of glasnost and the summits, even the most optimistic observers could not have known just how historic 1989 would be. Robert Gates, who played important roles in national security and intelligence under Reagan and Bush, wrote in his popular history of the era, "I know of *no one* in or out of government who predicted early in 1989 that before the next presidential election Eastern Europe would be free, Germany unified in NATO, and the Soviet Union an artifact of history."[108] John Lewis Gaddis used a memorable metaphor to describe this momentous year: "The Soviet Union, its empire, its ideology . . . was a sandpile ready to slide. All it took to make that happen were a few more grains of sand."[109] These grains of sand would be the ordinary citizens of Eastern Europe. Gorbachev's decision to withdraw troops from Afghanistan and the Warsaw Pact nations had a major impact on these citizens' assertiveness in 1989, as nationalists, liberals, dissidents, and many others tested the bounds of the Kremlin's hands-off approach. Demonstrations broke out in Eastern Bloc capitals, communist governments fell in free elections, and eventually the Berlin Wall itself came crashing down. All the while, the Soviet leadership responded with unprecedented restraint.

Although President George H. W. Bush had served under Reagan for eight years, he put a different face on America's approach to the world. Above all else, his foreign policy reflected his interest in maintaining stability and order in international affairs. In this sense, he was perhaps more an heir apparent to Richard Nixon than he was to Ronald Reagan. He was neither a doctrinaire democrat nor a realist; rather, he tended to favor the existing order. In James Mann's words, "There was rarely a status quo Bush didn't cherish."[110] Many of his foreign policy decisions reflected this desire for order, including assembling a coalition to eject Saddam Hussein from Kuwait and sending troops into Panama to arrest Manuel Noriega on drug charges. Bush was an able and consistent thinker in foreign affairs, but he lacked somewhat in creativity and rarely led in the human rights and democratization arena. He responded cautiously to unexpected human rights crises in Eastern Europe, China, and the Baltic republics, though the second half of his presidency did see some halting moves toward broader humanitarian interests, such as promotion of market reforms and democratization in Eastern Europe, support to international economic institutions, and a humanitarian mission in Somalia.

Bush's early approach to Eastern Europe reflected his cautious nature.[111] Rather than engage with Gorbachev right off the bat, he waited until his administration completed a lengthy study of Eastern European affairs. Thus despite the momentum of the Reagan-Gorbachev détente, Bush did not hold a summit with the Soviet leader until December 1989. Nor did his administration press the Soviets very hard on internal reforms. He did offer rhetorical support for democracy and the free market in spring and summer 1989, largely in response to events in the Eastern Bloc. Speaking at the Coast Guard Academy in May, he declared that the United States sought "a growing community of democracies anchoring international peace and stability, and a dynamic free market system generating prosperity and progress on a global scale." He called on the Kremlin to take more steps to achieve "a lasting political pluralism and respect for human rights. . . . Mr. Gorbachev, don't stop now!"[112] But he was reluctant to go beyond words.

Bush's slow movement in 1989 owed to a few factors. As a political moderate, he had to appear tough in order to placate his party's right wing. He also needed to establish his own reputation and get out from under the shadow of Reagan. Thus he did a thorough housecleaning, replacing essentially the entire Reagan cabinet. He named a retired Air Force officer and alumnus of the Ford administration, Brent Scowcroft, as national security adviser. Another veteran of the Ford White House, Dick Cheney, became secretary of defense. One of the few Reagan confidantes who continued into the Bush presidency was Reagan's treasury secretary, James A. Baker, III, whom Bush had known for decades. He became secretary of state. This hawkish foreign policy team did not fully trust the Soviet leadership, nor did they fully support arms reductions. Bush generally liked Gorbachev's direction, but some of his advisers counseled that the Soviet leader was working to save communism, not end the Cold War.[113] The president's advisers were also aware that Russian and Soviet history showed a tendency toward periods of liberalization followed by brutal crackdowns. The Kremlin's violent response to protests in Tbilisi, Georgia, in April 1989, in which security forces killed nineteen people, seemed to legitimize this view. Although such violent responses would prove to be rare under Gorbachev, mistrust of the Kremlin remained strong. The Bush administration simply did not take Gorbachev's statements at face value in 1989.

At the outset of his presidency, George H. W. Bush was more interested in strengthening relations with China than in engaging with Moscow. He worried that a close relationship with Moscow could imperil Sino-American relations, and he feared that Gorbachev's efforts to normalize relations with China might do the same. His outlook was partially sentimental: he had close ties with Chinese officials dating from his earlier stint in the U.S. liaison office. But he and his adviser, Brent Scowcroft, also believed that China required a different policy than Eastern Europe. The firmly entrenched Chinese government had more legitimacy than those of the Eastern Bloc, and dissent in China did not have the same international implications as did dissent in Europe. (Gorbachev had to manage internal opposition as well as dissent in the Eastern Bloc, while the Chinese had only the internal problem.)[114] Chinese dissidents had never played a prominent role in Sino-American relations, but as Eastern European governments were learning to tolerate previously unimaginable levels of opposition, dissidents in China unexpectedly entered into Sino-American diplomacy.

Bush's first presidential trip was to Asia in February 1989. When he and Scowcroft met with Deng Xiaoping and Premier Li Peng in Beijing, Bush reassured his hosts that he supported continued market reforms and more trade. Deng and Li reciprocated by stressing their desire for close ties and emphasizing the long-standing Chinese quarrel with Moscow. But they also noted China's long history of humiliation at the hands of foreign powers, and they made it clear that the Chinese people would consider outside criticism to be interference in their internal affairs. Bush politely explained Americans' interest in human rights, but he also clarified that he was uninterested in "lecturing" the Chinese or "unleashing an endless barrage of public criticism."[115]

While in Beijing, Bush planned a Texas-style barbeque banquet for prominent Chinese and American figures. Accordingly, Ambassador Winston Lord proposed a guest list that included China's most prominent advocate of democratic reforms, the astrophysicist Fang Lizhi. Fang's antigovernment writings had angered the regime, but he was also a respected scientist with a post at a government research institute. Lord thus assumed that Beijing would not protest his inclusion, and further reasoned that his presence would help the new president to establish his bona fides in the human rights arena. When he sent the list to Washington, he warned the White House that Fang and two other dissidents were vocal advocates who "could very well speak to the media at the banquet and cause some annoyance on the part of the Chinese authorities." Despite these warnings, Fang remained on the list. By the time Bush reached Asia, the Chinese foreign ministry had learned of the invitation and had warned that Chinese leaders would boycott if Fang attended. This would have been a major embarrassment for Bush, who wanted the presidential visit to be an apolitical, "welcome home" affair, but it would have been equally shameful to rescind Fang's invitation. Bush would appear to be caving to the Chinese, and he would seem soft on human rights. A compromise soon emerged: the

Chinese would allow Fang to attend, but he was to have no contact with any of the dignitaries.[116]

When the banquet finally took place in a Beijing hotel, Bush learned firsthand where the Chinese stood on dissident matters. They reneged on the compromise and used force to prevent Fang and his wife from attending. James Mann later estimated that in two decades of Sino-American meetings "there had never been such an ugly moment." As the Western press assailed the Chinese and the Bush administration, the president's other accomplishments were quickly overshadowed. One Chinese graduate student at Harvard lamented the apparent double standard: "The United States has been an acquiescent spectator to human rights violations in China, an attitude markedly different from the one it displays toward the Soviet Union." How could Bush so brazenly neglect Fang, the student asked, when Reagan had consistently embraced Sakharov?[117] The criticism was so sharp that Scowcroft somewhat disingenuously blamed the U.S. embassy in Beijing for the mix-up. To Ambassador Lord, it was clear that the White House wanted him to fall on his sword so that the administration could maintain relations while also expressing "regret" for Fang's treatment.

Then came a series of events that would test the very foundations of the Sino-American relationship. Occasional student demonstrations for political reforms had been taking place for over two years, inspired in part by Gorbachev's liberal reforms in the Soviet Union. This discontentment reached a new level in April 1989, when the former Chinese Communist Party general secretary Hu Yaobang died of a heart attack. Hu's reformism had led hard-liners to oust him, after which he became the spiritual leader of Chinese reformers. His death set off a new round of demonstrations centered in Tiananmen Square, during which protestors assembled a list of demands for more political freedom and an end to corruption. Winston Lord offered a prescient explanation of these events in his final cable as U.S. ambassador. With perestroika and glasnost on the march in Eastern Europe, he noted, Chinese leaders saw free expression as a source of instability. The intermingling of Asian and Western values had become the "most prickly problem" in the Sino-American relationship, and there was "palpable Chinese nervousness about domestic dissent." Quite unexpectedly, dissident activity had replaced Taiwan as Beijing's chief international relations problem, and as economic troubles mounted, there was "disaffection among the people and malaise among the leaders. . . . Cynicism is rampant," wrote Lord. The American public was beginning to ask about China, where mainstream human rights issues like freedom of expression commingled with China-specific ones, such as Tibet and the one-child population control policy. Lord recommended a tough, pragmatic U.S. response that struck a balance between American values and other interests. Washington could use carrots and sticks while keeping in mind China's challenges in bringing such a large population into a market economy. "We should protect our values, maintain contact with activists, and register our disapproval concerning abuses," he counseled. After spending a few weeks in Beijing, Lord's replacement, Ambassador James Lilley, presciently observed that the oppositional phenomenon "has a permanence about it. It is not going to go away."[118] Both men considered these events to be momentous.

The Chinese government's violent crackdown at Tiananmen Square proved to be the watershed moment that Lord and Lilley feared. In a six-week period between April and June, hundreds of thousands of Chinese took to Beijing's streets to demonstrate for a better economy, less corruption, and more political and individual freedom. These protests accelerated during Mikhail Gorbachev's visit from May 15 to 18, leading the government to impose martial law and send troops into Beijing. The U.S. embassy advised President Bush to distance himself from the Chinese leadership because a crackdown seemed imminent, but a characteristically cautious Bush simply affirmed the American belief in democracy and counseled restraint on both sides.[119] However, speaking in West Germany on the last day of May, he was uncharacteristically provocative: "Democracy. . . . This one idea is why the communist world, from Budapest to Beijing, is in ferment." The leaders of the East, Bush declared, would find this force "difficult to channel or control."[120] Back in China, the hard-liners prevailed. On the evening of June 3, the army's tanks and infantry fired on demonstrators who tried to slow their progress toward the city center. They shot hundreds of citizens and eventually delivered an ultimatum to the Tiananmen demonstrators to vacate the square. Student leaders fled, but the next day many more were shot on the square's periphery after challenging the army's authority. News cameras caught the image of one man defiantly standing his ground in front of a tank just yards from the carnage. This image of the "tank man" would become perhaps the most memorable symbol of the modern international human rights movement. Death toll estimates for the events of June 3 and 4 ranged from several hundred to several thousand.

Official Washington reacted harshly. Virtually everyone in the executive and legislative branches lodged a public protest and called for everything from economic sanctions to the severing of relations. While global critics dubbed Deng Xiaoping "the butcher of Beijing," demonstrators at the Chinese embassy on Connecticut Avenue hanged Deng in effigy and erected a replica of the Tiananmen Square "Goddess of Democracy." President Bush's public demeanor was comparatively moderate. He stated that he deplored the decision to use force, but he also invoked the Nixon-Kissinger logic of the 1970s, emphasizing that the Sino-American relationship was too important to jettison.[121] "Now is the time to look beyond the moment to important and enduring aspects of this vital relationship," he stated. Convinced that "the forces of democracy" would overcome the "unfortunate events" in Tiananmen Square, he declared that the United States should "encourage the further development and deepening of the positive elements of that relationship and the process of democratization."[122] Bush also had to refute Beijing's claim that Americans were spurring student activism. The U.S. embassy warned that the Chinese saw the United States as "an intrusive actor" and that they had "signaled us to watch our step or else"—meaning that they would crack down harder if outsiders interfered.[123]

Bush did enact some tough policies. He suspended arms sales, military contacts, and technology transfers, and announced that his administration would also oppose multilateral development bank (MDB) loans to China, as required by law. (Administration lawyers concluded that the massacre had met the requirement for a "gross violation of human rights.") The administration soon added more sanctions and banned all high-level bilateral contacts in response to the uproar from Congress and the Chinese government's televised show trials, draconian sentences, and executions. These sanctions clearly hurt the Chinese. Not only had the United States and China been developing a political and military relationship for years, but China had relied on huge American and MDB loans to fund its modernization.[124]

But even in the immediate aftermath of Tiananmen Square, Bush sought to put the incident behind both countries.[125] At the July 1989 G7 summit in Paris, the American and Japanese delegations succeeded in softening the official criticism. Bush later wrote that although he was greatly troubled by the events in Beijing, he believed that China was changing for the better and that the forces of reform were still intact. Unsure of how to offer appropriate condemnation while also engaging with Beijing, he sent Deng a long letter. Insisting that he was "simply writing as a friend," Bush laid bare his "heavy heart" at the recent turn of events. He then asked Deng "to remember the principles on which my young country was founded. Those principles are democracy and freedom. . . . It is reverence for those principles which inevitably affects the way Americans view and react to events in other countries." Public opinion was the source of the sanctions, Bush suggested, and he wanted the two countries to move beyond this difficult time.[126]

With Deng's agreement, on July 1 Bush secretly sent Scowcroft and Deputy Secretary of State Lawrence Eagleburger to Beijing as his emissaries. The mission was unpublicized because of the ban on high-level contacts and because the American public was still livid over the massacre. (The trip was so secret that nervous Chinese air force pilots nearly shot down Scowcroft's plane as it entered Chinese airspace.) Bush had several justifications for the Scowcroft mission. He wanted to open a direct channel in order to implore Beijing to ease up on its crackdown, and he wanted to assure the Chinese leadership that he intended to promote the relationship and revoke the sanctions once the outcry over Tiananmen died down.[127] Scowcroft and Eagleburger were instructed to clarify that Bush was deeply troubled by the crackdown and that "he believes deeply that a solid relationship between the PRC and the U.S. is in the interests of world peace and international stability."[128]

Their meeting with Deng and Li Peng was intense. Deng complained that the sanctions amounted to undue interference and that the United States had "cornered" China at a time when revolutionaries threatened the state. He essentially repeated what Li had earlier emphasized to Ambassador Lilley: "No government in the world would tolerate this kind of disorder in the middle of its capital city." The rebels must be punished, said Deng, and China would never allow outsiders to interfere in their affairs. He then quoted a Chinese proverb to suggest that the fallout from Tiananmen Square was the fault of America and the West: "It is up to the person who tied the knot to untie the knot." Scowcroft responded by explaining Bush's delicate political position. The crux of the president's problem, said Scowcroft, was that Americans "naturally and inevitably respond emotionally" when their values are attacked. Bush had to cope with this strong domestic reaction. While the Chinese had assailed Bush's "interference" in their affairs, most in Congress had attacked Bush for not doing enough. Still, the president wanted the relationship back on track, and Chinese restraint would assist him tremendously while also improving Beijing's global image. In the end, Scowcroft found his hosts too obsessed with security to budge on human rights. In another letter to Deng, President Bush disagreed with the "knot" analogy, arguing instead that the hard-liners were responsible for inciting world opinion: "We feel that those actions taken against peacefully demonstrating (nonviolent) students and the nationwide crackdown against those simply speaking for reform 'tied the knot.'" He went on to suggest that China's "forgiveness" of the demonstrators would allow Bush to offer a public statement of support for a restoration of relations. "If there is to be a period of darkness," wrote Bush, "so be it; but let us try to light some candles."[129]

Ambassador Lilley backed a cautious continuation of relations despite Beijing's animosity. The Chinese authorities, he wrote in a candid cable, were engaged in a "numbing propaganda campaign" to blame the United States for Chinese dissent, but at the same time they wanted U.S. trade and technology and enough of a security tie to dissuade the Soviet Union. Chinese authorities were ignoring the fact that most of their citizens detested the regime and wanted "a good shot of consumerism and more fun in life." The administration would have to acknowledge congressional misgivings, wrote Lilley, but it was better to move forward with some business, such as commercial aircraft sales. "We are not rewarding the murderers of Tiananmen by selling Boeing aircraft for hard cash," he argued. Lilley did suggest that America would have to be tough on the Chinese propaganda campaign and the lure of trade: "Our message should be if you want American business you also get VOA [Voice of America]."[130] But the Chinese were unwilling to reciprocate, and the noose continued to tighten around dissenters. All the while, Bush tried to keep China policy in the executive's hands. At the end of November, Congress passed a bill granting over forty thousand Chinese students the right to remain in the United States beyond their visas rather than return home and face possible recriminations. Despite overwhelming support in Congress, including a 403 to 0 vote in the House, Bush vetoed the bill and issued an executive order that allowed the students to stay.

In December, Bush sent Scowcroft and Eagleburger to Beijing for a second time to convince the leadership to lift martial law and free some dissidents. This time there were weightier economic issues at stake, including a potentially lucrative Hughes satellite deal and future sales of Boeing airplanes. Beijing wanted desperately to restore the multitude of international relationships that had been lost, and President Bush was confident enough that public and congressional anger had subsided that he decided to publicize the trip. Unfortunately, he had underestimated the level of American resentment. The news media and a bipartisan cross-section of Congress assailed the mission. House Majority Leader Richard Gephardt (D-MO) called it "precisely the wrong signal to the world. At a time when America's bipartisan commitment to freedom is bearing fruit in Eastern Europe, the last thing he should be doing is wavering in our commitment to freedom in China."[131] The administration's cause was further damaged by photos of Scowcroft toasting the Chinese foreign minister at a state banquet. Things then got worse for Bush when reporters broke the story of the earlier Scowcroft mission. The two trips made Bush appear like a court toady kowtowing to the emperors, yet his administration had precious little to show for their engagement with Beijing.

One of the dissidents in question was Fang Lizhi. He and his wife had been granted entry to the U.S. embassy in the wake of the massacre, with the predictable result that the Chinese demanded his return. But the Bush administration followed protocol and used international law as a defense for keeping them in the embassy. President Bush acknowledged in his diary that the decision would be "a real stick in the eye to the Chinese," but added that the United States had no choice but to grant asylum.[132] Fang then became a sticking point in Sino-American relations much as Sakharov, Solzhenitsyn, and Shcharansky had been to the U.S.-Soviet relationship in the 1970s and 1980s. When Fang had been in the embassy for a month, Ambassador Lilley wrote that he was "with us as a constant reminder of our connection to 'bourgeois liberalism' and puts us at odds with the regime here. He is a living symbol of our conflict with China over human rights."[133] After five months, Bush sent Henry Kissinger to meet with Deng, and the two men worked out a framework whereby the Chinese would allow Fang to leave the country as long as Washington did not use him to criticize China. (Kissinger had to remind Deng of the U.S. government's limited power over public speech.) When Ambassador Lilley informed Fang about these conditions, Fang took the initiative and wrote a bogus "confession" that would allow the Chinese authorities to save face.[134]

One month later, it looked like Fang would have his day when Brent Scowcroft visited Beijing, but the two sides disagreed on Fang's significance. The Chinese sought to link his release to the resumption of loans, the lifting of sanctions, and an invitation to high-level officials to visit Washington, but the American side rejected this lopsided "package option" in the belief that Fang's release would be a humanitarian gesture unrelated to the sanctions. As a result, Fang spent six more months living in the embassy compound and became a cause célèbre among activists and scientists. His case was finally resolved in June 1990 when the Japanese government promised to resume loans to China in exchange for his release. Fang and his wife left the country, and Fang took up a teaching post at the University of Arizona.

The events of 1989 greatly altered the Sino-American relationship and American perceptions of human rights in China. Long gone was the double standard whereby Soviet violations were publicized and the Chinese avoided scrutiny. The strategic nature of the Sino-American relationship also changed. While the massacre laid bare Beijing's authoritarianism, developments in the Soviet Union and Eastern Europe were proving that the Kremlin was not the threat it had once been. Soviet troops were out of Afghanistan, the communist governments of Eastern Europe were barely clinging to power, and Soviet leaders were proposing the most sweeping arms reductions in history. By summer of 1989, few Americans considered the Soviet Union an immediate military threat, and as events would prove, the Soviet leadership was willing to allow their empire to dissolve largely peacefully. As the Soviet Union became less menacing, China took its place in many Americans' minds. Tiananmen Square showed that the waning global ideological battle did not mean the end of human rights violations. Not only did Beijing crack down on dissent, but soon China also became more active in exporting weapons and nuclear technology. Thus for the Bush administration, a continuing Sino-American relationship was no longer justifiable as a deterrent against the Soviet Union, but rather as a way to increase trade and contain China's weapons exports.[135]

The American public, Congress, and news media were especially slow to forgive. Since Nixon's time, presidential administrations had been able to count on a largely quiescent Congress, but the days of congressional compliance with presidential China policies were over. Legislators voted to withdraw or severely restrict China's most-favored-nation status. Among the Bush administration's chief critics were Senate Majority Leader George Mitchell (D-ME), Congresswoman Nancy Pelosi (D-CA), and Congressman Stephen Solarz (D-NY). Even the conservative Republican Jesse Helms criticized his own party's president while unceasingly painting the Chinese leaders as murderers.

Chinese human rights became an issue in America in part because the Beijing movement focused on democracy at a time when successive Republican administrations had put democracy at the center of their human rights approach. But more significant was Beijing's undeniable brutality and the technologies that allowed it to be publicized. The Chinese government used wholesale violence against civilians to maintain power, and the global news media instantly spirited the film and images around the world. Polls showed that over 75 percent of Americans had followed the events in Tiananmen Square "closely" or "very closely" on television.[136] Just as significant was the Western public's perception of a waning Soviet threat. By the end of 1989—and certainly over the course of 1990 and 1991—the hoary old image of the Soviet Union as the world's worst abuser of human rights evaporated. Meanwhile, Chinese leaders were bewildered by this unprecedented attention and the "inconsistency" in American attitudes. Tiananmen Square would continue to loom large in Sino-American relations for the next decade, and bilateral economic, military, and political cooperation would take years to recover. Economic sanctions would remain a central issue until 1994, and would even have ramifications until the end of the 1990s.[137]

The Wall Comes Down

Back in Europe, a series of events in summer and fall of 1989 demonstrated just how different Mikhail Gorbachev was from his predecessors. The loosening of the Kremlin's grip led to cracks in the Soviet edifice, especially in Poland and Hungary—arguably the two most independent-minded Warsaw Pact states. Hungary had maintained some independence from the Soviet orbit through its decentralizing economic reforms and liberal cultural policies. When Prime Minister Miklos Nemeth told Gorbachev in March 1989 that the Hungarians were planning multiparty elections, Gorbachev disliked the idea but also made it clear that this was a Hungarian concern, not a Soviet one. Given the presence of eighty thousand Soviet troops (and popular memory of the 1956 invasion), Hungarians took Gorbachev's assurance as an unprecedented signal. The people of Poland also challenged Moscow. After years of suppression, the Polish authorities finally recognized Solidarność in February 1989 and agreed to allow parliamentary elections. Thus it came about that in the summer of 1989—the same week as the Tiananmen Square massacre—Solidarność won ninety-nine of one hundred Senate seats in the first free Polish elections since before the Nazi-Soviet partition of 1939. The new prime minister, Tadeusz Mazowiecki, was so overwhelmed that he nearly fainted at his own installation ceremony. True to his word, Gorbachev did not interfere in either country. His foreign affairs spokesman Gennady Gerasimov soon dubbed Gorbachev's policy the "Sinatra Doctrine"—the Kremlin, he mused, was letting the Eastern Bloc states do things "their way."

Meanwhile, yet another clear sign of change was the Soviets' renewal of large-scale emigration following a major drop-off in 1980–1986. Fewer than one thousand Jews emigrated in 1986, but in 1987–1988 there were over a thousand exits per month. So profound was this increase that in 1989 former congressman Charles Vanik declared that the climate was right to consider waiving Jackson-Vanik, and the National Conference on Soviet Jewry stated that it would support a waiver if the president received assurances on sustained emigration levels.[138] Bush granted a temporary waiver, and by fall the State Department was overwhelmed with entry applications. Negotiation of a formal waiver would have to wait until Bush and Gorbachev had rekindled relations, but there was no denying that the Soviet Union was now allowing many more émigrés. (Between 1989 and 1991, nearly half a million Jews left the Soviet Union; well over a million would emigrate in the 1990s.)

President Bush became more vocal about democracy when he visited Eastern Europe in July 1989, but he did not take a leading role in the unfolding events. Three months earlier he had pledged U.S. support to Poland if reforms continued, but after seeing firsthand just how quickly things were moving, he realized that Washington and Moscow must work together to manage the changes. The administration also feared a reversion to authoritarianism—in Scowcroft's formulation, "dying empires rarely go out peacefully."[139] Not only was Bush unsure of where these extraordinary events might lead, but he also wanted to avoid the appearance of American interference or triumphalism. The United States and Eastern Europe were within grasp of a historic opportunity, he argued, but his administration was reluctant to force the pace of change or to go beyond token support to demonstrators. The U.S. embassy in Warsaw warned that the unprecedented Solidarność victory might lead to "frightening instability," a crackdown, and even civil war.[140]

By the fall, the administration's lengthy policy review and the developments in Poland and Hungary had encouraged a major shift in Bush's outlook. The United States had long favored Yugoslavia and Romania for their independence from Moscow, but the new test was the extent of internal liberalization. Thus Poland and Hungary would now get the most U.S. support, while Romania would get the least.[141] In November, with prodding from the administration, Congress passed the Support for East European Democracy (SEED) Act to assist trade liberalization, economic stability, and democracy in these two nations. SEED funds were modest at first, but the amount for Poland alone would total over $400 million in three years. These efforts demonstrated a human rights interest, but there was also more than a touch of traditional Cold War anticommunism afoot. Poles' and Hungarians' election of noncommunist governments met not only the U.S. desire for democracy, but also its long-standing interest in antileftism. One gets the sense here that many policymakers wanted to help the fledgling Polish government stave off a reversion to communist rule. Earlier administrations had also granted immediate recognition and economic support to regimes that replaced left-wing governments, such as Castelo Branco in Brazil (1964) and Pinochet in Chile (1973), though now Bush could at least claim that he was supporting democratically elected governments. Anticommunist sentiment remained pervasive in part because the Eastern Bloc was still dominated by hard-liners who sought to preserve the status quo—Erich Honecker in East Germany, Nicolae Ceauşescu in Romania, Gustav Husak in Czechoslovakia, and Todor Zhivkov in Bulgaria. The seventy-seven-year-old Honecker's party was even "reelected" in May 1989 with 98.5 percent of the vote. Dissenting citizens feared that these dictators would maintain their power with a series of Tiananmen-like crackdowns.

It was quite fitting that the true testing ground in the fall of 1989 was East Germany, for Germany and Berlin had so often stood as the focal point of the entire Cold War. As thousands of East Germans began to flee the country via Hungary, state security forces crushed demonstrations in several cities. When seventy thousand gathered in Leipzig, the East German Politburo halted the crackdown and removed Honecker from power. Three weeks later, on November 9, the government lifted restrictions on travel to the West, a move that precipitated the most memorable scenes of the era. Berliners rushed to the Berlin Wall checkpoints, the guards opened the gates, and the masses poured through. The other Warsaw Pact governments fell like dominoes. Bulgaria's long-reigning dictator Todor Zhivkov stepped down and elections were planned. Czechs and Slovaks peacefully overturned their government and sent the dissident playwright and former prisoner Václav Havel to Prague Castle as the nation's president. The Czechs called it the *sametová revoluce*—the Velvet Revolution. The peaceful nature of the revolutions of 1989 showed the world just how popular these movements were, though Romania proved to be an aberration. Even after the region's other governments had fallen, Nicolae Ceaușescu ordered his troops to fire on demonstrators. When riots broke out during a pro-regime rally, he fled the capital, and over a thousand were killed in the ensuing factional fighting. On Christmas Day 1989, Ceaușescu and his wife were arrested, tried, and immediately led from the improvised "courtroom" and executed. It was a striking end to an extraordinary year. At the beginning of 1989, no one could have imagined that the year would end with Ceaușescu dead, Havel as president, and Berliners dancing on the Berlin Wall.

Gorbachev's restraint in the face of Eastern Europeans' defection was remarkable. On the first day of December 1989, he became the first Soviet leader to meet with the pope in the Vatican. Ever the tough negotiator, he emphasized his adherence to "ethics" rather than monotheism, and he cautioned the pope not to use Reagan's "prosecutorial" tactics. But he also promised to expand religious liberty in the Soviet Union and to legalize the Ukrainian Catholic Church, which had been suppressed for seventy years. Although he complained that some in the West were "trying to export [their] values," he also delivered perhaps the most liberal defense of religious freedom ever given by a Soviet leader: "The people are the highest authority. Everything depends on the choice of the people. . . . We start from the principle that the faith of believers must be respected."[142] The next day, Gorbachev and Bush began a summit in Malta. By this time, Bush was much more forthright about promoting (in the words of his summit briefing) "a Europe that is whole and free" and defined by "free, open elections and market economies." At Malta, Bush would insist on individual rights and the free exchange of goods and ideas, but he would also extend a commercial olive branch by proposing support for MFN restoration, a waiver of Jackson-Vanik, and extension of credits. He also followed precedent by handing Gorbachev a list of people who wanted to emigrate. For his part, Gorbachev showed that he was willing to accept democratically elected governments in Eastern Europe, and he signaled a reversal of forty years of Soviet foreign policy by stating that he wanted the United States to stay on the continent.[143]

Perhaps the most fascinating thing about the Malta Summit was the two sides' philosophical discussions of the changes sweeping through

Europe. Sitting aboard a Soviet cruiser in a stormy Mediterranean, the two men played true to character—Gorbachev the embattled pragmatist who was not ready to abandon his ideological view of the world, and Bush the moderate democrat who was unwilling to see his beliefs as ideological. Gorbachev insinuated that Americans were using the rhetoric of universalism to mask the self-interested imposition of their values. Eastern Europe was going in the direction of "greater openness, democracy, and rapprochement toward general human values," he argued, and it would be dangerous "to force artificially or to push the processes" in order to satisfy "certain unilateral interests." Bush countered that free speech, open debate, and the free market were no threat. He also pointed out that although some Americans accused him of being too cautious, he would not "climb the Berlin Wall" to make triumphal declarations. Unmoved, Gorbachev stressed that the Kremlin's painful decision to allow Eastern Europeans to choose their leaders did not give Americans permission to force their social and economic system onto others. "Let other people decide for themselves which God, figuratively speaking, to worship," he implored. Bush agreed that this should not be the source of conflict, and called for them to focus on "the content of these values. From the bottom of our hearts we welcome the changes that are taking place."[144] The Malta Summit showed that Gorbachev continued to share his predecessors' misgivings about American domination of Europe, while Bush sincerely believed that these values were universal, and thus not a threat to the new Soviet Union.

At the end of 1989, Bush and Gorbachev were in the unusual position of having to jointly manage the revolutions and navigate a future course for Central and Eastern Europe. In marked contrast to the Stalin-Roosevelt-Churchill era, these negotiations would have to heed the wishes of ordinary Europeans. Gorbachev disliked the idea of German reunification, but his regional policy was to decrease the Soviet military presence in Europe, not increase it. He also had his hands full with his domestic problems and worrisome separatist movements. The peoples of the Soviet periphery were growing more assertive and even violently nationalistic. In January 1990, nearly two hundred civilians were killed in anti-Armenian skirmishes in Azerbaijan. The new Lithuanian Seimas (parliament) took a provocative step by declaring independence from the Soviet Union in March 1990; by the end of the year, Latvia, Estonia, Armenia, and Georgia would see their communist parties turned out of office. President Bush remained cautious about these developments. In his January 1990 State of the Union address, he announced the vindication of President Harry Truman's containment doctrine and declared that "freedom" had won out over socialism. But he emphasized that there was still a considerable Soviet threat, and announced that the United States would continue military modernization and SDI while it lowered its European troop levels.[145] The CIA director briefed a Senate committee that the Kremlin still threatened some U.S. interests. The bulk of the evidence, he asserted, showed "a vigorous, broad-based modernization effort that is improving their overall strategic capabilities."[146]

A Final Dilemma: The National Independence Movements

National independence for the Baltic republics of Lithuania, Latvia, and Estonia became one of the last significant human rights issues confronting American policymakers in this era. The U.S. government had never recognized Stalin's forced annexation of these republics in 1940, and in the Cold War era they were referred to as "captive nations." Americans had long considered them a special cause, and American public opinion and congressional sentiment still favored their independence. By contrast, the Kremlin was not only extremely sensitive to outside interference in their nationality issues, but also argued that the Baltic peoples were an integral part of the Soviet Union. By 1990, Gorbachev was privately willing to acknowledge a right to self-determination, though he would not agree to an immediate separation. (He estimated that the Lithuanian "divorce proceeding" would take five to seven years.)[147] Still, nobody in the Kremlin wanted to oversee the dissolution of the empire. When Lithuania declared independence in March 1990, Moscow challenged this decision with an economic blockade, an energy cutoff, and more troops on the border.

The scholar Alex Pravda has noted that although Western governments sympathized with Baltic peoples' aspirations for autonomy, they also feared instability that might imperil Gorbachev, his reforms, and his international relationships. Western leaders were unable to prevent the Lithuanians from declaring independence, though they did convince Vilnius to place a hundred-day moratorium on any independent action, which in turn convinced the Kremlin to lift the economic blockade. Despite the Soviets' sensitivity to outside interference, in 1990–1991 they would continue to seek Western governments' help in reining in the republics' nationalistic tendencies.[148] Although the United States had never recognized these states' incorporation into the Soviet Union, formally recognizing them as independent states was a touchy matter. Standard practice was to wait until a government controlled the territory, was able to function, and was fulfilling international obligations. Naturally, Bush was careful. He wanted a peaceful resolution of the Baltics issue, but he also sought regional stability, close East/West relations, and Gorbachev's continued tenure. He hoped to continue nonrecognition of Soviet annexation while preventing these republics from going too far too fast. He also wanted to be forthright enough to please the American public and prevent Congress from legislating ahead of him, but he had to do so without provoking a Soviet crackdown.

The Lithuanian cause attracted a broad cross-section of Americans. With the bloom now coming off the Gorbachev rose, conservatives and liberal activists were willing to join forces to criticize Bush's "abandonment" of the Baltic republics. The *Detroit Free Press* accused Bush of betraying liberty in Lithuania, just as he had in Tiananmen Square: "A half century of brave words about captive nations has been shown as so much cheap talk. . . . The Bush administration has somehow gotten into its head the notion that appeasement is now the best policy."[149] These criticisms were largely unfounded. Although it was true that Bush and Gorbachev had forged a closer working relationship, Bush also met with Baltic leaders and Baltic-American organizations on multiple occasions. In April 1990, he clarified to an audience of ethnic representatives that he supported independence but feared a repeat of the Soviets' violent 1956 crackdown on Hungary. "We may differ on how we get there," he said, "but there is no disagreement on self-determination."[150]

He also discussed the Baltic issue with Moscow throughout 1990 and 1991. Much as Reagan had pressed Gorbachev on freedom of religion and the release of dissidents as a means of winning U.S. support, Bush regularly told Gorbachev that freeing the Baltic states would be the best thing he could do for bilateral relations. Continued tough measures against the Baltics would make it much harder to win congressional support for a trade treaty and a Jackson-Vanik waiver. Meanwhile, administration insiders feared that the harsh Soviet reaction in Lithuania might signal the end of reformism or show that the Soviet Union was, as one adviser put it, "an empire that has not yet totally lost its nerve." Indeed, Gorbachev appeared to be drawing the line at Lithuanian independence because the declaration created an existential crisis for the Soviet state. If the Kremlin accepted their independence, then the entire Union would be imperiled. Given that Gorbachev did not want to oversee his nation's dissolution, he had every reason to resist American meddling. Why, he asked Bush, did Americans view the Baltics as a special American interest? "If you want to undermine the relationship, to worsen the attitude of our people to the United States," he said, "then you should encourage separatism."[151]

It is worth pondering what human rights issues were at stake here. National self-determination and sovereignty were internationally accepted principles, though there was no accepted right to regional secession. Would Soviet leaders have to recognize that ethnic Lithuanians had always had a right to independence? Did the Soviet government have a right to enforce the union's territorial integrity? Did individual Lithuanians have a right to withdraw from an artificial confederation in which they were dominated by ethnic Russians? On this final point, who would protect Lithuania's ethnic Russians if Lithuania were independent? And were Americans supporting independence in the name of national self-determination and democracy, or simply to weaken an adversary? Since much of America's Cold War foreign policy had been aimed at weakening the Soviet Union, it is safe to say that this impulse continued to inspire at least some of the broad bipartisan agreement on Lithuania.

With the Bush administration unenthusiastic about the Baltics' independence, congressional and NGO activists brought the Lithuanian question into U.S.-Soviet trade negotiations. When several announced that they would not support MFN status if the Soviets used violence or otherwise prevented independence, Bush declared two conditions for a new trade agreement. The Kremlin would have to lift the remaining sanctions against Lithuania and allow freedom of emigration for all Soviet citizens. (A draft emigration law had been tabled in the Supreme Soviet for months.) Bush told Gorbachev that he had "no choice now but to identify with our strongly held convictions about Lithuania's self determination and the right to control its own destiny."[152] When they met in Washington in May and June 1990, Bush continued to emphasize that his policies reflected domestic opinion. "We are in favor of you resolving [Lithuania] on the grounds of your own laws," he said, but Americans were criticizing their president for supporting Gorbachev and "abandoning" the principle of self-determination. A Lithuanian leader had even compared Bush to Neville Chamberlain. Bush reiterated that neither the American public nor Congress would accept a trade agreement if the Soviets stalled on emigration or Lithuania. "It does not make sense to present this agreement to an unfriendly Congress," he said. "They would just tear it apart."[153]

Of course, Gorbachev's domestic difficulties were far worse than Bush's. He stood firm in his belief that Lithuania was an internal matter, and he insisted that there could be no agreement as long as Americans connected trade to the status of the Baltic republics. "We lived for decades without a trade agreement," he told Bush, "and we will survive now as well." Bush decided to drop the Lithuanian conditions and sign the trade pact because he wanted to give Gorbachev a sign of support, though he also made it clear that he would not send it to Congress until the Politburo passed an emigration law. So once again, MFN status for the Soviet Union was being tied to its emigration policies. When reporters asked Bush why he had signed the agreement despite the differences on Lithuania, he emphasized that "the overall relationship" was in America's interest.[154] Throughout the rest of 1990, the Supreme Soviet and the Politburo stonewalled on emigration, while Congress dragged its feet on the trade pact. But because the emigration floodgates were already open, Bush issued a presidential waiver of Jackson-Vanik at year's end.

These accomplishments were overshadowed somewhat by Saddam Hussein's invasion of the former Soviet ally, Kuwait, in August 1990. As American attention shifted to the Middle East, Gorbachev pursued a tougher domestic policy in the fall and winter of 1990–1991, perhaps believing that he had no choice but to follow the hard-liners' advice. He may also have thought that he could act more boldly because Moscow gave unprecedented consent to the U.S.-led Gulf War coalition that ousted Hussein from Kuwait. This war, it is worth noting, was motivated in part by human rights concerns. Although President Bush justified it in traditional terms—the invasion violated Kuwait's sovereignty—it was also true that activists had long criticized Hussein for a variety of rights violations. Bush was able to assemble a coalition by stressing both the realist and idealist/activist justifications, though Hussein remained in power after the war.

While Gorbachev's international popularity remained high, it was plummeting at home. Economic troubles were endemic, and Soviet citizens were becoming increasingly disillusioned with the gap between the promises of perestroika and its results. Public anger about the slow pace of reform put Gorbachev between a rock and a hard place. His adviser, Anatoly Chernyaev, wrote in his diary early in 1991, "Never did I think that the inspiring processes started by Gorbachev could come to such an ignominious end."[155] Just as the Gulf War was beginning in January 1991, the Soviets used military force in Lithuania and Latvia in response to demonstrations against inflation and the continued presence of ethnic Russians. Over a dozen civilians were killed in each country, spurring Western governments to issue harsh criticisms and threats of rescinding aid and cooperation. In a referendum held less than a month later, 90 percent of Lithuanians voted for complete independence. The Bush administration was characteristically circumspect about these developments, but by spring 1991 they were firmly behind independence, and even began to stress the inevitability of a separation during talks with Moscow. Since the Baltics would not voluntarily remain in the Soviet Union or join a federated state, said Bush, an amicable split would head off further violence and would avoid a mass emigration of ethnic Russians. But Bush also explained his position as a reflection of Americans' special interest in the Baltic peoples' independence. "The best thing [Gorbachev] could do for the Baltics is to free them," he told Shevardnadze.[156]

Bush's July and August trip to the Soviet Union placed him right in the middle of these events. The Supreme Soviet had finally lifted restrictions on emigration, and Congress had approved a trade deal that had great potential to strengthen the Soviet economy. But the administration also cultivated the republics. While in Kiev—the capital city of an increasingly restless, independent-minded Ukraine—Bush's entourage went to great lengths to emphasize that he was visiting the *nation* of Ukraine, not the Ukrainian Soviet republic. Deliberations, speeches, and toasts were held in English and Ukrainian, not Russian, and all political parties were invited to the events. Yet Bush would not meet with nationalist or independence party leaders, as he did not want to appear to be endorsing full independence or abandoning Gorbachev. This ambivalence reflected the divide in his administration. Bush still considered the breakup of the Soviet Union to be a potentially dangerous endpoint, and he contrasted the Ukraine with the Baltics—to Bush, the former was an internal Soviet issue, while the latter was an international issue. But many Americans considered the Ukraine to be a "captive nation," and even relished the possibility of the enemy superpower's ultimate dissolution. Unfortunately for Bush, on this symbolic occasion his caution and his loyalty to Gorbachev got the best of him. In a speech penned by Condoleezza Rice, who was then a director at the NSC, Bush declared that the United States would not turn its back on the Soviet Union's independence-minded leaders, but he also made it clear that the United States would maintain a strong relationship with Gorbachev's government in Moscow. This was hardly music to the ears of Ukrainian nationalists, who hoped to hear a rousing defense of Ukrainian sovereignty. Bush did stridently defend human freedom, but he bordered on sanctimony in cautioning his audience that "freedom is not the same as independence." Americans would not support "those who seek independence in order to replace a far-off tyranny with a local despotism. They will not aid those who promote a suicidal nationalism based upon ethnic hatred."[157]

Bush was trying to balance his interest in stable political transitions and Gorbachev's continued tenure with the popular American interest in the republics' independence and the myriad interests within the republics themselves. His reference to "suicidal nationalism" suggests that he also had in mind the ethnic separatist violence that was then breaking out in Yugoslavia and the Caucasus. But Ukrainian nationalists and American conservatives were angry; columnist William Safire even dubbed it Bush's "Chicken Kiev" speech. Brent Scowcroft countered that the Kiev speech was intended to send all of the republics a message of Americans' "excitement with grass-roots forces" and the republics' "sometimes raucous, but always exciting, debate over what are in fact basic American values: freedom, democracy, and economic liberty."[158] It was no coincidence, of course, that democracy, free market capitalism, and civil liberties happened to be the values that the Bush administration found the most appealing and the most universal. If the republics' nationalism veered in the direction of authoritarianism, anti-Semitism, or anticapitalism, then the administration would pressure their leaders to put things back on track.

With the world asking whether the remaining Soviet republics deserved the same independence and sovereignty as the former Eastern Bloc states, the sclerotic Soviet economy forced the issue. Gorbachev later wrote that he and his fellow reformers "rightly chose freedom, democracy, *glasnost'* and pluralism," but they got one thing wrong: "People judged the state of the country by what they could or could not buy in the shops."[159] Gorbachev had tinkered with free market incentives but had also tried to maintain many aspects of the planned economy; in the end, even reformed socialism could not deliver the goods. The ambitious party member Boris Yeltsin, who in June 1991 was elected president of the Russian Republic, took advantage of the economic crisis to argue that glasnost and perestroika had overpromised and underdelivered. It was now Gorbachev's turn to be on the wrong side of history. Yeltsin began pressing for an independent Russian Federation, assuming that other republics would also be independent if they so chose—which, of course, they would. Meanwhile, Gorbachev's refusal to sanction force in the Baltics had set Soviet hard-liners down a more radical path. When they launched a coup attempt in August 1991 and placed Gorbachev under house arrest, Yeltsin heroically stood atop a tank in front of the Russian parliament building and denounced the coup. Gorbachev was saved, but the torch had passed to Yeltsin.

The United States formally recognized the Baltic states in September, and soon also backed independence for Ukraine and Belarus. "You know our tradition as a democratic people," Bush confided to Gorbachev. "We must support the Ukrainian people." A combative Gorbachev reminded Bush that it was the Soviet people who would have to live with these decisions, not the Americans. When Russia, Ukraine, and Belarus agreed to become independent as a commonwealth in December, ten million people became minority citizens of a foreign country overnight. While most Americans saw the independence movements in a positive light, Gorbachev was prescient in pointing out that the problems of nationalism and minority rights were yet another potential powder keg.[160] His resignation on Christmas day effectively dissolved the Soviet Union. Despite this ignominious end to his career, he remained a figure of admiration. John Lewis Gaddis concluded that Gorbachev's dual goal of saving socialism without coercion was essentially incompatible, but his unwillingness to use force made him "the most deserving recipient ever of the Nobel Peace Prize."[161] As for the former Soviet republics, their problems were now their own to solve.

Epilogue: Human Rights in the Post–Cold War World

The revolutions of 1989 to 1991 were the capstone of a global trend in which parliamentary democracy became the world's most common form of government. Nations in every region were now holding multiparty elections under constitutions that included liberal protections for citizens. These political transitions were paralleled by changes in the prevailing economic wisdom and a growing belief that state-directed economies were insufficiently productive. This perspective first took hold in North America and Western Europe, and then in China, Eastern Europe, and beyond. Alongside this mounting criticism of statism, dissidents' desire for personal liberty and political democracy had much more resonance. Powerful authoritarian states like China and the Soviet Union sought integration into the global marketplace as a means of enhancing national wealth and, they hoped, solidifying state power. But as more citizens and societies demanded a higher standard of living, they also demanded more individual and political freedom.

Scholars still debate the role of human rights norms, policies, and activism in spurring communism's collapse in Eastern Europe. They also debate the significance of American policies. Surely the most important factors were internal: as the Western world transitioned to a techno-service economy, the socialist states did not demonstrate a sufficient degree of adaptability or efficiency. Jack Matlock is close to the mark in arguing that Gorbachev cooperated in ending the Cold War because the Soviet Union could not be reformed or enriched if the East/West conflict continued or escalated.[1] Although the weak economy was Gorbachev's primary motive for implementing reforms, it is also true that he believed the state should be less restrictive. The combination of Soviet economic problems and the reformers' acceptance of some human rights norms meant that by 1989 these leaders were willing to let the Warsaw Pact states manage their problems without interference. Once Gorbachev had allowed the Poles and Hungarians to force their communist parties out of power, it was only a matter of time before other states and republics asserted their national ambitions. Soviet leaders had always discouraged national and religious identification, and they had consistently crushed nationalist and separatist movements, but Gorbachev and the reformers hoped to hold together the Eastern Bloc without force. This turned out to be impossible. Securing freedom from foreign domination was a powerful motivating force. Nationalism was arguably the most prominent mass mobilizational theme in this period, and each case had far-reaching regional effects through a process that Mark R. Beissinger has called "the transnationalism of nationalism."[2]

The Soviet leadership could have chosen economic reforms at the expense of political and liberal ones, much as the Chinese had done. They could have cracked down on dissent and separatism, but they did not. As Daniel C. Thomas has suggested, in the 1980s these leaders increasingly realized that Europeans' acceptance of the Soviet Union would rely upon Moscow's compliance with Western human rights norms. The reformers not only began to express misgivings about limits on human liberty, but they also recognized that integration with Western Europe required more respect for individual freedom and national sovereignty in the entire Eastern Bloc. As reformers began to implement changes, activists grew ever bolder in their demands, some even challenging the party's monopoly on power. The combination of "top-down reform" and "bottom-up social mobilization," writes Thomas, was instrumental in the collapse of Soviet communism.[3] Scholars have also given dissidents and activists a prominent role in the story.[4] Sarah B. Snyder emphasizes activists' relentless cataloguing of abuses in the Conference on Security and Cooperation in Europe (CSCE) process and via the formation of international networks. This activism meant little when hard-liners dominated the Kremlin, but Gorbachev's accession changed the dynamic. Moscow abandoned its agitprop defensiveness and instead used reforms to win favor with the more prosperous West. Releasing prisoners and boosting emigration numbers won concessions and undercut foreign criticism.[5]

It seems clear, then, that the Helsinki Accords and the CSCE process played a role in Eastern Bloc affairs after 1975, though it is not so clear that Helsinki was all that important to human rights in American foreign policy, or even very important in ending the Cold War. To the extent that the "Helsinki effect" may have changed states' behavior, this effect was largely the work of domestic actors in the East. And although Helsinki-inspired norms and agreements were part of international relations from 1975 to 1991, they were not necessarily decisive. A few counterfactual questions are worth pondering. How would Europe have evolved after 1975 if the Helsinki Accords had not included human rights provisions, or if there had been no accords at all? Would dissidents have desired freedom less? Would Americans, Britons, and others have been more accepting of communist governments' authoritarianism? Would émigré ethnics have been less interested in liberating their captive ancestral homelands? Would broader global economic and technological changes have ceased to challenge the inefficient systems of the East? Would Gorbachev's momentous reforms have been necessary if the Soviet Union's economy had been growing at the same rate as China's? The Helsinki process mattered in Europe, but its role in ending the Cold War should be seen as ancillary to the far more significant economic, technological, and political changes sweeping the globe in the eighties. And when we consider the entirety of U.S. human rights policies from the 1960s to the 1990s, Helsinki's importance wanes in comparison with America's many other bilateral relationships and concerns outside of Europe.

In some international human rights cases, the United States played an important role in offering incentives for reform, either as part of a multination effort (as in South Africa) or with Washington taking the lead (as in Poland). Indeed, America's most important policymaking role was using its economic power to encourage change. In the case of states transitioning to democracy (e.g., Chile, South Korea, and the Philippines), the United States used a combination of encouragement and mild threats to speed the process. But we must be careful not to overstate America's role in the global human rights story. Individuals living under oppressive, autocratic governments were the primary figures making demands, whether in Brazil, South Korea, or the Soviet Union. American policies had an effect in Poland, for example, but more important were that country's internal realities—a stagnant economy, limits on personal freedom, a dearth of consumer goods, and anger over Soviet domination—as well as major changes in Soviet foreign policy after 1985.

George H. W. Bush responded to the international crises of his tenure by asserting that economic liberalization and the free exchange of goods and ideas were the best ways to gradually increase a nation's freedom. In this sense he was a realist like Nixon and Kissinger, because he did not believe that draconian American policies could force meaningful changes in other societies. With respect to China, it would be unfair and inaccurate to say that Bush was unmoved by the Tiananmen Square massacre, or that he was only influenced by business lobbyists or personal connections from his earlier stint in Beijing. He believed that a closer relationship would give the United States more leverage and that economic liberalization and trade would benefit both countries and enhance freedom in China. Congress, on the other hand, expressed clear displeasure at the massacre, the ongoing repression, and China's exporting of missiles and nuclear technology. Yet this indignation had its limits. Although the United States showed that it was willing to use sanctions, congressional activists were unable to muster a veto-proof majority to halt MFN status. Once the anti-Soviet security motive had dissipated, the economic relationship took precedent in Sino-American relations.[6] Chinese leaders soon realized that if they placated their own population with strong economic growth and mollified the West with trade, they could strengthen their country and increase their control over it without a major challenge from Washington.

Unfortunately for Bush, his reelection campaign did not benefit from the democratization of Eastern Europe, the collapse of communism, and the dissolution of the Soviet Union. Considering how few political dividends have accrued to activist policymakers since the sixties, it is doubtful that a tougher global human rights posture would have boosted his chances. To Bush's credit, history has vindicated his caution in Eastern Europe. Given this region's tumultuous history, there was no guarantee that the Eastern Bloc's breakup or the Soviet republics' transition to independence would be peaceful. Recognizing that small states could be dangerous to global order, Bush argued that a careful, orderly transition was more likely to bring about the kind of regional stability that was ultimately more important to America than any economic interest in such small markets as Estonia and Latvia.

As for the role of American policies and international activism in the global South, the end of the Cold War engendered new possibilities here as well. With the waning of the East/West conflict, the South African government could no longer rely on its standing as a regional anticommunist power. Believing that his government had to implement long-term reforms in this new world order, President F. W. de Klerk announced that Pretoria would begin negotiations on a new constitution. He also lifted the ban on outlawed parties and announced that Nelson Mandela and hundreds of other political prisoners would be freed. In a different day and age, the freeing of a figure like Mandela might have been a cause for alarm in Washington. Americans had long been wary of left-of-center nationalists, whether Fidel Castro, Jacobo Árbenz, Mohammed Mosaddeq, or Salvador Allende. But after 1989 this logic no longer applied. Mandela's summer 1990 visit to America brought out rapturous crowds, including 750,000 along Broadway in New York, 100,000 in Harlem, and 300,000 in Boston. In Washington, he met with President Bush and addressed a joint session of Congress. There were some uncomfortable questions about Mandela's earlier support of violence and his ties to Castro and Arab dictators, but overall his visit was lauded as a testament to the triumph of human freedom.[7]

The global community responded positively to the South African negotiations. The U.N. arms embargo remained intact, but the European Community lifted its sanctions and the International Olympic Committee ended its Olympic ban. In July 1991, Bush accepted the latest South African reforms as "suitable progress" (per U.S. human rights statutes) and lifted the sanctions that he had never supported in the first place, a decision that angered those activists who wanted to entice more rapid changes. They asked why he had supported opposition parties and had granted large aid packages to Poland and Hungary but did not extend the same favors to South Africa. In the bigger picture, though, the United States played only a supporting role in the difficult transition to a democratic South Africa between 1990 and 1994; by and large, the process was carried out by South Africans.[8] Yet the international antiapartheid movement definitely played a part in South Africa's path to reform, and the U.S. government and businesses played an important part in this movement from 1985 onward. The fading of the Cold War was the final straw.

The waning of East/West tensions also influenced events in Central America. As the Soviets and Cubans grew less interested in funneling money to rebel groups via Nicaragua, moderates in Washington considered other approaches. Particularly significant to this change in outlook was the February 1990 Nicaraguan election that ended Sandinista rule and brought to power an anti-Sandinista coalition led by Violeta Chamorro. Although it is hard to prove that U.S. involvement in the election was a decisive factor in her victory, the Bush administration did lend considerable financial support to the opposition parties, and Bush himself made it clear to Nicaraguans that the United States would lift its trade embargo if Chamorro won. This posture was consistent with U.S. democracy initiatives and the Reagan/ Bush challenge to the Sandinista government, but it was also a quite transparent effort to influence a sovereign nation's election.[9] Most in Washington saw Chamorro's victory as an American triumph, as evidenced by congressional willingness to send large amounts of aid to Managua, but others were troubled that democracy promotion could so easily veer into interference in Nicaraguan affairs. Either way, the Sandinistas' loss and the weakening of Cuban support made both sides in El Salvador more open to a settlement of their civil war. U.S. pressure on San Salvador served as yet another impetus to constructive peace talks. The settlement in the final days of 1991 finally ended the violence, disappearances, and torture, though the long-term effects of this terrible war would linger for years.

It is somewhat less clear what inspired South America's democratization trend. The international human rights and democracy movements may have played a part, but of course local activism and local developments were the most important factors.[10] In the 1970s and 1980s, American intercession freed some South American political prisoners and wrested a few liberal concessions from authoritarian regimes. The United States also played an important role in encouraging democracy in Chile during Reagan's second term. But these governments generally expressed a stolid indifference to American policies, and the democratic transitions in Argentina, Brazil, and Uruguay were largely the work of South Americans.[11]

As Greg Grandin notes, there remains a fundamental disagreement about the effects of U.S. policies in Cold War–era Latin America. One version of events depicts the United States as a progressive force in Central America and the Caribbean. In this narrative, Washington supported relatively stable, anticommunist regimes and encouraged economic growth and political reforms in the face of hostile insurgencies, Cuban interference, and a regional history of violence. After President Carter almost "lost" the region to Cuban-backed rebels, the Reagan administration restored intergovernmental relations and challenged the left-wing regimes in Cuba, Nicaragua, and Grenada. Reagan not only prevented communist incursions, but also pressured right-wing authoritarians to democratize. However, an opposing narrative finds the United States culpable for much of the region's

suffering through its interference in domestic reform efforts and its inser-
tion of huge amounts of military aid and weapons.[12] In Walter Lafeber's
formulation, decades of neo-imperial policies and rapacious business deals
left Washington all but incapable of supporting the kind of domestic
reforms that might have averted these "inevitable revolutions." Because
the Reagan administration preferred military responses to socioeconomic
problems, the United States flooded the region with arms and looked the
other way while friendly governments committed atrocities. "Cold War terror," writes Grandin, "either executed, patronized, or excused" by the
United States, "fortified illiberal forces, militarized societies, and broke the
link between freedom and equality."[13]

And indeed, from a twenty-first-century perspective, some of Washington's policies in Central America remain troubling. Too often, the fear of
another Castro in the hemisphere served to justify strong security policies
over potentially transformative social and economic ones. In the eighties,
the Reagan administration supported Nicaraguan rebels who committed
acts of terror against civilians, and also backed a Salvadoran government
which, for a time at least, had ties to brutal death squads. But behind the
scenes Reagan's advisers were greatly distressed, and far from unified, in
their evaluations of the region. After 1983, the most common theme in
their internal discussions was not optimism at the prospect of halting the
leftward drift, but rather exasperation at the near-impossibility of curbing
the violence while also alleviating social ills, encouraging democratic
reforms, and preventing insurgent victories. As one State Department official stated in 1987, "Arguments [have] raged within the administration over
every presidential speech on Central America."[14] Moreover, although
human rights tended to be a secondary interest, both democracy promotion
and human rights were intertwined with Washington policies from 1983
onward. Thomas Carothers has accurately concluded that Reagan's anticommunist policy in El Salvador was "successful" in the sense that leftist
insurgents did not win. Likewise, his democracy policy did help facilitate
multiparty elections that made the Salvadoran government more account-
able to the people. But these policies exacerbated America's political divides
and cost taxpayers over $4 billion, and even then they did not succeed in
eliminating the rebels or healing El Salvador's internal divisions. Liberties
like free association and free speech were limited, and the Salvadoran government never had majority support. These problems were not all the fault
of the United States, but it is safe to say that Reagan, Bush, and Congress

never squared the contradiction of desiring democracy and human rights while also involving America in another nation's internal affairs and granting huge amounts of support to a military in a brutal civil war.[15]

The policymaking environment changed substantially after 1991. With the end of the ideological polarization that had long defined human rights debates, activists faced a new paradox. The lack of a competing superpower meant that Washington had much less of a need to trumpet its vision to the world, and as ideological battles waned (and as state-sponsored violations seemed to decline), so did Washington's attention to international human rights. Without the communist adversary in the Kremlin, conservatives and moderates could no longer benefit from attacks on the now-nonexistent Eastern Bloc, nor could they assail liberals for being "soft" on communism. Some human rights norms had been institutionalized in American diplomacy, but there was no consensus that post-1991 foreign policy should include more activism. Some have chalked up this American retreat to the conservative trend in U.S. politics, but the explanation lies elsewhere. The American pursuit of human rights after 1967 was almost always done in America's national interest and in pursuit of traditional American "rights"—democracy, civil liberties, religious freedom, and private property. Those nations that fell outside of America's traditional economic sphere or security interests were rarely a part of human rights debates in Washington, and major trading partners were rarely sanctioned. The expansion of democracy and the end of the ideological struggle (parallel processes memorably described by Francis Fukuyama as "the end of history") meant that American policymakers had much less of an incentive to use human rights to gain advantages over political adversaries. Activists' alternative vision of a foreign policy geared toward human concerns rather than traditional national interests had a limited appeal in Washington, and among the public, both during and after the Cold War.[16]

Even without strong leadership from Washington after 1991—or leadership from any other nation, for that matter—the human rights pantheon expanded to include many new concepts. In the age of globalization, activists would give much more attention to the growing power of non-state actors, such as multinational corporations, international terrorist networks, human traffickers, arms dealers, and drug cartels. American policymakers and activists also shifted their attention away from Latin America and Eastern Europe and toward the Middle East, Asia, and Africa. Of the perennial violators that remained, some were American adversaries (Iran, North

Korea, Cuba), while others were commercial or strategic partners (Saudi Arabia, China, Egypt). China's human rights record would be the source of much political debate in Washington in the 1990s, though much less so in the 2000s.

Even without the superpower dynamic, Americans faced much the same dilemma that they had confronted three decades earlier. Did moral concerns belong in diplomacy? Did America's wealth, military power, and liberal traditions create a special obligation to promote liberal democracy? Did democracy promotion and rights activism mask American "meddling" in other nations' affairs? Should Americans follow the principles of realpolitik and pursue a narrow set of national interests? These questions elicited widespread disagreement. Yet in contrast to the global environment of the sixties, after 1991 there was much more agreement that human rights protections were an integral part of modern state legitimacy. People even began to speak of the international community's "responsibility to protect," and states and multilateral bodies established legal provisions for humanitarian interventions. Given this substantial change in global attitudes, as well as the important role that the United States played in fostering it, it was clear that such humanistic concerns would continue to play a part in the making of American foreign policy. In the twenty-first century, it remains to be seen just how significant that part will be.

Notes

The following abbreviations appear in the notes.

AIUSA   Papers of Amnesty International USA, Center for Human Rights Documentation and Research, Columbia University, New York, NY.

AJG   Arthur J. Goldberg Papers, Library of Congress, Washington, DC.

ASKGB   Andrei Sakharov KGB File, Yale University Annals of Communism Series, ed. Joshua Rubenstein and Alexander Gribanov, www.yale.edu/annals/sakharov.

CDP   Chile Declassification Project of the Central Intelligence Agency, Department of State, Department of Defense, Department of Justice, White House, foia.state.gov, www.foia.cia.gov.

CSM   *Christian Science Monitor.*

DMF   Donald M. Fraser Papers, Minnesota Historical Society, St. Paul.

EBB   Electronic Briefing Book, National Security Archive, Washington, DC, nsarchiv.gwu.edu.

FAS   Federation of American Scientists, Intelligence Resource Program, www.fas.org.

FRUS   Department of State, *Foreign Relations of the United States* series, history.state.gov/historicaldocuments.

GBL   George H. W. Bush Library, College Station, TX.

GFL   Gerald R. Ford Library, Ann Arbor, MI.

HJP   Henry M. Jackson Papers, Allen Library, University of Washington, Seattle.

HRC   Human Rights Collection, Houghton Library, Harvard University, Cambridge, MA.

HRQ   *Human Rights Quarterly.*

IHRC   Immigration History Research Center, University of Minnesota, Minneapolis.

JCL   Jimmy Carter Library, Atlanta, GA.

LAT   *Los Angeles Times.*

LBJ   Lyndon Baines Johnson Library, Austin, TX.

LOC   Library of Congress, Manuscript Division, Washington, DC.

NARA   National Archives II, College Park, MD.

NSA   National Security Archive, George Washington University, Washington, DC.

NYT   *New York Times.*

PPP   *Public Papers of the Presidents*, ed. Gerhard Peters and John T. Woolley, American Presidency Project, www.presidency.ucsb.edu.

RNL   Richard M. Nixon Presidential Library, Yorba Linda, CA.

RRL   Ronald Reagan Presidential Library, Simi Valley, CA.
WP   *Washington Post.*
WPP   William Proxmire Papers, Wisconsin Historical Society, Madison.
WSJ   *Wall Street Journal*

Introduction

1. William J. Butler and Georges Levasseur, *Human Rights and the Legal System in Iran* (Geneva: International Commission of Jurists, 1976).

2. Linda Charlton, "Clashes and Tear Gas," *NYT*, 16 November 1977; Paul Valentine, "Pro-, Anti-Shah Partisans," *WP*, 15 November 1977.

3. Jimmy Carter, *Keeping Faith: Memoirs of a President* (New York: Bantam Books, 1982), 433.

4. "Visit of Muhammad Reza Pahlavi," 15 November 1977, *PPP*, 6934.

5. Daniel Yergin, *The Prize: The Epic Quest for Oil, Money, and Power* (New York: Free Press, 2008), 627–628; Stephen J. Lynton and Courtland Milloy, "Shah Violence Sporadic," *WP*, 17 November 1977.

6. "Toasts," 15 November 1977, *PPP*, 6938.

7. John M. Goshko, "Human Rights Policy Test," *WP*, 16 November 1977.

8. Carter, *Keeping Faith*, 436–437; Vernon J. Vavrina, "The Carter Human Rights Policy: Political Idealism and Realpolitik," in *Jimmy Carter: Foreign Policy and Post-Presidential Years*, ed. Herbert D. Rosenbaum and Alexej Ugrinsky (Westport, CT: Greenwood, 1994), 104.

9. "Toasts," 15 November 1977, *PPP*.

10. Carter, *Keeping Faith*, 434.

11. "Remarks," 31 October 1969, *PPP*, 2302.

12. "Universal Declaration," 6 December 1978, *PPP*, 30264.

13. Cf. Paul Gordon Lauren, *The Evolution of International Human Rights: Visions Seen*, 2nd ed. (Philadelphia: University of Pennsylvania Press, 2003); Micheline Ishay, *The History of Human Rights: From Ancient Times to the Globalization Era*, 2nd ed. (Berkeley: University of California Press, 2008); Peter N. Stearns, *Human Rights in World History* (New York: Routledge, 2012).

14. Barbara Keys, *Reclaiming American Virtue: The Human Rights Revolution of the 1970s* (Cambridge, MA: Harvard University Press, 2014); Jan Eckel and Samuel Moyn, eds., *The Breakthrough: Human Rights in the 1970s* (Philadelphia: University of Pennsylvania Press, 2013); Kenneth Cmiel, "The Emergence of Human Rights Politics in the United States," *Journal of American History* 86 (December 1999): 1231–1250.

15. Samuel Moyn, *The Last Utopia: Human Rights in History* (Cambridge, MA: Harvard University Press, 2010).

16. "A Century of Death," *National Geographic* 209 (January 2006): 30.

17. Joshua S. Goldstein, *Winning the War on War: The Decline of Armed Conflict Worldwide* (New York: Dutton, 2011), 236–238.

18. Roland Burke, *Decolonization and the Evolution of International Human Rights* (Philadelphia: University of Pennsylvania Press, 2010), 109–110, 129–130; Kathryn Sikkink, *Mixed Signals: U.S. Human Rights Policy in Latin America* (Ithaca, NY: Cornell University Press, 2004), 54, 90–91.

19. Anatoly Dobrynin, *In Confidence: Moscow's Ambassador to America's Six Cold War Presidents* (New York: Times Books, 1995), 265.

20. David F. Schmitz, *Thank God They're on Our Side: The United States and Right-Wing Dictatorships*, 1921–1965 (Chapel Hill: University of North Carolina Press, 1999), 3–4.

21. Michael Ignatieff, "Human Rights," in *Human Rights in Political Transitions: Gettysburg to Bosnia*, ed. Carla Hesse and Robert Post (New York: Zone Books, 1999), 321.

22. Cmiel, "Emergence of Human Rights Politics," 1234.

23. Keys, *Reclaiming American Virtue*, 33.

24. Peter N. Carroll, *It Seemed Like Nothing Happened: America in the 1970s* (New Brunswick, NJ: Rutgers University Press, 1990).

25. Julie Mertus, *Bait and Switch: Human Rights and U.S. Foreign Policy* (New York: Routledge, 2004), 1–2, 17, 33.

26. Clair Apodaca, *Understanding U.S. Human Rights Policy: A Paradoxical Legacy* (New York: Routledge, 2006), xiii–xx.

27. David Forsythe, *Human Rights in International Relations* (Cambridge: Cambridge University Press, 2000), 145–148.

28. Noam Chomsky, *Hegemony or Survival: America's Quest for Global Dominance* (New York: Owl Books, 2004), 112–113.

29. Aryeh Neier, *The International Human Rights Movement: A History* (Princeton: Princeton University Press, 2012), 150–153.

30. Stearns, *Human Rights in World History*, 126–127, 132.

31. Adamantia Pollis and Peter Schwab, eds., *Human Rights: Cultural and Ideological Perspectives* (New York: Praeger, 1979).

32. Daniel Whelan, *Indivisible Human Rights: A History* (Philadelphia: University of Pennsylvania Press, 2010).

Chapter 1. The Crisis of Confidence

1. Paul Gordon Lauren, *The Evolution of International Human Rights: Visions Seen*, 2nd ed. (Philadelphia: University of Pennsylvania Press, 2003).

2. Elizabeth Borgwardt, *A New Deal for the World: America's Vision for Human Rights* (Cambridge, MA: Harvard University Press, 2005); Johannes Morsink, *The Universal Declaration of Human Rights: Origins, Drafting, and Intent* (Philadelphia: University of Pennsylvania Press, 1999).

3. Akira Iriye et al., eds., *The Human Rights Revolution: An International History* (New York: Oxford University Press, 2012), 3–24; Stefan-Ludwig Hoffmann, ed., *Human Rights in the Twentieth Century* (Cambridge: Cambridge University Press, 2010), 1–26; Susan Sontag, *Regarding the Pain of Others* (New York: Picador, 2003).

4. Tony Smith, *America's Mission: The United States and the Worldwide Struggle for Democracy in the Twentieth Century* (Princeton: Princeton University Press, 1994), 179.

5. William P. Bundy, "Dictatorships and American Foreign Policy," *Foreign Affairs* 54 (October 1975): 56.

6. Hans J. Morgenthau, *Politics Among Nations: The Struggle for Power and Peace*, 3rd ed. (New York: Knopf, 1960), 6.

7. Peter N. Stearns, *Human Rights in World History* (New York: Routledge, 2012), 126–127, 132.

8. Mary Dudziak, *Cold War Civil Rights: Race and the Image of American Democracy* (Princeton: Princeton University Press, 2000).

9. Aryeh Neier, *The International Human Rights Movement: A History* (Princeton: Princeton University Press, 2012), 162.

10. Gal Beckerman, *When They Come for Us, We'll Be Gone: The Epic Struggle to Save Soviet Jewry* (New York: Mariner, 2011), 39–85, 125–171.

11. Lauren, *Evolution of International Human Rights*, chap. 8.

12. Ryan M. Irwin, *Gordian Knot: Apartheid and the Unmaking of the Liberal World Order* (New York: Oxford University Press, 2012), 147–151, 187.

13. U.S. Policy Toward Southern Rhodesia, 25 January 1967, "NSC Meetings Vol. 4 (49)," box 2, NSC Meetings, NSF; Roche to Moyers, 6 September 1966, "CO 250 Rhodesia," box 65, GEN CO 237, LBJ.

14. Joseph to Watson, 14 December 1987, "CO 250 (1)," box 65, GEN CO 237; Ervin to East, 12 December 1966, "IT 47," box 11, GEN IT 47, LBJ.

15. Irving Kristol, "We Can't Resign,'" *NYT*, 12 May 1968.

16. Jeremi Suri, *Power and Protest: Global Revolution and the Rise of Détente* (Cambridge, MA: Harvard University Press, 2003).

17. Dominic Sandbrook, *Eugene McCarthy and the Rise and Fall of Postwar American Liberalism* (New York: Anchor, 2004), 135, 141.

18. Richard Sobel, *The Impact of Public Opinion on U.S. Foreign Policy Since Vietnam* (Oxford: Oxford University Press, 2001), 36.

19. "Address," 31 March 1968, *PPP*, 28772.

20. Neil Sheehan et al., eds., *The Pentagon Papers* (New York: Bantam, 1971), 580.

21. Peter Arnett, "Ben Tre's Destruction," *NYT*, 20 February 1968.

22. Robert Elegant, "How to Lose a War: The Press and Vietnam," *Encounter* 57, no. 2 (August 1981): 73–90.

23. Gregory Allen Olson, ed., *Landmark Speeches of the Vietnam War* (College Station: Texas A&M University Press, 2010), 93–113.

24. Telcon, Laird and Kissinger, 21 November 1969, EBB 123, NSA.

25. Packard to Nixon, 4 September 1969, "Calley Case (2)"; Moynihan to Nixon, 25 November 1969, "Calley Case (1)," box 118, Vietnam Subject, NSC, RNL.

26. "Notes and Comment," *New Yorker*, 20 December 1969, 27.

27. "Vietnam—My Lai Incident" folder, box 184, Senate, 1964–72, HJP; Peter Steinfels, "Calley and the Public Conscience," *Commonweal*, 12 April 1971, 128.

28. "The Great Atrocity Hunt," *National Review*, 16 December 1969, 1252.

29. "My Lai Incident" folder, HJP.

30. Daniel to Nixon, 3 April 1971, "Calley Case (1)," RNL.

31. Richard Nixon, *RN: The Memoirs of Richard Nixon* (New York: Grosset & Dunlap, 1978), 449–450.

32. Richard R. Moser, *The New Winter Soldiers* (New Brunswick, NJ: Rutgers University Press, 1996), 111.

33. *Causes, Origins, and Lessons of the Vietnam War*, Committee on Foreign Relations, U.S. Senate, 92nd Cong., 2nd sess. (Washington, DC: GPO, 1973), 41.

34. Daniel P. Moynihan, "An Erosion of Trust," *American Spectator*, November 1970, 6–7.

35. Don Luce, "Vietnam's Infamous Tiger Cages Revisited," *National Catholic Reporter*, 1 September 1995.

36. See Barbara Keys, *Reclaiming American Virtue: The Human Rights Revolution of the 1970s* (Cambridge, MA: Harvard University Press, 2014), 48–74.

37. Niall Ferguson, "Crisis, What Crisis? The 1970s and the Shock of the Global," in *The Shock of the Global: The 1970s in Perspective*, ed. Niall Ferguson et al. (Cambridge, MA: Harvard University Press, 2010), 14–15, 20.

38. John Lewis Gaddis, *The Cold War: A New History* (New York: Penguin, 2005), 212.

39. Humphrey Taylor, "Harris Poll #71," 30 December 1998, http://www.harrisinter tive.com/harris_poll/index.asp?PID = 13 6.

40. Memcon, 2 March 1971, "Kissinger University Student Body," box 1025, Presidential/HAK Memcons, RNL.

41. Hunter S. Thompson, *Fear and Loathing on the Campaign Trail '72* (New York: Warner Books, 1983), 86.

42. Daniel Yankelovich, "A Crisis of Moral Legitimacy?" *Dissent* (Fall 1974): 526–532.

43. Barbara Keys, "Anti-Torture Politics: Amnesty International, the Greek Junta, and the Origins of the Human Rights 'Boom' in the United States," in Iriye et al., *Human Rights Revolution*, 205.

44. "Who Speaks for Greece?" *NYT*, 17 May 1969.

45. Peter Schwab and George D. Frangos, eds., *Greece Under the Junta* (New York: Facts on File, 1970), 127–128.

46. Vournas to Manatos, 22 March 1968, "Greece 11/67–7/68," box 36, CO 94, LBJ; Benjamin Welles, "Papandreou, In Capital," *NYT*, 10 March 1968; Israel Shenker, "Ball and Papandreou," *NYT*, 5 December 1968.

47. John O. Iatrides, "The United States and Greece in the Twentieth Century," in *Greece in the Twentieth Century*, ed. Theodore A. Couloumbis et al. (London: Frank Cass, 2003), 92.

48. Telegram, 22 April 1967, doc. 277, *FRUS*, 1964–1968, XVI.

49. Brewster to Rockwell, 27 April 1967, "POL 1 Greece," box 2146, Central Foreign Policy 1967–69, RG 59, NARA.

50. James Edward Miller, *The United States and the Making of Modern Greece: History and Power, 1950–1974* (Chapel Hill: University of North Carolina Press, 2009), 152.

51. Konstantina Maragkou, "Favouritism in NATO's Southeastern Flank: The Case of the Greek Colonels, 1967–74," *Cold War History* 9, no. 3 (August 2009): 347–366.

52. Miller, *United States and the Making of Modern Greece*, 148–149.

53. Rostow to Johnson, 22 July 1967, "Greece Memos (1) Vol II," box 126, Cyprus/Greece Country, NSF, LBJ.

54. State to Ambassador, 31 January 1968, "Greece (2) Vol III," box 127, LBJ.

55. Rostow to Johnson, 31 May 1968, "Greece 3–11/68 (IV), box 127, LBJ.

56. Rostow to Johnson, 8 October 1968, "Greece 3–11/68 (IV)," LBJ.

57. Keys, "Anti-torture Politics," 202, 205.

58. Ibid., 211–214; William F. Buckley, "Understanding Greece," *National Review*, 16 July 1968.

59. Memo, U.S. Committee for Democracy in Greece, n.d., box 1, Minnesotans for Democracy in Greece, IHRC.

60. McCarthy Statement, 29 March 1968, IHRC.

61. Fraser to Hess, 20 June 1968, "Greece 1967–1968," box 87, DMF.

62. *Executive Sessions of the Senate Foreign Relations Committee* (Historical Series) XX, 90th Cong., 2nd sess. (Washington, DC: GPO, 2010), 862–865.

63. Committee for the Restoration, "The Greek Coup," 8 May 1967, "CO 94 10/66"; Biddle to Johnson, 4 January 1968, "Greece 11/67–7/68," box 36, CO 94, LBJ.

64. "Appeasing the Greek Junta," *NYT*, 19 March 1968.

65. I am relying here on James N. Green, "Clerics, Exiles, and Academics: Opposition to the Brazilian Military Dictatorship in the United States, 1969–1974," *Latin American Politics and Society* 45, no. 1 (2003): 87–117; and Martha K. Huggins, *Political Policing: The United States and Latin America* (Durham, NC: Duke University Press, 1998), 141–185.

66. Memcon, 28 March 1964, "Brazil, Volume 2 (2)," box 9, Country Brazil, NSF, LBJ.

67. "Message," 2 April 1964, *PPP*, 26136.

68. Embassy to Secretary, 7 August 1965, "Codel Fulbright," box 9, LBJ.

69. Economic Assistance Program, n.d. (1966), "Brazil Volume 6 (3)," box 11, LBJ.

70. Rostow to Johnson, 16 February 1968, "Brazil Volume 7a (2)," box 12, LBJ.

71. Rex A. Hudson, ed., *Brazil: A Country Study* (Washington, DC: GPO, 1997), 325.

72. Belton to State, 14 December 1968; Rusk to Embassy, 17 and 25 December 1968, docs. 236, 237, 241, *FRUS*, 1964–1968, XXXI.

73. James N. Green, *We Cannot Remain Silent: Opposition to the Brazilian Military Dictatorship in the United States* (Durham, NC: Duke University Press, 2010), 97.

74. "Brazil Volume 8," box 12, Country Brazil, NSF, LBJ.

75. Transcript, Nixon and Haldeman, 15 June 1972, doc. 29, EBB 95, NSA.

76. Interview, 24 September 1968, "Don McGaffin," box 98, Speech File, RNL.

77. *United States Policies and Programs in Brazil: Hearings*, Subcommittee on Western Hemisphere Affairs, 92nd Cong., 1st sess. (Washington, DC: GPO, 1971), 290.

78. Jacob Heilbrunn, *They Knew They Were Right: The Rise of the Neocons* (New York: Doubleday, 2007), 144.

79. "First Annual Report," 18 February 1970, *PPP*, 2835.

80. Henry A. Kissinger, *American Foreign Policy: Three Essays* (New York: Norton, 1969), 46–48, 53, 57.

81. Memcon, 22 September 1971, "Henry Kissinger, Herbert Stein," box 1025, Presidential/HAK Memcons, RNL.

82. Robert Dallek, *Nixon and Kissinger: Partners in Power* (New York: Harper Perennial, 2007), 439.

83. Barbara Keys, "Henry Kissinger: The Emotional Statesman," *Diplomatic History* 35, no. 4: 587–609.

84. Gerald Strober and Deborah Strober, *Nixon: An Oral History of His Presidency* (New York: HarperCollins, 1994), 124.

85. Dallek, *Nixon and Kissinger*, 610.

86. Christopher Hitchens, *The Trial of Henry Kissinger* (New York: Verso, 2001); William Burr, ed., *The Kissinger Transcripts: The Top-Secret Talks with Beijing with Moscow* (New York: New Press, 2000).

87. Nixon, *RN*, 344.

88. "Inaugural Address," 20 January 1969, *PPP*, 1941.

89. Michael Ignatieff, "Human Rights," in *Human Rights in Political Transitions: Gettysburg to Bosnia*, ed. Carla Hesse and Robert Post (New York: Zone Books, 1999), 317.

90. G. Arbatov, "Soviet-American Relations Today," *Pravda*, 3 August 1977.

91. Cargo to Kissinger, 17 August 1970, Presidential Directives, doc. 00538, NSA.

92. *Hearings on the Nomination of Henry A. Kissinger*, SFRC, 93rd Cong., 1st sess. (Washington, DC: GPO, 1973), 42.

93. Roberta Cohen, "People's Republic of China: The Human Rights Exception," *HRQ* 9, no. 4 (November 1987): 447–549.

94. "Memcons Feb. 1972," box 164, Briefing Books 1958–1976, RG 59, NARA.

95. Margaret MacMillan, *Nixon and Mao: The Week That Changed the World* (New York: Random House, 2007), 123.

96. Memcon, 9 July 1971, doc. 139, *FRUS*, 1969–1976, XVIII.

97. Dallek, *Nixon and Kissinger*, 364.

98. MacMillan, *Nixon and Mao*, 322.

99. Linda Bridges and John R. Coyne, *Strictly Right: William F. Buckley, Jr. and the American Conservative Movement* (Hoboken, NJ: John Wiley, 2007), 142–143.

100. Memcon, 30 June 1973, "HAK & Presidential (4)," Box 1027, Presidential/HAK Memcons, RNL.

101. Briefing Papers, February 1972, "Visit of Nixon to China," box 149, Briefing Books 1958–76, RG 59, NARA; Americans Imprisoned in China, n.d. (1972), NLN-NSC-847–5–1–9, RNL.

102. Memcon, 13 November 1973, doc. 59, *FRUS*, 1969–1976, XVIII.

103. MacMillan, *Nixon and Mao*, 337.

104. Iatrides, "United States and Greece," 93–94.

105. Derwinski to Kissinger, 29 January 1969; Danielopol to Klein, 29 May 1969, "CO 55 Greece," boxes 32–33, Subject, WHCF, RNL.

106. Memcon, 31 March 1969; Papadopoulos to Nixon, 6 April 1969, "POL 7 Greece," boxes 2146–2147, Central Foreign Policy 1967–69, RG 59, NARA.

107. Hughes to Secretary, 1 July 1969, "POL 2 Greece," box 2146, NARA.

108. Report by the Ambassador, 31 March 1970, doc. 273, *FRUS*, 1969–1976, XXIX.

109. Memcon, NSC Meeting, 17 June 1970, doc. 283, *FRUS*, 1969–1976, XXIX.

110. Rodgers to Fulbright, 28 September 1970; Sisco to Ellsworth, 10 February 1970, "1970–74 Chron," box 1, Davies, RG 59, NARA.

111. Memcon, 17 June 1969; "State Stand Against Greek Dictatorship Praised," 7 August 1969, "Minnesotans for Democracy in Greece," box 1, IHRC.

112. NSC Review Group, 2 October 1969, doc. 256, *FRUS*, 1969–1976, XXIX.

113. "Greece 1967–1968" folder, box 87, DMF.

114. "Foreign Relations 15" folder, box 186, Senate, 1964–72, HJP.

115. Iakovos to Rogers, 29 June 1973, "1970–74 Chron," box 1, Davies, RG 59, NARA.

116. "Greece 1967–1968" folder, box 87, DMF.

117. Nakis to McGovern, n.d. (August 1972), "AHEPA Banquet," box 23, Rogers Office, RG 59, NARA.

118. *Implementation of Homeporting in Greece*, House Foreign Affairs Committee, 93rd Cong., 1st sess. (Washington, DC: GPO, 1973), v–vii.

119. Briefing Book, July 1972, "Visit of Secretary Rogers to Greece," box 132, Briefing Books 1958–76, RG 59, NARA.

120. Remarks to American Community, 5 July 1972, "SEATO, ANZUS," box 22, Rogers Office, RG 59, NARA.

121. Memcon, 20 March 1974, doc. 12, *FRUS*, 1969–1976, XXX.

122. C. L. Sulzberger, *An Age of Mediocrity* (New York: Macmillan, 1973), 335.

123. Miller, *United States and the Making of Modern Greece*, x.

124. Mark Atwood Lawrence, "History from Below: The United States and Latin America in the Nixon Years," in *Nixon in the World: American Foreign Relations, 1969–1977*, ed. Fredrik Logevall and Andrew Preston (New York: Oxford University Press, 2008), 269–271.

125. Greg Grandin, *The Last Colonial Massacre: Latin America in the Cold War* (Chicago: University of Chicago Press, 2004), 188.

126. Juan de Onis, "Rockefeller Visits Brazil's Congress," 18 June 1969; "Rockefeller Raises Civil Rights," *NYT*, 19 June 1969.

127. Nelson A. Rockefeller et al., *The Rockefeller Report on the Americas* (Chicago: Quadrangle Books, 1969), 23–24, 143–144.

128. A. J. Langguth, *Hidden Terrors* (New York: Pantheon, 1978), 158.

129. Walter LaFeber, *Inevitable Revolutions: The United States in Central America* (New York: Norton, 1993), 202.

130. Andreas Feldmann and Maiju Perala, *Nongovernmental Terrorism in Latin America* (South Bend: Kellogg Institute, 2001), 3–5.

131. Cutter to State, 1 June 1970, "POL 23–9 BRAZ," box 2133, Subject-Numeric 1970–73, RG 59, NARA.

132. Manuel Hevia Cosculluela, *Pasaporte 11333: Ocho Años con la CIA* (Havana: Editorial de Ciencias Sociales, 1978).

133. Thomas E. Skidmore, *The Politics of Military Rule in Brazil, 1964–1985* (New York: Oxford University Press, 1988), 104, 155.

134. David Forsythe, *Human Rights and World Politics*, 2nd ed. (Lincoln: University of Nebraska Press, 1989), 142; Lars Schoultz, *Human Rights and United States Policy Toward Latin America* (Princeton: Princeton University Press, 1981), 6.

135. Kathryn Sikkink, *Mixed Signals: U.S. Human Rights Policy in Latin America* (Ithaca, NY: Cornell University Press, 2004), 60–61; Green, *We Cannot Remain Silent*, 156–158.

136. Margaret E. Keck and Kathryn Sikkink, *Activists Beyond Borders: Advocacy Networks in International Politics* (Ithaca, NY: Cornell University Press, 1998), 97–101.

137. "Oppression in Brazil," *WP*, 28 February 1970.

138. Frank Mankiewicz and Tom Braden, "Brazilian Blood on Our Hands," *WP*, 23 March 1971.

139. Tanya Harmer, *Allende's Chile & the Inter-American Cold War* (Chapel Hill: University of North Carolina Press, 2011), 10, 17.

140. "Brazil: Reports of Torture," 28 January 1970, "POL 23–9 BRAZ," box 2133, NARA.

141. Memo, 14 December 1970, doc. 134, *FRUS*, 1969–1976, E-10.

142. Abshire to Fulbright, 21 May 1978, "POL 29 BRAZ," box 2133, NARA.

143. Juan de Onis, "End of Direct Aid," *NYT*, 12 September 1969.

144. *Congressional Record*, 18 May 1970.

145. Ellis to Secretary, 11 May 1970, "POL 29 BRAZ," box 2133; 19 May 1970, "POL 7 BRAZ," box 2130, NARA.

146. "Brazil: Choosing Between Democracy and Efficiency," Intelligence Note, 11 November 1970, "POL 15 BRAZ," box 2131, NARA.

147. Telegram, 31 July 1970, "POL 29 BRAZ," box 2133, NARA.

148. Rountree to Secretary, 22 January 1971, "POL 29 BRAZ," box 2133, Subject-Numeric 1970–73, RG 59, NARA; Docs. 1–5, EBB 478, NSA; Langguth, *Hidden Terrors*, 60; "U.S. Has a 45–Year History of Torture," *LAT*, 3 May 2009.

149. See Cosculluela, *Pasaporte 11333*; "Prisoner Abuse: Patterns from the Past," EBB 122, NSA.

150. Green, *We Cannot Remain Silent*, 241, 243–244; *United States Policies and Programs in Brazil*, 1; Sikkink, *Mixed Signals*, 63.

151. *United States Policies and Programs in Brazil*, 39, 290–295.

152. Sikkink, *Mixed Signals*, 63.

153. Green, *We Cannot Remain Silent*, 248–252.

154. Rountree to State, 1 July 1972, doc. 3, EBB 478, NSA.

155. Rogers to Nixon, 2 December 1971, "Visit of President Medici," box 92, Briefing Books 1958–76, RG 59, NARA II.

156. Rountree to State, 17 June 1971, "POL 15 BRAZ," box 2131, Subject-Numeric 1970–73, RG 59, NARA.

157. Memcons, 7 and 9 December 1971, "Medici Visit (2)," box 911, VIP Visits, NSC, RNL.

158. Rountree to State, 21 December 1971, "POL 7 BRAZ," box 2130, Subject-Numeric 1970–73.

159. Memcons, 7 and 20 December 1971, docs. 11, 15, EBB 71, NSA; Harmer, *Allende's Chile*, 257.

160. Benjamin Welles, "Brazilian President Welcomed," 8 December 1971, *NYT*; "Visit of General Médici," 11 December 1971, *NYT*.

161. Cushman to Kissinger, 29 December 1971, doc. 3, EBB 282, NSA.

162. Schoultz, *Human Rights and United States Policy*, 6; Forsythe, *Human Rights and World Politics*, 142.

Chapter 2. The Congressional Challenge and the Ethnic Revival

1. David P. Forsythe, *Human Rights and U.S. Foreign Policy: Congress Reconsidered* (Gainesville: University of Florida Press, 1988), 2.

2. Robert David Johnson, *Congress and the Cold War* (New York: Cambridge University Press, 2006), xiv–xxvi.

3. Ibid., 190–207.

4. William P. Bundy, "The National Security Process: Plus ça Change?" *International Security* 7, no. 3 (Winter 1982–1983): 94.

5. Forsythe, *Human Rights and U.S. Foreign Policy*, 37, 49–50, 61, 78, 122.

6. *Congressional Record*, 4 March 1965.

7. Thomas Carothers, *Aiding Democracy Abroad* (Washington, DC: CEIP, 1999), 23.

8. "Two Decades of Foreign Aid," 23 September 1966, "Foreign Aid General Materials Magazines (5)," box 44, Campaign 1968 Research, RNL.

9. "Foreign Aid" folder and "Foreign Relations 4" folder, boxes 186, 189, 197, Senate, 1964–72, HJP.

10. Patricia W. Blair, ed., "World Development in the Seventies," "Economic Assistance 1971–1972," box 88, DMF.

11. Congressional Budget Office, "The Role of Foreign Aid in Development" (Washington, DC: CBO, May 1997), xii, 10.

12. Transcript, 16 September 1971, doc. 11, EBB 95, NSA.

13. Richard Sobel, *The Impact of Public Opinion on U.S. Foreign Policy Since Vietnam* (Oxford: Oxford University Press, 2001), 37.

14. CBO, "Role of Foreign Aid," xii, 10.

15. Edward M. Kennedy, "Beginning Anew in Latin America," *Saturday Review*, 17 October 1970, 19–20.

16. Transcript, 3 December 1974, EBB 110, NSA.

17. Johnson, *Congress and the Cold War*, xxiv–xxv.

18. *Hearings on the Nomination of Henry A. Kissinger*, SFRC, 93rd Cong., 1st sess. (Washington, DC: GPO, 1973), 2, 3, 7, 13–14, 40, 103.

19. Kathryn Sikkink, *Mixed Signals: U.S. Human Rights Policy in Latin America* (Ithaca, NY: Cornell University Press, 2004), chap. 3.

20. *Human Rights in the World Community: A Call for U.S. Leadership*, Subcommittee on International Organizations and Movements, 93rd Cong., 2nd sess. (Washington, DC: GPO, 1974), 9–12.

21. Ibid., vii, 53.

22. "Foreign Affairs—International Human Rights Hearings," box 2, lot 149.G.12.5B, DMF.

23. Aleksandr Solzhenitsyn, "Nobel Lecture," http://nobelprize.org.

24. Milan Kundera, *Immortality* (New York: HarperCollins, 1999), 139–140.

25. Stefan-Ludwig Hoffmann, ed., *Human Rights in the Twentieth Century* (Cambridge: Cambridge University Press, 2010), 23.

26. "News Conference," 25 February 1974, *PPP*, 4367.

27. "Solzhenitsyn and Détente," 15 February 1974, "Détente and Human Rights," box 244, Foreign Policy and Defense, 1941–83, HJP.

28. William Greider, "Hill Audience Hears Solzhenitsyn," *WP*, 16 July 1975.

29. Lou Cannon, *Reagan* (New York: Putnam, 1982), 199.

30. Douglas Brinkley, *Gerald R. Ford* (New York: Times Books, 2007), 109.

31. Sikkink, *Mixed Signals*, 10–12; Forsythe, *Human Rights and U.S. Foreign Policy*, 2–3, 11–12.

32. P.L. 87–195, sec. 32.

33. Foreign Assistance Act of 1974, sec. 26 (P.L. 93–559).

34. Minutes, 22 October 1974, doc. 244, *FRUS*, 1969–1976, E-3.

35. Memcon, 17 December 1974, doc. 245, *FRUS*, 1969–1976, E-3.

36. "Human Rights in the Republic of Korea," "Human Rights—Korea," box 3, HU 1975, RG 59, NARA.

37. Memcon, 22 November 1974, box 7, Memcons, National Security Adviser, GFL.

38. *Department of State Bulletin* 73, no. 1880 (7 July 1975): 123–126; Sandy Vogelgesang, *American Dream, Global Nightmare: The Dilemma of U.S. Human Rights Policy* (New York: Norton, 1980), 128.

39. Memcon, 26 November 1975, doc. 17, EBB 193, NSA.

40. Memcon, 6 December 1975, doc. 4, EBB 62, NSA.

41. Habib to Deputy Secretary, 27 June 1975, "Human Rights—Indonesia," box 3, HU 1975, RG 59, NARA.

42. Samuel Moyn, *The Last Utopia: Human Rights in History* (Cambridge, MA: Harvard University Press, 2010), 173.

43. Brad Simpson, "The Carter Administration, Indonesia, and the Transnational Human Rights Politics of the 1970s," in *The Human Rights Revolution: An International History*, ed. Akira Iriye et al. (New York: Oxford University Press, 2012), 181–182.

44. "Veto," 7 May 1976, *PPP*, 5952.

45. Ennals to Ellsworth, "International Secretariat Correspondence 1977–78 (1)," box 3, series I (Hawk), RG II, AIUSA.

46. James M. Wilson, "Diplomatic Theology—An Early Chronicle of Human Rights at State," "Wilson Memoir," box 1, Wilson, GFL.

47. Forsythe, *Human Rights and U.S. Foreign Policy*, 15, 120.

48. Wilson, "Diplomatic Theology."

49. Memcon, 29 September 1975, CDP (State).

50. Bernard Gwertzman, "U.S. Blocks Rights Data," *NYT*, 19 November 1975.

51. "Human Rights Today," n.d., "Human Rights—General," box 1, HU 1975, RG 59, NARA; Barbara Keys, "Congress, Kissinger, and the Origins of Human Rights Diplomacy," *Diplomatic History* 34, no. 5 (November 2010): 844–848.

52. Executive Director to Nominations Committee, 31 August 1977, "Correspondence (1) 1977 (21)," box 1, series I (Hawk), RG II, AIUSA.

53. Morris and Hawk to Congress, 10 December 1975, "U.S.S.R.—Trials," box 5, series I (Hawk), RG II, AIUSA.

54. Margaret E. Keck and Kathryn Sikkink, *Activists Beyond Borders: Advocacy Networks in International Politics* (Ithaca, NY: Cornell University Press, 1998), 90.

55. Barbara Keys, *Reclaiming American Virtue: The Human Rights Revolution of the 1970s* (Cambridge, MA: Harvard University Press, 2014), 192–195.

56. Hawk to Ivan, n.d.; Draft Resolution, n.d.; Draft Resolution, 17 December 1974, "Balance Question" (10), box 1, series I (Hawk), RG II, AIUSA.

57. Tanya Harmer, *Allende's Chile & the Inter-American Cold War* (Chapel Hill: University of North Carolina Press, 2011), 8–10, 17, 110; Lars Schoultz, *Human Rights and United States Policy Toward Latin America* (Princeton: Princeton University Press, 1981), 170–174; Mark Atwood Lawrence, "History from Below: The United States and Latin America in the Nixon Years," in *Nixon in the World: American Foreign Relations, 1969–1977*, ed. Fredrik Logevall and Andrew Preston (New York: Oxford University Press, 2008), 277–278.

58. Jan Eckel, "'Under a Magnifying Glass': The International Human Rights Campaign Against Chile in the Seventies," in Hoffmann, *Human Rights in the Twentieth Century*, 324.

59. Keck and Sikkink, *Activists Beyond Borders*, 91.

60. Eckel, "'Under a Magnifying Glass,'" 326–328, 338.

61. See the work of Matthew C. Price, Robert Alexander, and Jonathan Goldberg.

62. See the work of Armando Uribe and James Petras.

63. Paul Sigmund, *The United States and Democracy in Chile* (Baltimore: Johns Hopkins University Press, 1993), 106, 110.

64. Ibid., 80, 85.

65. Ibid., 90; Schoultz, *Human Rights and United States Policy*, 185–188; Harmer, *Allende's Chile*, 18, 249.

66. Transcript, 7 October 1971, EBB 95, NSA.

67. Memcon, 1 October 1973, EBB 110, NSA.

68. Popper, Ambassador Overview, 27 June 1974, CDP (State).

69. Harmer, *Allende's Chile*, 251.

70. David F. Schmitz, *The United States and Right-Wing Dictatorships* (Cambridge: Cambridge University Press, 2006), 105; Johnson, *Congress and the Cold War*, 197.

71. *United States and Chile During the Allende Years, 1970–1973*, House Subcommittee on Inter-American Affairs (Washington, DC: GPO, 1975), 101.

72. *Human Rights in Chile*, Subcommittees on Inter-American Affairs and International Organizations, 93rd Cong., 2nd sess. (Washington, DC: GPO, 1973, 1974), 129–135.

73. Johnson, *Congress and the Cold War*, 197; Jonathan Goldberg, "Captive Audience," *American Prospect*, 27 February 2003.

74. *Human Rights in Chile*, pt. 2, 17–18.

75. Seymour Hersh, "Censored Matter," *NYT*, 11 September 1974.

76. Hersh, "Kissinger Is Challenged," *NYT*, 28 September 1974.

77. Memcon, 5 December 1974, EBB 110, NSA.

78. Memcon, 23 December 1974, EBB 110, NSA.

79. Memcon, 18 July 1975, CDP (State).

80. Kissinger to Carvajal, 5 August 1975; Memcon, 29 September 1975, CDP (State).

81. Bloomfield to Rogers, 11 July 1975, EBB 212, NSA.

82. Wilson, "Diplomatic Theology."

83. Memcon, 1 June 1976, doc. 259, *FRUS*, 1969–1976, E-3.

84. Memcon, 8 June 1976, CDP (State).

85. Goldberg, "Captive Audience."

86. Sikkink, *Mixed Signals*, 10–12.

87. Arthur J. Goldberg and Richard N. Gardner, "Time to Act on the Genocide Convention," *ABA Journal* 58, no. 2 (February 1972): 141–145.

88. Paul Valentine, "Panthers to Press," *WP*, 10 January 1970.

89. Bruno V. Bitker, "Genocide Revisited," *ABA Journal* 56 (January 1970): 73, 75.

90. Samantha Power, *A Problem from Hell* (New York: Harper Perennial, 2002), 79–85, 155–169.

91. Goldberg and Gardner, "The Genocide Convention," *NYT*, 28 March 1972.

92. *Congressional Record*, 5 October 1972, S16921–S16922.

93. Ad Hoc Committee memo, 3 July 1973, folder 6, box I:66, AJG.

94. Jack L. Goldsmith and Eric A. Posner, *The Limits of International Law* (New York: Oxford University Press, 2005), 108, 120–121, 225.

95. Raymond L. Garthoff, *Détente and Confrontation: American-Soviet Relations from Nixon to Reagan* (Washington, DC: Brookings Institution, 1994), 527–533; Cathal J. Nolan, *Principled Diplomacy: Security and Rights in U.S. Foreign Policy* (Westport, CT: Greenwood, 1993), 139–142; Daniel C. Thomas, "Human Rights Ideas, the Demise of Communism, and the End of the Cold War," *Journal of Cold War Studies* 7, no. 2 (Spring 2005): 110–141.

96. Anatoly Dobrynin, *In Confidence: Moscow's Ambassador to America's Six Cold War Presidents* (New York: Times Books, 1995), 345–346.

97. Steven F. Hayward, *The Age of Reagan, 1964–1980: The Fall of the Old Liberal Order* (Roseville, CA: Prima, 2001), 436; "Jerry, Don't Go," *WSJ*, 23 July 1975; Kim Willenson, "Ford's Big Gamble," *Newsweek*, 4 August 1975, 16.

98. Memcon, 8 August 1975, "August 8, 1975—Cabinet Meeting," box 14, Memcons, National Security Adviser, GFL.

99. Willenson, "Ford's Big Gamble"; Memcon, 28 April 1974, "Memcons (1)," box 1028, HAK/Presidential, RNL.

100. Brinkley, *Gerald R. Ford*, 108.

101. "Address," 1 August 1975, *PPP*, 5137.

102. John Prados, *How the Cold War Ended* (Dulles, VA: Potomac Books, 2010), 86.

103. Andropov to Central Committee, 15 November 1976, doc. 8, EBB 191, NSA; "What Lies Behind the Furor," *Pravda*, 12 February 1977, 4.

104. Thomas, "Human Rights Ideas," 125–131.

105. Sarah B. Snyder, *Human Rights Activism and the End of the Cold War: A Transnational History of the Helsinki Network* (New York: Cambridge University Press, 2011), 81–114.

106. David Farber, *The Age of Great Dreams: America in the 1960s* (New York: Hill & Wang, 1994), 265–266.

107. Charles Mathias, Jr., "Ethnic Groups and Foreign Policy," *Foreign Affairs* 59, no. 5 (1981): 981.

108. Alexander DeConde, *Ethnicity, Race, and American Foreign Policy: A History* (Boston: Northeastern University Press, 1992), 1.

109. Matthew Frye Jacobson, *Roots Too: White Ethnic Revival in Post–Civil Rights America* (Cambridge, MA: Harvard University Press, 2008), 26.

110. European Commission of Human Rights, *Report of the Commission*, vol. 1 (Strasbourg: Council of Europe, 10 July 1976), 72–74, 163–167; Nasuh Uslu, *The Cyprus Question as an Issue of Turkish Foreign Policy and Turkish-American Relations* (Hauppage: Nova, 2003), 151–165.

111. Memcon, 8 August 1975, doc. 339, *FRUS, 1969–1976*, XXXIX; DeConde, *Ethnicity, Race*, 172–174.

112. Uslu, *Cyprus Question*, 151.

113. Zinovia Lialiouti and Philip E. Muehlenbeck, "Ethnic Nationalism in the Cold War Context," in *Race, Ethnicity, and the Cold War: A Global Perspective*, ed. Philip E. Muehlenbeck (Nashville: Vanderbilt University Press, 2012), 239–240.

114. Anton to *Milwaukee Sentinel*, 9 April 1976, 94/24, box 94, mss 738, WPP.

115. Memcon, 31 July 1975, doc. 183, *FRUS, 1969–1976*, XXX.

116. "Ethnic Lobbying: An American Tradition," Background Memorandum, February 1976, "Jewish," box 3, Novak, IHRC.

117. Göran Rystad, "Congress and the Ethnic Lobbies: The Case of the 1974 Arms Embargo on Turkey," in *Hyphenated Diplomacy: European Immigration and U.S. Foreign Policy, 1914–1984*, ed. Helene Christol and Serge Ricard (Aix-en-Provence: Université de Provence, 1985), 107.

118. John Lewis Gaddis, *Strategies of Containment: A Critical Appraisal of Postwar American Security Policy* (New York: Oxford University Press, 1982), 331.

119. Lialiouti and Muehlenbeck, "Ethnic Nationalism," 230, 241–242, 248.

120. "First Annual Report," 18 February 1970; "Second Annual Report," 25 February 1971, *PPP*, 2835, 3324.

121. "Second Inaugural," 20 January 1973, *PPP*, 4141.

122. Koval to Nixon, 16 October 1972; Kalynyk and Stankievic to Nixon, 11 October 1972 (no folder title), box 1, Association for Liberation of Ukraine, IHRC.

123. Lettrich to Nixon, 17 September 1969, 25, box 109, ACEN, IHRC.

124. Telegram, 26 September 1970, "Yugoslavia," box 45, Subject, WHCF, RNL.

125. "Toasts," 28 October 1971; "Joint Statement," 30 October 1971, *PPP*, 3202, 3203.

126. "Nixon in Chicago," *NYT*, 18 September 1970.

127. Mazewski to Nixon, 19 April 1972, "Polish American Congress," box 4, Balzano, WHCF, RNL.

128. I am relying here on Bennett Kovrig, *Of Walls and Bridges: The United States and Eastern Europe* (New York: NYU Press, 1991), 118–120; James Feron, "East Hopes Talks," *NYT*, 22 May 1972; "Joint Communique," 1 June 1972, *PPP*, 3449; and William Bundy, *A Tangled Web: The Making of Foreign Policy in the Nixon Presidency* (New York: Hill & Wang, 1998), 328.

129. "The Polish Question," April 1972, "Polish Americans," box 7, Balzano, WHCF, RNL.

130. Rogers to Nixon, 19 April 1972, 15 May 1972; Memcon, 31 May 1972, "Visit of Richard Nixon to Poland," boxes 103 and 164A, Briefing Books 1958–76, RG 59, NARA.

131. Memcon, 1 June 1972, "POL POL-U.S.," box 2554, Subject-Numeric 1970–73, RG 59, NARA.

132. Donald E. Pienkos, *For Your Freedom Through Ours: Polish American Efforts on Poland's Behalf, 1863–1991* (Boulder, CO: East European Monographs, 1991), 152–156.

133. Tony Smith, *Foreign Attachments: The Power of Ethnic Groups in the Making of American Foreign Policy* (Cambridge, MA: Harvard University Press, 2005), 57.

134. Dusko Doder, "Watergate Baffles E. Europe," *WP*, 11 November 1973.

135. Gal Beckerman, *When They Come for Us, We'll Be Gone: The Epic Struggle to Save Soviet Jewry* (New York: Mariner, 2011), 7–8.

136. Dobrynin, *In Confidence*, 334.

137. Gregory L. Freeze, ed., *Russia: A History* (Oxford: Oxford University Press, 1997), 370–393.

138. Hughes to Secretary, 19 February 1968, MS Russ 79 (3483); Denney to Acting Secretary, 24 February 1969, MS Russ 79 (3487), HRC; Tsvigun to Central Committee, 26 August 1968, doc. 6, ASKGB.

139. Andropov to Central Committee, 5 October 1970, 13 January 1971, docs. 15, 21, ASKGB.

140. Benjamin Nathans, "Soviet Rights-Talk in the Post-Stalin Era," in Hoffmann, *Human Rights in the Twentieth Century*, 180–190.

141. R. J. Vincent, *Human Rights and International Relations* (New York: Cambridge University Press, 1986), 63–65.

142. Freeze, *Russia*, 380–381.

143. Bernard Lewis, "The Anti-Zionist Resolution," *Foreign Affairs* 55, no. 1 (October 1976): 60–64.

144. Ibid.

145. Jacobson, *Roots Too*, 26, 222.

146. Jacob Heilbrunn, *They Knew They Were Right: The Rise of the Neocons* (New York: Doubleday, 2007), 67, 70.

147. Beckerman, *When They Come for Us*, 224–242.

148. Paula Stern, *Water's Edge: Domestic Politics and the Making of American Foreign Policy* (Westport, CT: Greenwood, 1979), 30–65.

149. Dobrynin, *In Confidence*, 268.

150. Noam Kochavi, "Insights Abandoned, Flexibility Lost," *Diplomatic History* 29, no. 3 (June 2005): 509.

151. Stern, *Water's Edge*, 14–15.

152. "Nixon Aides," *NYT*, 20 April 1972; Kochavi, "Insights Abandoned," 514; Dobrynin, *In Confidence*, 268.

153. Beckerman, *When They Come for Us*, 270–271.

154. Memcon, 23 May 1972; telegrams, 31 May 1972, "Moscow, Bonn," box 20, Rogers Office, RG 59, NARA.

155. Frank Lynn, "A Strong Defense," *NYT*, 27 September 1972.

156. Henry Kissinger, *Years of Upheaval* (Boston: Little, Brown, 1982), 249–250, 252; Richard Nixon, *RN: The Memoirs of Richard Nixon* (New York: Grosset & Dunlap, 1978), 876, 1034.

157. Henry L. Feingold, *Silent No More: Saving the Jews of Russia, the American Jewish Effort, 1967–1989* (Syracuse, NY: Syracuse University Press, 2007), 72–73; Robert Gordon Kaufman, *Henry M. Jackson: A Life in Politics* (Seattle: University of Washington Press, 2000), 268.

158. Adam Nagourney, "In Tapes, Nixon Rails," *NYT*, 10 December 2010.

159. Kaufman, *Henry M. Jackson*, 249, 251.

160. Johnson, *Congress and the Cold War*, 199.

161. "US-Soviet Trade Prospects," June 1973, "Brezhnev Visit (2)," box 940, VIP Visits, NSC, RNL.

162. Bernard Gwertzman, "U.S. and U.S.S.R.," *NYT*, 8 October 1972.

163. "Détente and Human Rights," 11 October 1973, "Pacem in Terris," box 244, Speeches and Writings, Senate, HJP.

164. Henry M. Jackson, "First, Human Détente," *NYT*, 9 December 1973.

165. Bundy, *Tangled Web*, 409.

166. Kaufman, *Henry M. Jackson*, 267.

167. "Trade—Jackson-Vanik" folder, box 199; "Foreign Relations 9" folder, box 197, Senate, 1964–72, HJP.

168. Memcon, 25 September 1973, "Memcons—April–Nov 1973 (3)," box 1027, Presidential/HAK Memcons, RNL.

169. Kissinger, *Years of Upheaval*, 253; Dobrynin, *In Confidence*, 269–270; Bundy, *Tangled Web*, 407–408.

170. "US-Soviet Trade Prospects," RNL.

171. William Burr, ed., *The Kissinger Transcripts: The Top-Secret Talks with Beijing and Moscow* (New York: New Press, 2000), 225–226.

172. "Remarks," 5 June 1974, *PPP*, 4236.

173. Secretary Kissinger's Statement, 19 September 1974, "Human Rights—USSR," box 4, HU 1975, NARA.

174. Dobrynin, *In Confidence*, 334–337; Kaufman, *Henry M. Jackson*, 280.

175. Memcons, 24 October 1974, "Kissinger/Brezhnev Talks (1)"; 30 July 1975, "Ford/Brezhnev Meetings (CSCE)," box 1, USSR Memcons and Reports, National Security Adviser, GFL; Hartman to Kissinger, 23 October 1975, "Human Rights—USSR," box 4, HU 1975, NARA.

176. Memcon, 28 May 1974, doc. 182, *FRUS*, 1969–1976, XV.

177. Kissinger, *Years of Upheaval*, 254.

178. Wilson, "Diplomatic Theology."

179. Kochavi, "Insights Abandoned," 521–522.

180. Kaufman, *Henry M. Jackson*, 6–7.

181. Ibid., 3, 6, 248, 281.

182. Murray Friedman and Albert D. Chernin, eds., *A Second Exodus: The American Movement to Free Soviet Jews* (Hanover, NH: University Press of New England, 1999), 1, 8; Adam Ulam, *Dangerous Relations: The Soviet Union in World Politics, 1970–1982* (New York: Oxford University Press, 1983), 81, 120–124.

183. Carl Bon Tempo, *Americans at the Gate: The United States and Refugees During the Cold War* (Princeton: Princeton University Press, 2008), 141.

184. Andrew Preston, *Sword of the Spirit, Shield of Faith* (New York: Anchor, 2012), 574–579.

185. Malcolm D. MacDougall, *We Almost Made It* (New York: Crown, 1977), 44.

186. Henry M. Jackson, "Where I Stand," *NYT*, 11 February 1976.

187. Davis W. Houck and Amos Kiewe, eds., *Actor, Ideologue, Politician: The Public Speeches of Ronald Reagan* (Westport, CT: Greenwood, 1993), 155–156.

188. "Remarks," 5 March 1976, *PPP*, 5672.

189. Colman McCarthy, "Governments that Rule," *WP*, 7 August 1976.

190. Zbigniew Brzezinski, *Power and Principle: Memoirs of the National Security Adviser, 1977–1981* (New York: Farrar, Straus and Giroux, 1983), 49.

191. Sidney Kraus, ed., *The Great Debates: Carter vs. Ford, 1976* (Bloomington: Indiana University Press, 1979), 479, 483–484, 490; Scott Kaufman, *Plans Unraveled: The Foreign Policy of the Carter Administration* (DeKalb: Northern Illinois University Press, 2008), 12.

192. "Text of Remarks," 25 July 1975, *PPP*, 5106; "Remarks," 2 April 1976, *PPP*, 5781; Sarah B. Snyder, "Through the Looking Glass: The Helsinki Final Act and the 1976 Election for President," *Diplomacy and Statecraft* 21, no. 1 (March 2010): 87–106.

193. House Committee on House Administration, *The Presidential Campaign 1976* (Washington: GPO, 1978–1979); vol. 1, pt. 1, 117; pt. 2, 1004–1005.

194. Elizabeth Drew, *American Journal: The Events of 1976* (New York: Random House, 1977), 464–465.

195. Presidential Campaign Debate, 6 October 1976, *PPP*, 6414.

196. Jules Witcover, *Marathon: The Pursuit of the Presidency, 1972–1976* (New York: Viking Press, 1977), 602, 607.

197. Drew, *American Journal*, 465.

Chapter 3. The Carter Human Rights Policy

1. Scott Kaufman, *Plans Unraveled: The Foreign Policy of the Carter Administration* (DeKalb: Northern Illinois University Press, 2008), 4.

2. Stephen B. Cohen, "Conditioning U.S. Security Assistance on Human Rights Practices," *American Journal of International Law* 76, no. 2 (April 1982): 249.

3. Barbara Keys, *Reclaiming American Virtue: The Human Rights Revolution of the 1970s* (Cambridge, MA: Harvard University Press, 2014), 243, 252–254.

4. Cf. Joshua Muravchik, *The Uncertain Crusade: Jimmy Carter and the Dilemmas of Human Rights Policy* (Lanham, MD: Hamilton Press, 1986); Donald S. Spencer, *The Carter Implosion: Jimmy Carter and the Amateur Style of Diplomacy* (New York: Praeger, 1988).

5. John Dumbrell, *The Carter Presidency: A Re-evaluation* (New York: Manchester University Press, 1993); Robert Strong, *Working in the World: Jimmy Carter and the Making of American Foreign Policy* (Baton Rouge: Louisiana State University Press, 2000); Mary E. Stuckey, *Jimmy Carter, Human Rights, and the National Agenda* (College Station: Texas A&M University Press, 2008).

6. Elizabeth Drew, "A Reporter at Large: Human Rights," *New Yorker*, 18 July 1977, 37.

7. Jimmy Carter, *Keeping Faith: Memoirs of a President* (New York: Bantam Books, 1982), 144–145.

8. "Inaugural Address," 20 January 1977, *PPP*, 6575.

9. "Interview," 15 July 1977, *PPP*, 7820.

10. Cyrus Vance, *Hard Choices: Critical Years in America's Foreign Policy* (New York: Simon & Schuster, 1983), 46, 441.

11. Powell to Carter, 21 February 1977, "Soviet Dissidents," box 46, Counsel's Office, JCL.

12. Toon to Secretary, 13 February 1977, "Human Rights, 2–4/77," box 28, Subject File, NSA Brzezinski, JCL.

13. Central Committee to Brezhnev, 18 February 1977, doc. 12, EBB 191, NSA; Anatoly Dobrynin, *In Confidence: Moscow's Ambassador to America's Six Cold War Presidents* (New York: Times Books, 1995), 390.

14. Hartman to Embassy, 18 February 1977, "Human Rights, 2–4/77," box 28, Subject File, NSA Brzezinski, JCL.

15. Andropov to Central Committee, 9 February 1977, 18 February 1977, docs. 122–123, ASKGB; "What Lies Behind the Furor," *Pravda*, 12 February 1977, 4.

16. Vance, *Hard Choices*, 53–55.

17. "News Conference," 30 June 1977, 12 July 1977, *PPP*, 7751, 7786.

18. Memcon, 1 February 1977, "Memcons: President, 2/77," box 34, Subject File, NSA Brzezinski, JCL; Dobrynin, *In Confidence*, 386.

19. Carter to Brezhnev, 26 January 1977, 14 February 1977; Brezhnev to Carter, 4 February 1977, "USSR—Carter/Brezhnev Correspondence [1/77–5/77]," box 18, Brzezinski Donated; Brezhnev to Carter, 25 February 1977, NLC-128-4-24-6-3, JCL.

20. "Secretary Vance's News Conference," *Department of State Bulletin*, 21 February 1977, 138.

21. "Address," 17 March 1977, *PPP*, 7183.

22. Cyrus Vance, "Human Rights and Foreign Policy," *Department of State Bulletin*, 23 May 1977, 505–508.

23. "Address," 22 May 1977, *PPP*, 7552.

24. PD/NSC-30, Human Rights, 17 February 1978, FAS.

25. Joe Renouard, Review of Kristin L. Ahlberg, ed., *Foreign Relations of the United States, Volume II, Human Rights and Humanitarian Affairs, 1977–1980*, H-Diplo (April 2014), 3, http://www.h-net.org/~diplo/FRUS/PDF/FRUS24.pdf.

26. Cohen, "Conditioning U.S. Security Assistance," 264–276.

27. "Human Rights II" folder, box 36, Christopher, RG 59, NARA.

28. "Report of the Interagency Group," 30 April 1978, "PD 30 Response (Final)," box 41, Christopher, RG 59, NARA.

29. "Argentina: Military Aid, Trade," n.d. (1978), "Argentina Campaign," box 302, series II, RG VII, AIUSA.

30. Kaufman, *Plans Unraveled*, 30–31.

31. "The Prophet Carter," *WP*, 20 March 1977.

32. CIA, "Human Rights Performance," September 1978, NLC-11-3-6-9-1, JCL.

33. *Human Rights and U.S. Foreign Policy*, Subcommittee on International Organizations, 96th Cong., 1st sess. (Washington, DC: GPO, 1979), 114.

34. Daniel Southerland, "State Department Rights Groups," *CSM*, 27 June 1977.

35. Vernon J. Vavrina, "The Carter Human Rights Policy: Political Idealism and Realpolitik," in *Jimmy Carter: Foreign Policy and Post-Presidential Years*, ed. Herbert D. Rosenbaum and Alexej Ugrinsky (Westport, CT: Greenwood, 1994), 103.

36. William Michael Schmidli, "Institutionalizing Human Rights in U.S. Foreign Policy: U.S.-Argentine Relations, 1976–1980," *Diplomatic History* 35, no. 2 (April 2011): 366.

37. Graham Hovey, "Brzezinski, U.S. Diplomats' Guest," *NYT*, 12 December 1977; Alan Riding, "El Salvador's Dissidents," *NYT*, 8 May 1978.

38. Embassy to Secretary, 17 February 1978, "Memoranda 1978," box 18, Christopher, RG 59, NARA.

39. Tuchman to Brzezinski, 7 July 1978, "7/1/78," box HU-2, WHCF HU, JCL.

40. Tony Smith, *Foreign Attachments: The Power of Ethnic Groups in the Making of American Foreign Policy* (Cambridge, MA: Harvard University Press, 2005), 62.

41. David P. Forsythe, *Human Rights and U.S. Foreign Policy: Congress Reconsidered* (Gainesville: University of Florida Press, 1988), 78.

42. Kirsten Sellars, *The Rise and Rise of Human Rights* (Stroud: Sutton, 2002), 130.

43. "'Mischief' in Moscow's Front Yard," *Time*, 12 June 1978, 19.

44. PD/NSC-21, "Policy Toward Eastern Europe," 13 September 1977, FAS.

45. Mazewski to Carter, "Polish-American: Meeting," box 47, Staff Offices, Ethnic Affairs, Aiello, JCL.

46. Memorandum: Prospects for Eastern Europe, 10 June 1977, NLC-6-22-1-1-9, JCL.

47. "Remarks," 29 December 1977; "News Conference," 30 December 1977, *PPP*, 7074, 7075.

48. Brad Simpson, "The Carter Administration, Indonesia, and the Transnational Human Rights Politics of the 1970s," in *The Human Rights Revolution: An International History*, ed. Akira Iriye et al. (New York: Oxford University Press, 2012), 179–200; Joseph Nevins, *A Not-So-Distant Horror: Mass Violence in East Timor* (Ithaca, NY: Cornell University Press, 2005), 53–56.

49. Derian to Vance, 16 June 1977, "Human Rights—Don Fraser," box 32, Christopher, RG 59, NARA; Simpson, "Carter Administration,"183.

50. "Meeting with Suharto," 18 April 1977, Telegram 4890, EBB 242, NSA.

51. Simpson, "Carter Administration," 193–194; Nevins, *A Not-So-Distant Horror*.

52. Charlotte Saikowski, "South Korea: A Nation with Microwave Ovens but Little Democracy," *CSM*, 1 December 1983, 20.

53. Vance to Carter, n.d., "Human Rights 2–4/77," box 28, Subject, NSA Brzezinski, JCL; PRM/NSC 13, 29 January 1977, FAS.

54. Carter to Park, 14 February 1977, "Korea, Republic of, 2/77–12/78," box 12, Foreign Leaders Correspondence, NSA Brzezinski, JCL.

55. Memcon, 9 March 1977, "Memcons: President, 3/77," box 34, Subject File, NSA Brzezinski, JCL.

56. Embassy to Vance, 19 April 1977, NLC-16-11-1-26-3, JCL.

57. CIA, U.S.-South Korean Relations, 10 May 1978, NLC-4-39-1-1-3; Carter to Park, 17 May 1978, "Korea, Republic of, 2/77–12/78," box 12, Foreign Leaders Correspondence, NSA Brzezinski; Human Rights in the East Asia-Pacific, 31 October 1978, NLC-28-17-15-10-6, JCL.

58. "Toasts," 30 June 1979, *PPP*, 32564.

59. Gregg A. Brazinsky, *Nation Building in South Korea* (Chapel Hill: University of North Carolina Press, 2009), 228–230; Park to Carter, 31 July 1979; Brzezinski to Gleysteen, n.d.; Carter to Park, 13 October 1979, "Korea, Republic of: 1–10/79," box 12, Foreign Leaders Correspondence, NSA Brzezinski, JCL.

60. Carter to Chun, 27 August 1980, "Korea, Republic of: 8–12/80," box 12, Foreign Leaders Correspondence, NSA Brzezinski, JCL; Brazinsky, *Nation Building*, 233–240.

61. Daniel Patrick Moynihan, "The Politics of Human Rights," *Commentary*, August 1977, 23–24.

62. Jeane J. Kirkpatrick, "Dictatorships and Double-Standards," *Commentary*, November 1979, 34–45.

63. Carter, *Keeping Faith*, 143.

64. Carter to Tito, 11 May 1977, "Yugoslavia," box 21, Foreign Leaders Correspondence, NSA Brzezinski, JCL.

65. Paul Valentine and B. D. Colen, "Security Heavy," *WP*, 8 September 1977.

66. Kathleen Teltsch, "Rights Treaty Move," *NYT*, 11 December 1978.

67. Kenton Clymer, "Jimmy Carter, Human Rights, and Cambodia," *Diplomatic History* 27, no. 2 (April 2003): 246–247, 252–253; "Human Rights Violations," 21 April 1978, *PPP*, 30693.

68. Miklos to Vance, 24 February 1977, NLC 21-44-4-15-0; Carter to the Shah, 7 February 1977, NLC-15-20-1-2-0, JCL.

69. CIA, Impact of the U.S. Stand, 6 June 1977, NLC-28-22-8-1-8, JCL; Sullivan to Vance, 19 June 1977, NLC-10-3-4-4-9, JCL; Vance, *Hard Choices*, 318–322.

70. The U.S. Relationship with Iran, 10 November 1977, NLC-5-5-7-12-1; Vance to Carter, 10 November 1977, NLC-5-5-7-9-5, JCL.

71. "Remarks," "Toasts," 31 December 1977, *PPP*, 7079, 7080.

72. FBIS, World Media Reaction, 10 January 1978, NLC-4-9-3-14-0, JCL.

73. Betty Glad, *An Outsider in the White House: Jimmy Carter, His Advisors, and the Making of American Foreign Policy* (Ithaca, NY: Cornell University Press, 2009), 245; Terence Smith, "Rights Policy: Uneven Stress," *NYT*, 12 December 1978.

74. John Dumbrell, *American Foreign Policy: Carter to Clinton* (New York: Palgrave Macmillan, 1997), 34.

75. Vance, *Hard Choices*, 316.

76. Warren I. Cohen, *America's Response to China: A History of Sino-American Relations* (New York: Columbia University Press, 2000), 221.

77. Oksenberg to Brzezinski, 20 June 1977, NLC-15-41-6-1-3, JCL.

78. PRM/NSC-28: Human Rights, 15 August 1977, NLC-132-44-6-1-9, JCL.

79. CIA, Human Rights Performance, September 1978, NLC-11-3-6-9-1, JCL.

80. "News Conference," 30 November 1978, *PPP*, 30222.

81. James Mann, *About Face: A History of America's Curious Relationship with China* (New York: Knopf, 1999), 81–82.

82. Human Rights in the East Asia-Pacific, 31 October 1978, JCL.

83. Rosemary Foot, *The Practice of Power: U.S. Relations with China Since 1949* (New York: Oxford University Press, 1995), 108–111; Kaufman, *Plans Unraveled*, 140.

84. Foot, *Practice of Power*; Kreps to Brzezinski, 11 March 1977, "China: 3–6/77," box 8, Country File, NSA Brzezinski, JCL.

85. Memcon, 30 January 1979, doc. 208, *FRUS, 1977–1980*, XIII.

86. Robert Gordon Kaufman, *Henry M. Jackson: A Life in Politics* (Seattle: University of Washington Press, 2000), 380–381.

87. Memcon, 23 January 1979, NLC-7-37-2-3-9; Tarnoff to Brzezinski, 26 January 1979, NLC-5-3-1-11-0, JCL.

88. Kaufman, *Plans Unraveled*, 141.

89. "Democrats Move to Drop Ethnics," *GOP Nationalities News* 7, no. 5 (September 1977), folder 1, box 4, Novak, IHRC.

90. Anne Geyer, "Latin America: Carterites' Whipping Boy," *LAT*, 27 March 1978.

91. I am relying here on Kaufman, *Plans Unraveled*, 168–175.

92. Anthony Lake, *Somoza Falling* (Boston: Houghton Mifflin, 1989), 206.

93. Jeane J. Kirkpatrick, "U.S. Security and Latin America," *Commentary* 71 (January 1981): 29–40.

94. Kaufman, *Plans Unraveled*, 174–175.

95. "Los desaparecidos son eso, desaparecidos. No están ni vivos ni muertos; están desaparecidos."

96. Memcon, 7 October 1976, doc. 6, EBB 104, NSA; Schmidli, "Institutionalizing Human Rights," 359–363.

97. Schmidli, "Institutionalizing Human Rights," 368–369.

98. Cohen, "Conditioning U.S. Security Assistance," 275.

99. Notes, n.d. (April 1977); Memo, "Human Rights the Key," 4 May 1977; Memcons, 15 August 1977, docs. 1, 2, 4, 5, EBB 85, NSA.

100. Carter to Videla, 3 November 1977, NLC-16-101-1-8-3, JCL; Stedman to Deputy Secretary, 3 November 1977, doc. 6 (note), EBB 85, NSA.

101. Brzezinski to Carter, 31 May 1978, NLC-1-6-4-8-2, JCL; Vance to Embassy, 29 June 1978, "Human Rights—Argentina (III)," box 27, Christopher, RG 59, NARA.

102. Iain Guest, *Behind the Disappearances: Argentina's Dirty War Against Human Rights and the United Nations* (Philadelphia: University of Pennsylvania Press), 170–179; Lars Schoultz, *Human Rights and United States Policy Toward Latin America* (Princeton: Princeton University Press, 1981), 310–312.

103. Harrop to Christopher, 11 August 1978, "Memoranda 1978," box 18; Foreign Minister to Ambassador, 3 August 1978, "Human Rights—Argentina (IV)," box 28, Christopher, RG 59, NARA.

104. Renner to Brzezinski, 20 July 1978, "Human Rights 5/77–11/78," box 28, Subject File, NSA Brzezinski, JCL.

105. Guest, *Behind the Disappearances*, 165.

106. Argentina: Assessment, 1 January 1979, NLC-28-8-1-1-1, JCL; Sandy Vogelgesang, *American Dream, Global Nightmare: The Dilemma of U.S. Human Rights Policy* (New York: Norton, 1980), 77, 220.

107. "Address," 7 June 1978, *PPP*, 30915.

108. Christopher to Vance, 27 May 1978, "Memoranda 1978," box 18, Christopher, RG 59, NARA.

109. "Thousands of Political Prisoners," *Izvestia*, 14 July 1978, 3.

110. Memcon, 18 June 1979, NLC-128-5-5-9-0, JCL; Carter, *Keeping Faith*, 259–260.

111. Memcon, 23 September 1977, "Memcons: President, 9/77," box 35, Subject, NSA Brzezinski, JCL.

112. Raymond L. Garthoff, *Détente and Confrontation: American-Soviet Relations from Nixon to Reagan* (Washington, DC: Brookings Institution, 1994), 806.

113. Peter Osnos, "Détente Is Dead," *WP*, 30 December 1979.

114. Andropov to Central Committee, 26 December 1979, doc. 136, ASKGB; Situation Room to Brzezinski, 21 January 1980, NLC-1-13-8-20-6, JCL.

115. Dumbrell, *American Foreign Policy*, 32.

116. David Skidmore, *Reversing Course: Carter's Foreign Policy, Domestic Politics, and the Failure of Reform* (Nashville: Vanderbilt University Press, 1996), 51; Zbigniew Brzezinski, *Power and Principle: Memoirs of the National Security Adviser, 1977–1981* (New York: Farrar, Straus and Giroux, 1983), 145; Patt Derian, "Brzezinski's Tale," *WP*, 31 March 1983.

117. See Joe Renouard and Nathan Vigil, "The Quest for Leadership in a Time of Peace: Jimmy Carter and Europe," in *The Strained Alliance: Conflict and Cooperation in U.S.-European Relations from Nixon to Carter*, ed. Matthias Schulz and Thomas A. Schwartz (Cambridge: Cambridge University Press, 2010), 324–332.

118. Jack Donnelly, *Universal Human Rights in Theory and Practice*, 2nd ed. (Ithaca, NY: Cornell University Press, 2003), 171.

119. Carter, *Keeping Faith*, 144–145.

120. John E. Rielly, ed., *American Public Opinion and U.S. Foreign Policy 1979* (Chicago: Chicago Council on Foreign Relations, 1979), 14.

121. Anne Geyer and Robert Shapiro, "A Report: Human Rights," *Public Opinion Quarterly* 52, no. 3 (1988): 386–398; Vogelgesang, *American Dream*, 16.

122. Skidmore, *Reversing Course*, 90, 93.

123. S. Mahmud Ali, *U.S.-China Cold War Collaboration* (New York: Routledge, 2005), 166–179, 190; Mann, *About Face*, 102–103.

124. Vance to Embassy, 16 January 1980, NLC-16-120-2-10-8, JCL.

125. Kaufman, *Plans Unraveled*, 230–231.

126. Council of Europe, *Andrei Sakharov and Human Rights* (Strasbourg: Council of Europe, 2010), 129.

127. Kathryn Sikkink, *Mixed Signals: U.S. Human Rights Policy in Latin America* (Ithaca, NY: Cornell University Press, 2004), 142–147.

128. Kaufman, *Plans Unraveled*, 36.

129. Paul Sigmund, *The United States and Democracy in Chile* (Baltimore: Johns Hopkins University Press, 1993), 108, 111, 129–130.

130. Carter to Stroessner, 31 October 1977, NLC-16-101-1-7-4, JCL; Margaret O'Brien Steinfels, "Death and Lies in El Salvador: The Ambassador's Tale," *Commonweal* 128, no. 18 (October 2001): 14.

131. Jessica Gibbs and Alex Goodall, "Conflict and Cooperation: Cuban Exile Anti-Communism and the United States, 1960–2000," in *Anti-Communist Minorities in the U.S.: Political Activism of Ethnic Refugees*, ed. Ieva Zake (New York: Palgrave Macmillan, 2009), 233–253.

132. Pastor to Brzezinski, 19 July 1979, NLC-12-19-3-17-7, JCL.

133. Situation Room to Brzezinski, 16 June 1980, NLC-1-15-7-15-1, JCL.

134. John M. Goshko, "Argentinian Visits," *WP*, 20 May 1981; Christian Williams, "The Torture of Jacobo Timerman," *WP*, 22 May 1981.

135. Joseph F. Harrington, "American-Romanian Relations, 1977–1981," in Rosenbaum and Ugrinsky, *Jimmy Carter*, 89–101.

136. Ann Crittenden, "Human Rights and Mrs. Derian," *NYT*, 31 May 1980.

137. Vogelgesang, *American Dream*, 27, 251–252.

138. Coalition for a New Foreign and Military Policy, "International Human Rights," March 1978, "Country Evaluation Papers," box 32, Christopher, RG 59, NARA.

139. Derian to Vance, 16 June 1977, NARA.

140. Dobrynin, *In Confidence*, 389.

141. Cohen, "Conditioning U.S. Security Assistance," 271.

142. Sikkink, *Mixed Signals*, 143.

143. Schmidli, "Institutionalizing Human Rights," 375.

144. Bernard Gwertzman, "Canal Pacts," *NYT*, 7 September 1977.

145. Samuel Moyn, *The Last Utopia: Human Rights in History* (Cambridge, MA: Harvard University Press, 2010), 154–161.

146. "Remarks," 19 November 1980, *PPP*, 45506.

147. David Hawk, "Human Rights at Half Time," *New Republic*, 7 April 1979, 22.

148. Sarah B. Snyder, *Human Rights Activism and the End of the Cold War: A Transnational History of the Helsinki Network* (New York: Cambridge University Press, 2011), 81–106.

Chapter 4. Ronald Reagan and the New Conservative Internationalism

Epigraph: Mikhail Gorbachev, *Perestroika: New Thinking for Our Country and the World* (New York: HarperCollins, 1987), 158.

1. Second Annual Report, n.d. (1981), "Helsinki Watch," box 5, series II (Executive Director), RG II, AIUSA.

2. Robert M. Collins, *Transforming America: Politics and Culture in the Reagan Years* (New York: Columbia University Press, 2007), 232.

3. Odd Arne Westad, *The Global Cold War: Third World Interventions and the Making of Our Times* (New York: Cambridge University Press, 2005), 331.

4. Mikhail Gorbachev, *Memoirs* (New York: Doubleday, 1996), 409–410.

5. Stefan-Ludwig Hoffmann, ed., *Human Rights in the Twentieth Century* (Cambridge: Cambridge University Press, 2010), 21.

6. Davis W. Houck and Amos Kiewe, eds., *Actor, Ideologue, Politician: The Public Speeches of Ronald Reagan* (Westport, CT: Greenwood, 1993), 166.

7. Andrew Preston, *Sword of the Spirit, Shield of Faith* (New York: Anchor, 2012), 574–587.

8. Ronald Reagan, *A Time for Choosing: The Speeches of Ronald Reagan, 1961–1982* (Chicago: Regnery Gateway, 1983), 206.

9. "Presidential Debate," 28 October 1980, *PPP*, 29408.

10. Memo, n.d., "Debate File (Baker)—Issues—Human Rights," box 239, series VI: Debate (Baker), 1980 Campaign, RRL.

11. Ronald Reagan, "The Ethnic American," *Hungarian Times*, 23 October 1980; Letters, *Ukrainian Weekly*, 26 October 1980.

12. Ed Bruske, "Ethnic Leaders Call Polish Strike," *WP*, 22 August 1980.

13. "Statement," 22 August 1980, "Voter Groups (Hugel)—Nationalities," box 338, series X (Hugel), 1980 Campaign, RRL.

14. Donald E. Pienkos, *For Your Freedom Through Ours: Polish American Efforts on Poland's Behalf, 1863–1991* (Boulder, CO: East European Monographs, 1991), 182–184; "Remarks," 30 October 1980, *PPP*, 45395.

15. Party Platforms, 15 July, 11 August 1980, *PPP*, 25844, 29607.

16. "Remarks," 14 August 1980, *PPP*, 44909.

17. Vita Bite, "Human Rights and U.S. Foreign Policy" (Washington, DC: Congressional Research Service, 1982), 29; Tamar Jacoby, "The Reagan Turnaround," *Foreign Affairs* 64, no. 5 (Summer 1986): 1068–1069.

18. Carl Bon Tempo, *Americans at the Gate: The United States and Refugees During the Cold War* (Princeton: Princeton University Press, 2008), 167, 187–189.

19. Bernstein et al., to Reagan, 5 October 1981, "038000–046999," box 1, WHORM: Subject—HU, RRL.

20. Aryeh Neier, *Taking Liberties: Four Decades in the Struggle for Rights* (New York: Public Affairs, 2003), xxxiii–xxxiv, 152–153, 156.

21. Ibid., 187.

22. "A Message for Moscow," *Time*, 9 February 1981.

23. "Excerpts," *NYT*, 21 April 1981.

24. Lord to Allen, 19 February 1981, "000001–022999," box 1, WHORM: Subject—HU, RRL.

25. Andropov to Central Committee, 2 May 1981, doc. 146, ASKGB.

26. Douglas Brinkley, ed., *The Reagan Diaries* (New York: HarperCollins, 2007), 14–15.

27. Ernest W. Lefever, "The Rights Standard," *NYT*, 1 January 1977.

28. *Human Rights and U.S. Foreign Policy*, Subcommittee on International Organizations, 96th Cong., 1st sess. (Washington, DC: GPO, 1979), 230–231.

29. *Nomination of Ernest W. Lefever*, Committee on Foreign Relations, 97th Cong., 1st sess. (Washington, DC: GPO, 1981), 3–4, 117–118.

30. Neier, *Taking Liberties*, 182–185.

31. Press Release, 5 June 1981, "Lefever Material," box 6, Counsel to the President, RRL.

32. David P. Forsythe, *Human Rights and U.S. Foreign Policy: Congress Reconsidered* (Gainesville: University of Florida Press, 1988), 139.

33. Neier, *Taking Liberties*, 188–189.

34. Bernstein et al., to Reagan, 5 October 1981.

35. Forsythe, *Human Rights and U.S. Foreign Policy*, 122–128.

36. Clair Apodaca, *Understanding U.S. Human Rights Policy: A Paradoxical Legacy* (New York: Routledge, 2006), xvii.

37. "Excerpts," *NYT*, 5 November 1981.

38. Allen to Bush, 2 April 1981, box 153, "CO 126 Poland," WHORM: Subject—CO, RRL.

39. "Freeze," episode 19, *The Cold War*, CNN (1998).

40. Memcon, 22 December 1981, "NSC 00034," box 91283, NSC Meeting, Executive Secretariat, RRL; Kiron K. Skinner et al., eds., *Reagan: A Life in Letters* (New York: Free Press, 2004), 305–306.

41. Gregory F. Domber, "Transatlantic Relations, Human Rights, and Power Politics," in *Perforating the Iron Curtain: European Détente, Transatlantic Relations, and the Cold War, 1965–1985*, ed. Poul Villaume and Odd Arne Westad (Copenhagen: Museum Tusculanum Press, 2010), 195–214.

42. Ibid., 204–205.

43. Pienkos, *For Your Freedom*, 184–195.

44. George P. Shultz, *Turmoil and Triumph: My Years as Secretary of State* (New York: Scribner's, 1993), 286.

45. Eliana A. Cardoso and Ann Helwege, *Cuba After Communism* (Cambridge, MA: MIT Press, 1992), 31–32.

46. Casey to Haig, 12 May 1981, "El Salvador/U.S. Domestic," box 90502, Tillman, RRL.

47. Jessica Gibbs and Alex Goodall, "Conflict and Cooperation: Cuban Exile Anti-Communism and the United States, 1960–2000," in *Anti-Communist Minorities in the U.S.: Political Activism of Ethnic Refugees*, ed. Ieva Zake (New York: Palgrave Macmillan, 2009), 241–244, 250n39.

48. Greg Grandin, *Empire's Workshop: Latin America, the United States, and the Rise of the New Imperialism* (New York: Metropolitan, 2006), 81.

49. Soviet Objectives and Intentions, n.d. (April 1984), "207644," box 3, WHORM: Subject—HU, RRL.

50. Sandinista Violations of Human Rights, n.d. (February 1984), "207644," box 3, WHORM: Subject—HU, RRL.

51. Grandin, *Empire's Workshop*, 113, 115; Neier, *Taking Liberties*, 217, 220.

52. Americas Watch, *Human Rights in Nicaragua 1986* (New York: Americas Watch Committee, 1987), 141–142.

53. Ronald Reagan, *An American Life* (New York: Simon & Schuster, 1990), 476–481.

54. Thomas Carothers, *In the Name of Democracy: U.S. Policy Toward Latin America in the Reagan Years* (Berkeley: University of California Press, 1991), 21; Shultz, *Turmoil and Triumph*, 129.

55. Theberge to Meese, 15 April 1981, "El Salvador/U.S. Domestic," box 90502, Tillman, RRL.

56. Carothers, *In the Name of Democracy*, 32; "Cold War Termination," in *Encyclopedia of the New American Nation*, http://www.americanforeignrelations.com.

57. Margaret O'Brien Steinfels, "Death and Lies in El Salvador: The Ambassador's Tale," *Commonweal* 128, no. 18 (October 2001), 19.

58. Department of State, A Statistical Framework, 15 January 1982, "El Salvador—Human Rights," box 90502, Tillman, RRL.

59. Max G. Manwaring and Court Prisk, *El Salvador at War: An Oral History* (Washington, DC: NDU Press, 1988), 400.

60. Shultz, *Turmoil and Triumph*, 130, 290.

61. Moore to Ottinger, 28 April 1982, "052700–063999," box 1, WHORM: Subject—HU, RRL.

62. Summary of Current Concerns, January 1982; Abrams to McGee, 9 March 1982, "El Salvador/U.S. Domestic," box 90502, Tillman, RRL.

63. Cynthia Arnson, *Crossroads: Congress, the Reagan Administration, and Central America* (New York: Pantheon, 1989), 90–94.

64. Michael J. Kryzanek, *U.S.-Latin American Relations* (New York: Praeger, 1996), 216.

65. Guillermo Manuel Ungo, "The People's Struggle," *Foreign Policy* 52 (Fall 1983): 52–60.

66. Solarz et al. to Reagan, 14 July 1983, "150738–155399," box 2, WHORM: Subject—HU, RRL.

67. Forsythe, *Human Rights and U.S. Foreign Policy*, 80.

68. Arnson, *Crossroads*, 99; Bernard Weinraub, "Envoy of U.S.," *NYT*, 3 November 1982.

69. Skinner et al., *Reagan*, 392, 491–492.

70. Jacoby, "Reagan Turnaround," 1074.

71. Talking Points, 5 December 1983, "El Salvador Violent Right," box 18, Latin American Affairs, NSC, RRL.

72. "Vice-President Bush Visits Latin America," *Department of State Bulletin* 84, no. 2082 (February 1984); Shultz, *Turmoil and Triumph*, 404.

73. Carothers, *In the Name of Democracy*, 30.

74. Haig to Reagan, 13 March 1981, "Viola Meeting (2)," box 18, Fontaine, RRL, emphasis in original.

75. Selden to Meese, 26 August 1983, "156696–166999," box 3, WHORM: Subject—HU, RRL.

76. Margaret E. Keck and Kathryn Sikkink, *Activists Beyond Borders: Advocacy Networks in International Politics* (Ithaca, NY: Cornell University Press, 1998), 106–107.

77. Carothers, *In the Name of Democracy*, 6, 125–127, 134–135.

78. "Relations with China," 28 February 1983, "China 1983 (3)," box 2, series II: Subject, Sigur, RRL.

79. James Mann, *About Face: A History of America's Curious Relationship with China* (New York: Knopf, 1999), 103.

80. "Message," 2 June 1981, *PPP*, 43888.

81. "Joint Communiqué," "Statement on Arms Sales," 17 August 1982, *PPP*, 42861, 42862.

82. Department of State, *Country Reports on Human Rights Practices*, 98th Cong., 1st sess. (Washington, DC: GPO, February 1983).

83. Helms to Clark, 19 July 1983, "China 1983 (17)," box 2, series II: Subject, Sigur, RRL.

84. Skinner et al., *Reagan*, 531.

85. "Remarks," "Statement," 27–28 April 1984; "Remarks," 1 May 1984, *PPP*, 39831, 39833, 39849; Charlotte Saikowski, "Reagan, Deng Build Diplomatic Bridge," *CSM*, 30 April 1984.

86. Rosemary Foot, *The Practice of Power: U.S. Relations with China Since 1949* (New York: Oxford University Press, 1995), 234.

87. Richard V. Allen, "On the Korea Tightrope, 1980," *NYT*, 21 January 1998.

88. Allen to Reagan, 3 February 1981, "Chun Visit—Feb. 1981," box 90264, Sigur, RRL.

89. Haig to Reagan, 1–3 February 1981, doc. 2, EBB 306, NSA.

90. Allen to Reagan, 3 February 1981.

91. Allen to Reagan, 6 February 1981, "Chun Visit—Feb. 1981," box 90264, Sigur, RRL.

92. Gregg A. Brazinsky, *Nation Building in South Korea* (Chapel Hill: University of North Carolina Press, 2009), 243.

93. Shultz to Reagan, n.d., "Trip to Japan and Korea (1 &4)," box 10, series III, Sigur, RRL.

94. Brazinsky, *Nation Building*, 243; "Address," 12 November 1983, *PPP*, 40758.

95. Kathryn Sikkink, *Mixed Signals: U.S. Human Rights Policy in Latin America* (Ithaca, NY: Cornell University Press, 2004), 149.

96. Shultz, *Turmoil and Triumph*, 189, 261–262, 466, 509; Reagan, *An American Life*, 547–550; Frances Fitzgerald, *Way Out There in the Blue: Reagan, Star Wars, and the End of the Cold War* (New York: Simon & Schuster, 1999).

97. Skinner et al., *Reagan*, 380; Shultz, *Turmoil and Triumph*, 171; Anatoly Dobrynin, *In Confidence: Moscow's Ambassador to America's Six Cold War Presidents* (New York: Times Books, 1995), 540; Jack Matlock, *Reagan and Gorbachev: How the Cold War Ended* (New York: Random House, 2004), 55–59.

98. Shultz, *Turmoil and Triumph*, 265–266, 276–277; Dobrynin, *In Confidence*, 518–521.

99. I am relying here on Beth A. Fischer, *The Reagan Reversal* (Columbia: University of Missouri Press, 1997), 109–143.

100. Reagan, *An American Life*, 585.

101. Ibid., 585–586.

102. James Mann, *The Rebellion of Ronald Reagan: A History of the End of the Cold War* (New York: Viking, 2009), 42, 77.

103. "Remarks," 9 December 1983, *PPP*, 40848.

104. "Address," 16 January 1984, *PPP*, 39806.

105. Jack F. Matlock, Jr., *Autopsy on an Empire: The American Ambassador's Account of the Collapse of the Soviet Union* (New York: Random House, 1995), 83–86.

106. Reagan, *An American Life*, 597, 601.

107. Charlotte Saikowski, "Soviet Olympic Pullout," *CSM*, 21 May 1984, 5.

108. Samuel P. Huntington, *The Third Wave: Democratization in the Late Twentieth Century* (Norman: University of Oklahoma Press, 1991).

109. "Address," 8 June 1982, *PPP*, 42614.

110. Aryeh Neier, *The International Human Rights Movement: A History* (Princeton: Princeton University Press, 2012), 175–176.

111. Ibid.

112. Carothers, *In the Name of Democracy*, ix–x, 3, 7.

113. Makau Mutua, "Human Rights International NGOs: A Critical Evaluation," in *NGOs and Human Rights: Promise and Performance*, ed. Claude E. Welch, Jr. (Philadelphia: University of Pennsylvania Press, 2001), 151–163.

114. "Remarks," 6 September 1984, *PPP*, 40332.

115. Bernard Gwertzman, "Reagan Will Submit," *NYT*, 6 September 1984.

116. Press Release, 24 April 1985, AJC, "Bitburg Letters (1)," box 1, Breger, RRL.

117. B. Ivanov, "Homage to Butchers," *Izvestia*, 6 May 1985; Reagan, *An American Life*, 377.

118. Bennett to Holt, 23 May 1984, "146421," box 2, WHORM: Subject—HU, RRL.

119. "Remarks," 10 December 1984, *PPP*, 39473.

Chapter 5. Global Human Rights, Democracy, and the Cold War's End

1. Mikhail Gorbachev, *Memoirs* (New York: Doubleday, 1996), 168.

2. Margaret Thatcher, *Downing Street Years* (New York: HarperCollins, 1993), 452–453.

3. Fraser J. Harbutt, *The Cold War Era* (Malden, MA: Blackwell, 2002), 227.

4. Charlotte Saikowski, "Soviet Leadership Passes," *CSM*, 12 March 1985, 1.

5. George P. Shultz, *Turmoil and Triumph: My Years as Secretary of State* (New York: Scribner's, 1993), 532–533.

6. George H. W. Bush, *All the Best, George Bush* (New York: Scribner, 1999), 342–344.

7. Reagan to Gorbachev, 11 March and 30 April 1985; Gorbachev to Reagan, 24 March and 10 June 1985, docs. 2, 6, 9, 10, EBB 172, NSA; Ronald Reagan, *An American Life* (New York: Simon & Schuster, 1990), 612–619.

8. Shultz to Reagan, 16 September 1985, "Reagan-Shevardnadze Mtg. (4)," box 45, Matlock, RRL; Chernyaev Diary, 9 June 1985, EBB, NSA.

9. "Statement," 15 May 1985, *PPP*, 38637.

10. Anatoly Dobrynin, *In Confidence: Moscow's Ambassador to America's Six Cold War Presidents* (New York: Times Books, 1995), 568–569, 607.

11. Bennett Kovrig, *Of Walls and Bridges: The United States and Eastern Europe* (New York: NYU Press, 1991), 190.

12. Charlotte Saikowski, "Despite Failings, Helsinki Accords," *CSM*, 25 July 1985, 18.

13. Korengold to Matlock, 8 November 1985, "Talking Points (1)," box 45, Matlock, RRL.

14. Platt to McFarlane, 23 September 1985, "Shultz-Shevardnadze Mtg. (1)," box 45, Matlock, RRL.

15. Shultz, *Turmoil and Triumph*, 587–591.

16. Gromyko to Central Committee, 22 May 1984, MS Russ 79 (2930), HRC; Minutes, 29 August 1985, doc. 12, EBB 172, NSA; "Interview," 29 October 1985, *PPP*, 37990.

17. Kiron K. Skinner et al., eds., *Reagan: A Life in Letters* (New York: Free Press, 2004), 413.

18. Memcons, 19–20 November 1985, "Geneva Memcons [2/3]," Summit Memcons, RRL; Reagan, *An American Life*, 637–638; Gorbachev, *Memoirs*, 408; Jack Matlock, *Reagan and Gorbachev: How the Cold War Ended* (New York: Random House, 2004), 161–162.

19. Memcon, 20 November 1985 (afternoon), "Geneva Memcons [3/3]," Summit Memcons, RRL.

20. "Joint Statement," 21 November 1985, *PPP*, 38086.

21. Anatoly Chernyaev, *My Six Years with Gorbachev* (University Park: Penn State University Press, 2000), 52–53; Reagan, *An American Life*, 638–639; Gorbachev, *Memoirs*, 405–408.

22. Skinner et al., *Reagan*, 414–417; Reagan, *An American Life*, 641.

23. "Excerpts of Interviews," *LAT*, 23 November 1985.

24. "Address," 21 November 1985, *PPP*, 38088.

25. Reagan, *An American Life*, 641.

26. Ibid., 644–650; Matlock, *Reagan and Gorbachev*, 174–175.

27. John Lewis Gaddis, *The Cold War: A New History* (New York: Penguin, 2005), 229.

28. Serge Schmemann, "Greater Glasnost," *NYT*, 9 November 1986.

29. "Remarks," 10 December 1985, *PPP*, 38143.

30. NSDD 209, "Implementing Decisions," 4 February 1986, FAS.

31. Thomas Carothers, *In the Name of Democracy: U.S. Policy Toward Latin America in the Reagan Years* (Berkeley: University of California Press, 1991), 194.

32. I am relying here on NSDD 220, 2 April 1986, FAS; and Alex Stepick, "Unintended Consequences: Rejecting Haitian Boat People," in *Western Hemisphere Immigration and United States Foreign Policy*, ed. Christopher Mitchell (University Park: Penn State University Press, 1992), 125–156.

33. Shultz, *Turmoil and Triumph*, 621–623.

34. Carothers, *In the Name of Democracy*, 184–193.

35. "Remarks," 16 September 1982, *PPP*, 42990.

36. David F. Schmitz, *The United States and Right-Wing Dictatorships* (Cambridge: Cambridge University Press, 2006), 233.

37. Marcos to Reagan, 12 November 1983, 29 May 1984, "Philippines Marcos," box 27, Head of State, Exec Secretariat NSC, RRL.

38. Presidential Debate, 21 October 1984, *PPP*, 39296.

39. NSDD 163, 20 February 1985, FAS.

40. Don Oberdorfer, "U.S. Official Urges," *WP*, 23 February 1985.

41. Paul D. Wolfowitz, "Developments in the Philippines," *Current Policy* No. 760 (Washington, DC: Department of State BPA, October 1985).

42. Marcos to Reagan, 16 October 1985, "Philippines Marcos," box 27, Head of State, Exec Secretariat NSC, RRL.

43. Stephen J. Solarz, *Journeys to War and Peace: A Congressional Memoir* (Lebanon, NH: University Press of New England, 2011), 117–122.

44. Ibid., 122.

45. Nunn to Reagan, 13 February 1986, "CO 125 Philippines," box 152, WHORM: Subject—CO, RRL.

46. NSDD 215, 23 February 1986, FAS; Schmitz, *United States and Right-Wing Dictatorships*, 239; Sara Fritz and Eleanor Clift, "'The Time Has Come," *LAT*, 26 February 1986.

47. "Message," 14 March 1986, *PPP*, 36995.

48. Tamar Jacoby, "The Reagan Turnaround," *Foreign Affairs* 64, no. 5 (Summer 1986): 1084–1085.

49. Box 16, series III, Addington, RRL.

50. "Remarks," 11 March 1986, *PPP*, 36972; Skinner et al., *Reagan*, 504.

51. "The Sandinista Road to Stalinism," *NYT*, 10 July 1986.

52. Elaine Sciolino, "U.S. Group Finds No Improvement," *NYT*, 10 February 1987.

53. I am relying here on Alex Thomson, *U.S. Foreign Policy Toward Apartheid South Africa, 1948–1994* (New York: Palgrave Macmillan, 2008), 111–159; Chester Crocker, *High Noon in Southern Africa: Making Peace in a Rough Neighborhood* (New York: Norton, 1992), 85–117, 253–332; Ryan M. Irwin, *Gordian Knot: Apartheid and the Unmaking of the Liberal World Order* (New York: Oxford University Press, 2012); and David L. Hostetter, *Movement Matters: American Antiapartheid Activism and the Rise of Multicultural Politics* (New York: Routledge, 2006).

54. Hostetter, *Movement Matters*, 143.

55. Francis Njubi Nesbitt, *Race for Sanctions: African Americans Against Apartheid, 1946–1994* (Bloomington: Indiana University Press, 2004).

56. Crocker, *High Noon*, 18.

57. "US Policy in Southern Africa," n.d. (1985), "South Africa 1985," box 9, Raymond, RRL.

58. Joe Ritchie, "U.S. Details Terms," *WP*, 29 May 1981.

59. Crocker, *High Noon*, 77–82; "Documents Link," NYT, 30 May 1981.

60. Thomson, *U.S. Foreign Policy*, 112, 122, 123.

61. Sandra Evans, "Hill Panel," *WP*, 5 December 1984.

62. "Most Americans in CBS Poll," *NYT*, 1 September 1985.

63. Nesbitt, *Race for Sanctions*, 123; Thomson, *U.S. Foreign Policy*, 133.

64. "Proposed New Initiative," 24 July 1985; Crocker, "The U.S. and South Africa," 16 August 1985, "South Africa 1985," box 9, Raymond, RRL.

65. Crocker, *High Noon*, 256–259.

66. Nicolaides to Buchanan, 21 July 1986, "South Africa Background (7)," box 2, Buchanan, RRL.

67. Lincoln Institute, *TransAfrica: A Lobby of the Left* (Great Falls, VA: Lincoln Institute, 1985); Hostetter, *Movement Matters*, 84.

68. "Jailed South African Black Leader," Associated Press, 22 August 1985.

69. Nicolaides, "US-Africa Relations," May 1986, "South Africa Background (5)," box 2, Buchanan, RRL.

70. Eschel Rhoodie, "Americans Blinded," *Philadelphia Inquirer*, 21 July 1986; Lincoln Institute, *TransAfrica*, 28.

71. Rhoodie, "Americans Blinded."

72. Ryan M. Irwin, "Freedom's Other," *Diplomatic History* 36, no. 5 (November 2012): 795–796.

73. EO 12532; "Remarks," 9 September 1985, *PPP*, 39073, 39074.

74. "Remarks," 22 July 1986, *PPP*, 37643; Thomson, *U.S. Foreign Policy*, 146–147; Crocker, *High Noon*, 322–323; "Tutu Denounces Reagan," *NYT*, 23 July 1986.

75. Crocker, *High Noon*, 261.

76. See Sue Onslow, ed., *Cold War in Southern Africa: White Power, Black Liberation* (New York: Routledge, 2009).

77. Norman Kempster, "Shultz Upbeat," *LAT*, 30 September 1987.

78. Bonner to Reagan, 22 May 1986, MS Russ 79 (4718), HRC; "Proclamation 5484," May 20, 1986, *PPP*, 37310.

79. "Statement," 30 September 1986, *PPP*, 36511.

80. Gorbachev to Reagan, 15 September 1986, doc. 1; Politburo Session, 22 October 1986, doc. 22, EBB 203, NSA.

81. Shultz to Reagan, 2 October 1986; Issues Checklist, 9–12 October 1986; Instructions, 4 October 1986; Politburo Notes, 8 October 1986, docs. 4, 5, 7, and 8, EBB 203, NSA.

82. Memcons, 11 and 12 October 1986, "Executive Secretariat, NSC Records [Reykjavik]," Vertical File, RRL.

83. Reagan, *An American Life*, 675.

84. "Remarks," 10 December 1986, *PPP*, 36797.

85. Gregg A. Brazinsky, *Nation Building in South Korea* (Chapel Hill: University of North Carolina Press, 2009), 250.

86. Gregory F. Domber, "Transatlantic Relations, Human Rights, and Power Politics," in *Perforating the Iron Curtain: European Détente, Transatlantic Relations, and the Cold War, 1965–1985*, ed. Poul Villaume and Odd Arne Westad (Copenhagen: Museum Tusculanum Press, 2010), 206–207.

87. Shultz, *Turmoil and Triumph*, 873–875.

88. John Tagliabue, "Bush Asks Warsaw," *NYT*, 29 September 1987.

89. Aryeh Neier, *Taking Liberties: Four Decades in the Struggle for Rights* (New York: Public Affairs, 2003), 251–253.

90. Mann, *Rebellion of Ronald Reagan*; Shultz, *Turmoil and Triumph*, 887–889.

91. Shultz, *Turmoil and Triumph*, 886–887, 986–990; Matlock, *Reagan and Gorbachev*, 259.

92. Matlock, *Autopsy on an Empire: The American Ambassador's Account of the Collapse of the Soviet Union* (New York: Random House, 1995), 169–171; Chernyaev Diary, 4 December 1988, EBB 250, NSA.

93. Memcon, 8 December 1987, "Executive Secretariat, NSC Records [Washington Summit]," Vertical File, RRL; Chernyaev to Gorbachev, 16 December 1987, EBB 238, NSA; Reagan, *An American Life*, 698.

94. Memcons, 8 and 10 December 1987, "Executive Secretariat, NSC Records [Washington Summit]," Vertical File, RRL; Jack Nelson, "Gorbachev Whirls," *LAT*, 10 December 1987.

95. Whitehead to Embassies, 12 December 1987; Politburo Memcon, 17 December 1987, EBB 238, NSA.

96. Chernyaev, *My Six Years*, 143.

97. Background Book, 29 May 1988, doc. 10, EBB 251, NSA.

98. Beth A. Fischer, *The Reagan Reversal* (Columbia: University of Missouri Press, 1997), 148.

99. NSDD 305, 26 April 1988, FAS.

100. Memcon, Moscow, 21 April 1988, doc. 7, EBB 251, NSA.

101. Schifter to Shultz, 6 June 1988, doc. 25, EBB 251, NSA.

102. Memcon, 29 May 1988, "1988 Summit Memcons," Vertical File, RRL.

103. Reagan, *An American Life*, 706.

104. Ibid., 705.

105. Memcon, 31 May 1988, "1988 Summit Memcons," Vertical File, RRL; "Toasts," 30 May 1988, *PPP*, 35895.

106. "Remarks," 30–31 May 1988, *PPP*, 35894, 35897.

107. Memcon, 7 December 1988, "Executive Secretariat, NSC [Governor's Island]," Vertical File, RRL.

108. Robert M. Gates, *From the Shadows: The Ultimate Insider's Story of Five Presidents and How They Won the Cold War* (New York: Simon and Schuster, 1996), 449.

109. Gaddis, *Cold War*, 238.

110. James Mann, *About Face: A History of America's Curious Relationship with China* (New York: Knopf, 1999), 176.

111. Svetlana Savranskaya and Thomas Blanton, Introduction, EBB 261, NSA.

112. "Remarks," 5 and 12 May 1989, *PPP*, 17057, 17022.

113. David F. Schmitz, *Brent Scowcroft: Internationalism and Post–Vietnam War American Foreign Policy* (Lanham, MD: Rowman and Littlefield, 2011), 91–96.

114. Mann, *About Face*, 177–183.

115. Schmitz, *Brent Scowcroft*, 103–107; George Bush and Brent Scowcroft, *A World Transformed* (New York: Knopf, 1998), 89–97.

116. Mann, *About Face*, 177–183.

117. Pei Minxin, "As Mr. Bush," *NYT*, 28 February 1989.

118. Lord to Secretary, 21 April 1989, doc. 6, EBB 47, NSA; James Lilley, *China Hands: Nine Decades of Adventure, Espionage, and Diplomacy in Asia* (New York: Public Affairs, 2004), 303.

119. Lilley to Assistant Secretary, 21 May 1989, doc. 8, EBB 47, NSA; "News Conference," 21 May 1989, *PPP*, 17047.

120. "Remarks," 31 May 1989, *PPP*, 17085.

121. "Statement," 3 June 1989, *PPP*, 17101.

122. "News Conference," 5 June 1989, *PPP*, 17103.

123. Schmitz, *Brent Scowcroft*, 107.

124. Mann, *About Face*, 196–197.

125. Robert L. Suettinger, *Beyond Tiananmen: The Politics of U.S.-China Relations 1989–2000* (Washington, DC: Brookings Institution, 2003), chap. 4.

126. Bush and Scowcroft, *World Transformed*, 98, 100–102.

127. Mann, *About Face*, 207–209.

128. "Themes," 29 June 1989, doc. 33, EBB 16, NSA.

129. Bush, *All the Best*, 435–437; Bush and Scowcroft, *World Transformed*, 106–111; Lilley, *China Hands*, 300.

130. Lilley to Secretary, 11 July 1989, doc. 11, EBB 47, NSA.

131. Michael McQueen, "Bush Defends," *WSJ*, December 9, 1989, 1.

132. Bush and Scowcroft, *World Transformed*, 99.

133. Lilley to Secretary, 11 July 1989.

134. Fang Lizhi, "My 'Confession,'" *New York Review of Books*, 23 June 2011.

135. Mann, *About Face*, 216, 224–225, 228.

136. Rosemary Foot, *The Practice of Power: U.S. Relations with China Since 1949* (New York: Oxford University Press, 1995), 244.

137. Jack Donnelly, *Universal Human Rights in Theory and Practice*, 2nd ed. (Ithaca, NY: Cornell University Press, 2003), 163.

138. News Release, 13 June 1989; Vanik Statement, 8 March 1989, "Jackson-Vanik," box 1, Subject USSR, Rice, NSC, GBL.

139. "Remarks," 17 April 1989, *PPP*, 16935; Bush and Scowcroft, *World Transformed*, 115, 120, 130–131.

140. Talking Points, 27 June 1989, "Polish-American Groups," box 19, WHORM: Subject—HU, GBL; Embassy to Secretary, 19 April 1989, doc. 1, EBB 42, NSA.

141. Schmitz, *Brent Scowcroft*, 97.

142. Memcon, 1 December 1989, doc. 8, EBB 298, NSA; Gorbachev, *Memoirs*, 509.

143. "President's Initiatives," n.d. (December 1989), "Lithuania (1)," box 1, Subject Soviet Union, Rice, NSC, GBL.

144. Memcons, 2–3 December 1989, docs. 9–10, EBB 298, NSA.

145. "Address," 31 January 1990, *PPP*, 18095.

146. Testimony of William Webster, 23 January 1990, FAS.

147. "News Conference," 3 June 1990, *PPP*, 18549.

148. Alex Pravda, "The Collapse of the Soviet Union, 1990–1991," in *The Cambridge History of the Cold War*, vol. 3, ed. Melvyn Leffler and Odd Arne Westad (New York: Cambridge University Press, 2010), 366–370.

149. Harry G. Summers, Jr., "Lithuania: A Shameful Betrayal," *Detroit Free Press*, 3 May 1990.

150. Memcon, 11 April 1990, "Country—Baltic (2)," box 2, Hutchings, NSC, GBL.

151. Rodman to Scowcroft, 19 April 1990, "Lithuania," Subject, Rostow; Gorbachev to Bush, 3 May 1990, "Situation in Lithuania," box 1, Subject 1989–90, Rice, NSC, GBL.

152. Bush, *All the Best*, 467–469.

153. Excerpts, 31 May and 1 June 1990, docs. 10, 12, 13, EBB 320, NSA.

154. Excerpt, 1 June 1990, doc. 12; "Exchange with Reporters," 2 June 1990, *PPP*, 18546.

155. *Chernyaev Diary, 1991*, 53.

156. Memcon, 6 May 1991, "POTUS Meeting with Shevardnadze," box 1, Burns and Hewett; Talking Points, n.d., "POTUS Trip Briefing Book," box 3, Subject CFO, Burns, NSC, GBL.

157. "Remarks," 1 August 1991, *PPP*, 19864.

158. Scowcroft to Cox, n.d., "Political Situation Union-Republics," Subject Russia, Burns, NSC, GBL.

159. *The Cold War*, episode 24, CNN (1998).

160. Telcon, 30 November 1991, "Bush-Gorbachev Correspondence (1)," box 2, Subject CFO, Burns, NSC, GBL.

161. Gaddis, *Cold War*, 257.

Epilogue

1. Jack Matlock, *Reagan and Gorbachev: How the Cold War Ended* (New York: Random House, 2004), 316, 327.

2. Mark R. Beissinger, "Ethnic Nationalism and the Collapse of Soviet Communism," in *Race, Ethnicity, and the Cold War: A Global Perspective*, ed. Philip E. Muehlenbeck (Nashville: Vanderbilt University Press, 2012), 283–299.

3. Daniel C. Thomas, "Human Rights Ideas, the Demise of Communism, and the End of the Cold War," *Journal of Cold War Studies* 7, no. 2 (Spring 2005): 129–131, 138–139.

4. Aryeh Neier, *The International Human Rights Movement: A History* (Princeton: Princeton University Press, 2012), 184, 14; John Prados, *How the Cold War Ended* (Dulles, VA: Potomac Books, 2010), 77–78, 181–192. See also the work of Peter Schweizer, Jay Winik, James Mann, John Lewis Gaddis, Melvyn Leffler, and Odd Arne Westad.

5. Sarah B. Snyder, *Human Rights Activism and the End of the Cold War: A Transnational History of the Helsinki Network* (New York: Cambridge University Press, 2011), 244–245; "Principles Overwhelming Tanks," in *The Human Rights Revolution: An International History*, ed. Akira Iriye et al. (New York: Oxford University Press, 2012), 266, 270–271.

6. Robert Sutter, "Domestic American Influences," in *Tangled Titans: The United States and China*, ed. David Shambaugh (New York: Rowman & Littlefield, 2013), 109; Rosemary Foot, *The Practice of Power: U.S. Relations with China Since 1949* (New York: Oxford University Press, 1995), 244–248.

7. Francis Njubi Nesbitt, *Race for Sanctions: African Americans Against Apartheid, 1946–1994* (Bloomington: Indiana University Press, 2004), 160–165.

8. Ibid., 168.

9. William M. LeoGrande, *Our Own Backyard: The United States in Central America* (Chapel Hill: University of North Carolina Press, 2000), 526–578.

10. Neier, *International Human Rights Movement*, 15.

11. Thomas Carothers, *In the Name of Democracy: U.S. Policy Toward Latin America in the Reagan Years* (Berkeley: University of California Press, 1991), chaps. 4–5.

12. Grandin, *Empire's Workshop*, 104–108; Grandin, *The Last Colonial Massacre: Latin America in the Cold War* (Chicago: University of Chicago Press, 2004), xiii–xiv.

13. Walter Lafeber, *Inevitable Revolutions: The United States in Central America* (New York: Norton, 1993); Grandin, *Last Colonial Massacre*, xiii–xiv.

14. Elaine Sciolino, "Contras on the Defensive," *NYT*, 15 March 1987.

15. Carothers, *In the Name of Democracy*, 40–46.

16. Ole Holsti, "Public Opinion on Human Rights in American Foreign Policy," in *The U.S. and Human Rights: Looking Inward and Outward*, ed. David Forsythe (Lincoln: University of Nebraska Press, 2000), 131–173.

Index

A c k n o w l e d g m e n t s

This project would not have been possible without the generous support of some exceptional foundations and academic institutions. Emory University and the Gerald R. Ford Foundation provided research travel grants during the initial stages, while the George C. Marshall Foundation, the Dirksen Congressional Center, and the Citadel Foundation granted research support that enabled me to finish the project. I cannot thank these fine organizations enough.

Many people assisted at various levels. I am indebted to Fraser Harbutt, Patrick Allitt, Joe Crespino, Holger Afflerbach, and Bob Dallek for reading portions of this manuscript when my ideas were still in their infancy. Their friendship and professional advice have been invaluable. Ambassador Patrick Duddy and Ambassador Peter DeShazo offered fascinating insights into the world of diplomacy. My thanks also go out to Peter Agree at the University of Pennsylvania Press for his guidance throughout the process, and to the anonymous readers who offered useful comments for further revision. I am also grateful for the assistance of the skilled archivists at the National Archives, the Library of Congress, the presidential libraries, and the many other research centers that I visited over the course of this project.

As always, I owe the most thanks to my family for their encouragement—Mom, Dad, Kathy, Sharon, Doug, Mike, Dan, Dave, Mike B., Pattie, Nikki, Chen Chen, and all the kids—and to Rebecca for her kindness and support.